Persuasion as a Critical Activity

Application and Engagement

Second Edition

Omar Swartz

University of Colorado Denver

Kendall Hunt
publishing company

Kendall Hunt
publishing company

www.kendallhunt.com
Send all inquiries to:
4050 Westmark Drive
Dubuque, IA 52004-1840

Printed in the United States of America
10 9 8 7 6 5 4 3

CONTENTS

PREFACE

I began teaching a course in persuasion in the early 1990s when I was a doctorial student at Purdue University in West Lafayette, Indiana, under the tutelage of Professor Charles J. Stewart. I was 25 years old at the time and without much world experience. I resembled more my students than the people who are now my colleagues. After graduating in May 1995, I taught persuasion for three years at the University of North Carolina, Greensboro, and at North Carolina State University. It was based on these experiences that I wrote the first edition of this textbook, while a law student at Duke University. The weaknesses of the first edition reflect both my limited experience at the time as well as the pressure and demands of law school which was a priority. Since 2001, I have regularly taught persuasion at the University of Colorado Denver (UCD). In the more than eight years I have been a professor at UCD, I have had the privilege of teaching thousands of students in my upper-division persuasion course. Working with these engaged and eager young women and men has been an unparalleled pleasure and has helped me to grow as a teacher, a scholar, and a cultural critic. That growth, I hope, will be reflected in this revised and much improved second edition.

Now, I am 41 and counting. The years have not changed my suspicion that, as the modern world grows increasingly complex, people tend to focus only on their small parts of it, ignoring the often harmful influences around them. This trend is growing as we prepare to move into the second decade of the twenty-first century, a decade that promises challenges more daunting than the last century. With so many demands placed on our time—family, work, and school demands, not to mention concerns that we have about war, the economy, terrorism, global warming, globalization, and a host of other national and international problems—it is no wonder that we hardly pay attention to the ceaseless messages embedded in the environment around us. While we are busy living our lives, we scarcely find the time to explore the ways in which others encourage us to live, with their subtle and not so subtle persuasions.

Much of this persuasion is understandable, even desirable, since there is a sense in which we have to think in common ways and work together as a nation and as a people to coordinate important tasks. Tradition and authority (i.e., order) have important roles to play in helping us to live our lives. We depend upon each other in many substantial, even essential, ways. However, all of us possess the ability to question the demands of others, to tread new ground, and to grow as mature human beings. As the English writer George Orwell once noted, "Orthodoxy of whatever color seems to demand a lifeless, imitative style." *Our* lives do not have to be so drab. This textbook and our course in persuasion will help us to accomplish this growth, this suspicion of orthodoxy, and to realize our potential as free thinking and socially conscious citizens of our immensely consequential nation.

Both this textbook and our course in persuasion stress the importance of a critical consciousness, "receptivity skills," or media literacy in living our lives. Such consciousness and skills involve the perceptional integration of language, community, memory, and history in order to grow strong and healthy, and to thrive in our mass-mediated, often soul-sapping, and deception-saturated environment. Any one of these variables, by itself, does not lead to a critical consciousness and such consciousness is not inevitable. Indeed, even together, we cannot assume that they equal a critical consciousness. By *critical consciousness* I mean the ability to see, in the positioning of the world, the seams of its construction, the political economy of its images and assumptions, and the resources of its communication. A critical consciousness enables us simultaneously to be here in the present and to be in the innumerable pasts as well. Perhaps most importantly, a critical consciousness allows us to envision the path to a more ethical, a more moral, and a more effective future for all of humanity. The past holds us, places demands on us, and limits us unless we are able to confront it. Notice that a critical consciousness accentuates our ability to understand how we are placed. Politics—and this course on persuasion is, in many ways, about the politics of everyday life—is always about *placement*. Persuaders or politicians in the most general sense of the term are always placing us—as consumers, as citizens, as passive spectators in a drama not entirely of our own making. We are placed in our schools, placed in our jobs, placed in our churches, placed in the "war on terror," and placed in countless hierarchies and social orders. Most of us assume that this is normal, and readily take what we can get, particularly if what we have is more than the next person (contentment, it seems, is relative). But it does not have to be this way. Human beings are unfinished creatures with the ability to recreate themselves continuously, adapting to the ebb and flow of life's happenstances and contingencies. We should not fear such contingency. This is our primordial strength as a species and the source of our perennial hope. In this very real sense, *communication is hope*. To hope is to be vulnerable and to be vulnerable is to love and to care.

While this course and textbook discuss rhetorical and social science perspectives on persuasion, it is fundamentally discussing the presence, parameters, and importance of critical thought in our society, as well as the necessity for being engaged, critical citizens during a period of time in which such engagement is difficult. Persuasion is an important dimension of a critical consciousness, and so, in discussing persuasion, we actually practice critical thought, and we practice rhetoric, as well. If the last sentence sounds confusing, then the pages of this textbook and course lecture that follow may provide a unique and hopefully joyful learning experience. If what was written above does not sound confusing, then the reader is well on the way toward understanding the lessons of this course and textbook.

Persuasion as a Critical Activity: *Application and Engagement* is intended to be a companion text to my course in persuasion, supplementing the daily lectures and course outlines provided. With the provided lecture notes and with this textbook, students will have the bulk of the course material with them at all times, which will make it easier for them to engage with the lecture. This is particularly important because most of the course involves more than 2,500 PowerPoint slides and other audiovisual examples of the theories and perspectives we will be discussing. To maximize their experience and education in this course, students are expected to come to class so that they can view and learn from the examples. Students also should come to class having read the appropriate chapter(s), be following the lecture with their packets, actively jotting down examples from the audiovisual material in the margins of their pre-printed lecture notes, and applying the course concepts to persuasive artifacts outside the class. If students become more mindful of what is going on around them, they will have an opportunity to internalize, experientially, the course material.

In effect, students have *three* opportunities to understand the theories and perspectives covered in the course: my live lectures and PowerPoint examples, the course lecture notes, and this textbook. Such triangulation, I believe, is a great strength of this course in helping students to learn what can be difficult material. To this "package" that I provide I would add a *fourth* resource—students' daily application of what they learn in this class to the persuasion saturating their lives.

As an educator, I am not unmindful of the expense associated with textbooks, even low-tech ones such as this without bells-and-whistles (the bells-and-whistles I have saved for class), which is out of the control of authors such as myself. I disagree strongly with the economics of our current publishing regime and am empathetic with the hardship this often places on students. For this reason, I donate *all* the royalties that I earn from the sale of this textbook to a student, merit-based scholarship fund that the Department of Communication has established for undergraduate students; this scholarship typically is awarded in late fall for the spring semester. While this money is not much when compared to rising tuition and other student fees, it represents an effort by the communication department to be as inclusive as possible for our students to be able to earn an education. This inclusiveness is in line with our departmental mission statement, which is "to guide students toward developing the skills, knowledge, and abilities necessary to use communication to create a more civil and humane world." In order to inspire our students, I encourage our faculty to practice what they preach and to lead by example.

I would like to thank my family, friends, and colleagues for the support they have provided me over the years as I have navigated the complexities of a difficult and convoluted tenure process; I appreciate everything they have done for me. Few things in my life have been more difficult or as consequential as earning a seat at the disciplinary table. I had no idea what I was getting into when I picked academia as a career; I was simply following my heart, as I advise my students to do. My wife, Rui Zhao, son, Avi Zhao Swartz, mother, Sue Swartz, and my best friend, Matthew Palmer, have been most patient, understanding, and generous with me; more generous, perhaps, than I have been with myself. I also want to acknowledge my deceased grandmother, Rose Forster, for all that she did for me.

Among my colleagues, I would like to thank Professor Michael Monsour for his reading and helpful comments on an earlier draft of this textbook and for his exceptional friendship, collegiality, and integrity. His early support of me in the department has proven invaluable and will never be forgotten. In an academic environment often filled with arrogant and self-serving faculty, Dr. Monsour's kindness, honesty, and humility is exemplary; I am proud to be his colleague. Likewise, Professor James Stratman deserves recognition for his kindness and stalwart support. I thank also Deirdre ("Dee") Morgenthaler, a UCD doctoral student in education and former teacher assistant for this course for her feedback, insight, and editing skills as I was writing this edition. It has been a pleasure to watch her blossom as an intellectual. She has a bright future ahead of her. Long-time communication consultant and steadfast instructor in our Department, Dr. James Hightshoe, read and commented on the penultimate draft of this manuscript, for which I am grateful. I hope some of his wisdom experience, and knowledge is reflected here. Some of my work has been informed by work I have done recently with Dr. Katia Campbell, an assistant professor at Metropolitan State College of Denver, and with Christina Pestana, a former graduate student.

This textbook consists of two parts. Part I, which comprises Chapters 1–5, introduces students to important philosophical, political, and critical questions fundamental to the study of communication, particularly of persuasion. Part II, Chapters 6–10, explores the component elements of persuasion in which we discuss theory, credibility, audience, language, and ethics.

Finally, and with all the gratitude I can muster, I want to again recognize and thank Professor Charles J. Stewart of Purdue University, whose decades teaching persuasion and his warm mentoring and belief in me inspired this project and whose spirit will guide this course for as long as I teach it (great teachers are "givers of eyes"). I wish him well in his retirement and I hope this textbook serves as testimony to his great love of students and of teaching.

PART ONE

ജ ഇ

CHAPTER 1

Persuasion in Our Democratic Society

Public discourse in democratic political theory is *talk* about politics; in particular, talk about the political status quo and the possibility for being different, better. We, in the United States, live in a society that has no firm *a priori* foundations, no metaphysical anchors connecting us with the One-True-Way or with Truth. No ideology, no religion, no economic philosophy is sacred or privileged in our society, and that, I argue, is a source of our strength as a nation. As U.S. citizens we have no guaranteed paths to follow and no God-given destinies to fulfill; we have only our own very human and fallible goals. What matters to us in our legal and political lives is the everyday expression of our hopes and dreams, our desire to make life better for our children and our grandchildren. What traditionally has made the United States unique among all the nations of the world is not our national narratives of "freedom," "democracy," and "dignity of the individual" that we repeat almost to the point of becoming platitudes, but the actual *diversity* found in our people and in our ideas. The United States, almost from its beginning, was a break with the past and a break from the limitations of tradition.

Yet, from a cultural point of view, what I wrote in the previous paragraph is not self-evident to many Americans living in this country. As we look around us, we see many different communities, each claiming to be the "official" voice or conscience of this nation. Politicians, religious leaders, and advertisers all try to sell us on the idea that the United States is *this*, *that*, or the *other* thing. If only we are patriotic enough, trusting in God enough, faithful enough in some religion or ideology, if only we purchase the right things, everything will be okay—there will be order under heaven and the great boogiemen (i.e., the communists, the terrorists, and the illegal immigrants) will be held at bay. By following God's will we will create a New Jerusalem out of the wilderness that was the New World.

Speaking as a communication scholar and as someone with a legal background, I have to disagree with such politicians, religious leaders, advertisers, and other powerful cultural persuaders. Rather than seeing them as voices of Truth, I see them as part and parcel of a rich tradition in this nation, of a robust American tapestry and dynamism that contribute much to the quality of life in this nation. Each different voice, including those with which I adamantly disagree, is uniquely valuable for the perspective it offers and for reminding us to take nothing for granted, but to publically and transparently argue our positions well. I am particularly heartened by an eloquent U.S. Supreme Court decision, perhaps the most beautiful ever articulated. In *West Virginia State Board of Education v. Barnette* the Court declared: "If there is any fixed star in our constitutional constellation, it is that no official, high or petty, can prescribe what shall be orthodox in politics, nationalism, religion, or other matters of opinion."[1] In writing this, the Court made it crystal clear that the Constitution does not recognize any official ideology, official religion, or privileged discourse. There are no sacred cows, no objects, people, or institutions to be accepted on faith.

The case before the Court specifically dealt with a West Virginia school district's attempt at coercing political uniformity among its students. A school district had mandated the saluting of the flag and the recitation of the pledge of allegiance. Students who refused were sent home and declared truant. Parents could then be arrested and fined for not sending their child to school. As the Court reviewed past attempts to achieve the uniformity that the school district was trying to achieve—church history, Nazi Germany, the Soviet Union—it went on to note wisely that "all efforts of enforcing uniformity have led to the uniformity of the graveyard."[2] Rather, what remains is, in the tradition of American philosopher John Dewey, a faith in ourselves to collectively work toward the common good. Otherwise stated, public discourse in our nation is the search not for perfection in an imperfect world, but for a gradual improvement in the quality of our lives based upon trial and error experimentation. The quest is not for certainty in a world of regrettable contingency, but for an increased sensitivity to the opportunities provided by contingency. Public discourse, how social meaning is created and maintained, is essential to this understanding. Without public discourse, we would have no society, no community, and we would experience a radically diminished sense of our humanity. Public discourse, therefore, needs to be rich, unimpeded, and intelligent. When the quality of public discourse suffers, we all suffer, and the resources of democracy grow stale.

Public discourse may involve approaching legislators with the aim of influencing legislation or talk of political cooperation with the aim of making minor or substantial changes in the structure of government. The guarantees of minority rights in the U.S. Constitution protect freedom of speech and of assembly in order to insure that people can come together to articulate their vision of the good society free of interference by the majority.[3] Even without these guarantees, democratic theory accords people similar prerogatives which "street democracy" (i.e., social movement persuasion) protects. Seen in this light, it is not the abstractions of the state or the symbols of power that we should honor; rather, we should honor that part of ourselves and our heroic ancestors that speak up for a better world. Speaking is a wonderful and consequential act of creation; when the ant calls for justice against the elephant and stands its ground, we have to recognize that the ant is not being foolish. Instead, we have to see that in its voice, in its stance, in its expression of anguish, it cultivates a power that is, in some significant ways, greater than the force that is often used to squash it. Recall the iconic image from June, 5, 1989, of the anonymous, lone Chinese unarmed student protester standing in front of four tanks near Tiananmen Square, Beijing, China, blocking their movement.[4] With his gesture of defiance, this protester exemplifies what Maya Angelou explains as why the "caged" bird sings: "his wings are clipped and his feet are tied, so he opens his throat to sing."[5] Beautiful quote!

Angelou, as well as that lone student protester, reminds us that sometimes the power of our voice is the only thing we have from which to draw strength. This is a rhetorical strength, the strength of persuasion, the tremendous resource of communication. Such was the strength cultivated by Martin Luther King, Jr., Mahatma Gandhi, César Chávez, and many other moral leaders, and expressed by countless people whose names we no longer remember who marched, chanted, went on strike, and fought against incredible odds for a better world. The power of our voice is the power of our *ideas* that become expressed in human speech and enacted in our daily lives. This quintessential humanist power is the power behind all national or ethnic liberation movements and the power behind the yearnings of all people to be free, no matter where they are and which government stifles their hopes. This freedom is an attitude that is expressed. The expression of freedom, even in the face of brutal repression, is itself an act of liberation. Above all, such expression represents a profound humanization.[6]

This textbook and course are about persuasion in a democratic society, *our* society, and is thus about our lives. But what do we mean by the term "democratic society"? We often use the term as a synonym for "the good society," for "justice incarnate on Earth" or some similar superlative, particularly in our political discourse, but few people appreciate fully what the term "democracy" means. Thus, for example, former President George W. Bush justified his 2003 invasion of Iraq, a country on the other side of the world, in part, by emphasizing the obvious fact that Iraq was *not* a "democracy" and, thus, did not *deserve* to have its territorial integrity respected. On the other hand, when Russia invaded its neighbor the Republic of Georgia in August 2008 in response to Georgian provocation, Bush strongly objected on the grounds that Georgia had a democratic government.

The term "democracy" comes from the Greek word *demokratia*, a derivative of *demos*, meaning "the people" (or "the common people") and *kratein* "to rule."[7] Thus, *democracy*, in its simplest connotation, is rule by the people. Democracy, however, is a pliable, multi-nuanced concept that allows for various interpretations and theories—variations include participatory democracy, direct democracy, and economic democracy. At a minimum, however, democracy springs from the idea that no one individual or no one group has the right to rule the rest at will, that public power flows from the citizens—defined inclusively—and that the citizens may challenge and change public policies and leadership when they believe these do not act on behalf of public opinion, and that they have a right and duty to do so. In other words, the state is only a creation of the citizenry to serve the common good, and when the state fails to serve the welfare of the public, it becomes self-serving and loses its authority. This democratic ideal animated, however imperfectly, the formation of the United States in the second half of the eighteenth century—the idea that the people came first, and from an association of the people the government gains authority. Along with political and civil rights, however, come the responsibility of shaping, monitoring, and critiquing the government. Democracy requires a commitment to, and involvement in, tangible, day-to-day civic action, in being the change, noted Gandhi famously, we want to enact. Communication, in its best expression, is democracy enacted. Within this context, communication and persuasion never stop, even in the most closed of societies, but the extent to which communication is *influential*, or has the potential to be influential, is dependent upon the degree to which freedom, in its various manifestations, is tolerated. Within any society there are *degrees* of openness. When we talk or write about the relative openness of communication and its relationship to the political philosophies of the modern nation-state, we are referencing a continuum. For instance, democracy in Ancient Greece was limited to males, excluding women and slaves. The United Kingdom, that "other" great democracy in the world, has historically been openly imperialistic as well as repressive of its working class and poor people. Finally, the U.S. government routinely bars people from visiting the United States or becoming citizens because of their political views.[8] As contentment is relative, so is democracy; we are often democratic in some sense and not in others. We can always be better.

Throughout this textbook and course I will sketch a description of persuasion grounded in a progressive or even libertarian sense of democracy and community, one grounded in my study of both rhetoric and law, and which extends from the potentials that are already implicit in current society, but which are often frustrated and remain under-actualized. In my vision of an edifying society, I embrace the potential of people individually and collectively to better perfect their communities and I remain suspicious of the ability of the machinery of the state political system to provide the guiding force and direction of our common future. This vision of democracy, what I, in a neopragmatic fashion call "creative democracy," is one in which diversity of ideas and meaningful participation of all groups in forming civic and political life is understood as an essential aspect. Therefore, persuasion and knowledge of persuasive tactics is central to political/cultural literacy and, ultimately, agency as informed and empowered citizens.[9] This conception of democracy is broadly positioned in terms of Martha Nussbaum's notion of *cosmopolitanism*.[10] Such profound cosmopolitanism, what Nussbaum describes as an escape "from the comfort of local truths, from the warm nestling feeling of patriotism, from the absorbing drama of pride in oneself and one's own,"[11] demands that we understand the individual in light of our power for self-reflection and redescription. Cosmopolitanism recognizes that all of our inherited characteristics, no matter how much beloved and important to us, are accidents of time and chance. Thus, as Nussbaum notes: Definition of cosmopolitanism.

> We should not allow differences of nationality or class or ethnic membership or even gender to erect barriers between us and our fel-

> low human beings. We should recognize humanity wherever it oc-
> curs, and give its fundamental ingredients, reason and moral cap-
> acity, our first allegiance and respect.[12]

Nussbaum continues by writing, "We should give our first allegiance to no mere form of government, no temporal power, but to the moral community made up by the humanity of all human beings."[13]

To be such a citizen, however, does not, notes Nussbaum, mean that we have to give up our local idiosyncratic quirks, as they remain quite important to us as individuals. All politics are, as the slogan states correctly, local. In a practical sense, our religious, political, and ethnic identifications matter very much. Such expressions of style animate our lives and help make human beings interesting—they are the spices and seasonings of social existence. While important, however, they are not enough. Rather, Nussbaum suggests that we think of ourselves as in the middle of ever larger circles:

> The first one is drawn around the self; the next takes in one's imm-
> ediate family; then follows the extended family; then, in order, one's
> neighbors or local group, one's fellow city-dwellers, one's fellow
> countrymen—and we can easily add to this list groupings based on
> ethnic, linguistic, historical, professional, gender and sexual iden-
> tities. Outside all these circles is the largest one, that of humanity as a
> whole.[14]

We are each, therefore, already connected to a larger whole. This largest circle represents that which is common to all humans. It transcends the local and is something to which we all can speak.

In the name of this humanity, the responsibility for social change, then, rests in citizens' perceptions, attitudes, and commitments, not in a faith in political institutions or in the benevolence of the power elite. As U.S. history has shown, social and economic justice are not inevitable.[15] Moral evolution is seldom driven by top-down initiative. When such evolution occurs, the driving force of change is usually the result of community vision and mass struggle, a disapproval and/or rejection of the status quo. The problem, however, is that people do not often struggle *en masse* and tend to accept the way things are as being inevitable. Humans, as well as other mammals, are remarkably able to adapt themselves to the most horrific of situations.[16] As a result, as confirmed in the social movement literature, leadership of oppressed communities tends to arise not from the oppressed themselves, but from members of the middle class who have the education, leisure, and foresight to help nudge the masses out of their passivity and acceptance of their conditions.

At the center of creative democracy and persuasion as a critical activity is a rejection of the *guardianship* theory of democracy and "epistemarchy," which claim that knowledge and what is "good," "right," and "just" are accessible only by certain groups and not others. As a society, we will make greater gains in social justice when such thinking is recognized for what it is and resisted, when more people are able to perceive the ways that they can use their agency for creative influence in shaping their local environments. This vision requires a communication of hope and resistance to dominating and oppressive ideologies and practices, including those embedded in commercial messages. For example, the abolition of slavery, the gaining of women's right to vote and to own property, and the winning of the 8-hour work day were all achieved through sustained and committed *resistance* to the accepted Truths of their respective times—that of a "natural order," a hierarchy "written" by some transcendent Authority, in which, for instance, Whites were considered superior to Blacks, men considered superior to women, and wealthy people considered superior to the working class and the poor.[17] These changes were also created through an alternative description of the way things can and should be. As American philosopher Richard Rorty notes, "The freer the imagination of the present the likelier it is that future social practices will be different from past practices."[18] An important point to consider is that the imagination is only free to the extent that communication among people is open and robust.

The neo-pragmatist tradition emphasizes the potential for change through the pedagogical and the dialogical—that is to say, persuasion. This tradition assumes that disparities in resources, enormous polarizations in perceptions, or intense conflicts of interest can be overcome by means of education and communication.[19] To engage in this creative work, people need opportunities for edifying education and communication that develop their communication imagination and heighten their critical perception.[20] Given that formal education, such as this course, is an important public space for communication, such education could empower future generations, starting with ourselves, to work toward and enact progressive social change.

This courageous dimension of an individual's self can be called the *critical* or *communicative imagination*. The critical imagination is about meaning, about understanding, about figuring out the place of humans in the world. The communication imagination is the progressive antithesis of the social manipulation of society by economic, political, or social elites (e.g., advertisers, the public relations industry, politicians, or religious leaders). It is worth remembering that Edward Barneys, an important early public relations pioneer, believed in what he called "enlightened social manipulation." He wrote in 1928 that it "was the astounding success of propaganda during the war [World War I] which opened the eyes of the intelligent few in all departments of life to the possibilities of *regimenting* the public mind."[21] In contrast, the critical imagination involves creating *our* place in response to theirs; *our* space for constructing a fair and just world out of the poverty and degradation that power alien to us has created. The critical imagination concerns the myriad of things that matter most to us as people—flesh and blood individuals—in our negotiations or fight over the conditions of community life.

The critical imagination is concerned with questions of *praxis* and power, issues that we engage with constantly without giving them much thought, thus giving up control of our destinies. *Praxis* is an important term in classical persuasion theory and remains so in critical theory today. In the Aristotelian/Ciceronian traditions, persuasion is seen as an art that lies on the boundary between ethics and politics and helps people to deliberate in the world of common affairs. *Praxis* involves knowledge of the subject matter, knowledge of the human psyche, and a political awareness within the constraints of materially determined conditions.

Whether we are cognizant of the fact or not, our day-to-day politics and behaviors are determined by how we contemplate or fail to contemplate *praxis* and power. This is why control over the mass media by corporate interests is consequential; why we should be concerned that the bulk of the mass media we consume is controlled currently by five corporations; why it is detrimental for citizens in our society to avoid asking hard questions of media ownership; why we should question the widespread use of public relations tactics by government to hoodwink and deceive us, and the lack of responsible, public, and independent reporting.[22] We can be different only if we can *think* differently and we can think differently only if we have information about alternative views which are often precluded by the monopoly of the mainstream press.[23]

The struggle for dissent and counter-discourse to be given a voice is to struggle against *public amnesia*. Public amnesia refers to events and actions once part of public discourse that, while bearing on a contemporary crisis, are not recalled.[24] The progressive lessons of the past, the struggles against power and for social justice, are subjugated by the powers of the present that define the "good" in its own terms, excluding the humanity of others. Progressive experiences by generations of activists as well as victims are thus ignored in policy debates, during political deliberation, by corporate media in their so-called "watch dog" function, and in school textbooks that tame the critical imagination and direct it into the service of the nation-state and the market. Public amnesia is present when challenges to established ways of talking about or understanding the world are voided by existing institutional and social arrangements that anchor the epistemological foundations of wealth and power.[25]

To fight public amnesia, champions of a critical imagination point out that human beings are enriched tremendously with the ability to vocalize and thus to actualize their worlds. Such thinkers take seriously the human capacity for liberation or at least, for making things better. There is no reality so reified, no system of thought so impenetrable, no political regime so entrenched that it cannot be overcome by the human will to freedom, the will to overcome one's self and the limitations of one's society. This phoenix-like will is the quintessential act of liberation. Contrary to many skeptics across the political spectrum, liberation is not a failed project, although its scope is more nuanced and less static than theorized previously by philosophers and critics. Simply put, *liberation* involves the humanistic act of breaking down normative beliefs and values that deprive us of our potential to grow as individuals and as a society.

As we problematize our world through the critical imagination—that is, to refuse to accept the world as we experience it as "given"—and engage in the progressive re-visioning of ourselves and our "places," we are engaging in society at the level at which it is constructed and we are denying the permanence of that construction. In the face of permanence we advocate change, a way of taking back the world to reorient and humanize our priorities—literally, to make sense anew. As illustrated by a paradigmatic insight from Lu Xun, an important figure in modern Chinese literature, this critical power is part of our libratory *telos* as inspired and thinking human beings who engage conscientiously with the power of our humanity.[26]

Lu Xun wrote in the beginning decades of the twentieth century, a period of time in which Chinese society was in utter disarray. The imperial and often grand dynasties that had ruled China for many thousands of years had come to an end, the National Republic that replaced the rule of the emperor was criminally corrupt and tyrannical, China had been invaded by marauding Japan, and, before that, by many of the European countries. In short, China had come to the point in its history in which its existence as a civilization was seriously imperiled. Considering the immense importance of Chinese culture in human affairs, and the sheer number of people on Earth who call themselves Chinese, the impending dissolution of China was no small event. It was out of this crisis—perhaps the largest social crisis in the twentieth century—that the communists eventually came to power in 1949 promising, and largely delivering, independence and national pride, although at the expense of human rights and the type of democratic *ethos* animating this textbook and course.

This context is important because Lu Xun said something very wise that greatly informs our discussion of hope and the power of a critical imagination. We often take for granted our world. We treat our world as if it were permanent, unchanging, and stable. When we make these implicit assumptions we forget that the world was created, constructed, and put together in a particular way by humans according to someone's interest. It is persuasion, or discourse, that puts together the world, but we do not see this clearly because our world is often constructed before we are born, and it takes some catastrophic event to unsettle our world enough for us to see its impermanence, how much at risk each of us is to the twists of contingency.[27] Such an event happened in China, once a world-consequential civilization, and enabled Lu Xun to comprehend a fundamental point. He looked at the death and chaos around him and wrote, "Hope cannot be said to exist, nor can it be said not to exist. It is just like roads across the earth. For actually the earth had no roads to begin with, but when many men pass one way, a road is made."[28] Hope, in other words, is not a *thing*, such as a God, a government, or a piece of technology. Such things, while themselves important, are "idols," externalizations of an inner human agency. Instead of seeing hope in this way, as most of us do, as a truth, Lu Xun sees it as a *practice*. We manifest hope through our actions. Hope, therefore, can never be lost as long as humans retain their freedom to act; it is through our actions that hope or despair comes into the world.

This pragmatic idea is implicit in the critical imagination; it is given its firmest expression by the French philosopher Michel Foucault. Foucault's work evidences some of the strongest historical or empirical documentations to support the power of a communicative understanding of human agency. In his many histories—he calls them "archaeologies" or "genealogies"—Foucault demonstrates the link between communication, knowledge, and power, illustrating how the progression of human intellectual history involves a series of raptures and breaks in thought, of discontinuities, rather than continuities.[29] In other words, we are not simply progressing (to the extent that we *are* progressing) as a culture because we are building on more and more rational or "true" types of discourse (e.g., capitalism, American values, conservatism, Rule of Law, God, etc). On the contrary, we have *always* been rational. What Foucault shows us, as German philosopher Friedrich Nietzsche did before him, is that the rules of the game, the norms of rationality, frequently change. Practically, this means that the way that we talk changes, and each change creates a whole new moral and psychological universe. This is what we mean by the concept of the "paradigm shift."[30]

Once we change, we lose our social and moral connections to the past. Yes, the artifacts remain but their meaning is lost. What is left is the subject of archeology—the bones, the fossils, the myths, but not the life. To understand the critical imagination, then, and to see the power of persuasion to create and reinforce meanings, is to understand the breath that animates a particular community in a specific historical context under a certain set of contingencies. As students and citizens in an era of a global "war on terror," the community we study is our own and the historical context is the present.

❧ Conclusion ☙

Communication is power, and persuasion is the application of that power; the coordination of the human will toward specific goals. The collective sum of these goals comprises the world, with all its pleasures and pains, glories and depravities. These goals can be beneficial or harmful; depending upon whose interest is involved. As Greek philosopher Aristotle made clear many centuries ago, rhetoric (or persuasion more generally) is amoral:

> And if it is argued that great harm can be done by unjustly using such power of words, this objection applies to all good things except for virtue, and most of all to the most useful things, like strength, health, wealth, and military strategy; for by using these justly one would do the greatest good and unjustly, the greatest harm.[31]

Following Aristotle, modern scholars have acknowledged several *functions* that the study of persuasion serves for citizens in our society.[32] First, the study of persuasion has an *instrumental* value; that is, it helps us to become more effective co-creators of our lives. Persuasion is the way social creation occurs and the way things get done. Second, it provides a *knowledge and information* function as those creations become codified and incorporated into human practice. Third, persuasion has a *control* function—as we come to define the world we place a sense of order upon it. Such order is the mechanism by which control is conceptualized. Fourth, persuasion has a *defense* (or reform/change) function or debunking function. With this function, persuasion circles back on itself; its creation can always be questioned, allowing the process of signification to begin anew. This dialectic, as I argue throughout this textbook and course, is a model for social health.

౸ Notes ౮

1. 319 U.S. 624 (1943). What made this case all the more unusual was that the Supreme Court was reversing itself from a few years earlier. In *Minersville School District v. Gobitis* (1940) the Court ruled against the students, also Jehovah's Witnesses, leading to increased violent (and substantial) persecution for the minority religious group.

2. Ibid.

3. See *United States v. Carolene Products Company*, 304 U.S. 144 (1938). In the famous Footnote #4, the Court suggested that run-of-the mill police power legislation aimed at discrete and insular minorities (i.e., those who lack the normal protections of the political process), should be an exception to the presumption of constitutionality that courts normally follow. The Court proposed a heightened standard of judicial review in such circumstances, greatly influencing the evolution of equal protection jurisprudence.

4. Reportedly, the first tank tried several times to maneuver around the protestor, but the protestor moved to prevent this. The man then climbed on the tank and spoke to the driver before disappearing into the crowd. No one knows, ultimately, what happened to the man. He may have been arrested and killed or he may have escaped the country. Both *Time* and *Life* magazines considered this photo to be among the most important and influential of the twentieth century.

5. *The Complete Poems of Maya Angelou* (New York: Random House, 1994), 194.

6. Essential tensions exist in any society between humanization and bureaucratization, between institutionalization and freedom, and between hierarchy and egalitarianism. These tensions become the resources for resisting reification and *stasis*.

7. Mogens Herman Hansen, *The Athenian Democracy in the Age of Demosthenes: Structure, Principles, and Ideology* (Norman: University of Oklahoma Press, 1999).

8. For an introduction to this phenomenon, see Jane Lampman, "Uncle Sam Doesn't Want You," *The Christian Science Monitor* (May 11, 2006), retrieved from http://www.csmonitor. com/2006/0511/p14s02-legn.htm. For a legal overview of the issue, see Mark W. Voigt, "Visa Denials on Ideological Grounds and the First Amendment Right to Receive Information: The Case For Stricter Judicial Scrutiny," *Cumberland Law Review*, 17 (1987), 139-166.

9. Neo-pragmatism is the branch of philosophy initiated by Richard Rorty starting in 1979 with the publication of his *Philosophy and the Mirror of Nature* (Princeton, NJ: Princeton University Press).

10. "Patriotism and Cosmopolitanism," in *For Love of Country: Debating the Limits of Patriotism*, Joshua Cohen, ed. (Boston: Beacon Press, 1991), 2–17.

11. Ibid., 15.

12. Ibid., 7.

13. Ibid.

14. Ibid., 9.

15. See Howard Zinn, *A People's History of the United States* (New York: Harper Perennial Modern Classics, 2005).

16. An example from the social sciences is *learned helplessness*, a theory which helps us to understand why victims of abuse and violence often lack the psychological resources for removing themselves from deleterious situations when they have a chance. See Martin E. P. Seligman and Stephen F. Maier, "Failure to Escape Traumatic Shock," *Journal of Experimental Psychology, 74* (1967), 1–9.

17. A telling, and perhaps underappreciated, sentiment is expressed in the bumper sticker slogan that reads, "The Labor Movement—The People Who Brought You The Weekend."

18. "Feminism, Ideology, and Deconstruction: A Pragmatist View," *Hypatia, 8* (1993), 100.

19. Cornell West, *Keeping Faith: Philosophy and Race in America* (New York: Routledge, 1993).

20. David Engen, "The Communicative Imagination and its Cultivation," *Communication Quarterly, 50* (2002), 41–57.

21. Edward Bernays, *Propaganda* (Brooklyn, NY: Ig Publishing, 2004), 54. Emphasis added.

22. Ben H. Bagdikian, *The New Media Monopoly: A Completely Revised and Updated Edition With Seven New Chapters* (Boston: Beacon Press, 2004).

23. Robert W. McChesney, *The Problem of the Media: U.S. Communication Politics in the 21st Century* (New York: Monthly Review Press, 2004).

24. Wenshu Lee and Philip C. Wander, "On Discursive Amnesia: Reinventing the Possibilities for Democracy Through Discursive Amnesty," in *The Public Voice in a Democracy at Risk*, Michael Salvador and Patricia M. Sias, eds. (Westport, CT: Praeger, 1998), 151–172.

25. "Epistemology" is the study of knowing; it is the attempt by philosophers to address the question of how is it that we know. From the perspective of a critical or communicative imagination we are discussing in this course, the epistemological foundations of wealth and power are protected by a "forgetting" of knowledge and information critical of the status quo.

26. A *telos* is the ends to which something strives, its locomotion. In Aristotelian theory, implicit in a seed would be a full grown tree, and the *telos* of the seed would be its struggle to reach its natural potential.

27. The concept of "exigency" and "rhetorical situation" will be discussed in Chapter 9.

28. *Selected Works* v. 1 (Beijing: Foreign Languages Press, 1985), 101.

29. *The Archaeology of Knowledge* (New York: Pantheon Books, 1972).

30. Historian and philosopher Thomas S. Kuhn argued that our understandings of the world are grounded in a set of beliefs that we hold and that these beliefs exist due to social factors. As the social factors change, the grounding or paradigms of our beliefs change, and with them changes our perception of the world. See his *The Structure of Scientific Revolutions* 3rd ed. (Chicago: University of Chicago Press, 1996).

31. *On Rhetoric: A Theory of Civic Discourse*, trans. George A. Kennedy (New York: Oxford University Press, 1991), 35.

32. See, for example, Robert H. Gass and John S. Seiter, *Persuasion, Social Influence, and Compliance Gaining* 2nd ed. (Boston: Allyn and Bacon, 2003), 8–9.

CHAPTER 2

Intersections Between Persuasion and Rhetoric

In this chapter we are going to explore the concept of rhetoric and why it is important for students studying persuasion. We need to address this question at the outset because rhetoric, as we will see throughout this textbook and course, is a shadow that pervades our understanding of persuasion. For our purposes here, rhetoric is the *gestalt,* in the general sense, the humanistic conceptualization and orientation behind both the practice and the informed critique of persuasion. In order for us even to begin to understand what rhetoric is and why it is important in the context of persuasion and a critical consciousness, we have to understand the two competing (albeit abstract and philosophical) ways of comprehending communication. From this discussion we can further understand *why* and *how* persuasion functions the way it does in our society. This discussion also helps us to appreciate the backdrop behind many of the cultural wars we experience frequently in this country.[1]

ಬ Two Ways of Approaching Our Understanding of Communication ೞ

For the purposes of our discussion in this textbook and course, there are two general ways of approaching an understanding of communication. The first one is the rhetorical, epistemological view, the view privileged in the discipline of Communication Studies and represented by the National Communication Association (NCA).[2] This view assumes that communication is a *heuristic* experience—that is, communication helps us to understand, learn, and grow. In this sense, communication is *epistemic,* leading to new knowledge.[3] Because of this, one can claim that the discipline of communication lies at the center of the humanities, and is essential for the practice of scientific inquiry as well.[4] It is, in short, fundamental—the resource upon which civilization is founded. The ancient Greek philosopher Isocrates reflects this view:

> For in the other powers which we possess… we are in no respect superior to other living creatures; nay, we are inferior to many in swiftness and in strength and in other resources; but because there has been implanted in us the power to persuade each other and to make clear to each other whatever we desire, not only have we escaped the life of wild beasts, but we have come together and founded cities and made laws and invented arts; and, generally speaking, there is no institution devised by man which the power of speech has not helped us to establish.[5]

Most people associated with the discipline of Communication Studies will not disagree with this proposition, at least initially; a strong social constructionist view pervades our discipline, animating our teaching and scholarship. As mentioned above, this dimension of communication makes our discipline indispensable to the academic community, and invests a sense of importance in our endeavors. With this view, we come to understand that communication is *how we* put things together; it is how we structure and order our lives and our societies. In a more bold sense, communication is how we find meaning in our lives and how we create ourselves.

This last statement is controversial for some people. How is it through "communication" that we find meaning in our lives? Is not this meaning located elsewhere? Clearly, many of us turn to other areas to find meaning: to religion, to government, to our families, to our jobs, and to our friends. Many people believe that meaning has been planted in them, that some divine spark animates them, and their job—or the job of a paternalistic government and other social institutions—is to help them look inward, to prevent them from distractions by purging society of illusion.

A defender of this progressive view of communication might respond that meaning is found in all those above places, God and country, for example, but not in the way we commonly think. Religious meaning does not come from God, but from the way we *talk* and *write* about God. Governmental or nationalistic meaning does not come from the Declaration of Independence or from the U.S. Constitution, but from the ways we *talk* and *write* about each of these documents and grant them meaning in our lives. Meaning is found in the *com-*

munication, not in the things about which we communicate. As media scholar Neil Postman explains:

> Knowledge of a subject mostly means knowledge of the language of that subject. Biology, after all, is not plants and animals; it is language about plants and animals. History is not events that once occurred; it is a language describing or interpreting events. And astronomy is not planets and stars but a special way of talking about planets and stars.[6]

Under such a view, the ways in which we communicate become important: communication is emotional, ideological, sensuous, sermonic, and critical. It contributes to our understanding of the world around us and entices others to join and work with us. Notice, I am *not* saying that communication *creates* the world. Clearly, there are rocks, plants, animals, stars, and events in history. While these things exist, they become meaningful to us only as we become socialized to accept their meaning in a particular way. Communication, in short, is empowering, humanizing, edifying and reifying. It infuses things with emotion so that value can be introduced into the world. Consider the following poem fragment from the great American bard, Walt Whitman:

> O the orator's joys!
> To inflate the chest, to roll the thunder of the voice
>   out from the ribs and throat,
> To make the people rage, weep, hate, desire, with
>   yourself.
> To lead America—to quell America with a great tongue.[7]

Notice the activity associated with communication as it is evoked by Whitman. Notice the veneration, potential, and joy that Whitman associates with talking, and perhaps with writing as well. In this case, talking is not petty; rather, it is grand. It is big and important; the people who practice it are necessarily robust, enthusiastic, passionate, and engaged. There is even something patriotic about talking as well, a sense of responsibility, ownership, agency, and presence. Orators lead, they quell, they embody an identification that reverberates powerfully throughout the nation. In short, communication for Walt Whitman is an enactment and celebration of community. Notice also the critical dimension being evoked here. This grand celebration of communication is not an end in itself. Rather, it integrates itself firmly into the American experience—it leads, it differentiates, it chastises. In short, communication *democratizes*. As suggested in Chapter 1, communication becomes a standard of shared perceptual reality, the humanization necessary for democratic societies to function smoothly and productively.

With Whitman, we have been exposed to a sense of the grandeur of rhetoric in serving as a life force animating our society. But we also have reason to be cautious in light of Whitman's enthusiasm, for the epistemic view of rhetoric claims for itself the realm of "meaning" and sets itself up as an alternative standard for "Truth," and for some people, meaning and Truth cannot be contested so subjectively. For many, perhaps most people, Truth's stipulated *a priori* status precludes such flexibility.[8]

one truth or one confirmed belief.

The legendary Chinese Taoist master, Lao Tzu, was one such person, and his experience serves as a counter-example to the above.[9] Lao Tzu had a different temperament than Walt Whitman. Where Whitman sang, Lao Tzu whispered. Where Whitman celebrated, Lao Tzu meditated. Where Whitman saw in expression a distinct form of understanding and a heightened awareness, Lao Tzu saw expression as a form of mystification and alienation from the "correct" way of life as determined by Nature. Where Whitman saw language as a critical resource, Lao Tzu viewed it as a threat, a disruption, a source of confusion and disharmony. In one of his famous philosophical poems, he wrote:

> Those who know do not speak; those who speak do not know.
> Keep silent and guard your senses.
> Temper your sharpness. Mask your brightness.
> Be at one with the dust of the earth. This is the holy union.
> He who has achieved this state is unconcerned with enemies,
> friends, good, evil, honor or disgrace.
> This is the pinnacle of humanity.[10]

Lao Tzu clearly does not have a high view of communication. For him, it is something that must be guarded against. Communication interferes with an essence that is more primal, pressing, or real. His view of communication is *ontological*, or at least, ontologically situated.[11] According to him, we have an essence that is more human than communication, something more essential to us than language, and some of us—the "wise" people (such as Plato's "Philosopher King") —can be more aware of what it is than others. The more that we sense this, the less we have to depend on communication to make sense of the world, and the more we realize that communication, itself, is part of the illusion of the world. Communication, for Lao Tzu, is the *problem*. Truth, in this case, is something unconcerned with human beings and their desires. It is unconcerned with human culture. Truth is out there, somewhere, and human beings, in order to be happy, have to find it and mold their experience to its demands. As another classical Chinese Taoist scholar, T'ao Ch'ien, wrote:

> I built my hut in a zone of human habitation,
> Yet near me there sounds no noise or horse or coach,
> Would you know how that is possible?
> A heart that is distant creates a wilderness round it.
> I pluck chrysanthemums under the eastern hedge,
> Then gaze long at the distant summer hills.
> The mountain air is fresh at the dusk of day;
> The flying birds two by two return.
> In these things there lies a deep meaning;
> Yet when we would express it, words suddenly fail us.[12]

Again, readers of this poem are struck by the notion that what is really important lies outside of human communities, and that the truly wise person needs to be intellectually and emotionally distant from the affairs of people. Such sentiment has been an important theme in much Eastern, and even in some Western, philosophical and religious thought. Philosophy, religion, and science, in general, have tended to be suspicious of language and seek some sort of experience that is more primal or transcendent than words. A modern Chinese scholar, Fung Yu-Lan, elaborates on the Taoist suspicion of language:

> According to Taoism, the *Tao* (the Way) cannot be told, but only suggested. So when words are used, it is the suggestiveness of the words, and not their fixed denotations or connotations, that reveals the *Tao*. Words are something that should be forgotten when they have achieved their purpose. Why should we trouble ourselves with them any more than is necessary?[13]

The problem with Fung's statement is that language is all we really have. There is no universal transcendent position that everyone recognizes as being valid.

In all of recorded history, and certainly since the Ancient Greeks set the philosophical stage for Western society, people have searched for those extralinguistic realities, and have failed to find them. What these efforts have led to are largely *incommensurable* positions. Conditions of incommensurability exist when there is no common quality between two or more different entities to ground a comparison or measurement between them. For example, one philosophical or religious system determines a universal Truth, and another philosophical or religious system determines another universal Truth, and it so happens that the two Truths are incompatible and mutually exclusive.

As an example of incommensurability, consider the following cartoon. A man stands before St. Paul at the Pearly Gates of Heaven. St. Paul's job is to evaluate each person's candidacy for Heaven. After analyzing the man's file, Paul declares, "You picked the wrong religion, period. I'm not going to argue about it." As this cartoon suggests, when two people or systems of thought reach an incommensurable position, there is nothing more to talk about. Our search for absolutes leads to fragmentation in the human community. It is at this point, usually, that people turn to violence and to war. While we lament this violence and war, we recognize that violence and war are often the inevitable result of ontological thinking and the search for something extra-human within us. Rather than to fear this condition, to see in incommensurability the source of one party's error, we need, like Walt Whitman, to learn to celebrate such *stasis* and learn to redescribe it creatively and joyfully. In this way, disagreement becomes a resource for transcendence and edification.

What people have come up with in their search to leave language behind them and to find other standards of meaning are philosophical and religious systems of metaphysics that have largely proven to be *social* (although a person committed to a metaphysical system would never admit this about *her* or *his* system). So, after more than twenty-five hundred years of hard work and a great amount of bloodshed—religious wars, crusades, inquisitions, and world wars—we are back where we started. In the pursuit of God and Truth, we are left, in the end, with a plethora of books—that is, *words* and arguments, claims and counter-claims, biases and prejudices and the rich diversity of human culture. The will-to-religion and the will-to-knowledge would not be possible without language. As Kenneth Burke explains:

> Purpose will have its origins in bodily desires, most notably the appetites of food and sex. In this respect, it will be grounded in man's

animality. But it will attain an immaterial counterpart in the principle of communication. Hence, purpose will have a secondary grounding in man's symbolicity. Add, next, the ways of empire that develop among the various societies of symbol-using animals and the conditions are set for the imagining of love, whether sacred or profane.[14]

This is not to say that the quest for Truth and Knowledge is not important, as our religious identifications and political commitments are often very dear to us, as they should be. However, we have to recognize that such commitments are primarily *cultural*; that is, these systems of thought change as society and culture change. They reflect not timeless essences but specific historical and political needs. In other words, people have this drive toward metaphysics and transcendence, but this drive is always contextualized in the history of ideas and in the needs of various historical contingencies. This takes us back to the importance of a rhetorical epistemology, as it thrives in the murky waters of a historical contingency.

☙ The Meaning of Rhetoric in Contemporary U.S. Culture ❧

The popular understanding of rhetoric in contemporary U.S. culture is pejorative. It is seen as empty discourse, or flowery language. Rhetoric is a type of talk and writing that exists at the expense of substance or action. Consider the politician who tells his audience, "We welcome every honest act of peace. We care nothing for *mere* rhetoric." This is a common sentiment in U.S. political discourse. Variations of it exist everywhere. For example, a recent book catalogue offers the following description of a new monograph: "The power of this book is in its balanced, common sense view of arms control negotiations: no rhetoric, no ideology, no silliness."[15]

What is going on in both of these examples? Most clearly, what we see are practical examples of the political tensions that exist between epistemeological and ontological world views. In both examples of the ontological view, we are being offered an absolute statement about what the world *is*—the person offering each observation has determined in advance what constitutes "Truth" and is aligning her or himself with it.[16] In the first example, "honest act of peace" is defined by the speaker in ways that are highly partisan and selfish. In this case, the words belong to President Dwight D. Eisenhower.[17]

Eisenhower's speech took place during the Cold War, and the president is speaking to Americans about Russia. For those students who do not remember, the Cold War was a condition of *stasis* that existed between the United States (and its proxies) and the Soviet Union (and its proxies). It lasted roughly from the end of the Second World War until the early 1990s with the dissolving of the Soviet Union and of the transition of the former Eastern Bloc nations to market economies and American influence. In this context, Eisenhower is trying to illustrate how his administration has made overtures of peace to the Soviets, but without success. He defines "honest" by his own standard, and measures the Soviets by these same standards. The word "rhetoric," in this instance, is used by Eisenhower to marginalize everything the Soviets say and do that does not meet *his* expectations, which *he* defines as the standard of Truth. He makes no effort to recognize that the Soviets have their *own* criteria of what is acceptable and their own standards of *decorum*; indeed, Eisenhower's primary assumption is that the Soviets, by definition of who they are, are not entitled to have a political interest. The Soviets are simply wrong.

Now it is not unreasonable for Eisenhower to be partisan in some regard—he is, after all, the president and he is speaking on behalf of U.S. "interests," and history, from our vantage point, has not looked kindly on the Soviet experience. What is less reasonable is his presumption that his way is the *only* way, and that the rest of us should believe his way. By refusing to recognize the Soviet subjectivity, Eisenhower places us *all* at risk, since negotiations, to be fruitful, have to be undertaken among *equals*, which is clearly something the United States was never willing to do, as far as the Soviet Union was concerned. We see a similar communication style in the eight years of the Bush Administration's stance toward Cuba, Iran, North Korea, Syria, Hamas, Hezbollah, and other political groups/nations that Bush defined as antithetical to our interests. Overtures from these nations and/or political entities are dismissed as irrelevant. As late as the 2008 presidential election, candidate Barak Obama found himself on the defensive for his willingness to talk directly with leaders from these countries/political groups.

The structure of Eisenhower's belief system, and the way he expresses it through his language, is similar to Lao Tzu's belief that the Tao stipulates correct and incorrect ways of behaving. Both believe that Truth is objective, that it corresponds to *their* politics, and, therefore, not much has to be said or argued; the other side simply has to act in the way that they have prescribed. If the other side does not agree to these conditions, then *they* are wrong and are acting against *nature*. Because Nature, Truth, God, or some similar power is on *our* side, we have the moral authority to "correct" the other party, which becomes the role of the military.

The assumption that there is one universal Truth or unquestionable set of principles situating and justifying an ideal human society is illustrated in the following quote from American political philosopher and Platonic rhetorician Richard Weaver, someone whose views on rhetoric and persuasion we will review in different places throughout this textbook and course. In this quote, Weaver exemplifies the principal belief that some external rationality grounds human institutions and that it can be understood, or misunderstood, at our peril. "Rational society," he writes, "is a mirror of the logos, and this means that it has a formal structure which enables apprehension."[18] Apprehension requires "the recovery of true knowledge" in order to "preserve society." He reasons that, in order to understand society, we must look for the structure and hierarchy that establish that structure. He calls this hierarchy and structure a "metaphysical truth" and issues a warning against the "declamations of the Jacobins," a reference to the political party responsible for instigating the French Revolution, the first modern revolution, which conservatives everywhere abhorred.[19] Your speech, he says, is inconsequential at best and hazardous at worst: it is foolish to rebel against the established order; to do so is to invite punishment.[20]

To the extent that we believe in Lao Tzu's, Eisenhower's, or Weaver's ontological assumptions about the nature of reality and politics, then it would appear as if each were speaking the Truth when, in fact, each is using an extreme form of language to set up his own standards of acceptable behavior. A similar language tactic is evident in the second quote. Here, "rhetoric" is lumped with "ideology" (a demonized term for most people) and deemed "silly," and it is opposed to "balance" and "common sense." Actually, both rhetoric and ideology have much in common, as both involve the ways that people derive their ideas, and how those ideas influence their behaviors. Neither is "silly" and both involve "common sense." Ideology constitutes common sense for the people who belong to that discourse community. Rhetoric, to be effective, must speak to the beliefs and values held by an audience.

However, the view of rhetoric and ideology, as just explained, is not shared by the person who writes that these concepts are "silly." This person privileges "balance" above all else and views balance as antithetical to rhetoric. But what is "balance"? Balance is the middle point between two extremes, and that is where this person positions her or his definition of Truth. This appears to be reasonable. After all, who wants to be "unbalanced"? Who wants to be "extreme"? These are positions that only our opponents/enemies hold. But here we have lost control of our language, and we are letting language use us. In reality, particularly in political reality, there is no such thing as a "balanced" position. What exists are competing interests, and balance is always *stasis* (or non-movement) which is quite often counter-productive. Thus, politicians always call for "balance" or "centralism," *their* privileged positions, which means little more than acquiescence to the status quo. Scholars are told to be "balanced" in their research, which means they should avoid challenging the status quo (i.e., stick to "bean counting"). "Balance," in short, is another name for what professionals commonly call "objectivity." While there are some important exceptions, most academic scholarship fits this conservative, anti-rhetorical, essentialist model. Similar to most people committed to a paradigm, scholars do not like to "rock the boat."

Weigh both sides—that is a good thing to do, but for what reason? Ultimately, a person is forced to judge based upon what she or he knows, and thus true balance and objectivity are never possible. But people who call for both believe that it is attainable, and usually expect balance and objectivity because judgment or criticism is the last thing they want. An "objective" stance frees a person from moral responsibility, it is simply the Way-Things-Are, and the mouthpiece for that Truth is not responsible for the implications of that Truth. In short, when scholars, politicians, religious people, or anyone else plays the politics of ontological Truth, they divide the world through definitions of "right" and "wrong," and they protect their definitions with highly emotive language that gives their positions a natural appearance—it keeps them from appearing coldhearted and self-interested. Everyone wants "reality" on her or his side, which is why "realism" is a rhetorical identification that all politicians strive for and which is why, during the centuries of religious wars between competing sects of Christianity that plagued Europe, all the armies claimed that God was on *their* side. The "war" currently between the "Christian" West and the Arab or Muslim world has a similar and tragic dynamic.

Rhetoric, as an idea, is always marginalized in such a game because it is a way of cutting, of slicing the world in a particular way and, thus, is a way of challenging the reifications of language that people use to control the world. Consequently, rhetoric is a potentially powerful tool in helping people to re-envision their lives and is for this reason frequently marginalized by the elites of our society. It is a way of emphasizing one set of relationships at the expense of others. Elites deny that they use rhetoric and try very hard to keep the rest of us from utilizing its resources by denying rhetoric's utility.

Rhetoric is frequently marginalized by a false distinction between "Truth" and "Appearance," as the two earlier examples suggest. Truth is what they believe, and rhetoric is that which promotes appearance. This position assumes that there is "the world," on the one hand, and language on the other, and that the two seldom interact. When they do interact, we should be on our guard, since nothing but trouble can follow. When the world is seen as existing independent of language, then our methods of knowing, themselves, must be purged of any linguistic connection. This means that we have to control what we say, so as not to fall prey to our perceptions, which, in a *de facto* manner, interfere with "Truth." If we cannot control what we say, and thus what we think, there is always someone else waiting to do this for us. The job of the censor and the executioner has always been to protect the explanation or justification given for the existing order.

Rhetoric is thus seen in our society as a threat. This is why it is demonized in the popular media. Rhetoric is, first and foremost, an invitation to change. It is a not-so-subtle reminder that the world is constructed through language and that it can be reconstructed if people are committed to talking about things differently. This sentiment is expressed beautifully in Foucault's poetic language when he writes that there "are times in life when the question of knowing if one can think differently than one thinks, and perceive differently than one sees, is absolutely necessary if one is to go on looking and reflecting at all."[21] Critical thinking, he adds, is "the endeavor to know how and to what extent it might be possible to think differently, instead of legitimating what is already known."[22]

ᔆ Difficulty of Defining Rhetoric ᔆ

Now that we have discussed the meaning of rhetoric in contemporary culture, we need to start training ourselves to think about rhetoric in a more *positive* fashion, since it can be a powerful tool in our lives to help us determine who we want to be and how we want to live. To aid in this process we will, in the next section, explore some of the more useful definitions of rhetoric. But before we do that, we need first to learn to appreciate how difficult it is to define rhetoric. To this end, please consider the following examples and try to determine whether or not each is a form of rhetoric or the extent to which it has a persuasive element:

1. A presidential inaugural address
2. The United States' flag
3. Burning the United States' flag
4. A textbook on physics or mathematics
5. Aristotle's *Poetics*
6. A personal diary
7. A physician's or professor's clothing
8. A piece of architecture

The first item on the list, the presidential inaugural address, seems to be a relatively straightforward, even paradigmatic, instance of rhetorical communication. Even given its negative connotations, rhetoric, in the popular mind, is usually associated with political discourse. As discussed earlier, politicians frequently extol their opponents to drop their "rhetoric" and to engage in "action." In this context, "simplicity" and "honesty" are usually antonyms for rhetoric. No matter how we look at it, a presidential inaugural address constitutes an act of persuasion.[23]

What about the U.S. flag? Is the flag, by itself, an instance of rhetoric? This question is more difficult to answer than the first. What about burning the flag? To what degree can that be considered an act of persuasion?

Clearly, the flag is a symbol; it speaks to something more than itself. Few symbols in our society evoke the intense emotional response that the U.S. flag evokes. As the recurring attempt in the U.S. Congress to pass a Constitutional amendment to "protect" the flag from desecration suggests, many Americans treat the flag as if it were dear to their *selves*, almost as if the flag were a *part* of themselves in ways that other institutions are not. Why else would the flag need to be protected, as if it were a child or a bald eagle that could be physically harmed or made extinct? What is it that we are trying to "protect" when we say the flag is "threatened"? What collective angst is generated when a citizen or foreign government publicly burns the U.S. flag? Surely, it is not the cloth we are protecting; the cloth is not a sentient being that can be harmed. Furthermore, people destroy fabric all the time without controversy. For example, we do not arrest people for ripped jeans or torn shirts.

Literally, we are protecting ourselves, or parts of ourselves, when we feel threatened by criticism directed toward the flag or the destruction of a particular flag through fire or mutilation. We are specifically protecting the preferred meanings of ourselves, meanings that correspond to our religious, national, and ideological ideals. Since the flag is an icon embedded with many of these ideals, it accentuates and even anchors much of our collective moral identity. In protecting the flag, we are trying to honor some part of ourselves that we feel is exemplary and praiseworthy. This is natural and healthy, a logical extension of our ability to use (and misuse) symbols. (Qoute of Kenneth Burke)

The flag is *iconic*. That is, it is a physical representation of an abstract entity—the United States of America. In nature, there is no such *thing* as the United States of America. The United States of America is an idea, a symbolic entity that is constructed on part of the land mass known as North America. The collective character of this entity is reified or represented by its symbols. These symbols, in turn, help call into being its presence and its meaning in our lives. To the extent that the U.S. flag convinces us that this abstract entity (our nation) has a material presence, and to the extent that it determines, in part, the way we will understand its presence, it is persuasion. That the flag incites patriotism (or hostility) is an example of its persuasive, or at least its communicative, power.

In a traditional sense, however, the flag is not rhetoric, since there is no speaker and no obvious intent. The flag is simply there; we read into it what we want. When someone burns the flag, however, she or he is consciously manipulating this symbol in a particular way. The element of intent is thus introduced.

But why would someone burn the flag? Is this not sacrilege or treason? There are, in fact, many reasons for wanting to do so. For example, by federal law, people are obligated to burn the flag if it becomes soiled or frayed.[24] The intent here is to protect the "honor" of the flag, or to enact the duty one feels on behalf of the law. Other people burn the flag because they respect what it represents, at least theoretically, which is openness, tolerance, and freedom. When flag burners look around and see that the United States often pursues policies, both domestically and internationally, that are contrary to its stated values, they destroy the flag to protest peacefully. In destroying the physical flag, these people are attempting to illustrate that the important values represented by the flag have been corrupted or are otherwise endangered. Persuasion is the main intent of these people.

The final group of people who burn U.S. flags are those who, for one reason or another, have been positioned as enemies of the United States. They burn the flag, usually in mass rallies to gather or otherwise galvanize support for their anti-U.S. resistance. Again, there is an element of a persuasive intent involved, but not so much as in the previous example. In this instance, the people burning the flag and their spectators already have made up their minds about the United States—burning the flag simply serves as a trumpet call to arouse the passions of the people against the United States. In contrast, when the second group of people mentioned above burn the flag, they are doing so in a strategic attempt to incite people to reconsider their values and to see the world differently.

The resources for persuasion in this context lie in the citizens' perception of their nation and are essential to their formulation of a collective national pride. In the United States, this collective perception often lacks a critical consciousness. As suggested in the previous chapter, a critical consciousness involves a multidisciplinary study grounded in the integration of narrative, philosophy, community, cultural memory, and history. By simultaneously involving us in the present as well as in the innumerable pasts, a critical consciousness enables citizens to appreciate the construction and manipulation of what are understood as narratives of normative history. In short, a critical consciousness helps to debunk the normative myths of our contemporary, consumer-oriented, mass-mediated culture.

What about a textbook on physics or mathematics? In what ways can this be considered rhetorical? What persuasive elements can it possibly have? What about knowledge in general? Unlike the two previous examples, we are on less clear footing here as we search for paradigmatic instances of rhetoric. Clearly, in its attempt to understand the natural laws of the universe, physics has been quite successful in many of its goals and mathematics is a useful tool for that end. In order to accomplish these ends, both have to be accurate and objective in terms of applying and understanding knowledge in the field and both books are dependent upon highly refined methods. In these major respects neither is rhetorical or persuasive. Nevertheless, there is still a sense in which all knowledge, including a knowledge of physics and math, does involve rhetoric and involves elements of persuasion.

To borrow a popular metaphor from the traditional philosophy of science, our minds are not "mirrors" (recall Weaver's evocation of the metaphor a few pages back) that we can polish with logic so that it can reflect back the universe as it *is*.[25] Rather, we use the tools of logic and analysis to help us in our understanding, and that understanding will always be limited and situated clearly in the subjective, in what Nietzsche called the "human-all-too-human." We are limited by our five senses. Even more so, we are limited by the structures and conditions of our own brains. One of those conditions involves human symbolicity. As Burke explains, "Man, qua man, is a symbol user. In this respect, every aspect of his 'reality' is likely to be seen through a fog of symbols."[26] We, in the sense that we think about ourselves, do not exist outside the conditions of this fog.

Simply, what we know and experience are only *representations* of the world. These representations are not exact copies of the world, but the world as filtered through our human subjectivities, which include our morals, perspectives, and beliefs. In other words, we never get the world the way it *is*; rather, we get it in the way that it makes sense to us as humans. When we communicate about the world, we communicate about it as humans—that is, highly selectively and with a large degree of anthropomorphism—we understand the universe only in relationship to our human features and needs. As Thomas Kuhn and others have demonstrated, the pragmatics of scientific advancement is often dependent upon political and other types of contingent and historical matters.[27] Whenever we are talking about contingency and history, we are talking at some level about rhetorical processes.

As we have discussed, knowledge in the scientific realm can often be considered rhetorical or at least considered to have an important rhetorical dimension. If this is indeed true, as scholars in the communication discipline argue, then it is even truer about knowledge in the humanities. Indeed, this is a less controversial claim. With this in mind, what can we say about Aristotle's treatise called the *Poetics*? In what ways can we say that the *Poetics* has a rhetorical dimension? Obviously it is rhetorical in the sense in which we claimed a physics textbook is rhetorical. But this book's rhetorical dimensions are even more pronounced than the previous example. Why?

Aristotle's book seems mistitled to our modern ears. The book is about what we would consider to be drama today, not poetry, although in Aristotle's day the method of drama was very much a form of poetry. A basic assumption that Aristotle makes about drama is that it exists in the service of the state. Drama serves an important propagandistic function of "draining" off dissent and unrest by providing audience members with an opportunity to vent and purge their frustrations, which might otherwise be expressed in undesirable political action. An important theory that comes out of his writings on poetry and drama is known as *catharsis*. For instance, in his explanation of tragedy, Aristotle writes that it "is the imitation of an action that is serious . . . in a dramatic, not in a narrative form; with incidents arousing pity and fear, with which to accomplish its catharsis of such emotions."[28] In other words, by experiencing these counterproductive feelings vicariously through art, audiences are given the opportunity to relieve themselves of any inclination they may have of expressing them through their lives.

Another reason the book can be regarded as rhetorical involves Aristotle's motivation for writing it. While he might have written the book for any number of reasons, the book clearly fits nicely with his overall political philosophy, one that is not altogether democratic. Aristotle believed in an aristocracy, one in which the government is ruled by its most capable citizens (read "richest" for capable). Rhetoric is central to his society because, although aristocratic, Aristotle is not as politically rigid as other theorists, such as Plato. Aristotle believed in a society that could keep itself happy if the rulers governed wisely. He believed in a fairly wide public sphere, but rationalized the exclusion of women and slaves. Unlike Plato, he did not feel that force was necessary to keep people in line; he felt that persuasion could accomplish this goal. Therefore, the theatre was an important political forum for Aristotle and for the Athenians more generally, because here was a place where people's ideas could be controlled in a non-obtrusive and even enjoyable manner.[29]

What about a personal diary? Can this be rhetoric if there is no sense of an external audience? Clearly, every major theorist of rhetoric discusses the importance of audience to the act of rhetoric or persuasion. Audience is a central part of all rhetoric as it is in persuasion more generally and will be discussed in some detail in Chapter 8. With this in mind, it is difficult to make a case for rhetoric existing in this context, with the clear exception being that we often engage in self-persuasion. The very act of writing supposes an audience, or else there would be no need to write. In many cases, that audience is our-selves or for some anticipated posterity. We write in order to reach some sort of understanding or clarity about something we have experienced. Journals are usually emotional and personal, but even if they are factual and descriptive, they are ways for us to understand what we have experienced. In most cases, writing is an act of self-creation and recreation.

Sometimes, however, these personal journals are shared. In that shar-ing they are sometimes persuasive in content and sometimes not. French phi-losopher Jean-Paul Sartre's war diaries, for instance, were probably never in-tended to be shared, but, nevertheless, they offer commentary on the Second World War, convey information about his private life and loves, and express the seeds of ideas that he later developed in his mature philosophical writ-ings.[30] The net result of this journal, at least in its published form, is a state-ment of autobiography and perhaps of philosophy. It may be persuasive in the sense that it expresses, at times, the ugliness of war, but this is not the primary intent of the text.

In contrast with Sartre's diary, the diary of the young Anne Frank and the diary of Anonymous (published as *Go Ask Alice*) are exceedingly rhetorical documents, even if they were not intended as such by their authors.[31] Both Anne Frank and Anonymous (dubbed "Alice" by her publishers) were young women who lived tragic lives. Anne Frank, the more famous of the two, was confined for two years in an attic in Holland with her family. They were Jewish and Holland was occupied by the Nazis. They hid above a warehouse, and young Anne had to spend her days without moving, for fear of being heard be-low by the workers and reported to the police. To pass her time, she wrote a remarkable journal, in which she detailed her daily existence, and pondered the significance of her experiences. Eventually her family was discovered by the German authorities, and Anne Frank, along with all of her family except her father, perished in Hitler's death camps. After the war, her father returned to their old hiding place and discovered her diary. It was subsequently published and remains an important twentieth-century testament to human courage, and a scathing indictment of human barbarity. Undoubtedly, the book is persuasive. Few people can read it and remain unmoved by the plight of people living un-der similar conditions of injustice.

Anonymous' diary is less worldly in its scope, but immensely relevant to aspects of U.S. culture since the late 1960s. The book was published in 1971 and has remained in print. The diary was purported to be written mostly on garbage bags and on other scraps of paper that were found after "Alice," a fifteen-year-old, died from a drug overdose. The diary chronicles "Alice's" life over her final turbulent years. It is a description of alienation, unhappiness, estrangement from one's family, despair, drug abuse, and sexual promiscuity. "Alice" is continually getting into trouble, running away from home, using drugs, and engaging in prostitution to support herself. Friends and family are not able to help her, and at the end of the book we are informed by the publisher that "Alice" has died.

The diary, at least as it is positioned as a published book that claims on its cover to be "a real diary," is clearly an attempt to warn young people of the dangers of rebellion against parental authority and the lure of counter-cultural traditions.[32] The book speaks the language of young people and it is persuasive, not because the persuasion is obvious but because it is not obvious, at least to young readers. Indeed, the moral lessons of the book are not lost to its young readers. When young adults read the book, they experience what "Alice" experiences, and it leaves a deeper impression on them than the overt injunction, "Just Say No." As a scholar of persuasion, I cannot imagine a more effective piece of propaganda to give to children to discourage them from using drugs, although it may have the *opposite* effect on older, more mature or experienced readers who may dismiss its anti-drug message and identify with the detailed and somewhat exciting descriptions of drug culture the book contains. Unlike the government's "Just Say No" campaign, or the Drug Abuse Resistance Education (D.A.R.E.) campaign in the schools that makes little effort to hide its dependence on a federal propagandistic source, the persuasive content of *Go Ask Alice* does not call attention to itself to younger readers. For a certain and vulnerable audience of young people, it is not overtly moralistic.

In what respect could a physician or professor's clothing be considered rhetorical? Imagine for a moment that you are feeling ill and have to go to the doctor. When you arrive at the doctor's office, you are greeted at the door by the receptionist wearing scruffy and dirty clothes, with unkempt hair and rough mannerisms. Imagine that the office is clean, but untidy with old, sagging furniture. Imagine further that when the doctor appears, he is dressed in cutoffs and a Metallica T-shirt, and his forearms are heavily covered with tattoos. Imagine that his teeth are not perfect, that his grammar is slightly off, and that perhaps he is unbathed. A farfetched scenario, to be sure, but, nevertheless, how would we feel about his advice? Or to take another example, assume that you needed surgery and, the night before the surgery, you are nervous and go to a local bar for a drink. There you meet your surgeon, hanging out with her friends in her casual street apparel. How would you feel? In neither case would patients feel very comfortable, even if there were no objective differences in the skills between either physician and other highly respected doctors. After all, many doctors go to bars, are free to dress as they like, and socialize with their friends. There is no law that requires doctors to wear their white coats, and often there is not even a need for it. Objectively, in medicine or any other field, personal appearance is incidental to professional competency.

In the abstract, appearance and competency are not connected, but in practice this is often the case. As we will discuss in further detail in Chapter 7 on credibility, the way we dress says a great deal about who we are and how people should treat us. For example, all of us have had experience with treating our clothes and our appearance as being something more than just comfort. In many cases there is actually a conflict between our *strategic* use of clothing and our desire to be comfortable. Simply put, we "dress for success." In other words, we often dress for *influence*; we dress for some sort of predetermined effect. The way we dress and present ourselves has much to do with our credibility, which, in turn, has much to do with our ability to persuade. This is why people who are in positions of responsibility, or otherwise want to be considered trustworthy, pay special attention to the way they dress and appear in public. For instance, I once teased one of my graduate students, Dee Morgenthaler, who is studying to be a critical scholar, for wearing high heels to class when she taught public speaking. Dee retorted, intelligently, that I wear a *tie* each day when I come to work, even when I am *not* teaching. High heels and ties are two examples of nonfunctional and uncomfortable garments that are essential for acceptance in most professional communities and are expected by the clients of most professions.

Finally, in what ways could we construe architecture as rhetorical? Humans, like most animals, are spatial creatures. Thus, we tend to be influenced by the relative space between us and other stimuli. Similar to animals, space makes or breaks us. Imagine, for instance, being confined in a zoo—no wonder wild animals, particularly mammals, look so lethargic and pathetic when they are held, for years at a time, in captivity. Or visit a prison. Inside, we find the same sorts of depressed, under-stimulated creatures. This is intentional—most of what we mean by punishment is confinement and an internalized sense of pain. While we take such confinement for granted when prisoners—society's "other"—are subjected to it, few of us stop to consider the way that our environment, specifically the spaces that are provided for us by our buildings and offices, conditions us to think and behave in certain ways. Indeed, many of the mechanisms of the prison operate throughout society more generally.[33]

From the beginning of Western culture, the Greeks and the Romans paid specific attention to the magnificence of their architecture. Not only that, but the European cultures that succeeded them would outdo themselves by lavishly spending money on palaces, cathedrals, and other magnificent public displays of architecture. Why? In a real sense, our architecture represents our society and our state. Such architecture helps us to define the national character of our society, and it even helps to influence the national psyche.

In all strong states—that is, states that are both bold and wealthy—architecture becomes even more accentuated. Hitler, for example, had detailed plans to rebuild Berlin in a way befitting his international empire.[34] In less extreme, but also well-ordered and collectivist societies, such as the former Soviet Russia and modern China, the physical center of their political worlds consisted of great plazas. Red Square and Tiananmen Square are places where millions could gather in patriotic displays of strength and solidarity (discussed more in Chapter 8). A similar place exists in the United States in front of the Lincoln memorial—the "Mall."

Even a quick glance around Washington, D.C., will show that many of its monuments are overtly suggestive of a particular attitude toward the federal government. Furthermore, a journey to our larger cities will quickly show that their skyscrapers communicate a certain reverence for the wealth and power of the corporations that constructed them. Space encourages certain behaviors, as do color and shape. Before any building can be built, the architect needs to have a detailed idea of what sort of function it is going to serve in the community.[35]

❧ Definitions of Rhetoric ❧

In the previous paragraphs, we have broadly discussed some of the dimensions of this concept we call "rhetoric." Now it is time to see how scholars have defined it in the past. Rhetoric is an old concept; indeed, it is the oldest formal area of study in Western culture.[36] Because it has been around so long, and because it is so central to our society, it has been defined by different people in divergent ways. What follows are some of the more popular definitions of rhetoric that remain influential.

We will start with Plato, the man who first coined the word in circa 385 BCE.[37] Plato defines rhetoric as "The art of leading the psyche through words."[38] Plato sees persuasion as a powerful tool for controlling or for inciting the passions. In fact, rhetoric is so powerful for Plato that he spends considerable time explaining why it needs to be guarded against by a wise philosopher-king, whose authority, while ostensibly extending from Reality or Truth itself, would, in fact, be backed by a powerful police state and the resources of public manipulation.[39]

Our next definition is from Aristotle. No one in history has had a greater influence in constructing the parameters of rhetoric than Aristotle. It is only a small exaggeration to say that all of rhetoric since Aristotle has been an extension or a refutation of his ideas; at least until recently. In the last few years there has been an explosion of perspectives on rhetoric, some of which bypass Aristotle completely.[40] Nevertheless, no one today can talk about persuasion for long without engaging with Aristotle on some level.

Aristotle differs from Plato, his teacher, in many areas, and this is particularly true in his view of rhetoric and persuasion. Whereas Plato seeks to control persuasion, and to direct its service to the strengthening of the state, Aristotle seeks to extend its power to a wide range of men (but not to women nor to slaves) so that it could be used in the service of collective governance. Aristotle defines rhetoric as "the counterpart of dialectic" and as "the faculty of discerning in every case the available means of persuasion."[41] What Aristotle means by this is that rhetoric is a dynamic that helps to structure our thought and perceptions. We are successful as persuaders when we can see the objective conditions under which persuasion can occur. People trained under Aristotle's system of rhetoric literally react to the world differently from people who are not similarly trained. Rhetorical action is also such that it directs sight, and Aristotle's system is designed to accentuate the structure of that sight.[42]

Kenneth Burke, the scholar who most closely approaches Aristotle in terms of his significance to the rhetorical tradition, defines rhetoric much more broadly. For Burke, rhetoric is the "the use of language as a symbolic means of inducing cooperation in beings that by nature respond to symbols."[43] More specifically:

> Paper need *not know the meaning* of fire in order to burn. But in the "idea" of fire there is a persuasive ingredient. By this route something of the rhetorical motive comes to lurk in every "meaning," however purely "scientific" its pretensions. Wherever there is persuasion, there is rhetoric. And wherever there is "meaning" there is "persuasion." Food, eaten and digested, is not rhetorical. But in the *meaning* of food there is much rhetoric, the meaning being persuasive enough for the idea of food to be used, like the ideas of religion, as a rhetorical device of statesmen.[44]

For Burke, the rhetorical motive is to be found wherever human beings are. In many senses, the rhetorical is the human. As he explains, rhetoric is "not rooted in any past condition of human society. It is rooted in an essential function of language itself, a function that is wholly realistic, and is continually born anew; the use of language as a symbolic means of inducing cooperation in beings that by nature respond to symbols."[45] In sum, Burke approaches rhetoric as a system of identifications and misidentifications (discussed in more detail in Chapter 6). Rhetoric is how we cooperate with each other, or otherwise form alliances against others.

Another theorist, I. A. Richards, defines rhetoric as "the study of misunderstanding and its remedies."[46] Richards, writing in Europe between two world wars, was under the impression that traditional notions of rhetoric and communication in the West bred a combative mentality which he saw reflected in the world around him. He correctly points out that classical rhetoric, meaning Aristotelian rhetoric, "was the theory of the battle of the words and has always been itself dominated by the combative impulse."[47] This impulse, and the tendency to miscommunicate in the ever-widening social universe, leads to conflict and social disease. To correct for this, and to exert a positive influence on the world that he saw being destroyed around him, Richards lectured and wrote that language could be cleared of certain structural differences that lead to political confusion or disagreement. For example, he tried to simplify the English language and he invented a range of marks and other signifiers with which to supplement the written language (things such as specialized quotation marks).[48]

Finally, in an influential essay, Donald Bryant defines rhetoric as the "art of adapting ideas to people and people to ideas." For him, rhetoric is "The rationale of informative and persuasive discourse."[49] Rhetoric is all these things, and it is more. It serves as strategic discourse, the structure of language, and as the regulator of social meaning. Rhetoric controls, and it transforms. Saints and sinners both use rhetoric and persuasion to enact their ends. As graffiti found on an ancient Greek wall from the sixth century BCE declares, the person who does not study rhetoric will likely be victimized by rhetoric.[50]

❧ Conclusion ☙

In this chapter, we discussed what rhetoric and communication are and why they are important. We looked at two general ways for approaching our understanding of rhetoric, and accentuated the epistemological view—the notion that rhetoric and communication create knowledge. We explored the meaning of rhetoric in contemporary culture and highlighted rhetoric's ability to help people change their political and social perspectives. For this reason, rhetoric is often downplayed or ridiculed by our politicians and cultural leaders, people who wish to stabilize society's preferred meanings. In an important sense, rhetoric is always the enemy of dogma and tradition, as it always asks the question "why?" Few religions or political regimes can long tolerate that simple question, for ultimately, they have no compelling answers. When "why" is answered with "just because," as is often the case, then the reification of the established order begins its slow eventual decline. Finally, we have discussed the difficulty of defining rhetoric, and then offered several influential definitions of rhetoric.

In the following chapter we are going to move beyond these theoretical discussions, that is, move from "rhetoric" to "persuasion" and explore the pervasiveness of persuasion in our daily lives. From there we will explore specific definitions of persuasion (Chapter 4) before extending to a study of the persuasion process (Chapter 5), which concludes Part I of this book.

໖ Notes ໕

1. Culture wars denote long situated and deeply divisive public conflict grounded in competing values. These values can be "liberal" and "conservative," or something more profound, but the point is that American society, while institutionally stable, is bitterly divided on a number of fundamental social issues—things such as war, abortion, gun control, separation of church and state, privacy and gay rights. See James Davis Hunter, *Culture Wars: The Struggle to Control the Family, Art, Education, Law, and Politics in America* (New York: Basic Books, 1992).

2. NCA is the oldest and largest professional communication association, founded in 1914. For information about its activities or how to join, visit its website at http://www.natcom.org.

3. Robert L. Scott, "On Viewing Rhetoric as Epistemic," *Central States Speech Journal*, 18 (1967), 9–17.

4. There is an important subdivision of Communication Studies known as the rhetoric of science. See Alan Gross, *The Rhetoric of Science* (Cambridge, MA: Harvard University Press, 1996).

5. In Patricia P. Matsen, Philip Rollinson, and Marion Sousa, eds., *Readings from Classical Rhetoric* (Carbondale, IL: Southern Illinois University Press, 1990), 55.

6. *Conscientious Objections: Stirring up Trouble About Language, Technology, and Education* (New York: Vintage Books, 1988), 23.

7. *The Complete Poems* (Middlesex, England: Penguin, 1983), 211.

8. The *a priori* is a philosophical concept that helps people to reason from "self-evident" propositions. It is an assumed knowledge that exists independent of observation. It is a form of pre-existing, non-human dependent form of knowledge, something held to be a contextual and universally valid.

9. No one knows for sure if Lao Tzu was an actual person. According to legend, Lao Tzu (which means "Old Man") was an imperial archivist in ancient China who became disgruntled with the affairs of the kingdom and retired to the frontier—what is now Tibet. As he passed from the kingdom, the final guard recognized Lao Tzu as a sage and begged him to record his teaching. Lao Tzu sat in the imperial outpost and composed the *Tao De Ching* (The Way of Virtue).

10. Lao Tzu, *Tao De Ching*, annotated by Guoqing Chen and Aidong Zhang, (Xi'an, China: San Qin Publishing House, 1995.) [Original translation from the Chinese by Dr. Rui Zhao for this textbook]. Incidentally, Lao Tzu's book is, after the Western Bible, the most widely trans lated book in the world, and is a central expression of traditional Asian life.

11. *Ontology*, the study of "being," is the branch of philosophy historically concerned with the search for essential forms to "ground" an objective reality. The question "What is Truth" would be an example of a concern for the time-independent boundaries of an object that can be known supposedly outside of human subjective bias. These types of questions have animated our ancestors but have tended, in the opinion of many modern philosophers, to have been misguided and counterproductive to the creation of inclusive and tolerant societies.

12. Quoted in Fung Yu-Lan, A *Short History of Chinese Philosophy* (New York: The Free Press, 1948), 23.

13. Ibid., 13.

14. *The Rhetoric of Religion: Studies in Logology* (California: University of California Press, 1970), 305.

15. The book is *Bargaining for National Security: The Postwar Disarmament Negotiations* by Lloyd Jensen. The book was advertised in a Sage Publications catalogue, and the quote was attributed to the *Journal of Politics*.

16. A note on my use of gendered pronouns. A careful reader will find that, almost without exception, all of the gendered pronouns used in the quoted sources are masculine. This reflects historical biases in learned discourse—up to relatively recently women were for the most part excluded from the community of learners that made up the audience for producing and consuming academic discourse. In more recent times, writers attempt to correct for this and typically add the feminine pronoun after the masculine pronoun. While this is an improvement, a tacit recognition of the other half of the human population, it still privileges the masculine over the feminine. In fairness, therefore, I have throughout this text inverted this sequence and will exclusively place the feminine pronoun before the masculine. While such a sensitivity to pronoun use may seem trite, it underscores a central point of this textbook and course. Language matters. The German philosopher Friedrich Nietzsche once wrote: "I am afraid we are not rid of God because we still have faith in grammar." What he meant by this is that language structures thought, that the words and relationship among words come first, and from that we have deduced metaphysical structures that we then force ourselves to accommodate. In other words, our metaphysics is a shadow of our language, and not the other way around as people often assume. Communication scholar Kenneth Burke, a student of Nietzsche, came to a similar conclusion. He cautions us to use language, and not to let language use us; that the words we use, and perhaps the languages we speak, condition us for seeing the world in a particular way and in acting in accordance with that view.

---

17. *Peace With Justice* (New York: Columbia University Press, 1961), 34–35.

18. *Ideas Have Consequences* (Chicago: University of Chicago Press, 1948), 35.

19. See Edmund Burke, *Reflections on the Revolution in France* (New York: Penguin Classics, 1986). Originally published in November 1790, this work provides a template for criticism directed at modern liberal and progressive political philosophy.

20. What Weaver means by metaphysics is the condition ascribed to the highest reality demarcated by "qualities of stasis, immutability, eternal perdurance" He adds, "That which is perfect does not change, that which has to change is less perfect." *Language is Sermonic*, edited by Richard L. Johannesen, Rennard Strickland, and Ralph T. Eubanks (Baton Rouge: Louisiana State University Press, 1970), 212.

21. *The Use of Pleasure* (New York: Vintage Books, 1990), 8.

22. Ibid., 9.

23. See Karlyn Kohrs Campbell and Kathleen Hall Jamieson, *Deeds Done in Words: Preidential Rhetoric and the Genres of Governance* (Chicago: University of Chicago Press, 1990), 14–36.

24. United States Code, Title 4, ¶8 (k) states, "The flag, when it is in such condition that it is no longer a fitting emblem for display, should be destroyed in a dignified way, preferably by burning."

25. For a description of this metaphor and its critique, see Richard Rorty, *Philosophy and the Mirror of Nature* (Princeton: Princeton University Press, 1979).

26. *A Rhetoric of Motives* (Berkeley: University of California Press, 1969), 136.

27. This point is made particularly salient in Thomas S. Kuhn, *The Structure of Scientific Revolutions 3rd ed.* (Chicago: University of Chicago Press, 1996). See also the work of Richard Rorty, in particular, *Philosophy and the Mirror of Nature* and Michel Foucault, *The Order of Things: An Archaeology of the Human Sciences* (New York: Vintage Press, 1970).

28. *Poetics* translated by Ingram Bywater (New York: The Modern Library), 230.

29. See my extended discussion of Aristotle on this point in *The Rise of Rhetoric and its Intersections With Modern Critical Thought* (Boulder, CO: Westview Press, 1998), 154–178.

30. *The War Diaries: November 1939–March 1940* (New York: Pantheon, 1984).

31. *Ann Frank, The Diary of a Young Girl: The Definitive Edition* (New York: Doubleday, 1991); *Go Ask Alice* (Englewood Cliffs, NJ: Prentice-Hall, 1971).

32. In fact, the book was written by Beatrice Sparks, a Mormon psychologist, who intended the book to be a "cautionary tale" or, as her critics would point out, propaganda. Sparks claimed to have based the book on the experiences of actual clients whose lives were being destroyed by drugs. In what ways does knowing this change our appraisal of the book?

33. Michel Foucault, *Discipline and Punish: The Birth of the Prison* (New York: Vintage, 1979).

34. See Albert Speer, *Alpert Speer: Architecture, 1932–1942* (France: Archives d'Architecture Moderne, 1985).

35. For a study of the rhetoric of architecture that reviews the relevant literatures, see Carole Blair, Marsha Jepperson, and Enrico Pucci, Jr., "Public Memorializing in Postmodernity: The Vietnam Veterans Memorial as Prototype," *Quarterly Journal of Speech, 77* (1991), 263–288.

36. See Goodwin F. Berquist, William E. Coleman, J. Michael Sproule, and Ruth Golden, *The Rhetoric of Western Thought 9th ed.* (Dubuque: Kendall/Hunt Publishing, 2007).

37. BCE stands for "Before the Common Era." It is synonymous with BC (Before Christ) in that it refers to dates before the year 1 as demarcated by the Western calendar; however, it is intended to be a dating system free from a Christian-centric world view. By evoking this phrase, I recognize the world-historical significance of the Christian cosmology in affecting our dating system, without reifying and, thus, giving tacit support to such a cosmology.

38. The context of Plato's coining of the word "rhetoric" is discussed in Edward Schiappa, *Protagoras and Logos: Studies in Greek Philosophy and Rhetoric* (Columbia: University of South Carolina Press, 1991). Plato discusses rhetoric throughout his corpus, but his most detailed discussions and definition appear in his *Gorgias*, trans. W.C. Helmbold (Indianapolis: Bobbs-Merrill Company, 1952) and in his *Phaedrus* trans. W.C. Helmbold and W.G. Rabinowitz (New York: Macmillan Publishing Company, 1956).

39. See Simona Forti, "The Biopolitics of Souls," *Political Theory, 34* (2006), 9–32.

40. See Karen A. Foss, Sonja K. Foss, and Cindy L. Griffin, *Feminist Rhetorical Theories* (Thousand Oaks, CA: Sage, 1999).

41. *On Rhetoric: A Theory of Civic Discourse*, trans. George A. Kennedy (New York: Oxford University Press, 1991), 28, 36.

42. For a wider discussion and illustration of this point through a discussion of *kairos* (timing) and *ornatus* (style), see Omar Swartz, "Understanding Rhetorical Timing By Means of an Analogy," *Speech Communication Teacher, 11* (1997), 12–13.

43. *A Rhetoric of Motives*, 43.

44. *A Rhetoric of Motives*, 173.

45. Ibid., 43.

46. *The Philosophy of Rhetoric* (New York: Oxford University Press, 1936), 3.

47. Ibid., 24.

48. *Richards on Rhetoric*: *I.A. Richards, Selected Essays, 1929–1974,* ed., Ann E. Berthoff (New York: Oxford University Press, 1991).

49. "Rhetoric: Its Functions and its Scope," *Quarterly Journal of Speech, 39* (1953), 404.

50. Discussed in James J. Murphy and Richard A. Katula, *A Synoptic History of Classical Rhetoric 3rd ed.* (Mahwah, NJ: Lawrence Erlbaum, 2003), 3.

CHAPTER 3

The Pervasiveness of Persuasion in
U.S. Society

In a democratic society such as ours, persuasion is a pervasive phenomenon and is central to understanding our sociological, commercial, and political identities as well as our much-vaunted "way of life." As we have been discussing so far in this textbook and course, it is the flow of communication and the controversy that often surrounds such flow that makes for a healthy and robust society. Indeed, one measure of how democratic any society is involves the degree to which communication is open and to which dialogue can affect or influence community norms. In an important sense, a quiet society is often a *closed* society. A public, civic society is necessarily noisy and rambunctious. [*open*]

Notice that in the word *deliberation*, the word *liberation* is found, and, in American philosopher John Dewey's view, liberation is the self-realization of a person developed through the process of contributing to a common good. This democratic vision engages a dialectical relationship between the self and community, in which Dewey argued that people's self realization could be achieved through the process of mutual inquiry, communication, and the moral development that accompanies such communion with others. The democratic process is one that both embraces and emerges from active dialogue among people with differing and diverse perspectives and values.[1] Under Dewey's views, we should seek liberation from the limitations of a limited world view.

Dewey, however, would probably be surprised and alarmed at the way communication is often practiced in contemporary society. He believed strongly in the ameliorative and edifying potential of communication to expand our moral and political consciousness. Dewey was critical of the advertisements of his day (he lived from 1859 to 1952) and fearful of the power of corporations to monopolize the public sphere. While Dewey believed fervently in the creative potential of each and every human being, he also recognized that education was fundamental for individuals to achieve the critical consciousness needed to actualize their creative potential. While open communication is a social good, it must be balanced against the need for preventing the manipulative power of media monopolies and unscrupulous commercial interests for using persuasion *against* us. As both a student of law and a communication scholar, I fear that we as a society have not yet struck this balance, as the following statistics suggest:

- *Advertising Age*, the industry flagship publication, along with other advertising professionals, estimates that people receive approximately 5,000 persuasive messages a day. These messages appear in newspapers, magazines, radio, television, cable, billboards, e-mails, as well as through interpersonal interactions.[2]

- The average American spends 11% of her/his life watching television.[3] That breaks down to approximately 4 hours and 35 minutes of TV viewing each day.[4] By the time the average American is 20, she/he has viewed one million commercials.[5] Those commercials add up: three years of the average American's life will be spent watching television *commercials*.[6]

- In 2005, credit card companies mailed 5.23 billion offers.[7] In 2006, marketers sent more than 114 billion pieces of direct mail—catalogues, credit card solicitations, coupons, and the like.[8] In the same year, marketers spent $1.5 billion to send out nearly 600 billion junk e-mail messages.[9]

- These messages can be extremely expensive, but they work. For instance, the cost of a 30-second spot for the 2009 Super Bowl will be $3 million.[10] The 2008 Super Bowl was viewed by 97.5 million people in the United States and advertisers received "a return of $1.25 to $2.74 for every dollar invested in Super Bowl advertising."[11]

Most of the 5,000 messages to which we are exposed are innocuous or insignificant and do not reach the level of our conscious awareness or are easily overlooked and/or dismissed. In fact, we are trained since birth to disregard most of what we hear and to which we are exposed, and these psychological filters are quite effective in distancing ourselves from the persuasive environment that clamors, constantly, for our attention. Without such filters, we would be overwhelmed by confusion, disorder, and paralysis. Yet many of these messages and some of these appeals are quite significant. Some can even be unhealthy. For example, many ads and cultural persuasions encourage people to smoke cigarettes, to drink alcohol, and to consume unhealthy foods.[12] Others encourage us to adopt lifestyles that are unsustainable, irresponsible, or deleterious to our self-images as well as to the environment.

We tend to take the communication environment described previously in stride, but we should not be so accepting or uncritical of its impact on us. Of course, any *one* ad or message is not going to have an effect on people; it does not work that way. We can easily dismiss any one ad as inconsequential; most, in fact, are silly and unbelievable, which we readily discard. Nevertheless, ads may well have a *cumulative* effect on people's consciousness. Exposure to a million *anything* is significant and viewing a million ads, particularly for young people, has an *inculcating* effect. One psychological theory—the theory of mere repeated exposure—recognizes that the more we experience things in our environment, the more natural they become.[13] We grow to take pleasure in the familiar and to measure our boundaries by what we see around us.

Imagine, for example, that you have an aunt who lives out-of-state who, one day, sends you in the mail a terrible and ugly painting that she lovingly created just for you. You take one look at the monstrosity and shove it immediately into the back of your closet, determined to never look at it again. Your aunt follows up with a phone call and asks if you like the painting, and you lie, saying that you enjoy the painting very much. You then forget about it for eight months when you receive a call from your aunt saying that she has flown in unannounced for a two-week visit. Before leaving the house to pick her up at the airport, you retrieve the painting and place it prominently on the wall in your living room. Your aunt is pleased to see it displayed. Two weeks later, your aunt leaves and you are too busy with work and school to take down the picture. Six months pass and you are hosting a holiday party for friends and co-workers. A guest asks about the painting. "My aunt painted this," you reply with pride, and with genuine sincerity.

I experienced this effect of repeated exposure directly when I was in college and taking an upper division course in persuasion, like readers are taking now. We were learning about the theory of mere repeated exposure when, walking across campus one day, I came across what appeared to be a block of rusted metal the size of a van. It looked like it fell from the back of a construction truck or that somebody had placed it temporarily on the lawn and had forgotten to remove it. I assumed it had been placed there inadvertently and expected it to be gone the next time I passed that way. It was not, and, as time passed, I realized it was *supposed* to be art and I made a point to register how ugly I thought it was, how it was a waste of money, etc. However, as the semester wore on, I found myself actually liking it. The purported reason for this is that familiarity leads to psychological comfort.[14]

Another way of discussing this effect of repeated exposure on a phenomenon is that the more we see things on television or reflected back at us by society, the more *real* they become, the more natural they appear. The technical term for this is *naturalization*. Naturalization occurs when people talk about things long enough that we assume that they have always existed. For example, the political entity that we know as the "United States" came into existence when people assumed and acted as if it existed. When seen from space, however, natural boundaries disappear. The United States exists, and we identify as American citizens, because everywhere we turn people and signs tell us that this is the case. Naturalization (or reification—from the German word *Verdinglichung* or "thingification") has occurred; an abstract concept has become "real." The more often we look at the American flag and reaffirm in our minds its primary meanings, the more substantial becomes our conceptual commitment to the reality it denotes.

Communication scholar Kenneth Burke once explained how persuasion works in the following way: "[W]e must think of rhetoric not in terms of some one particular address, but as a general *body of identifications* that owe their convincingness much more to trivial repetition and dull daily reinforcement than to exceptional rhetorical skill."[15] Key to understanding the importance of this quote is the emphasis on the words *trivial, dull,* and *reinforcement*. Our identities and worlds evolve over time, and the greatest influences on our lives are not the flashes of brilliance that we sometimes encounter, but the redundancy of our mundane experiences. Thus, we must not think about persuasion in the way that most of us tend to think about persuasion, as a gigantic hammer that we smash down on people's heads (the traditional metaphor of persuasion is of the fearful hypodermic needle or of the two mighty warriors embattled in the public forum). Rather, persuasion is often a "rhetoric," that is, a *strategic* and *subtle* positioning of people in light of specific values, beliefs, attitudes, and behaviors.

❧ An Average Day ❧

The theme of this chapter is that persuasion permeates everything we do and are. It is a powerful force that touches all aspects of our lives. To illustrate the ubiquity of persuasion in our society, this section walks us through an average day that a person might experience and illustrates how the environment in which we live bombards us, constantly, with persuasive messages and appeals.

We start the day by being wakened by our alarm clock. In many cases, we have clock-radios so the sound we hear is the music, talk, and background noise of the early morning broadcast. Perhaps, in fact, we are not really listening. But what are we tuning out? In most cases, unless we are listening to National Public Radio (NPR), we are being exposed to commercials. Even NPR spends an agonizing eight weeks a year on on-air fundraising campaigns where they make direct appeals for donations. Even if we are listening to NPR, it, like all mass media channels, is being *selective* in the types of news and information that it presents to us and is filtered through reporters and producers with a noticeably liberal bias. In any case, we often mistake what we see and hear in the media as *the* world, when it is actually the world as it is *presented* to us.

The above difference becomes very obvious when we talk about *demographics*, or the study of audiences based upon the tendencies of people to congregate based on their ideological predispositions. In important ways, we can identify the type of people we are by the media we consume. For instance, NPR listeners live in a different world than FOX News Network aficionados— no better, no worse, but different, often profoundly so, and this distinction is expressed in the hundreds of choices we make each day. Our view of the world is profoundly affected by such resources. We know, for instance, that people's misperceptions about the war in Iraq became reinforced depending on the source of their media consumption.

For example, in a study released in October 2003, conducted by the Program on International Policy Attitudes (PIPA) at the University of Maryland and Knowledge Networks, a national marketing firm, reveals that in the months prior to the U.S. invasion of Iraq, the majority of the people living in the United States held "significant misperceptions" regarding the root justifications given for the war and that these misperceptions affected *support for going to war*. Importantly, "48% incorrectly believed that evidence of links between Iraq and al Qaeda have been found, 22% that weapons of mass destruction have been found in Iraq, and 25% that world public opinion favored the US going to war with Iraq." [16] Further, nearly a quarter of the population believed that Iraq was "directly involved" in the September 11 attacks. The report concludes that "overall, 60% had at least one of these three misperceptions."[17] What makes this report particularly interesting is that it found that the *frequency* of these misperceptions varied "significantly according to individuals' primary source of news."[18] People whose primary news source was FOX News were found to significantly be more likely to nurture these misperceptions, "while those who primarily listen to NPR or watch PBS were significantly less likely."[19]

Once out of bed, we slowly make our way to the kitchen to prepare ourselves some breakfast. As we sit down to eat our breakfast we find, before us, a bowl, a carton of milk, a box of Kellogg's Frosted Flakes—or some other brand, like the more expensive "health" brands equivalents found at Whole Foods with names such as Amazon Frosted Flakes, Gorilla Munch, and Koala Crisp—and our spoon. In eating our cereal we are also consuming, or have had consumed, persuasion. In particular, the milk (or soy milk) carton and the box of cereal are loaded with persuasive appeals, particularly so-called "green products" that appeal to our health and environmental consciousness.[20] While such market-based approaches to protecting the environment are useful, and while consumers should have the choice to engage in green consuming, there has, in recent years, been the rise of what critics call *greenwashing*. As defined by the *Concise Oxford English Dictionary*, greenwashing is the "Disinformation disseminated by an organization so as to present an environmentally responsible public image."[21] Most companies these days, including oil companies, highlight their efforts to be good stewards of the Earth, even when such claims are negligible, misleading, or false.[22]

Perhaps we do not carefully study these objects, but it is instructive to do so, particularly the cereal box, where the grains of cereal are magnified to emphasize texture. The first thing that catches our attention is the bright colors. The background of the box is blue, and Tony the Tiger is a bright orange and white creature, wearing a bright red scarf. This tiger has no teeth or claws—far from being threatening as tigers generally are, this one is inviting and human-like, projecting safety and trust, fun and adventure. He is holding up his index finger; nonverbally, he is indicating that the product is number one. The non-verbal image is complemented by the verbal message, "They're gr-r-reat!" so there is an allusion here to the powerfulness of a (friendly) tiger's growl. The tiger is holding up a bowl of cereal. In the bowl can be seen what appears to be white milk, colorful fruit, and solid looking pieces of the cereal product.

Great example of critical description

The brightness of the box and the contrast of the colors are important for helping the product stand out in the crowded cereal section of the super-market, usually at eye level for children. The product itself looks wholesome floating in the milk, which is really glue. Every flake was carefully selected and positioned on the glue, which serves the dual function of holding the cereal in place and of not getting it soggy during the long hours under hot lights for the photo session. The appearance of the fruit in the photograph helps to con-vey this wholesomeness. In small print underneath the bowl it says "serving suggestion" (a legal disclaimer to preempt charges of misrepresentation), which simply means that fruit is not included in the package. But the favorable association with the fruit or garnishment may remain.

analysis

Taking this discussion a step further, the discerning consumer may no-tice that products tend to look better on the package than they do on our plates. In a sense, the photograph of the product is really of a sculpture created by a *food stylist*. Food stylists are professional artists who express themselves com-mercially using food as their medium of expression. They are hired by cor-porations to create appetite appeal in a product, whether it be for a cereal box, restaurant, or frozen dinner. Food stylists are skilled in crafting images of what appears to be freshly made and wholesome food coming straight from the kitchen; this despite the fact that food products spoil easily under the hot lights of photo or filming sets. The persuasive intent of the food stylist is to seduce our senses with the most irresistible, primal desire. In other words, to feed our-selves in an emotionally satisfying manner that goes beyond our need for nutri-tion.

Among the tactics of food stylists is to paint carrots and other vegeta-bles with glycerin to make them shine, glue rice or other grains into perfect shapes, put plastic cubes into glasses to simulate ice, use dough or mashed po-tatoes to simulate ice cream, use paper towel strips to perfect the positioning of gravy or syrup, and meticulously glue each and every sesame seed onto hamburger buns. For the meat itself, a common tactic is to cook only the outside and leave the center raw to keep it looking luscious. The burger may be painted with oil and brown coloring to enhance the same effects. To make grill marks, the meat is branded with a hot metal skewer so that it appears as if it were grilled. Paper towels may be used as a "diaper" for the meat to keep the juices from leaking onto the bun, making it soggy. Pancakes also bloat and disintegrate with syrup, and they can be protected by first spraying them with a fabric-protecting product. These sprays also work well for prolonging the freshly baked appearance of cakes and other pastries, which dry out easily and crumble.

On the back of the box of cereal is usually a coupon for more of the product and a game or fun story. There is also some sort of proof of purchase seal that a person can cut out and collect. The package tells us that if a person collects a certain amount, then she or he is eligible to receive (for an added cost) some auxiliary product, like a shirt, hat, or some more advanced toy than the plastic gadget that is actually in the box of cereal itself. In many instances, this material object becomes the impetus for consuming the product, particularly when young children are involved.

When the shirt, hat, or toy arrives, it often increases our identification with the product (i.e., the name of the product will be printed prominently on it). The more we identify with the product—and this is particularly true of children—the more the product becomes a lifestyle commitment, and the more likely we will consume the product without thinking *why* we consume it. The product simply becomes "breakfast." The ritual of eating the morning meal will not be the same without it. These identifications even continue, at various levels, from childhood into adulthood and are passed off to our own children. The old saying that "apples don't fall far from the tree" applies here. The best way we can protect our children from bad influences is to identify and correct for our *own* bad habits which we unintentionally bequeath to our children.[23]

Now that we have finished breakfast, it is time to go to school or to work. We get into our cars, or onto our bikes, or we walk through the neighborhood, and we see a great deal many persuasive messages. For example, there are signs stuck into people's front lawns advertising houses for sale. Businesses have large flashy signs so that cars going by can see who they are and what they have to sell. But these businesses do not just list their wares. They also offer a slogan to catch our attention. *Slogans* are "battle cries," short

[handwritten margin notes:]
other than outside appearance and food stylist this is another persuasive tactic

"common phrase" or

memorable (or mnemonic) sayings that reduce or package an idea for easy con-sumption.[24] An ad for Noble Roman's, a large pizza chain, reads, "Try the Best in the West, the Monster Express." Again, this may be insignificant by itself, but multiplied by the tens of millions, it has a coloring effect on our lives.

Let us look more closely at one particular persuasive appeal from the "Family Inns of America." Here we see the characteristically large sign to at-tract motorists from the highway featuring a silhouette of a middle class, white, 1950s type mother, father, and small child. In this case, the verbal and the non-verbal accentuate each other. The message is that this motel is whole-some and clean and, despite its cheap price, it is likely to be secure—notice the use of the European notion of "inn" which has connotations of being a cozy gathering place instead of the American word "motel" which denotes a much more soli-tary and seedy environment. To establish further the credibility of this econ-omy establishment, there is a prominently posted logo of the Automobile As-sociation of America (AAA), a well established and highly trustworthy organi-zation. This logo announces that the rooms are discounted for AAA members, and the endorsement (discussed as an ethos-building strategy in Chapter 7) also helps to build our enthusiasm for this unknown place in an unfamiliar city. Other attention-gaining devices posted in front of the motel are announcements of a pool, kitchenettes, cable TV, and a restaurant.

Taken together, the sign communicates to drivers passing by that the motel is safe, convenient, and comfortable. Whether or not it is all these things for such a cheap rate is another issue altogether. The point is that we may be *convinced* that this is true, and all because of the information presented to us by a persuader who may or may not have our interests at heart.

The traffic that drives by us is also filled with persuasive messages. Pepsi, Coke, UPS, McDonald's, and the entire realm of commercial enterprises in this country take advantage of the trucks they use to transport their mat-erials. McDonald's trucks have pictures of voluptuous hamburgers on them, and the soft drink trucks have pictures of bottles clothed in a lingerie of ice. The immediate function of these images and the names that we see everywhere is to remind us that these companies exist, that they are a natural (and reason-able) part of our world. But, more essentially, they are cumulatively creating an *ethos* for the company. It is part of what I call the "everydayness" of our lives and of the naturalization process mentioned above.

Even if a company has nothing to sell us, the public is often made aware of the company's name and logo, so that the company itself becomes a natural part of our environment. During the Second World War, for example, American automobile factories were converted into munitions factories. Corporations such as Ford and Chevrolet were making military hardware and consumers could not purchase new cars. Yet these companies still advertised during this period, associating, patriotically, their future commercial products with tanks and ships and with the war effort. The goal here is for a company to become familiar to us and trustworthy, as Joe Camel and Tony the Tiger are instantaneously familiar to children, even when, in the case of Joe Camel, they are not permitted to consume the product themselves.[25]

Another good example of this is the Mobil ads (called "observations") that have appeared weekly in *Time Magazine* since the mid 1970s.[26] These ads are short editorials that usually have little or nothing to do with gasoline. The editorials discuss an array of political, social, and economic concerns, and overtly urge us to support policies that the company supports. But they also do something more fundamental. Even if we do not own or drive an automobile, we basically start to associate Mobil Corporation with Americanism, with the "Right Way" to do business. We begin to associate the company logo with a natural part of world events. The ads exhort us to believe that what is good for Mobil is good for the United States. As communication scholars Richard E. Crable and Steven L. Vibbert explain:

> "Observations" presented Mobil with a superb rhetorical vehicle for premise-building. Superficial analysis of "observations" may result in the conclusion that, above all, these are non-controversial messages delivered on Sunday morning to people who already believe them. The importance of such messages is as easily overlooked as the role of speeches delivered on the Fourth of July by politicians and civic leaders in countless American communities. These messages, both on Sunday morning and in early July, function as epideictic.[27]

Epideictic discourse is discourse that attempts to reinforce common values in a community. The persuasiveness of the Mobil appeals are such that they seek to influence the American value system.[28] More overt forms of corporate advocacy must be grounded on centrally held values in the population. As Crable and Vibbert explain, the "intensification of the value-acceptance is accomplished, not while the public is at work, but while the public relaxes on the sofa on a Sunday afternoon reading 'the papers.'"[29] Again, the best persuasion conceals itself by posing to be something else, such as information, entertainment, etc. (discussed more fully in Chapter 4).

Continuing on our trek to school or work, we may pass various churches, synagogues, mosques, or shrines, most of which will have some sort of an announcement board by the side of the road. In large letters like those seen on movie marquees, the name of the church or other institution appears along with the name of the head pastor, announcements of when Sunday school or religious services start, and then, in an attempt to persuade us to attend, some catchy slogan to communicate some of the ideology of the church. For instance, "Come in! Share God's Love With Us" or "What will you say on judgment day?" are two of thousands of such examples.[30]

Later in this chapter, when we discuss the control function of persuasion in our society, we will explore more specifically the persuasive dimension of much organized religion. For now it is enough to write that, at some fundamental level, religion is connected to persuasion. This is true of Christianity, for example, since the time of St. Augustine of Hippo.[31] While many people have a desire for spirituality or an identification with some higher power, no one can agree on how to understand what that is or how to express that understanding to others. There have been hundreds of religions in the world, and, among the dominant religions, there have been and are many denominations. Why we go to one establishment of religion, and not to another, and why we switch from one religion to another, has to do with the accident of our birth and the religious identifications of our parents, as well as the types of messages, appeals, and persuasions that a particular church or religious establishment communicates. Religious sentiments are primarily *social* sentiments and social sentiments are nurtured through our communication environment.

Why, for example, are television evangelists or the corner fire-and-brimstone preachers we find on college campuses and in other places reprehensible to many people who, themselves, attend church on Sunday and consider themselves pious? Whenever this issue comes up in class, my students tell me that these preachers—people such as Oral Roberts, Pat Robinson, Jerry Falwell, Tammy and Jim Bakker, to name a few, not to mention the array of faith healers prevalent in our society—"give Christianity a bad name," and "do not reflect *true* Christianity." What are we to make of this? After all, the message that is promoted in established churches and that is promoted in fringe denominations is basically the same; what varies is the degree of a preacher's rhetorical sensitivity (or lack thereof).[32] Television evangelists, with their extravagance, and the fire and brimstone preachers that stand on our college campuses and harangue listeners with vivid and insulting language are simply, in many cases, not persuasive, or, at least, not persuasive to *us*. Such religious leaders often alienate potential converts with their anger or superficiality, rather than encourage people to join their community.

In other words, we worship in places where we feel most comfortable. Our places of worship, like our other community identifications, tend to reflect our cultural and socio-economic backgrounds. The controversy surrounding the remarks of Reverend Jeremiah Wright, Democratic presidential candidate Barak Obama's former pastor, is illustrative. In early 2008, video recordings of Pastor Wright surfaced from a 2003 sermon in which he denounced the United States for racism and blamed the United States for, among other things, the 9/11 attacks against it. This created a problem for Senator Obama, since he made it clear on many occasions that he takes advice from Reverend Wright, who is a close friend. Wright's comments, while extreme sounding to others, are part-and-parcel of the rhetoric found in many Black churches, and is certainly more plausible to African American audiences than it is to White audiences. "The fact that so many people are surprised to hear that anger in some of Reverend Wright's sermons," notes Obama in his major address on this issue, "simply reminds us of the old truism that the most segregated hour in American life occurs on Sunday morning."[33] One advantage of being a member of the dominant group is that a person can ignore safely the discourse of minority groups while minority groups are, by necessity, aware of the dominant group narratives.[34]

Another example of the persuasion that confronts us as we walk or drive to work is the billboard. As mentioned before, there are literally millions of billboards in this country, and a person cannot go anywhere without seeing some of them. Every aspect of our lives is appealed to in our billboard advertisements. From cradle to the grave, we have choices to make about how best to live our lives and what products can help us to do that well. From the prenatal care that a mother purchases for her developing child, to the burial plot where we finally rest at the end of our long lives, we are besieged by images of the ideal life that are held before us by cultural persuaders.

After the excitement of our commute, we finally arrive on campus. We express a sigh of relief for we have successfully navigated through the sea of persuasion that has engulfed us. But we should not be too hasty in letting down our guard. So far, we have only been exposed to a *fraction* of the thousands of persuasive messages to which we are exposed in a single day.

Once we arrive on campus, we usually spend time doing errands and socializing before rushing off to class. So we walk around doing our business and looking for our friends. One of the first things we may notice is that most college campuses have some sort of public announcement system. Either through the internet or other computer medium or with electronic billboards like those found at sports stadiums, schools promote the various groups or activities that are vying for the attention of students. In a less official and formal manner, a range of student interest groups produce fliers and post them on telephone poles, garbage cans, and doors. Some of these fliers may be political, announcing the meeting or formation of some activist group or organization, or some may be simply announcing a sale, activity, or speech that is occurring in the community.

While walking across campus, we unavoidably run into all kinds of ads that are produced commercially. Around spring break, travel companies plaster universities with spicy deals to Miami or Daytona Beach or to other undergraduate "hot" spots. In one ad, the persuader beckons, "Last year over 140 people had the time of their life." Similarly, credit card applications are frequently plastered in classrooms and in hallways. In one large lecture classroom at Purdue University where I did my doctoral work, someone placed Visa application forms on each of the nearly four hundred desks, so that every student who sat down for the eight a.m. class had her or his own personal copy. The prevalence and easy accessibility of these cards is no favor to students, or to the adult population more generally.[35]

In addition to this commercial material, student organizations decorate display cases in the university's student union. In these places, we often find what are known as "campus call-outs," particularly at the beginning of each semester, in which the various campus organizations attempt to galvanize support for their causes. Sometimes these organizations are a part of a national coalition to raise awareness for some problem or injustice in our society.

Walking the gauntlet of these appeals, students can be enticed to join the campus recreation center, a vast array of religious and political organizations, as well as cultural, academic, and social clubs. Also in many student unions, places exist where various professors advertise for upcoming special interest classes. Many times professors have the desire and the expertise to teach special classes that are not a part of the normal curriculum. Because these classes typically do not count toward students' graduation, they often serve as electives. But because there are so many electives from which to choose, professors often have difficulty attracting the necessary number of students to keep the class from being cancelled. In order to arouse interest for their courses, these professors make elaborate posters that appeal to the general student body. This is very much an example of persuasion.

Another source of persuasion as students walk across campus is the various political or religious speakers, organizations, and activists that constitute a medley of perspectives. In the more than 25 years I have been on college campuses as either a student or professor, I have seen neo-Nazis, Klansmen, an array of what I would consider to be extreme preachers, as well as a mixture of single-issue activists on a range of topics including anti-war, environmental protection, and human trafficking. After particularly bad disasters in foreign countries, there is usually a group of students who identify with that country who take up collections of relief to aid the victims, such as the terrible Asian tsunami of December 26, 2004 in which nearly 300,000 people died or the more recent earthquake in the Sichuan provenance of China, on May 12, 2008 which killed tens of thousands of people.

One particularly noteworthy character that was familiar on many college campuses when I was a student was a late middle-aged stocky man named Brother Max. Brother Max was a typical fire-and-brimstone preacher, and readers unfamiliar with him will easily recognize the character type that he represents. In class, I enjoy telling my students, somewhat jokingly, that I had a rather long relationship with Brother Max. When I was an undergraduate student at Humboldt State University (HSU), in Northern California, Brother Max was a staple figure on that campus. Twice a year he would appear on campus and enact a high-profile community presence for a few weeks. He would stand on the "quad," the central place on campus where students congregated between classes, and, like the well-known Christian preacher Jonathan Edwards centuries before him, shout at us how we were all sinners, that women should be barefoot and pregnant, and that a vengeful god wanted nothing more than to dangle us over the flames of hell like a cruel little boy who dangles spiders over candles.[36] As can be expected, Brother Max made quite a spectacle of himself, and it was not infrequent that he was surrounded by students, egging him on, playing his game, or simply making fun of him. While the students were busy ridiculing Brother Max, Brother Max was busy ridiculing the students, and the spectacle was not entirely unpleasant.

When I graduated from HSU, I went to the California State University, Fresno, for a semester, and was again confronted with the spectacle of Brother Max haranguing a crowd. From there I went to the University of California, Davis, to complete my master's degree, and, again, had the "pleasure" of witnessing the antics of Brother Max before the students. It seemed odd to me, at the time, that Brother Max spent his life running around Northern California, harassing and being harassed. It appeared to me that his presentation and delivery were not serving any purpose. To my eyes and ears, Brother Max appeared freakish and inconsequential. The world, I thought, was full of such kooks and crazies, and I accepted it all in stride as part of the campus experience.

After earning my M.A. degree, I left California for Indiana, where I enrolled at Purdue University as a doctoral student. There, I thought, at last I would be rid of Brother Max! But I was wrong. Lo-and-behold, he appeared one day on campus with his familiar demeanor! Brother Max, apparently, stacked out a territory for himself that was significantly larger than Northern California, one that included a significant portion of the United States.

Later, at a professional conference, I had the opportunity to talk with a former professor of mine from HSU. I mentioned to him my experiences with Brother Max, and I expressed how incredulous I felt that this man was so determined to be a public fool. As it turns out, the professor had felt similarly, and had asked Brother Max why he did what he did, when, clearly, his persuasion was not being successful. Brother Max's answer was as chilling as it was enlightening. He said, "Every time I leave a campus, I take *one* person with me."

In the end, we should never underestimate the Brother Maxes of the world, nor should we impute to other persuaders the standards or expectations that we hold for ourselves. To do so is to misjudge our positions in the social and moral universe that we share with others. Yet this is easy to do; there is a great deal of diversity and variance in a religion that claims the terrain of timeless historical truth. In the midst of all this variance, we like to believe that somehow, *our* church, *our* religion, and *our* interpretations are more real than those of the people down the street. It is typical of human beings to moralize from their community experiences. Our community involvements ground our knowledge commitments. Recognizing this point helps us to realize that *all* of our institutional practices, that is, our *official* connections with knowledge, are idiosyncratic and are not universal. To assert that X does not represent *true* Y is not to state a fact; rather, it is, as suggested in the previous chapter, an invitation to argue a point, to play the *politics of definition* (which will be discussed more in Chapter 9).

The above are only some of the types of persuasion a person is likely to come across on a typical day while walking across campus. As we have seen, persuasion occurs from the moment we get up to the moment we arrive on campus. Once on campus, the persuasive environment becomes enriched. But it does not end there. In addition to the above instances of public communication there is a whole other realm of persuasion known as *interpersonal communication.* When we talk to our friends, we frequently engage in persuasion. As social beings, we seek to involve ourselves in the lives of others, and we constantly strive to encourage others to involve themselves in our lives. Whether we are looking for dates, study partners, or someone with whom to socialize, we want to fit in and belong, and we seek to be acceptable to our peers. Certain manners of expression, linguistic style, and even dress, are encouraged and discouraged among various groups of people, and there is a constant negotiation of group norms within any social interaction.

By the time we arrive at class, we have run through the above gauntlet of persuasion. In some cases we are prepared for them, and in other cases, our exposure to persuasion comes as a great surprise to us. But when we walk into the classroom, we usually let down our guard completely. At least here, we often like to think, we are in the realm of "truth" and "objectivity." After all, knowledge is knowledge and classrooms are the neutral vehicles of its dissemination. Right? Maybe not. As we will discuss later in this chapter, one important function that persuasion serves in our society involves the accumulation and dissemination of what we understand to be "knowledge." But persuasion in an educational setting can be more crass. Take, for example, the commercialization occurring in many of our public schools. As Stuart Elliott notes, "The commercialization of educational culture, particularly in elementary schools, has long been a contentious issue. It has become more clamorous in the last decade as hard-pressed school districts seek to raise money for academic programs, sports and extracurricular activities without raising taxes."[37] Another recent *New York Times* article reports that "some school buses now play radio ads meant for children."[38]

Upon returning home, after our long day at school, the cycle of persuasion continues, with one more venue added: the mail (and in contemporary times we can add to this e-mail and the internet). The mail is a tremendous source of persuasion that we are exposed to each and every day. What American has not been inundated with junk mail of a vast variety? Everything gets sold through the mail, and every charitable or political organization has vast mailings in which they make appeals for donations. Within the last fifteen years, this trend has been exacerbated by credit card companies that send out their "elite" invitations to tens of millions of people. There are times in college when students may receive three or more credit card applications a week.[39]

Persuasion, in short, exists wherever we go. It is simply unavoidable. It is everywhere in our daily lives. Even if we do something special, like go to the beach or to a big recreation center, and we leave behind all the trappings of normal life, people will come to sell us soft drinks or popsicles.

Imagine sitting at the beach with a soft drink and popsicle. We think that we have freed ourselves from this octopus called persuasion. But guess again. Overhead we hear the roar of an airplane. It is not a jet, but one of those small propeller planes, and it is trailing a banner with a variety of persuasive messages. Or perhaps we see some group of people on strike, walking the picket line. Or perhaps on our way back from the beach or a park, we run into a protest or a demonstration. Operation Rescue, for example, is one persuasive movement that has had a high visibility throughout the United States in recent years.[40] Again, this is persuasion. The people of Operation Rescue, while physically trying to shut down abortion clinics late in the twentieth century by blocking entrances with their bodies and clogging the jails, spend most of their time creating persuasion, and in so doing, are trying to raise what they think is the moral consciousness of this nation. Seeing them, *en masse*, acting on the strength of their convictions, may be enough to convince some people that this is a cause worth joining.

⁊ The Moral Dimensions of Persuasion ⱥ

Now that we see that persuasion is everywhere, what can we say about its moral dimensions?[41] The first point relevant here is one that was acknowledged by the Greek philosopher Aristotle, more than twenty-five hundred years ago when he wrote the first recorded treatise on persuasion theory.[42] In this treatise he points out that rhetoric is *amoral*. Persuasion, we learn from Aristotle, is neither good nor bad. It is simply the way that people work in the world. Both sinners and saints use persuasion. Too often, however, we see persuasion (or rhetoric) as something that the bad people do. We seem, as a culture, to assume tacitly that people who do good things are acting in line with "truth," while the people who get us to do things that we should not do are tempting us with persuasion and "rhetoric." We often associate persuasion with the devil. The devil persuades us through the passions, with money, sex, glamour, and pride. The saints, however, do not persuade us, but simply point out the godliness of the good, which somehow "corrects" or overcomes evil. However we want to conceptualize it, we often have a difficult time separating the saints from the con-artists when it comes to persuasion.

What, for example, is the difference between the ethical and unethical uses of persuasion? It is not so easy to come up with an answer to this, so, instead, I am going to offer some questions, to illustrate how complex is this issue.

Is advertising ethical? As a personal and professional matter, I believe that much of it is *unethical* and would like to see it regulated better by the government; the information value of most ads, as opposed to their propagandistic value, is limited and can be conveyed sufficiently by generic packaging.[43] What about cigarette and alcohol advertising or other so-called "vice products"? Desire for these products is counter-intuitive and must be promoted rigorously, which is clearly against the public interest. Is presidential persuasion ethical? The short answer is "yes," we expect the president to be a master persuader. What about when the president convinces the nation to go to war on what turns out to be a flimsy pretext?[44] Or what if the president actually lied or fabricated evidence? We expect the president to make difficult decisions, but when can we say that she or he has gone over the line? And where *is* this line? What about public relations (P.R.)? Is that ethical? Certainly, companies have a right as well as an obligation to inform the public on matters important to the public, but what about when companies use P.R. to deceive the public or to cover up maleficent behavior? What about corporate propaganda? Should we allow corporate entities to be able to influence politics with their vast war chests? In terms of democratic theory and the experience of democratic life, there is a difference between one entity, say a multinational corporation such as General Electric devoting many millions of dollars to support some policy view, and millions of individuals giving one dollar to express the *opposite* view.

How do we understand each of the above questions/issues? Clearly, there is no simple way we can pass judgment in any absolute sense, as questions of "right" and "wrong," "good" and "bad," have no absolute standards (discussed more fully in Chapter 10). Rather, they are relative standards that become established in a community vis-à-vis communication. People, however, can make intelligent, well-informed decisions if they can understand the functions of persuasion in our society and its many strategies and tactics. The question then becomes: How are we going to pick and choose among the thousands of messages that bombard us each and every day? If persuasion is a morally neutral activity, it is important to become aware of the technical and ethical guidelines that control the use of persuasion.

One important guideline involves the relative openness of a society and of people participating in a communication interaction. This question of openness, democracy, and dialogics, has been with us for centuries. Since the advent of literacy in the fifth century BCE, and through the establishment of moveable type in the fifteenth century, and again in the twentieth century with the rise of the electronic media, the question of communication has always been tied to the question of social control as well as to the ability to think.[45]

Progress, social change, and moral development come from the ability to question and debate social assumptions of "truth." It is not the debate itself that frames this moral development, but the relative space in that society that allows for the debate to occur. Seen in this sense, issues such as pornography, equal access to the media, flag burning, hate speech, slander, sex and violence in the media, freedom of the press, and academic freedom become not ends in themselves, but *means* for reassessing our relationship with ourselves and others. By debating these issues we negotiate the parameters of how persuasion affects our lives.

✇ Conclusion ✇

Persuasion involves the art and science of influencing others. The oldest and most direct way to influence others is simply to affect them by force (e.g., I push you out of line so I can get to my seat first). This is not always practical (you may shove me back), and thus we have devised ways to influence each other in more symbolic and peaceful ways. But persuasion still involves a type of violence.[46] The Greek philosopher Plato went so far as to call rhetorical persuasion a type of rape.[47] While Plato and some other communication scholars offer the most extreme view on this matter, persuasion is indeed a force that constrains us and positions us in significant ways, often without our realizing it. Two representative examples of this positioning are the judge and the priest.

Most people do not think of judges and priests as persuaders or as controllers, but religion and law are two controlling forces in our society that are based heavily in persuasion. In both cases, judges and priests delineate morality. That in itself is significant. "Right" and "wrong," "good" and "bad," become prescribed for us by the forces of law and religion, and we have to be convinced that their characterization of morality is true.[48] In fact, we often take for granted that it is so. But is it? Do laws and religions describe the world as it *is*, or do they give us idealized visions of what some people think is true and acceptable? Are we not encouraged, in significant ways, to accept these ideas as truth, and to live our lives by them? Laws and religions use both the carrot and the stick to get us to conform to society in ways that are quite political (as opposed to natural).

In law and religion we are taught the values and ethics of a particular group of people and are urged to think of them as "universal." However, if we were to examine each carefully, we would find that laws and religious values are highly dependent upon *cultural* norms and identities. In any given historical context, our laws and our religions appear "real," but every new culture and every new generation needs to be taught and convinced that such religious and legal norms are relevant to their historical circumstances. The more that our legal and religious values are assumed and are unquestioned, and the more that a normified standard is enforced, then the more we have a *closed* society. When our religious and cultural standards are open and debated, when we change and grow to meet society's contemporary needs, then we have an *open* society, one in which human freedom and dignity have a chance to flourish, a society we like to think of as our own.

℅ Notes ℆

1. See John Dewey, *The Political Writings* (Indianapolis: Hackett Publishing Company, 1993); and David L. Hildebrand, *John Dewey: A Beginner's Guide* (Oxford, UK: Oneworld Press, 2008).

2. Charles Larson, *Persuasion: Reception and Responsibility 11th* ed. *(*Belmont: Thomson Wadsworth, 2007), 9. See also "Cutting Through Advertising Clutter," *CBS News* (September 17, 2006). Retrieved from http://www.cbsnews.com/stories/2006/09/17/Sunday/printable 2015684.shtml; and Louise Story, "Anywhere the Eye Can See, It's Likely to See an Ad," *New York Times* (January 15, 2007). Retrieved from http://www.nytimes.com/2007/01/15/business/media/15everywhere.html?pagewanted=print.

3. Bradley Johnson, "Day in the Life: How Consumers Divvy Up All The Time They Have," *Advertising Age* (May 2, 2005), 44.

4. Josh Getlin, "Time Spent Watching Television Increases," *Los Angeles Times* (September 22, 2006), retrieved from http://articles.latimes.com/2006/sep/22/business/fi-tv22.

5. Herbert Simons, Joanne Morreale, and Bruce Gronbeck, *Persuasion in Society* (Thousand Oaks, CA: Sage, 2001), 12.

6. Jean Kilbourne, *Can't Buy My Love: How Advertising Changes the Way We Think and Feel* (New York: Touchstone, 1999), 59.

7. Rebecca Lindsey, "Got Mail? A Record Six Billion Credit Card Offers Were Mailed Last Year!" *CardRatings.Com* (May 15, 2006), retrieved from http://www.cardratings.com/credit cardnews/2006/05/got-mail-record-six-billion-credit.html.

8. Louise Story, "Junk Mail is Alive and Growing," *New York Times* (November 2, 2006). Retrieved from http://www.nytimes.com/2006/11/02/business/media/02adco.html?sq=600% 20billion%20junk%20e-mail%20messages&st=nyt&scp=1&pagewanted=print.

9. Ibid. Recently, however, the number is starting to decline with the economic downturn of 2008–2009. Alex Mindlin, "Even Credit Card Offers Are Ebbing," *New York Times* (April 14, 2008). Retrieved from http://www.nytimes.com/2008/04/14/business/14drill.html?_r=1 &sq = Credit%20card%20offers&st=nyt&oref=slogin&scp=1&pagewanted=print.

10. Brian Steinberg, "Super Bowl Spots Hit $3 Million," *Advertising Age* (May 12, 2008), 4.

11. Ibid.

12. Kilbourne, *Can't Buy My Love;* Michael F. Jacobson and Laurie Ann Mazur, *Marketing Madness: A Survival Guide for a Consumer Society* (Boulder, CO: Westview, 1995).

13. Robert B. Zajonc, "Attitudinal Effects of Mere Exposures," *Journal of Personality and Social Psychology, 9* (1968), 1–27.

14. Scott A. Hawkins and Stephen J. Hoch, "Low-Involvement Learning: Memory Without Evaluation," *Journal of Consumer Research, 19* (1992) 212–225.

15. *A Rhetoric of Motives* (Berkeley: University of California Press, 1969), 26.

16. The report, "Misperceptions, The Media and The Iraq War," can be found on-line at http://65.109.167.118 /pipa/pdf/oct03/IraqMedia_Oct03_rpt.pdf.

17. Ibid.

18. Ibid.

19. Ibid.

20. The cereal brands just mentioned are produced by a company called *Nature's Path,* which invites children to become "EnviroKidz." Activities and information about being an Enviro-Kid appear on their website http://www.envirokidz.com which, like most cereal and other childrens' food websites, provides games, activities, and other ways to become involved with the product. The company claims that 1% of the sales of these products are donated to organizations that help the environment.

21. John Connolly, Pierre McDonagh, Michael Polonsky and Andrew Prothero, "Green Marketing and Green Consumers: Exploring the Myths," in *The International Handbook on Environmental Technology Management*, eds., Dora Marinova, David Annandale, and John Phillmore (Northampton, MA: Edward Elgar, 2006), 251.

22. William S. Laufer, "Social Accountability and Corporate Greenwashing," *Journal of Business Ethics, 43* (2003), 253–261.

23. As a parent, I realize that this is difficult to do, but small gains here may have a large impact on how the next generation sees itself. Few things, I believe, are more important so far as raising children are concerned. This is discussed in more detail in the conclusion of this book.

24. Robert E. Denton, Jr., "The Rhetorical Functions of Slogans: Classifications and Characteristics," *Communication Quarterly, 28* (1980), 10–18.

25. A study published in 1991 argued that Joe Camel was more recognized by children than other cartoon figures such as Mickey Mouse. See Paul M. Fischer, Meyer P. Schwartz, John W. Richards, Jr., Adam O. Goldstein, and Tina H. Rojas, "Brand Logo Recognition by Children Aged 3 to 6 Years. Mickey Mouse and Old Joe the Camel," *Journal of the American Medical Association, 266* (December 11), 3145–3148. As a result of pressure, the Joe Camel campaign was discontinued in 1997.

26. Mobil merged with Exxon in 1999 to become the ExxonMobil Corporation, becoming the largest publically held, and most lucrative, corporation in the world.

27. "Mobil's Epideictic Advocacy: 'Observations' of Prometheus-Bound," *Communication Monographs, 50* (1983), 383.

28. David M. Timmerman, "Epideictic Oratory," in *Encyclopedia of Rhetoric and Composition: Communication From Ancient Times to the Information Age*, ed., Theresa Enos (New York: Garland Publishing, 1996), 228–231.

29. "Mobil's Epideictic Advocacy," 394.

30. A collection of these signs with rhetorical/cultural analysis appears in Harold L. Goodall, Jr., *Divine Signs: Connecting Spirit to Community* (Carbondale, IL: Southern Illinois University Press, 1996). Perhaps the most interesting one that Goodall reports is from the cover: "Ch -- ch. What's Missing?"

31. James J. Murphy, *Rhetoric in the Middle Ages: A History of Rhetorical Theory From Saint Augustine to the Renaissance* (Berkeley, CA: University of California Press), 1974.

32. For a discussion of "rhetorical scrutiny," see Roderick P. Hart and Don Burks, "Rhetorical Sensitivity and Social Interaction," *Speech Monographs, 39* (1972), 75–91.

33. "Speech on Race," *New York Times* (March 18, 2008), 35. Retrieved from http://www.Ny times.com/2008/03/18/us/politics/18textobama.html?_r=1&pagewanted=print&oref=slo.

34. Peggy McIntosh, "White Privilege: Unpacking the Invisible Knapsack," in Monica McGoldrick, ed., *Re-Visioning Family Theory: Race, Culture, and Gender in Clinical Practice* (New York: The Guilford Press, 1998), 147–152.

35. A useful resource here is the film (2006) and the companion book (2007) *Maxed Out: Hard Times, Easy Credit and the Era of Predatory Lenders.* For a review of the movie see Ann Hornaday, "'Maxed Out': Serious Matters of Life and Debt, *The Washington Post* (March 9, 2007), C01.

36. Jonathan Edwards' actual words were: "The God that holds you over the pit of hell, much as one holds a spider, or some loathsome insect over the fire, abhors you, and is dreadfully provoked: his wrath towards you burns like fire; he looks upon you as worthy of nothing else, but to be cast into the fire." "Sinners in the Hands of an Angry God," in Ronald F. Reid, ed., *Three Centuries of American Rhetorical Discourse: An Anthology and a Review* (Prospect Heights, IL: Waveland Press, 1988), 72.

37. "Straight A's, With a Burger as a Prize," *New York Times* (December 6, 2007), 10. Retrieved from http://www.nytimes.com/2007/12/06/business/media/06adco.html?_r=1&scp=1&sq =%93Straigt+A%92s%2C+With+a+Burger+as+a+Prize%2C%94&st=nyt&oref=slogin. The subject of this article was McDonald's sponsoring of student report cards. In exchange for paying the cost of printing the cards, McDonald's had its logo and a coupon printed prominently on it. What McDonald's receives in return for its small investment is an increased level of branding with young people in vulnerable periods of their lives. Although dealing with a younger population than school-aged children, a recent research study found that, among children ages 3–5 years old, food tasted better if wrapped in McDonald's packaging. In other words, the McDonald's image is so powerful for children at such a young age, that children preferred the taste of food and beverages that looked like they came from McDonald's, even if they did not (for example, one food tested in the study was carrots). See Thomas N. Robinson, Dina L. G. Borzekowski, Donna M. Matheson, and Helena C. Kraemer, "Effects of Fast Food Branding on Young Children's Taste Preferences," *Archives of Pediatrics & Adolescent Medicine, 161* (2007), 792–797.

38. Louise Story, "Anywhere the Eye Can See, It's Likely to See an Ad," (January, 15, 2007). Retrieved from http://www.nytimes.com/2007/01/15/business/media/15everywhere.html?Pa gewanted=print.

39. This is not an entirely new phenomenon. Activist and radical Abbie Hoffman noticed this trend emerging in the 1960s and offered this advice for his countercultural followers. As these applications come with prepaid envelops, they can be fixated to bricks or other heavy objects and mailed (metal washers placed inside the envelope work as well). The post office, he noted, has to deliver the envelope and the company that is soliciting its credit cards or other gimmicks must pay the increased postage. Imagine, writes Hoffman, if everyone did this. *Steal This Book* (New York: Four Walls Eight Windows Press, 1996), 107.

40. Operation Rescue was founded in the late 1980s by activist Randy Terry and became frontline news during the 1988 Democratic National Convention in Atlanta, Georgia, in which they staged a massive campaign of civil disobedience.

41. A more detailed discussion of ethics will take place in Chapter 10.

42. *On Rhetoric: A Theory of Civic Discourse,* trans. George A. Kennedy (New York: Oxford University Press, 1991).

43. In *Virginia State Board of Pharmacy v. Virginia Citizens Consumer Council* (425 U.S. 748, 1976) the landmark Supreme Court decision extending First Amendment protection for advertising, reasoned that advertising is important due to its so-called "information value." The question faced by the Court was whether a pharmacist could advertise "X prescription drug at Y price." The Court acknowledges that commercial speech may have no other informative value. Most ads, not just for drugs, fall in this category of X is being sold for Y. However, the vast majority of what appears in any ad is emotive and seductive. Under the logic of the Court, therefore, the regulation of advertising should be permissible when the gist of the ad goes toward constructing an image, rather than the conveying of information, for which generic advertising is well suited.

44. As reported by Mark Mazzetti and Scott Shane, a 170-page study released in June 2008 by the Senate Subcommittee On Intelligence found that President Bush used exaggerated intelligence and ignored information contrary to his view, intentionally misleading the American public. "Bush Overstated Iraq Evidence, Senators Report," *New York Times* (June 6, 2008), retrieved from http://query.nytimes.com/gst/fullpage.html?res=9B00E7DF153BF935A3575 5C0A96E9C8B63&scp=1&sq=bush+overstated+iraq+evidence&st=nyt.

45. Paul E. Corcoran, *Political Language and Rhetoric* (Austin: University of Texas Press, 1979).

46. Sonja K. Foss and Karen A. Foss, *Inviting Transformation: Presentational Speaking For a Changing World.* 2nd ed. (Prospect Heights, IL: Waveland Press 2003); Cindy L. Griffith and Sonja K. Foss, "Beyond Persuasion: A Proposal for an Invitational Rhetoric," *Communication Monographs, 62* (1995), 2-18.

47. *Phaedrus*, trans. W.C. Helmbold and W.G. Rabinowitz (New York: Macmillian, 1956).

48. Speaking frankly for the Court, Justice Felix Frankfurter wrote in a 1962 dissent, "The Court's authority—possessed of neither the purse nor the sword—ultimately rests on sustained public confidence in its moral sanction," *Baker v. Carr*, 369 U.S. 186, 267.

CHAPTER 4

Definitions and Parameters of Persuasion

Throughout the first three chapters of this textbook I have skirted the definition and scope of persuasion. I have done this to create the conceptual and political context by which our approach to persuasion in this course can be understood and appreciated. I have written generally about how persuasion involves the art and science of influencing others and how this process is fundamental to understanding the construction of community and identity in our lives. With this chapter, I now introduce five prominent definitions of persuasion, plus one of my own, to guide our understanding as we work through this textbook and course. From there, I explore various paradigmatic communication types and their mixtures that we experience in communication every day. The goal of this chapter is to help students recognize that persuasion often exists where it is not so obvious, in the taken for granted assumptions about the lives we are living. We are all prepared, or should be prepared, for the persuasive appeals of the political speech or the proverbial used car salesperson, but it is much harder to appreciate, for example, the persuasive dimensions of a film or television show, the interactions of a loved one, a college lecture, or the military posturing of a nation's armed forces.

༄ Five Definitions of Persuasion ༄

What follows are five well-known definitions of persuasion taken from established textbooks in the field. I have added bold type to accentuate the key words in each that I will elaborate upon below.

First, persuasion is the "interactive **process** of preparing and presenting verbal or nonverbal messages to **autonomous** and often receptive individuals in order to alter or strengthen their attitudes, beliefs, and/or behaviors."[1] Second, persuasion can be understood as "the use of verbal and nonverbal symbols to affect an audience's **perceptions** and thus to bring about desired changes in ways of thinking, feeling, and/or acting."[2] Third, persuasion is "human communication designed to influence the autonomous **judgments** and actions of others."[3] Fourth, persuasion is an "intentional effort at influencing another's mental state through communication in a circumstance in which the persuadee has some measure of **freedom**."[4] Fifth, persuasion is the "**co-production** of meaning that results when an individual or group of individuals uses language strategies and/or other symbols (such as images, music, or sounds) to make audiences **identify** with that individual or group."[5]

As indicated above, central to the definitions offered are the concepts of *process*, *autonomy*, *perception*, *judgment*, *freedom*, *cooperation*, and *identification*. Taken together, what this means is that persuasion is a complex phenomenon involving many different variables which interact over time in a process that can be both comprehended and studied. The subjects of persuasion are autonomous individuals, people with a measure of freedom who exercise free will and have the power to make internalized decisions regarding a future state of mind or action. Within this process, individuals must be able to conceptualize as important some external factor (e.g., a threat or a promise) or set of factors and be able to reconcile this new information/events/arguments with what they already believe and know. In other words, they must be able to judge the new stimulus as important and thus determine that it is a good reason for thinking or acting differently. This entire process is influenced by an individual's sense of self and others.

❧ What Is and What Is Not Persuasion? ☙

Persuasive communication exists on a continuum. On one end of the continuum there are what can be considered *paradigmatic* cases of persuasion. Paradigms are archetypes, or defining examples of a category. As Herbert W. Simons, Joanne Morreale, and Bruce Gronbeck note, paradigmatic cases of persuasion "involve no complex admixture of motives, no masking of persuasive intent, no question about whether they are attempts at persuasion or some other form of influence."[6] Paradigmatic persuasion is usually taken to be activities such as sales presentations, campaign speeches, and advertising. These are instances of persuasion that most people would not doubt and do not need theory or much in the way of advanced education to perceive. On the other end of the continuum, there are instances of things which are clearly *not* persuasion. For example, art, expression, logic, description, coercion, and entertainment, often appear as if they have little to do with persuasion.[7] While these two extremes do exist, the more significant types of persuasion are the ones that do not fall clearly into either end of the continuum. Rhetoric is best; the old adage goes, when it goes unnoticed. Persuasion, to be effective, often conceals itself.

Throughout this textbook and course, we are interested in exploring how persuasion affects us without our being fully aware of what is happening. For example, while human emotions are natural and characterize the human condition, commercials often play upon our emotions to encourage us to purchase products. What may feel "natural" to us in terms of our emotions, may, in fact, be an instance of corporate persuasion (i.e., efforts by commercial entities to sell us consumer artifacts of dubious value). In such cases we find *expressive rhetoric*, or *expressive communication*. While all art (or commercials) are effective, that is, they *do* something to us or for us at some level, some art is intentionally effective or manipulative. As Kenneth Burke explains, literature (or art more generally) constitutes "equipment for living."[8]

What Burke means is that art and cultural expression influence our lives in many ways. As he explains, "Art forms like 'tragedy' or 'comedy' or 'satire' [can] be treated as equipments for living, that size up situations in various ways in keeping with correspondingly various attitudes."[9] In other words, artistic expression is a "rhetoric," a strategic extension of the human desire to find or to create order and meaning in human existence. Art, in this sense, is a transcendence or a definition. Art equips people for living by helping them to define or otherwise to interpret their lives. With this understanding, Burke recognizes that art—and, by extension, advertising—is not inconsequential. Burke acknowledges that the potential danger, as well as the potential beneficence, of art can be characterized in two ways—the Platonic "ideological" way and the Aristotelian "aesthetic" way.[10]

Another way we can talk about the Platonic and Aristotelian principles mentioned above is as the "censorship principle" and as the "lightning rod principle."[11] These principles are just as relevant today for understanding our social and political relationships and the role of communication within them as they were in Ancient Athens when they were first articulated. According to Plato's perspective, art is overtly ideological and serves, in Burke's words, "as a means of lining us up in behalf of the state, a theory now generally associated with totalitarian governments."[12] The idea here is to control people by controlling their communication environment, neutering, as it were, their communicative imagination. (Remember, as discussed in the Preface, the communicative imagination is the ability to see in communication the resources of our humanity and the social freedom associated with those resources.)

On the other hand, Burke explains that, in line with Aristotle's theory of *catharsis* (which I discussed in Chapter 2 as the idea that art can psychologically "purge" us of certain feelings, tensions, or anti-social tendencies), art is potentially therapeutic, as well as at least inadvertently ideological—it purifies society "by draining-off dangerous charges, as lightning rods are designed, not to 'suppress' danger, but to draw it into harmless channels."[13] As political tensions are worked out and resolved on stage, the audience is thus purified and less likely to harbor grudges against the government. A variation of this was practiced during the Roman era of "bread and circus" (*panem et circenses*) social control, in which costly public entertainment was provided by the government to distract people from their troubles and provide an outlet for their anti-social urges, supplemented with free bread for poor people—again, with the idea of keeping the masses satisfied and distracted.[14]

A modern view of this Roman practice can be found described in a portent book—*Amusing Ourselves to Death: Public Discourse in the Age of Show Business*—in which communication scholar Neil Postman argues that Americans have given up public civic engagement in exchange for a steady regimen of mindless, pacifying, entertainment.[15] Postman uses two benchmarks to argue his point that we are destroying ourselves as a society by succumbing to the seductions of the entertainment industry. The first is George Orwell's dystopian novel *1984* and the second is Aldous Huxley's equally terrifying (but for opposite reasons) *Brave New World.*[16]

Along with Postman, I remember the anxiety that was expressed in popular culture during the year 1984 regarding Orwell's predictions. The dreadful year had arrived. When it passed, we released our collective breath when Orwell's hell failed to materialize (i.e., the smothering omnipotent and utterly dehumanizing regime of Big Brother). Again we smiled, five years later in 1989, when the last remnants of Orwell's fear faded for good with the demise of the Soviet Union, a society associated frequently with Orwell's vision. We congratulated ourselves with winning the Cold War. A mistake we made, however, was to assume that Orwell's monster was uniquely embodied in the Soviet edifice—or that the Soviet model was *the telos* of the developing world—ignoring that Orwell was concerned about trends he saw developing in the *Western* democracies. Orwell was warning us against ourselves; we might have won the Cold War in the sense that neo-liberalism is now the model of development throughout the world, but that does not mean we have escaped the twentieth century's collective fear of dystopia.

Assuming, for the moment, that we escaped Orwell's hell; that is, ignoring our tactics in the war against terrorism—the secret prisons, the tortures, the military occupations, the domestic surveillance—we must remember, as Postman was correct in pointing out, that Orwell had competitors for the business of outlining our future dystopia. The competitor Postman highlights is, as already mentioned, Aldous Huxley, but I have identified another—Ray Bradbury, author of the 1953 classic, *Fahrenheit 451*.[17] Under Orwell's vision the human will is smothered by external oppression—Big Brother or the oppressive, omnipotent state, in command of language and thus in command of the past, present, and future, squanders humanity to feed itself. Huxley, however, as well as Bradbury, recognized that the oppressive force of the state is not required to enforce submissiveness and invite totalitarianism. Other threats exist to our autonomy, sense of self, and history; there are other ways to squash one's soul other than through fear. In Huxley's and Bradbury's worlds, people "come to love their oppression, to adore the technologies that undo their capacities to think."[18] Indeed, in this sense, Bradbury's vision is more in line with Postman's point—books became illegal in Bradbury's tale because books are frequently contradictory, they may make people confused and frustrated; so people stopped reading. On their own, without government pressure, they stopped reading and found themselves to be "happier." More than half a century since the novel was originally published, fire chief Captain Beatty's apologia to Guy Montag, the disgruntled fireman, is even more resonate:

> Ask yourself, What do we want in this country, above all? People want to be happy, isn't that right? Haven't you heard it all your life? I want to be happy, people say. Well, aren't they? Don't we keep them moving, don't we give them fun? That's all we live for, isn't it? For pleasure, for titillation? And you must admit our culture provides plenty of these.[19]

As the preceding quotation suggests, the propagandistic functions of art and entertainment are not as easy to perceive in our society as they are in less democratic societies, like that of the former Soviet Union. This fact does not make the Aristotelian "lightning rod" principle any less substantial in influencing people's beliefs, attitudes, values, and behaviors. With Postman and Burke's observations in mind, I focus in this chapter on those aspects of our lives that can be categorized as "scientific persuasion," "expressive persuasion," "persuasive art," "persuasive entertainment," "coercive persuasion," "information persuasion," and other cultural areas that influence us in a myriad of ways.

Clearly, not everything involves persuasion, and not everything is rhetorical. Mountains, rivers, hurricanes, tornadoes, the death of a family member, and pestilence are examples of things that happen in the material world that do not have much in the way of a persuasive dimension. They just happen and we have to deal with the consequences. Further, things like traffic signals, light switches, and much phatic communication have, at times, only limited persuasive and/or ideological dimensions; perhaps they have none at all. Some things have no discernable agendas and it would be silly to look for one. For instance, in graduate school we used to joke about something we called the "rhetoric of fire hydrants." As a practical matter, there is no such thing; or at least, nothing important to talk about. To borrow the sentiment, if not the words, of psychologist Sigmund Freud, "sometimes a cigar is just a cigar."[20]

The danger in writing the above, however, is to assume that rhetoric or persuasion is a *thing*. Something *is* or is *not* persuasion. A better way of looking at rhetoric or persuasion is as a *perspective*, a dimension of experience that human beings introduce into the world. It involves a way of interpretation, a way of understanding, a way of reading (literally, a way of "seeing," as in Aristotle's sense).[21] For example, while death as a phenomenon is real, the "meaning" of death is not real in any universal sense. While death creates an absence and a disturbance for the living, it is, and will remain, quite incomprehensible. While many groups of people (e.g., religions) will try to give meaning to this experience, all give simply their *interpretation*, which millions take far too seriously. Aside from its biological breakdown of cell function, "death" has no meaning. The dead, simply, cease to exist.

In the human struggle for meaning over a particular death, or even of death in general, we are involved in persuasion. From eulogies, the stories we tell each other about our deceased loved ones, to the religions we follow to give meaning to our lives, we are engaged in the rhetorical.[22] Our legal, moral, ethical, and behavioral patterns and norms are situated here.[23] In the same way, while hurricanes, mountains, and famine exist at a level beyond human symbolization, they are all forces that can be contextualized in some way, or influenced, by the actions of humans, and thus assume an ideological and rhetorical significance at certain times and under certain conditions. Humans *can* move mountains, they *can* influence the weather, and they *are* often responsible for famines, not to mention global warming and other environmental derogations. In this sense the world never exists in its "God-given" or natural state, but in a state that is constantly mediated by human rhetorical and political activity. Nature is no longer raw and human beings are no longer innocent (if they ever were)—that is, existing outside of morality in some pure, perfect state. There is no "garden" from which we have come and no place outside of time and this earth to which we can return. We have only the present with all of its challenges and opportunities and our dearest hopes for what might come tomorrow.

Let us turn now to practical examples of rhetorical dimensions in our lives in order to discern the relative degrees of persuasion that exist in a range of everyday phenomena that we often take for granted.

∞ Information and Persuasion ∞

In the realm of information and knowledge there are a variety of ways in which we can talk about the rhetorical and the non-rhetorical. In some sense, persuasion does serve a knowledge function. What counts as knowledge in our society is simply authority plus evidence—or at least the relationship between authority and evidence, neither of which is objective; both are constructed entities, what I affectionately call *habits of convenience*. "Knowledge," in other words, "is never static, but in a continual dynamic dialogue with social issues and politics."[24] But we can also talk about knowledge in its simpler form—a belief we hold about a set of symbols that states something meaningful about phenomena in the world. Consider, for example, a sign we may see on our university campuses that lists upcoming events. While the sign is not the thing (the word is not the event), the range of possible readings of the sign, and the experiences that it is encouraging us to have, is limited and clear enough that we are not encouraged to think beyond it. What appears in the sign simply *is*, and to talk about what is *not* there would be a little odd.

Still, we *could* talk about exclusion, and we could talk about authority as well. The sign authorizes, in a sense, what constitutes a bona fide campus event. It also serves to popularize and normalize an *approved* event. The sign reifies what authority designates and contributes to the popularization of some bona fide or official activity. By offering publicity, the sign literally makes it possible, in part, for people to attend the event. In fact, since these signs are so limited in their definition of community, when we talk of exclusion, we really mean that a good deal has been left out, and, thus, we can discuss the politics of suppression. As legal scholar Catherine MacKinnon notes in her analysis of Jim Crow or anti-Semitism, signs matter profoundly:

> Social inequality is substantially created and enforced—that is, *done* —through words and images. Social hierarchy cannot and does not exist without being embodied in meanings and expressed in communications. Segregation cannot happen without someone saying "get out" or "you don't belong here" at some point. Elevation and denigration are all accomplished through meaningful symbols and communicative acts in which saying it is doing it.[25]

Signs are important, argues, MacKinnon because "[w]ords and images are how people are placed in hierarchies, how social stratification is made to seem inevitable and right, how feelings of inferiority and superiority are engendered, and how indifference to violence against those on the bottom is rationalized and normalized."[26] Rationalization and normalization establish the precondition for hatred and violence. While most people do not engage in overt acts of violence against others, we acquiesce in the *symbolic* violence imbedded in our structures of social signage. We do not realize it, but many things serve as exclusionary signs and exemplify the functions identified by MacKinnon. For example, there is a growing literature called Whiteness Studies, composed of critical race scholars. These scholars trace the embeddedness of White power in various property relations, thus connecting the ideology of White supremacy to its material anchors in order to critique and condemn it.[27]

Still, on another level, a sign is just a sign and all these other levels of meaning collapse under its primary significance. The interpretation above, like all interpretations in this textbook and course, is not exclusive of other interpretations. Nothing that I say or write in this course, or throughout my teaching and scholarship more generally, should be taken as definitive. My arguments, while informed by research experience, professional training, and years of interdisciplinary study are not intended to be exclusionary. Everything, I maintain, is open for argument; better or worse arguments exist for or against any contingency. As students, your job is to learn how to recognize, analyze, and/or articulate such arguments for yourself.

The *practice* of persuasion, as opposed to its theory, is always an art and not a science, although it can be studied scientifically. While human behavior can be quantified, human meaning cannot be quantified in any significant fashion. When we talk about persuasion, we never talk about "truth." But that does not mean that we are lying. It means that we talk about "meaning" and "meaning" is not the same thing as "truth." For example, I can write the words "The keys are on the table" and that would, under some conditions, be true. But did I say anything meaningful about the world? In a small sense, yes, although such talk does not get us very far. More importantly, in saying that sentence, we (meaning I as speaker and you as audience) had to assume a common understanding of the words "key," "table," and "on." Thus, for the statement to be "true," we already had to agree on its "meaning."

Some signs are *performative*. That is, some signs are so simple in their expressions or declarations that there is little room for subjectivity. Uttering them or witnessing them constitutes or initiates a moral, spatial, or conceptual universe. According to John L. Austin, the "issuing of the utterance is the performing of an action—it is not normally thought of as just saying something."[28] Saying "I do" at a wedding, for example, or pleading guilty at a trial, positions a person in a community with specific moral and legal relationships. These are examples in which *saying* something is *doing* something. MacKinnon argues that pornography falls into this class of performative speech acts. She argues that pornography is a harm, not an idea, a performative act of subordination of women through images. Pornography is a "sign" that announces the presence of patriarchy and the potential for sexual violence. It places women on notice that certain things can, and often will, happen to them. If nothing else, pornography announces to women that men make the rules in society and that their bodies do not belong solely to them.

The information content of a message, as opposed to its persuasive content, is determined by the degree to which its "meaning" is not contested.

The more that the meaning is contested, however, the more the sign will appear to be "persuasive" and not "informative." In addition, some signs point beyond themselves and then persuasion is clearly involved. Some signs, however, do not point beyond themselves, and in such cases, persuasion may be involved when the things omitted are more significant than the things highlighted.[29] On the other hand, some persuasion is so tired, and has been around so long, and so many people are convinced of its "reality," that we no longer think of it in terms of persuasion. In such cases we have that which for all intents and purposes we can consider to be "information."

✍ Expression and Persuasion ✍

The ways of thinking described in the previous paragraphs can also be used to explain our relationship to human expression. Not all human expression is important communication, and not all of it is persuasive. But much of it clearly is. An important function of all human communication is to ground the objects in the external world with human subjectivity. In a fundamental sense, to "know" is also to "feel," to be physically present, to have a sensual, even tactile relationship with an idea. To state the words "I see" or even "I understand" literally means to relate to the material world at the level of our bodies. To "see" or to "stand under" something is to express one's relationship with it, to experience it as only a human can. Objective knowledge, or what we commonly call "empirical" knowledge, is simply our appraisal of the world in relationship to our cognitive capacities—our ability to perceive. This is another way of saying that our ability to perceive relates to our ability to express.

So when a group of middle-class, middle-aged men follow the poet Robert Bly into the woods to beat on drums and to express their love or solidarity with other men, or when a group of religious men join the "Promise Keepers" and celebrate their identities through prayer and hugging, they are simultaneously expressing a very real human need—to communicate and to be understood at the emotive level—as well as at a fundamentally persuasive level.[30] This should not be taken as suggesting that paradigmatic cases of expression do not exist, as they clearly do. People cry. People call out. People hurt. People celebrate. This is both real and it is primordial. Indeed, many animals experience life at these levels; in our animality, we act in kind. Nevertheless, we often cry for a *reason*, we often suffer for a *reason* (and we often suffer from *symbolic* causes from which no animal would ever suffer),[31] and we celebrate and rejoice also for *reasons*. We collectively express these emotions as well. We are, above all else, *emotional* creatures. While humans hold forth the pretense of being logical creatures, our primary experience of the world is emotional. Our logical and rational potential must be carefully cultivated and learned, an artificial restraint we place over our emotions. Our pretense of being logical and rational creatures is often maintained at great psychological cost.

℘ Coercion and Persuasion ℘

Coercion is a type of action intended by a change agent to instigate a material effect by bringing force to bear on a subject in such a way that she/he experiences the loss or nullification of free choice.[32] Alternatively, coercion can be defined as the "manipulation of the target group's situation in such fashion that the pursuit of any course of action other than that sought by the movement will be met with considerable cost or punishment."[33] Beating down a speaker, throwing a brick through a window, or smashing someone with a stick or a club, are paradigmatic forms of coercion. To blow up a building, to burn down an abortion clinic, to shoot people or to lynch them, to drop napalm on them or to corral them into "protective" hamlets is to bring about an "order" through violence. Violence is one way of establishing order, although it may not be the most effective way of doing so in terms of long-term goals.

Violence, however, is not always bad. In our pursuit of health, we do violence to microorganisms and few people seem to argue that medicine is unethical. We do violence to the animals we eat, and whose skins we wear, and we do violence to them with the cosmetic and medical testing we do on them. Another way of seeing violence in a positive sense is as a transformation of material. We transform material all the time, for example, when we convert the iron ore we drill from rocks into the skeletons of buildings, and so does nature (e.g., predators kill and consume prey). However, some human-influenced transformation is symbolic when it involves persuasion—the demonization of our enemies, for example.

Naked violence is a transformation that is done without the aid of persuasion. As such, violence is quick and easy. Violence requires little skill and patience. Furthermore, to the extent that a person has the power to make the world in her or his image by force, violence is a direct way to establish that influence. So we must not disparage violence just because it is violence. While "violence" is such an ugly word, we must remember that when we like its effect, we call it something else—"liberation," for example, "protecting our national interest," or "promoting democracy abroad."

Similar to the other categories of behavior that we are discussing in this chapter, violence has its limitations. Violence fails when force fails, and the violence that we do tends to beget more violence. Thus, coercion has as its major disadvantage that it is usually inappropriate, and it is often unavailable. When one side has a monopoly on the use of force, the other side has to come up with a different strategy. For example, the success of Mahatma Gandhi's much celebrated "non-violent" resistance (read "symbolic" or "persuasive" resistance) to the British was determined by three interdependent factors. First, the British had all the guns—their monopoly on the use of force was overwhelming; to confront the British with violence would be to invite a devastating retaliation and guarantee an even *harsher* future imperial rule. Second, the British, to their credit, were resistant to the idea of slaughtering all of the rebellious Indians. The self-image of the British had evolved to the point where it was no longer possible for them to imagine massive slaughter of disrespecting but nonviolent protesters to buttress their imperial goals (which might have been done in earlier decades of the British Empire). This new self-image encouraged restraint when dealing with the restive Indian population. Third, and finally, the British were politically weak because of turmoil and resistance in their other colonies, and because of conflicts with other Western nations, leading to two disastrous world wars.

In sum, the British had neither the resolve nor the resources for an extended defense of their far-away colony. In contrast, the Indians were inspired and fighting for their own interest in their own communities. Rejecting violence as counter-productive in their situation allowed them to develop other more creative alternatives for resistance. With this context in mind, the experience of Gandhi in India does not prove that non-violence is better than violence; the relative success of Gandhi's movement only proves that the persuasive tactics of nation building are dependent upon historical circumstances, such as those discerned correctly by Gandhi. Gandhi's strength as a leader was dependent upon his astute appraisal of Britain's tactical and moral positions at the time that he was advocating the independence of India. Other conflicts, such as the Japanese invasion of China in the 1930s and the subsequent political revolution among the Chinese peasants, may demand other tactics. As the famous ex-slave abolitionist leader Frederick Douglass noted in 1857:

> If there is no struggle, there is no progress. Those who profess to freedom and yet deprecate agitation are men who want crops without plowing. They want rain without thunder and lightning. They want the ocean without the awful roar of its mighty waters. Power concedes nothing without a demand.[34]

In addition to its limited availability and to its frequent lack of appropriateness, coercion tends to create conflict. As we will see in the next section, conflict tends to create polarized situations in which one party's loss is the other party's gain. Because of the constant struggle over relative advantages, both sides in a coercive relationship are constantly on their guard to get an edge over the other. Violence tends to be a zero-sum game—one person wins and one person loses. The use of coercion also tends to create ill-will toward the persuader and the organization that the perpetrator of violence represents. The Israeli/Palestine conflict is grounded here—neither side has a strategy that reflects, practically, the constraints and opportunity of the current historical context. Until one side decides to change, the two parties will remain locked in a paralyzing and intractable stasis.

ꙅꙨ Paradigmatic Persuasion ꙅꙨ

Persuasion is the final example of a communicative effort that can exist, theoretically, in a paradigm state. But what do we mean by persuasion? This textbook and course are intended to be an answer to that question. In the sense that we are discussing the term here, with the five definitions at the start of this chapter in mind, persuasion, as I define it, can be understood as *suasory discourse—an attempt by a person to encourage another to move, cognitively and freely, from one mental position to a different one, so as to affect, ultimately, that person's behavior.* So, for example, one bumper sticker from a blood bank reads, "Give blood so we won't run out on you" and couples that verbal message and pun with a visual counterpart—the letters on the top row of the verbal message are white, and, as we read the second row of letters we see that three fourths of the characters are red, and one third is white, and the top of the red has waves, indicating that it is the blood supply that is slowly decreasing. The overall effect of the visual image is to highlight the fact that three-fourths of the blood in this picture is *gone*, and that it is diminishing further. Indeed, there may not be any *real* blood left when *we* need it.

This appeal for blood donation is what we may call a classical or a paradigmatic example of persuasion. Nobody would look at this appeal and fail to see that it is, in fact, a persuasive message, although many people may look at it and not be persuaded. Another example of paradigmatic persuasion would be most ads for commercial products. In these cases, we can identify the persuader, the intent, and the motives involved. Consider the following ad for a generic perfume. This ad features a picture of a beautiful and elegant woman drinking wine by a fireplace with a bright fire burning. She wears what appears to be expensive jewelry. In front of the woman there is another glass, half full, indicating that there is a man lurking somewhere just outside of our view. The caption reads, "When was the last time he wanted to be alone with you over the holidays?"

As with the bumper sticker, there is no other way to read the perfume ad *except* as an instance of persuasion. The product (perfume) is linked to sex and romance (and to wealth) and women are asked to imagine themselves in this model's shoes. The ad strongly implies that the desirability of a woman (in terms of a man who is the implied standard of normality) is dependent upon the use of the product. The fact that there may be other ways to experience sexuality (or even friendship) and fun, or another way to celebrate a holiday, is ignored. We are given an image and are told that the image represents the sole opportunity we have to fulfill the expectations that it itself upholds. The ad does not appeal to logic, but to our emotions and to our desires which previous ads have already manipulated, making us more receptive to this appeal. The ad reduces and it misrepresents—it falsifies and it conceals. In short, it is normally what we take to be persuasion.

A more graphic example of paradigmatic persuasion can be seen in the following appeal for the anti-abortion movement which positions two photographs against each other. On the left side is a healthy baby, approximately eight months old, sucking his finger and gazing inquisitively and somewhat innocently past the camera. This picture is contrasted with a bloody and mangled corpse of a fetus that had been aborted at nineteen weeks. The ad goes on to tell us that the choice is ours: life or death! The overt appeal is to "Be the voice of the unborn." Provide support for the movement to overturn *Roe v. Wade*.[35]

Paradigmatic persuasion involves the above instances, and it is more. It is, for example, the president, or the preacher, the woman or man who stands before an audience and exhorts us to think, to be, to feel in a particular way. It may be ourselves as well as we attempt to impose our will on others and on the world.

Similar to the use of coercion, persuasion has its advantages and its disadvantages. For example, it is usually coactive in nature. That is, persuasion is not a thing that we do *to* others, but an activity that we do *with* them. Simons, Morreale, and Gronbeck describe coactive persuasion as an umbrella term "for the ways that persuaders might *move toward* persuadees psychologically so that they will be moved, in turn, to accept the persuader's position or proposal for action."[36] Coactive persuasion includes efforts of communication that emphasize similarities between the persuader and the persuadee. The basic premise behind coactive approaches to persuasion is Burke's theory of identification (see Chapter 6). Persuasion works best when audiences see persuaders as they see themselves. For example, the more others appear similar to ourselves, the more we have common agreements and mutual understandings, the more our ideas and behaviors will match the values and beliefs that others honor, the more that we appear similar to others, and the more that others will like us and be receptive to our ideas. Far from breeding contempt, familiarity—or at least the perception of it—suggests a tendency toward affinity. Indeed, one of the more consistent findings in the literature concerning "interpersonal attraction" is that commonality or similarities between two or more people increases the level of attraction between those two individuals.[37]

Persuaders who utilize a coactive approach to persuasion seek to correct what they consider the "misunderstandings" that separate their ideas from their audience. "This may sound controversial," a persuader may claim, "but when you think about it, it is *really* an extension of what we, as a nation, already believe." Notice the appeal to common ground in this example. If a persuader can illustrate that her or his proposal falls within our national beliefs, then we may reach some sort of agreement based upon this shared understanding or experience.

In order for coactive persuasion to work, however, the assumption the persuader has to make is that disagreements or dissimilarities between the two parties are lightly held, inconsequential, and that they are not essential to either's self-identification or self-image. Even more crucially, the persuader has to assume that the similarities between her/him and her/his audience are merely unknown or unrecognized. The goal, then, is to uncover and build up these connections and to capitalize upon them. Persuaders who utilize this approach accentuate the ties that bind us to one another. We can always argue for differences; that is easy to do. It is much more civil and humane, I think, to argue for commonality and inclusion, which is the hallmark of this perspective.

To summarize, coactive persuasion is *receiver* oriented—focused on the terms of the persuadee. It is necessarily situation specific in that different people respond differently to persuasion in different contexts. The practice of coactive persuasion is particularly artful in that it combines images of similarity between persuader and persuadee while promoting images of the persuader's unique expertise and trustworthiness (discussed further in Chapter 7). Lastly, coactive persuaders ground controversial material in premises acceptable to the audience. The persuader strives to be perceived as "reasonable."[38]

The Reverend Jesse Jackson's 1988 speech at the Democratic National Convention in Atlanta, Georgia, is a clear example of how appeals to common ground can be operationalized. In one telling section of the speech, Jackson makes an overt appeal for inclusion and unity within the ranks of the Democratic party:

> Common ground! That is the challenge to our party tonight… The Bible teaches that when lions and lambs lie down together, none will be afraid and there will be peace in the valley. It sounds impossible. Lions eat lambs. Lambs sensibly flee from lions. But even lions and lambs find common ground. Why? Because neither lions nor lambs want the forest to catch on fire. Neither lions nor lambs want acid rain to fall. Neither lions nor lambs can survive nuclear war. If lions and lambs can find common ground, surely, we can as well, as civilized people.[39]

Of course not all persuasion fits this coactive model. As Charles J. Stewart, Craig Allen Smith, and Robert E. Denton, Jr. argue, conflict is often necessary for meaningful growth and change. Confrontational strategies emphasize dissimilarities, diverse and antithetical experiences and conflict.[40] The experience of civil rights persuasion teaches us that it is not enough to change laws; more fundamentally, the civil rights persuaders found that they had to reach people's hearts if social progress was to occur. As Dr. Martin Luther King, Jr. instructed, the way to affect people's consciousness is to dramatize and thus highlight an unjust situation. This dramatization, which includes the naming of villains, saints, struggle, and the like was the symbolic function of much of the civil unrest that characterized the Civil Rights Movement.

As the above suggests, we almost never persuade people by ignoring their subjectivities, by reducing them to objects to be manipulated. Persuasion starts, always, with the individual, with what she/he thinks or feels, with, in effect, her or his humanity. Violence, on the other hand, starts from the suppression of this humanity. Persuasion is about sharing; violence is about forcing. As such, persuasion is almost always appropriate. Few people, and few institutions, as a matter of policy, will exclude the potential for persuasion. Built into nearly all social systems is some procedure to hear people's complaints and some apparatus to see people as *people*, in spite of the institutionalization and bureaucratization that often surrounds them. The more that these conditions exist in any system, the more democratic and open a society becomes, and the more human and less bureaucratic its expression of living. It is always an important struggle to humanize bureaucracies; else we become tyrannized by instrumental language.[41]

Finally, persuasion has the advantage of creating the possibility for good will to be cultivated for the persuader and the organization that the persuader represents. People tend to appreciate the skill, the intelligence, and the difficulties involved in persuasion, and often even respect the challenge that persuaders have in our society. A strong bias in our society is that we tend to attribute intelligence to people who can speak well and influence us verbally. To be a persuader, particularly a cultural persuader, is to be, in an important sense, part of a venerable tradition in this country, one that can be traced back to the foundation of this country and has roots in what we have reified as the "Golden Age" of Greece and the birth of Western civilization.[42]

The disadvantages of persuasion are, as can be imagined, that it takes time and skill. It takes patience. Often, circumstances do not allow us to engage in persuasion. Most importantly, persuasion requires a *reasonable* audience (as our earlier discussion of Gandhi's persuasion illustrated). During the Civil Rights Era, for example, Martin Luther King Jr.'s strategy was premised (correctly, for the most part) on the notion that this country *could* change, that people fundamentally did not want to mistreat African-Americans, and that the best of people could withstand the worst of people. Most essentially, King understood that the capacity of African-Americans to suffer was greater than the capacity of others in this society to inflict suffering on them, that despite a long history of violence directed against slaves and the descendents of slaves, or perhaps because of that history, Americans could be different. Without a firm belief in this assumption, King never would have been successful as the pre-eminent civil rights leader. As King himself explained to White America, "We will not only win freedom for ourselves, we will so appeal to your heart and conscience that we will win you in the process, and our victory will be a double victory."[43]

To his credit, and to ours, King was right. This passage exemplifies beautifully an important spiritual resource that King makes clear with regard to the Civil Rights Movement. The movement is about integration—not just physical integration, but moral integration; it is about the resources and promises of the American law, and the cruel, contradictory, and exclusionary practices of that *same* law. Another way King cultivates this sense of inclusion—of this appeal to reason—to encourage his White audience to accept African-Americans as full-fledged members of the national community, is when he carefully situates his "dream" in his celebrated "I Have A Dream" address. He declares that his dream is "deeply rooted in the American dream." This, along with his wider, powerful metaphors of inclusion, helps us as audience members to visualize the integration he urges us to accept—one law, one justice, one people. Apartheid, King reminds us time and again, is morally and spiritually wrong; more importantly, it goes against the grain of what almost every American holds to be true about what it means to be an American.

Continuing in this vein, King likens the U.S. Constitution to a "promissory note" that all Americans are entitled to receive, and one which, through government mismanagement and bad business practices, has failed to materialize for members of the African-American community. According to King, the founders of the United States, those who drafted the Constitution, had guaranteed to all Americans certain unalienable rights—rights to freedom, equality, liberty, and dignity. This was a promise made to *all* future Americans. He argues that this is a "promissory note" that now is past due. King concludes his argument in this section by playing out the metaphor of the "check" to its natural argument for inclusion:

> It is obvious today that America has defaulted on this promissory note in so far as her citizens of color are concerned. Instead of honoring this sacred obligation, America had given the Negro people a bad check; a check which has come back marked "insufficient funds." [44]

All of us can understand this metaphor. Such persuasion turns the question away from what African-Americans *want* to what they *deserve* as citizens of the United States, and as long-suffering human beings. King's metaphor forces the rest of us to realize that the civil rights *disturbances*—that is, the "inconveniences" and "disrespect" for law and order put on the country by the protesters with their marches, sit-ins, and boycotts—were not about causing trouble; rather, and fundamentally, they were dramatizing and resolving a trouble in the national culture that *already existed*. The Civil Rights Movement was about dispensing medicine, using heat to cauterize a festering sore that existed for so long in this country that it seemed normal.

What people frequently refer to as "racial tension" has been a fact of life from the beginning of colonization in North America. With European colonization, there arrived individuals from a variety of nations who confronted a heterogeneous indigenous population. These Europeans—themselves bitterly divided along racial, class, and religious lines—fought each other as they fought and exterminated the Native population of North America. In addition, the Europeans soon imported slaves from Africa. The first Africans appeared in Virginia in 1619, and slavery attained a formal legal status after 1660.[45] In short, from the seventeenth century forward, what we now call the United States has seldom experienced racial peace or social justice. Rather, a more accurate characterization, historically, is that the United States was founded on the principle of social intolerance.[46] Marginalized communities symbolically and literally bled for generations, living with open sores. The Civil Rights Movement was about healing wounds that have been around for a long time. In this respect, King's message was about more than Black liberation; rather, it was (and is) about *human* liberation from our injured past—from intolerance and inequality.[47]

In contrast to King's tactics, imagine what possibility a Jew would have had in Nazi Germany to build from the assumptions that we find in the strategy of the civil rights protesters. What worked for the Black people in the United States in the 1950s and 1960s would not have worked for the Jews in Berlin during the 1930s and 1940s. The Jewish appeal for tolerance and inclusion would appear to be "nonsense" within the context of the period. In the Nazi frame of mind, the Jew was antithetical to "Aryan" success.[48] The more tolerance that was shown to Jews, the less healthy the Aryan community appeared. The identity and strength of the Aryan was defined by the destruction of the Jew.[49]

In stark contrast, King was successful in his ability to encourage the majority of Americans to look inside themselves, to explore their actions, and to reconcile the differences between their self-identities and their actions. King's Jewish counterpart would have failed because Hitler was also successful in his task of getting the majority of Germans to look into themselves, to explore their heart-of-hearts, to look at their actions, and to conclude that the Jews were a threat to their well-being. King bet, successfully, that the more he could put the sufferings of the African-American community in the national and international spotlight, often through confrontational strategies, the more able he would be to arouse the moral as well as pragmatic conscience of the United States.[50] Hitler was successful in doing the exact opposite—he evoked the moral indignation, rather than the moral responsibilities, of the Germans. As a result of both men, the world experienced dramatic change, testimony to the power of persuasion.

Applying the above line of reasoning to a contemporary context, I suggest that it is a mistake to dismiss the claims of so-called terrorist groups or other opponents of the United States as self-delusional. For example, a memo from the U.S. Department of Homeland Security entitled "Terminology to Define the Terrorists: Recommendations From American Muslims" went to great lengths to deny so-called "terrorist" groups religious or moral legitimacy, as did the rhetoric of the Bush administration more generally. While understandable from our perspective (we do *not* want them to have legitimacy), we have to realize that this is wishful thinking. Clearly, these groups *do* have legitimacy and credibility in some circles and they must be engaged, to some extent, *on their terms* or we will fail to appreciate their considerable symbolic resources, which is why labeling all of our geo-political opponents as "terrorists" is not very useful. As a practical matter, we cannot legislate their terms for them. We can blow them up, but we cannot control how others may perceive them.

ಏ Mixed Communication Efforts ಞ

Now that we have looked generally at the ways we can conceptualize the different types of communication efforts, we turn now to explore some examples of how such communication efforts frequently mix and overlap in the world around us. As suggested above, it is somewhat artificial to talk about paradigmatic cases of anything—the world is a much messier place than our sterile intellectual classifications can often contain. The more rigid the classification, the more we drain the life out of that which we study.

The first blending of communication efforts we will discuss is *information-persuasion*. For example, politicians regularly mail out newsletters to their constituents, keeping them informed of what their representatives are doing, and generally commenting upon political affairs. This is information, and it also is persuasion. In reading the newsletter, citizens learn about what is happening in their district, but they are also being encouraged to continue supporting the politician, or to support that politician in the future.

We also find examples of information-persuasion in many ads. While some ads are devoid of information (such as the perfume ad discussed earlier), many ads try to present, in a relatively rational way, the benefits of their products. Some hotel ads, for instance, discuss or even detail the types of food a customer can eat, describe the rooms and the services customers can expect, and provide pictures that idealize the hotel experience. Many of these ads contain a great deal of information, but they are also persuasive—their intent is to make real one type of hotel experience so that it becomes the person's standard and the focus of her/his future behavior.

Much information-persuasion originates in public relations firms. Approximately 40% of all the material we receive through the broadcast and print news agencies is derived, frequently unedited, from public relation agencies.[51] Indeed, one function and goal of public relations in our society is to manage information so that it serves certain agendas. When General Colin Powell went on television in the early 1990s in front of a map of Somalia, at a time when American military involvement in that country was accelerating, he was not just showing Americans where Somalia was on the map. He was not just explaining to his television audience what U.S. troops were doing there and why they were there. Rather, he was trying to convince us or to reassure us that what we were doing there was justifiable. Likewise, in his shameful performance before the United Nations in February 2003, to argue that Iraq possessed weapons of mass destruction (WMDs) in the Bush Administration's final attempt to acquire the Security Council's backing for the planned military invasion of Iraq, Powell, in his capacity as Secretary of Defense, was informing the world of the imminent threat posed by Iraq's Saddam Hussein. This was both an attempt to inform and to persuade, although Powell later apologized for his speech admitting that he deceived the public on behalf of the Bush Administration.[52]

Earlier I alluded to the persuasive dimensions of entertainment. As advertising scholar Susan B. Kretchmer notes, "Advertising and promotion have evolved to the point where the line between what can be considered strictly entertainment as opposed to what can be seen as commercial persuasion has become extremely flexible and blurred."[53] Obvious examples of *entertainment-persuasion* include the political/editorial cartoons found in our nation's newspapers, movies such as Michael Moore's *Fahrenheit 9/11,* Leni Riefenstahl's *Triumph of the Will,* and the U.S. government's World War II *Why We Fight* film series.[54] Entertainment-persuasion can be found in other mediums as well. Take for example a Spider-Man comic produced in conjunction with the American Cancer Society. In this comic, Spider-Man, with Storm and Power Man, battle a foe called Smokescreen, an evil-doer who peddles cigarettes to a high school track and field team. The theme of the story is that smoking is bad for young people, and that to smoke is to be a loser. In case anyone misses the message that is enacted in the drama of the text, the last page of the comic has a list of smoking-related facts, and each of the superheroes comments in one of the following ways: "Not even I can fly in the face of facts; Smoking has serious side-effects; All this adds up to a heavy load on your system; Smoking is too big a burden to bear—even for a superhero."[55]

With *coercive-persuasion,* the final mixed communication effort discussed here, persuaders "bring about desired change by convincing that force is likely to follow noncompliance."[56] As Parke Burgess explains, the "victim must be convinced that dire consequences are likely… before he can feel forced to comply, just as he must become convinced of the coercer's probable capacity and intent to commit the act… before he can conclude the act is likely to follow non-compliance."[57]

A typical example of coercive-persuasion is called *military persuasion*. Political scientist Stephen J. Cimbala defines military persuasion as "the threat or use of armed force in order to obtain desired political or military goals. It is basically a psychological strategy intended to influence the decisions of other parties without necessarily having to destroy their armed forces or societies."[58] He goes on to explain that "the object of military persuasion is to induce the party being influenced to want to comply with the demand of the influencer and, having achieved that result, to act in accord with the influencer's demands."[59] Military persuasion is the common practice of using armed force to support diplomacy, deterrence, crisis management, unconventional conflicts, peace operations, and other military activities short of major conventional war. For instance, in early June, 2008, Israel staged a massive military operation over the Mediterranean ocean, displaying 100 warplanes. This was widely seen by the world as a warning against Iran to cease immediately what Israel perceives as Iran's effort to build nuclear weapons. Note, to be successful here, military persuasion requires that policy makers and diplomats understand the subtle interaction between force and diplomacy. Poor judgment in this area can have cataclysmic consequences.

Coercive-persuasion is also prevalent in *social movement persuasion* where confrontational communication strategies are important for, among other things, creating attention, discrediting an enemy, provoking violence, fostering identification, and providing catharsis.[60] In the 1980s, for example, many farmers in the United States were having problems surviving and the number of family-owned and family-run farms was dramatically reduced. The farmers turned to the Reagan Administration for relief, and found little. In response, the farmers organized and staged a mass rally in Washington, D.C., to emphasize their concern. They rode their tractors to the nation's capital, disrupting traffic, and created a spectacle. The tractors added a concrete dimension to their rally and brought a sense of heaviness and seriousness to the farmers' cause. While tractors are not tanks, they are formidable machines, and while the farmers were peaceful, the fact that they gathered, *en masse*, and with their heavy machinery, communicated a sense of urgency to the federal government. Later, they burned an old tractor to reemphasize their basic point: government inaction and non-concern were destroying them.

Again, the implicit threat is real—the threat to *any* property is a threat to *all* property. When groups of people gather together and burn an official in effigy or destroy, however symbolically, a piece of property, people take notice—a symbolic destruction of the social fabric is almost as real, and as significant, as the actual disruption. Any time people gather, focused on a cause, the message they send collectively is greater than their individual voices. This was as much true in the Solidarity Movement in Poland in the early 1980s as it was during the student protest in China in 1989. The same is true for the anti-Vietnam War and civil rights protests in the United States in the 1960s.

ℬ Conclusion ℭ

Now that we have defined persuasion—five definitions plus my own and looked at what is and is not persuasion, and have seen how there is a persuasive dimension to most forms of communication, we are ready to see in the next chapter how persuasion can be conceptualized as a *process*. Once we see how persuasion is a process involving a range of interrelated variables and perspectives (Chapter 5), and once we have explored some of the theories that help us to appreciate how persuasion works (Chapter 6), we can look more closely at some of its component parts—the persuader (Chapter 7) and the audience (Chapter 8). We will then explore the power of language in persuasion (Chapter 9) before tackling the issue of ethics (Chapter 10).

℘ Notes ℧

1. Gary C. Woodward and Robert E. Denton Jr., *Persuasion and Influence in American Life* 5th ed. (Prospect Heights, IL: Waveland Press, 2004), 6.

2. Charles J. Stewart, Craig Allen Smith and Robert E. Denton Jr., *Persuasion and Social Movements* 5th ed. (Long Grove, IL: Waveland Press, 2007), 21.

3. Herbert W. Simons, Joanne Morreale, and Bruce Gronbeck, *Persuasion in Society* (Thousand Oaks, CA: Sage, 2001), 7.

4. Daniel J. O'Keefe, *Persuasion: Theory and Practice* 2nd ed. (Thousand Oaks, CA: Sage, 2002), 5.

5. Timothy A. Borchers, *Persuasion in the Media Age* (Boston: McGraw-Hill, 2005), 17.

6. *Persuasion in Society, 6.*

7. This discussion is adapted from Herbert Simons' "persuasion map." See his *Persuasion: Understanding, Practice, and Analysis* (New York: Random House, 1986), 116.

8. *The Philosophy of Literary Form: Studies in Symbolic Action* (Berkeley: University of California Press, 1973), 293.

9. Ibid., 304.

10. See Omar Swartz, "Kenneth Burke's Theory of Form: Rhetoric, Art, and Cultural Analysis," *Southern Communication Journal, 61* (1996), 312–321.

11. *Counter-Statement* (Berkeley: University of California Press, 1968).

12. Ibid., 160.

13. Ibid., xii.

14. The term originates from the Roman poet Juvenal who wrote: "Already long ago, from when we sold our vote to no man, the People have abdicated our duties; for the People who once upon a time handed out military command, high civil office, legions—everything now restrains itself and anxiously hopes for just two things: bread and circuses" (*Satire* 10.77–81).

15. (New York: Penguin, 2005).

16. Aldous Huxley, *Brave New World* (New York: Harper Perennial Modern Classics, 2006); George Orwell, *Animal Farm and 1984* (New York: Harcourt, 2003).

17. *Fahrenheit 451* (New York: Ballatine Books, 1953).

18. *Amusing Ourselves To Death*, vii.

19. *Fahrenheit 451*, 59.

20. Sigmund Freud (1856–1939) was a cigar-smoking psychologist who founded the field of psychoanalysis. Freud was famous for his discussion of the unconscious and its connection to the sexual drive. He presumed to find in everyday innocuous behavior signs of a repressed sexuality.

21. Remember, in Chapter 1 we discussed Aristotle's definition of rhetoric being "the faculty of seeing in any given case the means of persuasion." Those means are discussed throughout this textbook and course as *ethos, pathos, logos,* and *mythos.* (Note, *mythos* does not appear in Aristotle and was added by later theorists).

22. Donovan J. Ochs, *Consolatory Rhetoric: Grief, Symbol, and Ritual in The Greco-Roman Era* (Columbia: University of South Carolina Press, 1993).

23. James Boyd White, *Heracles' Bow: Essays on the Rhetoric and Poetics of the Law* (Madison: University of Wisconsin Press, 1985).

24. Marouf A. Hasian, Jr. and Thomas K. Nakayama, "The Empires Strike Back: The Sokal Controversy and the Vilification of Cultural Studies," *Journal of Communication Inquiry, 21* (1997), 46.

25. *Only Words* (Cambridge, MA: Harvard University Press, 1993), 13.

26. Ibid., 31.

27. See for example, Cheryl L. Harris, "Whiteness as Property," in *Critical Race Theory: The Key Writings That Formed the Movement*, eds., Kimberly Crenshaw, Neil Gotanda, Garry Peller, and Kendall Thomas (New York: The New Press, 1996), 357–383.

28. *How to Do Things With Words* (New York: Oxford University Press, 1962), 7.

29. See Philip C. Wander, "The Third Persona: An Ideological Turn in Rhetorical Theory," *Central States Speech Journal, 35* (1984), 197–216.

30. Robert Bly is a popular author and poet, who co-founded the mythopoetic men's movement in the United States, a psychological and spiritual self-help group for men. The Promise Keepers is a Christian organization of men committed to reinforcing the traditional male role in family life.

31. This is a fundamental Burkean notion, central to the unique human capacity to use symbols.

32. See Parke G. Burgess, "Crisis Rhetoric: Coercion vs. Force," *Quarterly Journal of Speech*, *59* (1973), 61–75.

33. Ralph H. Turner and Lewis M. Killian, *Collective Behavior* (Englewood Cliffs, NJ: Prentice Hall, 1972), 291.

34. Cited in Raymond Arsenault, *Freedom Riders: 1961 and the Struggle for Racial Justice* (New York: Oxford University Press, 2006), 517.

35. *Roe v. Wade*, 410 U.S. 113 (1973) is the landmark United States Supreme Court decision recognizing that a woman's right to privacy protected her decision to have an abortion.

36. *Persuasion in Society* (Thousand Oaks, Sage, 2001), 74.

37. See Michael Monsour, "Similarities and Dissimilarities: Constructing Meaning and Building Intimacy Through Communication," in Steve W. Duck (Ed.), *Dynamics of Relationships* (Thousand Oaks, CA: Sage, 1994), 112–134.

38. *Persuasion in Society*, 75.

39. "Common Ground and Common Sense," in *African American Communications: An Anthology in Traditional and Contemporary Studies*, ed. James W. Ward (Dubuque, IA: Kendall/Hunt, 1993), 311.

40. *Persuasion and Social Movements*, 67-69.

41. Examples of instrumental language in bureaucracies include "precision," "speed," "cost/-benefit analysis," and "accountability."

42. For a critical discussion of this tradition, see Omar Swartz, *The Rise of Rhetoric and Its Intersection With Modern Critical Thought* (Boulder, CO: West View Press, 1998). For a sampling of the canonical texts of the American rhetorical tradition, see Ronald F. Reid, ed., *Three Centuries of American Rhetorical Discourse: An Anthology and a Review* (Prospect Heights, IL: Waveland Press, 1988).

43. *The Words of Martin Luther King, Jr.* (New York: Newmarket Press, 1983), 72.

---

44. In *I Have a Dream: Writings and Speeches that Changed the World*, ed. James M. Washington (Glenview IL: Harper Collins, 1986), 104.

45. For a rhetorical study of this process, see Omar Swartz, "Codifying the Law of Slavery in North Carolina: Positive Law and the Slave Persona," *Thurgood Marshall Law Review*, *29* (2004), 285–310.

46. See Omar Swartz, "Hierarchy, Values and Political Identities in the Imperial Practices of the United States," in *Transformative Communication Studies: Culture, Hierarchy, and the Human Condition*, ed. Omar Swartz (Leicester, UK: Troubador Publishing, 2008), 249–279.

47. This dimension of King was downplayed for strategic reasons during the civil rights struggles of the late 50s and early to mid-60s but emerged publically in the final year of his life and is evident in his *The Trumpet of Conscience* (New York: HarperCollins, 1989), which consists of five radio broadcasts on the Canadian Broadcasting Corporation in the last two months of 1967. King was assassinated on April 4, 1968.

48. For elaboration, see Omar Swartz, "Symbols and Perspectives in Burkean Rhetorical Theory: Implications for Understanding Anti-Semitism," *World Communication*, *24* (1996), 183–190.

49. Ibid.

50. Aside from its obvious moral repugnance, segregation had two major practical problems. First, it was expensive (e.g., two separate college systems of supposedly equal resources). Second, in a fundamental fashion, segregation frustrated the United States' Cold War foreign policy goals in trying to counter the influence of the Soviet Union throughout the largely "colored" developing world. See Mary Dudziak, "Desegregation as a Cold War Imperative," 41, *Stanford Law Review, 61* (1988), 61–120.

51. Mark Dowie, "Torches of Liberty," introduction to *Toxic Sludge is Good For You: Lies Damn Lies, and the Public Relations Industry* by John Stauber and Sheldon Rampton (Monroe, ME: Common Courage Press, 1995), 2.

52. In a February, 2005, interview with Barbara Walters on ABC News' *20/20* program, Powell himself admitted that this speech was a blot on his reputation.

53. "Advertainment: The Evolution of Product Placement as a Mass Media Marketing Strategy," *Handbook of Product Placement in the Mass Media*, ed. Mary-Lou Galician (New York: Routledge, 2004), 39.

54. Moore's *Fahrenheit 9/11* is familiar to most readers, as it was his attempt to discredit President George W. Bush in the 2004 election. Less familiar to readers today is Leni Riefenstahl's *Triumph of the Will*, the most influential piece of propaganda to come out of the Nazi Third Reich. The *Why We Fight* film series was a well-known collection of seven propaganda films commissioned by the U.S. government to gain American support for the Second World War.

55. Stan Lee, Marvel Comics, 1995.

56. Burgess, "Crisis rhetoric," 69.

57. Ibid.

58. *Military Persuasion in War and Policy: The Power of Soft* (Westport, CT: Praeger, 2002), 1.

59. Ibid., 25.

60. J. Dan Rothwell, "Verbal Obscenity: Time for Second Thoughts," *Western Journal of Communication*, 35 (1971), 231–42. The strategy of polarization is also a factor here. See John W. Bowers, Donovan J. Ochs, and Richard J. Jensen, *The Rhetoric of Agitation and Control* (Prospect Heights, IL: Waveland Press, 1993).

CHAPTER 5

Understanding Persuasion as a Process

In this chapter we are going to explore persuasion as a complex unfolding, as a movement toward the co-construction of meaning in a communication interaction. In other words, persuasion is not merely a product—it is not simply the behavioral act itself—as many people assume. Persuasion cannot be so easily quantified in this manner, just as rhetorical "meaning" cannot be so quantified as we discussed in Chapter 2. Rather, persuasion is fundamentally a *process* that involves an interrelated system of multiple variables, factors, concerns, and tendencies that contribute, ultimately, toward a state of mind, an internalized situatedness on behalf of the persuadee. While behavior and action are obviously important in terms of persuasion, they mean little if they are not grounded firmly in some more substantial internalized state. Persuasion that affects behavior alone and does not settle itself in our attitudes, values, and beliefs, has only a short-term relevance to our lives.

For example, in class I can ask a student to pick up and place into a trash receptor an empty soft drink bottle on the floor near her or his desk, even if it did not belong to the student. The simplicity of the act, my authority as a college professor, and peer pressure due to the public announcement and reasonableness of my request will likely ensure compliance from the student. But what have I really accomplished? I have had only a minimum impact (if that) on the student's sense of self and her or his relationship to the environment or to myself. As we will discuss in Chapter 6 in the famous attribution theory study involving school children and littering, behavioral change can be grounded more substantially in the self-image of an individual, leading to greater permanence.[1]

Persuasion, therefore, to be more substantial can best be seen in terms of its interrelated variables that reflect deeply who we are as individuals. Skill in persuasion involves how these aspects interact with each other, and combine for an overall series of influences that help structure our perceptions and enact substance within our lives. In addition to being a process, persuasion is a state of mind, or at least a tone we take in our relationships with each other. Persuasion is an attitude, and, as I have been emphasizing in this textbook and throughout this course, it is a *critical sensitivity* that can be cultivated and practiced. In understanding the process of persuasion, we can protect ourselves from unwanted or undesirable persuasion and achieve a better sense of who we are as living, breathing, human beings and not merely as consumers or abstract political supporters. We do not have to be objects for elite manipulation; our lives have integrity on our *own* terms. We are, I maintain as a humanities scholar, *more* than our money or our votes and much more than a collection of drives to be satisfied. We can live our lives more richly by focusing on the ingredients of persuasion, which is the function of this chapter.

ᔧ Persuasion Is a Mutual Activity ᔦ

Part of the multi-varied aspect of persuasion is the relationship between the *persuader* and the *persuadee*; in other words, the person who is doing the persuasion and the person who is being encouraged to be something other than what she or he is currently. More specifically, persuasion must be approached as a *mutual* rather than as an *individual* activity in which the persuadee participates in the process. As Kenneth Burke explains:

> The individual person, striving to form himself in accordance with the communicative norms that match the cooperative ways of his society, is by the same token concerned with the rhetoric of identification. To act upon himself persuasively, he must variously resort to images and ideas that are formative. Education... exerts such pressure upon him from without; he completes the process from within. If he does not somehow act to tell himself (as his own audience) what the various brands of rhetorician have told him, his persuasion is not complete. Only those voices from without are effective which can speak in the language of a voice within.[2]

All persuasion, in other words, is a form of *self*-persuasion. Persuasion is done *with*, not *to* another. As we will discuss in Chapter 6 with self-persuasion and the enthymeme, and as we saw in our discussion of coactive persuasion in the previous chapter, people are rarely persuaded unless they participate in the process. Furthermore, persuasion is an *incremental* activity, not a "one-shot" effort—it involves the slow, subtle, building up of identifications, of beliefs, and of commitments. When we hear a speech, watch a commercial, interact with our partners, or even read a book, the manner in which we are being influenced involves more than a direct correlation between "exposure" and "effect," in what is classically known as the "hypodermic needle" model of persuasion.[3] Scholars once believed that the mere experience of a persuasive message, like a political propaganda poster or a commercial, was itself enough to affect us in a significant way. One Bizarro cartoon, for example, depicts a man running out of the door, leaving his surprised wife in front of the television where an ad shouts "sex, youth, sex, youth." His parting words, "I'm off to buy a red sports car, don't wait up."

Such, however, is not the case. By paying attention to the process of persuasion, we find that there is a more subtle influence than the old exposure-effect model was able to comprehend. Broadening our perspective, we find that persuasion involves the sum of the parts of a complex relationship. In other words, our understanding of exposure means little, if it is not coupled with an understanding of how that exposure interacts with our psychological dispositions—our sentiments, schemes, and values—or perhaps within our physiological constitution (i.e., in our need for water, food, and procreation). Indeed, one reason why persuasion, particularly our television advertising, is often so effective is that it lulls us into thinking that we are secure against its effect—any *one* message can easily be rejected. Because we are conscious of this power of ours to dismiss *particular* appeals, we tend to think we are immune to *all* appeals. We tend to think that other people are the fools who get taken in by persuasion. *We* are much too *smart* for that!

In the social science literature, this is known as the *self-serving bias*. The majority of people believe they are smarter and better looking than average, that they are free from the depersonalizing trends that affect others.[4] As individuals, we tend to see ourselves as outside the norm, as unique or, alternatively, as common, depending on the circumstance. For example, when successful, people may attribute that success to internal reasons that she/he is *better* than others, or works *harder* than others, as opposed to some external cause, such as luck, unearned privilege, or the helpful influence of a relative (i.e., nepotism). One's failures, on the other hand, are attributed outside ourselves, implying that we are no different than the average. So, for example, we tend to recognize that the media affects other people, not ourselves.[5] In fact, the effects of persuasion are often concealed from us. What we see or feel is often not what is happening to us. In the end, the apparent transparency of *some* persuasion convinces us that *all* (or most) of it is innocuous. We are ill-served by this belief, since it makes us compliant in our conditioning, disinclining us to be critical. Such a view allows us to take our advertising/commercial culture for granted as inevitable and necessary.

Most of us are adept at tuning out messages that we do not like to hear (i.e., selective perception). In so many ways, we can rationalize away the influence of persuasion in our lives ("it's only a commercial," we tell ourselves as we drink a can of Coca-Cola and eat our Big Mac hamburger). Yet each of these encounters is important in encouraging us to know, to be, to think differently. When seen cumulatively, any amount of exposure is significant. This is an important assumption behind the area of study known as *cultivation theory*, which considers how public beliefs are often colored by what is emphasized in the news and entertainment media that surround them. For instance, the more television one watches, the more likely she/he will over-emphasize the amount of violent crime there is in society,[6] fear people with mental disorders and be more likely to reject them,[7] have skewed and socially detrimental notions of male and female sexuality and greater acceptance of sexual stereotypes,[8] as well as display sexual callousness toward women.[9] This leads to what theorists call "the mean world syndrome," as such beliefs "may eventually translate into opinions and even socially relevant behaviors."[10] We are, in other words, what we watch as much as we are what we eat!

It may take a while, and it may never be completely influential, but the fact that we have seen an idea, heard an appeal, felt the pull of a different perspective in our minds, means that we have the potential to be different. While we can deny it, repress it, or even consciously forget it, the new perspective has become a part of us. A phrase here, a gesture there, a random piece of information that does not quite fit anywhere—these are often the parts of significant attitudinal or behavioral change. What starts as an itch might contribute one day to the molting of old skin. Such growth is part of the learning model of persuasion that we will discuss in more detail in Chapter 6.

In an important respect, this opportunity for growth is what persuasion is and how it works: it is the promise, the potential, and the ability to be different if we allow it, or if we become conscious of how environmental factors affect us. Without our acquiescence, the persuasion we hear and see will not change us. At a fundamental level, we change because that is how we *feel*. This means, in effect, that the best persuasion is often indiscernible to us. If we hear a message and we think to ourselves, "Wow, that is the most reasonable thing I have heard all day," we have been persuaded and have not noticed it. Persuasion can usually be seen, from the perspective of the audience, in its vulgarity. Persuasion is most apparent to us when it does *not* work. This is why we often feel immune to persuasion. The part we see, however, is only the "tip" of the proverbial iceberg. The significance of persuasion lies in the persuader's ability to make it appear "natural." When it works, it does so because persuasion has been made to fit seamlessly into the backdrop of our lives.

❧ Realms of Persuasive Interactions ❧

For the purpose of this textbook and course, there are three general realms of interaction that will contextualize our study of persuasion. While all three are discernable in the abstract, they tend to blur into each other in the real world. These three types are: interpersonal, public, and mass communication.

The most pervasive type of persuasive interaction with which we engage is *interpersonal persuasion*. This level involves at least two persons in the interaction, but can involve many others. However, as suggested above, at a certain point interpersonal communication turns into public communication, but where this line exists is difficult to discern. Furthermore, public communication, to be effective, must have a strong element of interpersonal communication, or else people will not be able to identify with the speaker. Again, how much interpersonal communication is needed in a particular context of public communication cannot be rigidly stipulated and is dependent upon the dynamics of the people involved. The important point is that in *all* communication, even in mass communication, the illusion of interpersonal communication must be present. Persuaders must *appear* to be talking to us and appear to *care* about us if we are going to invest our time in listening. Because of the need for audiences to identify with the person communicating, I am going to treat interpersonal communication as the prototype of persuasion in the paragraphs below.

People engaged in interpersonal communication and persuasion can constitute a variety of different relationships—indeed, they run the entire gamut of human cultural relationships. For example, a conversation between a patient and her/his doctor, between a teacher and her/his student, between a parent and her/his child, between two lovers or friends, or between two strangers chatting while waiting at a bus stop for a late bus all constitute examples of interpersonal communication. One difference between interpersonal persuasion and the myriad of other types of persuasion discussed in this textbook and course is the *saliency* of those messages. Saliency, in this context, means that messages from relational partners, people we know and trust are more important and have more of a sense of urgency than do persuasive messages embedded in ads, commercials, political rhetoric, and sales presentations. Public and mass persuaders, therefore, need to cultivate the sense of interpersonal trust in their audiences to have a chance at being successful.

To make matters more interesting, two people involved in an interpersonal relationship can be communicating through a *medium* such as the telephone or e-mail. As many of us probably realize, at least intuitively, the *medium* greatly impacts the type of communication that can be experienced. For instance, computer-mediated communication (CMC), particularly as it relates to online initiation and maintenance of romantic relationships, is probably best described as having both liberating features as well as limiting ones. As for liberating features, CMC allows an otherwise shy person with little confidence to come out of her or his shell, unhampered by, for example, negative conceptions about her/his physical appearance that might stop a romance before it gets started.[11] Along these same lines, however, CMC makes relationship building difficult because, unlike face-to-face communication, detecting deception or other emotional nuances is more difficult. Two examples from my personal life illustrate the pros and cons of CMC.

The first example involved my mother who was well into her 60s when, under pressure from her employer, she reluctantly purchased her first computer. She used her computer for her bookkeeping work and was resistant to learning how to use e-mail. After many months of my explaining to her that this is what people did these days, that I would be able to communicate with her more, she relented and gave it a shot. After sending me her first e-mail, and receiving my immediate response, I did not hear from her for some time. When I called her on the phone to see what was wrong I could tell that she was mad; I had inadvertently insulted her. "You don't love me" she said. "What! Of course I do. What makes you say that?" The upshot was that my e-mail message seemed to her cold and impersonal, lacking the emotional depth and sensibility that she remembered from my youthful college letters—which I had carefully and lovingly typed out on an old electric typewriter. Because that was the primary way I communicated with her—long distance phone calls were expensive back then—the letters were an *event* for both her and me. In writing the letters each week, I placed significant emotional life into them and my mother enjoyed the tactile experience of receiving, opening, and reading them. Now that we talk on the phone with some regularity, the fact that e-mail communications are not privileged or protected legally in ways that are regular letters, and my practice of approaching e-mail as a running open-ended conversation with multiple people, the emotional intensity in most e-mails I send has been greatly reduced. There is one notable exception to this, which is the topic of my second example.

The second example involved the woman who is now my wife. I met my wife in graduate school at Purdue University where she was studying biology, but we knew each other only superficially. We were both members of a campus student social organization that met once a week. I graduated a year before she did and left the state to assume my first faculty position. It took a couple of months for me to get e-mail (I did not start using e-mail until after I graduated from my Ph.D. program), and when I did I wrote to the group to say hello. It so happens that the woman who has come to be my wife was chosen by the group to write me back. This prompted the exchange of a flurry of e-mails and within three weeks of receiving her initial e-mail, she and I were engaged to be married. We kept those e-mails. Reading them over, nearly 15 years later, reveals that the medium freed us from the restraints common in face-to-face communication, although it undoubtedly imposed other constraints not apparent in face-to-face communication.[12]

In any case, an important condition that exists between two people engaged in interpersonal communication is that they experience a frequent switching of roles during their interaction; neither party is allowed to monopolize the discussion for long. Within the dialectic that defines the relationship, both parties define themselves and the other. In an important and complementary sense, each participant in a conversation needs the other.[13]

Contrast the above with coercion and coercive relationships. The more coercive the relationship, the more authoritarian and dictatorial, the less frequently the roles switch during communication interactions. The classic model of this is the classroom, at least in its more traditional manifestations. Teachers talk, students listen, and knowledge "flows" uni-directionally from the teacher to the student. This flowing knowledge fills "the students with the contents of [the teacher's] narration—contents which are detached from reality, disconnected from the totality which engendered them and could give them significance."[14] Such communication practices contribute to passive and uninspired audiences:

> The more students work at storing the deposits entrusted to them, the less they develop the critical consciousness which would result from their intervention in the world as transformers of that world. The more completely they accept the passive role imposed on them, the more they tend simply to adapt to the world as it is and to the fragmented view of reality deposited in them.[15]

As the pedagogue "deposits" information in the mind of the student, that knowledge becomes sterile—it is not knowledge that the students make for themselves. Knowledge, to be significant, particularly knowledge of "the Other" and knowledge of one's place and functioning in society, has to be created in the experience of two speakers mutually interacting with each other. In an important sense, a person has to *earn* knowledge—we can never expect it to be digested for us and handed to us on a plate. Knowledge, like other social pheneomona, has to be negotiated, constantly, and made into one's own image. Knowledge has to be experienced. It makes no sense to talk about "knowledge," or "communication" outside the experience of them. Both are experiential and, for that reason, potentially transformational.

To the extent that education is edifying it must be dialogical (i.e., it must have a shared communicative element). Likewise, in order for our interpersonal relationships to be meaningful they must involve a sort of interactiveness, one that quickly breaks down when one of the parties behaves egotistically or coercively. In other words, communication has to be truly free if we are to be free.

℘ Communication Levels ℘

Within all communication there are *levels* of interaction which change depending upon the *type* of communication with which we are involved. In interpersonal communication there are three levels of interaction. The first level, common to all communication types, involves the safe, superficial, and socially acceptable level. At this level, the door to our innermost sense of self is slightly ajar. We have constituted minimal awareness of each other and we agree to address the other with at least a degree of respect.

In interpersonal communication, unlike public or mass communication, it is necessary to go beyond this level of superficiality if meaningful persuasion or influence is to occur. For significant relationships to develop and to be maintained, people need to experience each other on deeper levels of understanding. Mutual trust, bonding, and developed commonalities are essential parts of meaningful identification—significant modifications of our values and beliefs are impossible without some sort of influence at this level. The orator can arouse our awareness of a subjectivity, or get us to question or at least to entertain the possibility of being different, but the real change in our experience comes from the day-to-day interactions we have with our significant others.

The second level of communication that we can reach is more risky than the first. Here the door is half open and our subjectivities start to become animated—we start to become multi-dimensional. Here we begin to reveal ourselves. Our thoughts and our feelings become more pronounced and clear. Our hopes and our fears become more accentuated. Our vulnerabilities begin to suggest themselves and, correspondingly, we begin to see opportunities for growth and change. To some extent, this level can be approached in public communication, and there is a sense in which it must be approached if significant persuasion is to occur—for example, the concept of speaker or teacher immediacy. By *immediacy*, I mean an awareness of the psychological distance between the speaker and the audience (or the teacher and a class) and the conscious effort to reduce it.[16] It behooves us as agents of influence to come across as caring about the people we are working to reach. As students are sometimes resistant to instructions from college professors, how an instructor interacts with her/his students is often crucial for impact. Studies continually show that the "construct of immediacy appears to be the unifying element between teachers' compliance-gaining attempts and students' resistance."[17] No matter what our credentials as teachers or communicators, without care and concern for the genuine well-being of our students and/or audiences, we will be fighting an uphill battle to be effective. In short, we have to be excited by what we see in each other, and to be reminded that there is something in ourselves about which it is good to feel excited. Good persuaders get us excited by awakening or reanimating our internal desires to feel inspired.

By the time we reach the third level of interaction, however, it is exceedingly difficult to proceed with public communication. When we do we often hurt our public credibility and/or appear somewhat compromised in terms of our leadership abilities. In our society, it is unacceptable to show our vulnerabilities in public, to convey our innermost thoughts and feelings, and to express, in an obvious way, the type of care and concern that we show to each other as individuals. Such emotional displays do not communicate well or appear sincere on television.[18]

Two noteworthy examples illustrate the above point. The first occurred in 1972 when Democratic Senator Edmund Muskie was the front-runner in the primaries for his party's nomination for president. His campaign was cut short, in part, because he was pictured on television in Manchester, New Hampshire, in the dead of winter, angrily reacting to an attack on his wife that had been promoted in a newspaper. While Muskie claimed to have been wiping snow from his eyes, viewers at home interpreted his nonverbal gestures as crying, and his credibility dropped significantly.[19] If Muskie was a man who could not keep his composure when people attacked his wife, how could we expect him to keep his composure during delicate political negotiations or crises?

More recently, former Vermont Governor Howard Dean had a similar experience when running in the 2004 Democratic primary. Addressing a post-Iowa caucus rally of supporters disappointed by his third-place finish in the Iowa caucuses, Dean ended by shouting: "And then we're going to Washington, D.C., to take back the White House! Yeeaarrgghh!" On television and on radio, this sounded like a *howl* and made him seem angry and out of control. Moreover, he appeared scary. Clips of Dean's howl were seen by millions of people on television and, repeatedly, on the internet, making Dean look like a lunatic.[20]

When employing the medium of mass communication there is little opportunity for either of these last two levels of communication to be reached successfully, as the Muskie and Dean examples illustrate. What is communicated on the airwaves is often incomplete. While emotions might be communicated, they do not become communicated in the way that their experience can be appreciated, as they would in a strictly interpersonal context. The medium, in effect, changes the way that we appreciate or understand a person. While we feel we know our celebrities from the television, what we really know is only one dimension of them, one that has been fitted for the constraints of the television cameras. We may think we know them, but we do not, a point lost to many fans of soap operas who mistake the actors for the fictional characters they are portraying.[21]

The type of communication interaction that a communicator can achieve depends upon a multitude of variables such as self-concept, risk, necessity, motivation, trust, cost, relational dimensions, and situation. In other words, the degree to which self-disclosure is possible, or necessary, involves a plethora of conditions. The point is that self-disclosure is always an invitation for the audience to let down its guard, and thus must be undertaken responsibly by the ethical persuader.

The crafty persuader, however, often manipulates her or his way into our trust by disclosing or fabricating enough common ground to put us at ease, so that when it comes time to reciprocate, we may do so without being aware that we are being manipulated and that what we say may unscrupulously be used against us. Beware of the person who listens a little too much, gives too little, or consistently asks the sorts of questions that make us vulnerable without putting her or himself in a similar position of vulnerability. When people we just meet smile and nod when we talk to them, it is easy for us to imagine that they are our friends. We simply enjoy being friendly and making friends. However, all of us can probably remember a time when we shared with people who we thought were our friends, or with strangers whom we hoped would return our gesture, only to find ourselves manipulated when we discovered that the person had used us for her/his own ends. Spiritually and psychologically, we feel degraded, weak, vulnerable, and violated in such situations.

Keep in mind also that these levels of self-disclosure interaction exist at the verbal and nonverbal levels. It is not just what a person *says* that reveals who that person *is*. In actuality, every aspect of the person *speaks*, and what is not spoken often gives us significant insight into what that person *is*. Behavioral acts and attitudes convey messages, and we can often "read" a person simply by viewing with care what is exuded from that person's attitude. We consciously and unconsciously promote these attitudes—from the clothes we wear, to things we say, to the expressions we put on our faces. In effect, we are all walking endorsements of our attitudes, projecting our idealized selves on the world. Once, when shopping with my son, we encountered a man with a shirt that read "Don't Smoke, Don't Drink, Eat Right, Die Anyway." Wow, I thought to myself, what a terrible message.

Even not speaking is significant—silence itself has a whole range of communicative dimensions of which persuaders often take advantage. First, silence communicates emotional and relational messages of need, meaning, safety, and understanding. Silence acknowledges a person's subjectivity, thus setting the ground for respect. For example, silence may help us to attain and maintain attention, particularly when it is unexpected (e.g., "strategic politeness.")[22] By standing in front of a noisy classroom and not uttering a word, a teacher may regain the students' attention. Silence also can show interest in what the audience has to say. It invites the illusion of the dialectical environment that must exist between a speaker and her/his audience. In some cases, an actual dialogue may emerge between a speaker and an audience, but, to the extent that public communication is taking place, the locus of control will remain with the speaker.

In addition, silence shows respect for the event and the place. The first thing we do when we walk into a church, temple, or mosque is to lower our voices out of respect. We do the same thing in cemeteries and even in government buildings. Speakers sometimes enact a few moments of silence after they are introduced and before they begin their speech in an effort to acknowledge their respect for the audience. Silence also tactfully communicates belief or disbelief, as when parents coax the truth out of their children by sternly looking at them, silently, as the children vainly try to explain, in as acceptable terms as possible, where they were and why they were out so late. Silence also communicates feelings when words are inadequate. So, for example, we remain quiet when listening to someone talk about a dreadful trauma they have endured or share their awareness of an awesome natural event such as a serene coastal sunset. Silence is the appropriate behavior in these contexts so that our ordinary, phatic verbalizations do not appear cheap or cheapening of these experiences. In addition, events such as silent vigils express a sense of urgency and community that language cannot always express. Silence also communicates a sense of uncertainty or mystery, which often is useful in cultivating interest or anticipation in communication. A further function of silence is that it allows "feed forward" to occur, a sort of inner speech equivalent of "looking before we leap." Finally, and most importantly, silence allows time for self-persuasion to occur.[23]

In sum, good persuaders can allow silence when it is effective or appropriate. To do this we have to be comfortable with silence and to understand its many uses. For example, persuaders can avoid being pressured into "spilling" when silence is used manipulatively, such as during an employment interview—novice job seekers are often pressured into saying more than they want to say by such interviewing techniques as silence or nonverbal probes. Conscientious persuaders can offer silence as a gift or sign of respect. To be successful in these tasks, we must learn to interpret the silence of others appropriately, and understand how other cultures use silence.

❧ Listening and Feedback ❧

Listening and feedback are other important variables in the process of communication and for understanding persuasion. Listening and feedback go hand-in-hand—one cannot exist without the other, in any meaningful sense. Just as we have to learn to write by reading, we have to learn to speak by listening. However, as communication consultant Robert Bolton explains:

> [F]ew people are good listeners. Even at the purely informational level, researchers claim that 75 percent of oral communication is ignored, misunderstood, or quickly forgotten. Rarer still is the ability to listen for the deepest meanings in what people say. How devastating, but how common, to talk with someone about subjects of intense interest to oneself only to experience the stifling realization that the other person was not really listening and that his responses were simply automatic and mechanical.[24]

As Bolton goes on to discuss, good hearing and, thus, effective persuading, is dependent upon three skill clusters, what he identifies as "attending," "following," and "reflecting" skills.

Attending skills involve the posturing of the persuader's body so that it is physically coordinated with the body of the audience. While this sounds obvious, and while communication is not necessarily a physical experience, the way the body is positioned vis-à-vis the other helps either to facilitate or to hinder the communication interaction. Further, attending skills involve the degree to which listeners engage themselves psychologically and physically in the persuasive interaction. Strong signs that the audience is attending to the speaker is its unwillingness to distract the speaker (i.e., absorption in what the speaker is saying), its intolerance for unruly or destructive members of the audience (i.e., desire to protect the speaker), and the increased amount of eye contact it has with the speaker (i.e., psychological reciprocity). The more time people spend looking at the speaker, the more attention they are giving her or him. Generally speaking, the closer one physically moves to her/his audience, offering gestures of physical immediacy, the more that the audience will return goodwill through open gestures and supportive eye contact. The end result is that the overall communication interaction will be more fluent, natural, and meaningful, an ideal situation for any persuader. Signs that the audience is not attending to the speaker are tuning out, vigorously crossing one's arms, and, in the most extreme of cases, getting up and leaving the room.

According to Bolton, *following skills* and behaviors go beyond attending to the speaker's message. These involve ways that the audience has of encouraging certain types of behaviors from the speaker or communicator. One type of following behavior is the use of questions designed to open doors in the mind of the other and to increase the level of self-disclosure in the relationship. While it may seem counter-intuitive to those of us who loathe the strangers who talk at us for hours on the airplane, the fact remains that most communicators need encouragement in order to continue talking. As communication scholar Alice Ridge explains:

> Experience alone has shown that lack of feedback to a speaker is often times interpreted as ignoring the speaker, disagreeing with the speaker, or, in the extreme, decimating the speaker. Thus, skills involved with responding would seem to be no less important than others when one discusses the total listening setting.[25]

As all listening and talking are relational—that is, they only make sense in the context of a relationship—the speaker's only reason for being as a speaker is to engage meaningfully with the audience. Within this context, attentive silence, accentuated with infrequent questioning, and the related non-verbal behaviors such as head-nodding and smiling, all encourage the conversation and let the speaker know that it is appropriate to continue. In fact, these types of communication behaviors help regulate the interaction as well as reward the speaker, who is investing time, energy, and emotional commitment into the relationship. Unreceptive audiences can destroy a communication as much as an unprepared speaker. Audience communication with the speaker is just as important as speaker communication with the audience.

Indeed, audiences can have a strong influence on a speaker. To take one example, if a class agrees, before the instructor enters the room, they can manipulate the movement of the instructor by listening attentively on one side of the room and by acting disinterested on the other side. Over the course of the class period, one side shifts gradually its attention from the instructor and the students toward the middle switch on and then they switch off and the ones on the other end of the room switch on. In a case like this, an unwitting speaker may likely physically follow the interest of the class.

Reflecting skills, which are necessary for the communication dialectic and for responsible persuasion, involve paraphrasing, statements reciprocating emotional commitment and commitment to the "meaning" being constructed, and summative reflections to indicate that the listener is following through with her or his responsibility in holding up the conversation.[26] It is a sign of a poor persuader to talk and then stop without comprehending where the audience is in relationship to the communication environment and to the persuasive appeal. More generally, it is a sign of poor persuasion to fail to engage in these types of behaviors as the communication progresses.

The above listening skills apply to classroom teaching under a dialogical model as well. Students, like audiences in general, learn not by the inundation of knowledge (or, more specifically, of *words*) but by the instructor's gentle positioning of information into their schemas of understanding. *Schemas* are knowledge structures that we assemble in our minds for the purpose of organizing and applying information. Schemas are directly impacted by communication, and, in turn, schemas direct and guide communication.[27] The good persuader procures the agreement of the audience as she/he moves through a proposition, and teachers encourage students to learn and to grow, not at the end of the lesson, but in the development of the ideas that constitute the lesson.

Punctuated throughout the educational process, as they are throughout a carefully organized speech, are internal summaries and statements forecasting the ideas and the structure of the lesson. However, in educational and in general public speaking environments there are also summative reflections and mental paraphrasing that go on in the minds of the audience. Students, to be learners, need to be *active learners*, and audiences, to be good audiences, need to be *active analyzers* of the speech. Being an effective audience member is no less a structural task than being an effective speaker. Without such structure on behalf of both parties, communication (persuasion or rhetoric) is reduced to a performance, its informational or transformational content compromised by irrelevance or informational overload.

Another, but related, problem arises when members of an audience criticize a speaker's delivery rather than her or his message. Such people approach communication literally as a "performance" rather than as a process. However, it is particularly disruptive of a communication interaction when the speakers *themselves* view their communication as a performance. As communication scholar Michael Motley explains:

> One implicit goal of a "performance" is to get a positive evaluation from the audience. This focus on evaluation is bound to produce anxiety. It is better to concentrate on other goals.... . A non performance orientation helps speakers realize that their real objective is to communicate. Unlike our school classmates who counted the number of times we said "uh" during book reports, most audiences are more interested in hearing what we have to say than in evaluating our speech skills.[28]

In listening to a message, members of an audience may become too emotionally stimulated, and that might detract from their ability to become effective listeners. On the other hand, people can listen only for the "facts" and miss the larger message of a communication. While all public speaking (and communication more generally) has to start from facts (from the *logos*), a speech fails as an event when all it purports to do is to communicate the said facts. The larger purpose of public communication or persuasion more generally is to take the "facts" and to situate them into a human emotional base; that is, into the *pathos* of our experience. Facts, after all, never make sense when they are divorced from the human communities and situations that give them their significance. Historian of social thought Russell Jacoby best captures this sentiment when he writes:

> The transmission of knowledge across generations is more delicate than one would suppose. To remain a vital force, knowledge… requires the living contact of teachers and students. Knowledge is bathed in emotions, desires, and commitments. Without these nurturing fluids, it withers into empty words. Texts can be saved and studied, but they lose their urgency; they drift out of the public culture to the library shelves.[29]

To listen only for the facts, even within the context of a scientific communication, is to miss the larger narrative or structure that gives those particular facts a significance over another set of competing facts. Behind any presented "fact" is a judgment, usually based on the authority of the communicator, which maintains that one particular fact is important to emphasize. By implication of this judgment, which is partisan, other facts may be ignored (and, practically speaking, are often ignored). The German philosopher Friedrich Nietzsche went as far as to claim that "there are no facts, only interpretations."[30] Even if we do not agree with Nietzsche, still, even in the most scientific of discourses, there exists a tension between ideas and a narrative structure that conceals its own persuasion.[31]

Another common listening problem occurs when we answer questions or react to ideas before fully hearing or understanding them. We often hear what we want to hear, and, as mentioned earlier, we tend to overcompensate for perceived similarities, so it is not difficult to imagine a situation in which our positive (or negative) initial view of another person clouds our understanding of her or his message, and we find ourselves responding prematurely, often in ways that we later regret. This problem is compounded because listeners often allow their attention to be diverted by connotatively loaded words or *ideographs*—language that greatly excites us or angers us but does not encourage self-reflexive thought. As rhetorician Michael McGee explains, an ideograph is a collective abstraction which signals or denotes a community's commitment to essential but broad values or goals. An ideograph is normative:

> It warrants the use of power, excuses behavior and belief which might otherwise be perceived as eccentric or antisocial and guides behavior

and belief into channels easily recognized by a community as acceptable and laudable.[32]

For example, words such as *capitalism, democracy, free market,* and
the like invite the audience to register an emotional agreement or bond with the
persuader or with the persuader's goals. The inverse is also true. Words like
socialism, welfare, and *government regulation* invite audience revulsion toward something the persuader is attacking. In this way, ideographs short-circuit
critical thinking by substituting emotionally laden words for concrete propos-
als. Because we tend to listen only to that which we easily understand, and because we are distracted by our prejudices and deep-seated convictions, words
or ideas that challenge our understandings, or fall outside of what we can easily
digest become incomprehensible and dismissible. This is how ideographs
work. They simplify the abstract and the complex so that we do not have to
spend much time contemplating any particular idea. What we already believe
becomes further enforced in our consciousness, and what we already detest is
given further substantiation of its unworthiness. In both cases, our world becomes more manageable and the energy we have to expend to get along with
our lives is drastically reduced.[33] As communication consultant Bill Scott explains, "It takes energy to concentrate on understanding what has been heard,
and to make an objective evaluation of what has been understood."[34]

There are ways, however, that we can improve our ability to listen and
to comprehend. The first thing we have to do is to realize that communication
is transformational and that to be an effective listener is, foremost, to allow
oneself to be open to change.[35] If we approach listening as an approach against
thinking—as when people look to be told what to do and be—then we will
never be good listeners, because listening is primarily about *thinking,* and
thinking is about *responsibility.* Thus, to be a good listener one has to open
oneself up to the possibility of being affected or moved by the communication.
The goal here is to, together, as speaker and audience, explore mutually a subject from a range of perspectives and/or moral vantage points in order to discover what they know collectively about it and how to allow themselves to be
transformed by a richer knowledge of the subject.

Listening for transformation involves our ability to discern critical content in what we hear. Listening is, as mentioned above, about thinking, and this
is different from simply letting ourselves become bamboozled by what we normally think of as "eloquent" speech. This distinction is another way of discern-

ing between communication or persuasion as "performance" and communication or persuasion as a "critical activity." As rhetorical scholar Carole Blair explains, we fundamentally misconstrue eloquence when we reduce it to a smooth performance or use it as a "window dressing" to dazzle, amaze, or bewitch an audience. Rather eloquence "finds its source not in the convincingly smooth delivery of an actor or in gimmicky flourishes of language, but in a cogency, precision, and dignity of thought that engages and inspires audiences."[36]

This is why listening for feelings is as important as listening for "facts," because the "facts" never make sense outside of the moral, subjective, and human universe that constitutes them. Or, as legal scholar James Boyd White explains, "Our thoughts about ethics and justice, about our practical social and political lives, must acknowledge that the facts, the imperatives, and the motives of ourselves and others are not fixed but uncertain, in a sense always made by us in conversation with each other."[37]

Another way to become a better listener is to discern and pay attention to all cues, verbal and nonverbal, that emanate from a source. Keep in mind that there may be contradictions between the verbal and the nonverbal, in which case it is usually better to trust the nonverbal.[38] We listen not just with our ears, but with our eyes as well.

Good audiences let the speaker know that it is listening. The speaker will be watching constantly the audience, judging it, exploring it for cues, reading it. When we involve ourselves in the communication by nodding, by responding, and by establishing eye contact, we encourage the dialectics of the interaction to continue. There is no talking without listening and there is no listening without talking. The more actively one engages in listening, the more rewarding the communication becomes. Audiences, therefore, should be mentally and physically ready to listen. They should be patient, particularly when they are exposed to ideas that challenge fundamental assumptions in their world view. Finally, it helps if we focus our attention on the speaker and on the message, not on the surroundings. It is easy to be distracted by external and internal barriers, such as fatigue, bias, prejudice, or ideology. But by focusing attention on the communication and not on the various environmental factors that vie for our attention, we can more readily involve ourselves in the symbolic world that the persuader is attempting to construct for us.

Situational variables are another component of the communication process. These variables have an *implosive* effect. They not only constrain the types of things that can be said, but they constrain the types of things that can even be thought about. Situational variables are similar to the atmospheric pressure that surrounds us. Few of us think of this pressure against us, but without it our bodies would literally explode.

❀ Function of Perception ❀

Central to all three types of persuasive interactions (i.e., interpersonal, public, and mass media) is the role or function of perception in mediating the relationships we establish with others. All members of a communication interaction have perceptions of themselves and of others. In addition, we have perceptions of the event and of the context in which we are communicating. It is the influence of these perceptions that creates the experience of persuasion and establishes the preconditions or terms of our communication. Indeed, in any given conflict or persuasive encounter each member of the relationship will contextualize the conflict, self, and other differently depending upon their perceptions of it.[39]

Many popular cartoons in our culture illustrate graphically the role of perception in mediating our interpersonal relationships. One such cartoon features a young U.S. or state senator talking with an older, more seasoned senator, and the young senator is drawn viewing himself as a fearless knight in shining armor slaying a ferocious dragon, who is drawn in the image of the older statesman. The older official is pictured as perceiving his younger colleague as a small baby crying with his lollipop. Given this scenario, what sort of meaningful discussions can the two men have? Each man perceives himself and the other in ways that are not shared and are not even compatible. Inherent in their perceptions, and thus in their mental articulations, is an implicit antagonism.

In another cartoon, there is a picture of a young man interviewing for a job. He sees himself as small, undeserving, pitiful, and he is drawn with his hat clutched meekly in his hands, beads of sweat dripping from his forehead. Towering over him is a teeth-gritting, immense, and brutal potential employer in a strikingly terrifying pose. Both images are caricatures. Yet, how often do we feel in the one position or in the other? In neither case are we engaging in a healthy communication interaction, and our persuasion, if it is successful at all, involves the submissiveness of one and the dominance of the other. Such power differential can only be considered unhealthy.

A clearer way to think about this process of perception involves the levels of identification that we cultivate in each other. Each individual's subjectivity is like a circle, and when we communicate, we each try to attain as much overlap between each circle as possible (a kind of empathy). Sometimes the overlap is great, and sometimes the overlap is small, but there always has to be *some* overlap if any type of significant communication is to occur. Effective persuaders will try to take advantage of this perceptional overlap and turn it toward their advantage. Such persuaders recognize that audiences tend to *overcompensate* for perceived similarities.[40] That is, the larger the apparent overlap, the more likely we are to attribute a greater similarity between us and the person attempting to persuade us. The less overlap that exists, the more the persuader is dependent upon overt persuasion—that is, a conscious positioning of our subjectivities in order to create the appearance of similitude. Without this appearance, the persuader will remain "the Other" and will be ignored by us.

Ideally, the best persuasive situation would be the one in which the two circles overlapped completely. This would be a state or condition of complete identification. While being a theoretical possibility, such a position is practically impossible to achieve as each of us is a different individual. In such a state, the two people involved would have such a complete identification that they could communicate without talking, understanding each other on a fundamental and primordial level. Language would be unnecessary, deception would be unthinkable, and persuasion would be non-existent—we would simply exist for each other.

To the extent that *no* overlap exists between the two people, a state of incommensurability exists (as discussed in Chapter 1). Within this scenario, both people would literally be speaking different languages—linguistically, morally, and socially. No persuasion is possible here. In order for persuasion to occur, there has to be some common ground, some agreed upon standards, if only a term or two or a common commitment to each other's humanity, otherwise there is nothing to say; both of us simply pursue our own material interests, our own "will to power" at the expense of others.

As I have been suggesting, perceptions of self and other play a significant role in understanding how persuasion works. In a sense, when we talk about theories or perspectives in persuasion, when we talk about the strength of rhetoric or of rhetorical thinking in our society, we are talking about the *role of perceptions* in the determination of what we understand to be reality. The same point applies to criticism and to the critical act. Persuasive communication is the quintessential critical act (hence the title of this textbook and the tone of the course). We communicate to understand and to convince people that we understand. But more importantly, we communicate to construct who we *are* out of the many possibilities of which we can *be*. As White explains:

> This is all a way of saying that while we cannot have the certainties we yearn for, we ought not on that account be afraid, for we have in fact always lived, and can only live, with radical uncertainty. We make the best sense we can of things, the best judgments we can make, always checking our account against experience, against our sense of our own disposition to err, against the suggestions and imaginations of others. We are always tentative or presumptive, always revising; in all of this we are always making and remaking our culture. This is what we know how to do.[41]

Communication is our way of knowing, being, and seeing; it is all we have to make sure that we are really "here," that we are who we think we are, that we can master ourselves. Communication is a way of shaping our sensibilities, of selecting and deflecting vision.[42]

How can communication affect our vision? Think of the situation in which a couple sits across from each other. The woman is thinking, "I can't stand it—we never talk about our relationship anymore." The man thinks, "I can't stand it—all we ever talk about is our relationship." Who is correct in this situation? Within this context, it does not make sense to ascertain who is "right" or who is "wrong." Both members of the dyad simply see the relationship differently.

Or consider our own self-images. We often idealize ourselves. Sometimes this is negative, such as when we think we are fat, ugly, unintelligent, or otherwise unattractive. Other times we idealize ourselves in more positive ways—substituting in our mind well-defined abs for the excess flab when we look in the mirror. In either case, what we see when we look in the mirror is not "ourselves" per se, but ourselves as filtered through our idealized and/or romanticized consciousnesses—our hurts, fears, loves, and hopes. Imagine our surprise when we see photographs or videos of ourselves, especially if a few years have passed and we no longer remember the specific mental state we were experiencing at the time the photograph was taken. How do we feel? Usually we feel alienated. While we recognize the person in the picture as being us, something does not feel right. Something is missing. What is missing are those prior interpretations and subjectivities that, at the time the picture was taken, assigned meaning and interpretation to our lives which we have long since forgotten.

Psychologists have developed simple ways to highlight the role of perception in determining how we see. The classic example of this is the two faces/vase picture. What appears to be two faces in black speaking to each other against a white backdrop is, for another, a white vase against a black backdrop. Clearly, the picture involves both images—depending upon how we focus our gaze, one image or the other will come into relief.

If we look hard enough, we can eventually learn to discern the two images. But in everyday life, when we scramble about hectically to get things done, few of us take the time to explore the different ways of seeing an object or an event. By talking through the object or event, that is, by using guiding communication and persuasion, we can help each other to see things differently. When a person engages in persuasion or in rhetorical communication, that person does not make up the world in a vulgar relativism. Rather, that person is simply highlighting one aspect of life over another in a different way. In so doing, we often experience moral, spiritual, or cognitive growth. Such growth is an important aim of communication in general.

The importance of perception on persuasion can be found in a series of experiments starting in 1953 by psychologist Solomon Asch.[43] Asch assembled people to participate in what he said were "vision tests" and showed a roomful of people a series of lines on a board. The group was to determine a match between the ones on the board and a second one presented by a technician. All of the people in the room were working for Asche except for the true subject, who was misled into thinking that s/he was no different than the others in the room. Asch was interested in how the subject would react to being a minority of one against a unanimous majority; in other words, "an individual in a relation of radical conflict with all the other members of a group."[44] What Asch found was that there "was a marked movement toward the majority. One third of all the estimates in the critical group were errors identical with or in the direction of the distorted estimates of the majority."[45]

Asch recorded three types of reaction, the first being *distortion of perception*. Here were a few subjects who yielded to the distorted views of the group but were not aware that they had done so. Rather, "they came to perceive the majority estimates as correct."[46] Second is the *distortion of judgment*. This was the largest category. Important to this group of yielding subjects is the decision they make "that their perceptions are inaccurate, and that those of the majority are correct. These subjects suffer from primary doubt and lack of confidence; on this basis they feel a strong tendency to join the majority."[47] The third type of reaction is the *distortion of action*. The subjects here have not had their perceptions modified, nor do they believe that they made a mistake and that the majority was correct. Rather, they "yield because of an overmastering need not to appear different from or inferior to others, because of an inability to tolerate the appearance of defectiveness in the eyes of the group."[48] In other words, these "subjects suppress their observations and voice the majority position with awareness of what they are doing."[49]

Asch's findings should give us pause. One third of the subjects he tested, and this experience and its variations were repeated many times, said, in effect, "black is white" when clear evidence suggested otherwise. A small portion of those individuals believed sincerely that black *was* white, and that is scary in itself. But the rest of the people *knew better*. That is, they could tell the difference between black and white, but had so little confidence in themselves and wanted so hard to please the group that they accepted the group's determination. George Orwell was not far off when he grounded the dystopia he outlined in the novel *1984* in three lies that became accepted by its citizens: "War Is Peace, Freedom Is Slavery, Ignorance Is Strength."

A final construct that we will discuss in this context is *agenda setting*.[50] According to agenda setting theory, the press and the media do not reflect the world as we find it, as does a mirror; rather, the media filters and shapes it. Media concentration on a few issues and subjects, usually the most easily commercialized and commodified (i.e., easily packaged), lead the public to perceive those issues as more important than other issues. Audiences not only learn about public issues and other matters from the media, they also learn how much importance to attach to an issue or topic from the emphasis the media place on it. Something that does not fit the medium or the politics of the medium does not become communicated. As Bernard C. Cohen famously declared, "The press may not be successful much of the time in telling people what to think, but it is stunningly successful in telling its readers what to think about."[51]

℘ Conclusion ℀

We have in this chapter explored the dynamics and process of persuasion. Persuasion involves two or more parties with a degree of role change between them. The relationship between the persuader and the persuadee is mediated by the perceptions of each toward themselves, the other, and the situation. There are levels of interaction that fluctuate depending upon the type of communication, the situation, and the conditions of the audience. There are degrees of feedback, with the channels severely constrained in mass communication. The entire process is further contextualized by the situation. The larger context for this process involves the perceptions that ground our awareness.

With this chapter, we have completed Part I of this text. Specifically, we have explored how persuasion is essential in the construction and maintenance of our democratic society. We have explored definitions of persuasion and rhetoric as well as the important relationship between them. In so doing, we have highlighted two important philosophical ways we can approach an understanding of communication. Through these chapters, we have understood persuasion as a process involving mutual influence and have learned to look for the persuasive elements that lie in a range of diverse phenomena, such as seemingly informative, expressive, or coercive messages.

In Part II of this text, we will study contemporary theories of persuasion as well as the role and dimensions of source credibility. We will study the importance of audience in the construction of persuasive messages, the power of language, and the necessity for an ethical perspective when engaging and evaluating persuasive discourse.

℘ Notes ☙

1. Richard L. Miller, Philip Brickman, and Diana Bolen, "Attribution Versus Persuasion as a Means for Modifying Behavior," *Journal of Personality and Social Psychology, 31* (1975), 430–441.

2. *A Rhetoric of Motives* (Berkeley: University of California Press, 1969), 39.

3. Shearon A. Lowery and Melvin L. DeFleur, *Milestones in Mass Communication Research* 3rd ed. (New York: Longman, 1995).

4. Dale T. Miller and Michael Ross, "Self-Serving Biases in the Attribution of Causality: Fact or Fiction?" *Psychological Bulletin, 82* (1975), 213–225.

5. W. Phillips Davison, "The Third-Person Effect in Communication," *Public Opinion Quarterly*, 47 (1983), 1–15; W. James Potter, *Media Literacy* (Thousand Oaks, CA: Sage, 1998), 29.

6. Nancy Signorielli, "Television's Mean and Dangerous World," in Nancy Signorielli and Michael Morgan, eds., *Cultivation Analysis: New Direction in Media Effects Research* (Newbury Park, CA: Sage, 1990), 85–106.

7. Matthias C. Angermeyer, Sandra Dietrich, D. Pott, and Herbert Matschinger, "Media Con sumption and Desire for Social Distance Towards People With Schizophrenia,"*European Psychiatry, 20* (2005), 246–250.

8. Elizabeth Hall Preston, "Pornography and the Construction of Gender," in Nancy Signorielli and Michael Morgan, eds., *Cultivation Analysis: New Directions in Media Effects Research* (Newbury Park, CA: Sage, 1989), 107–122.

9. Dolf Zillmann and James B. Weaver, "Pornography and Men's Sexual Callousness Toward Women," in Dolf Zillmann and Jennings Bryant, eds., *Pornography: Research Advances and Policy Considerations* (Hillsdale, NJ: Lawrence Erlbaum, 1989), 95–126.

10. William P. Eveland, Jr., "The Impact of News and Entertainment Media on Perceptions of Social Reality," in James Price Dillard and Michael Pfau, eds., *The Persuasion Handbook: Developments in Theory and Practice*, eds. (Thousand Oaks, CA: Sage, 2002), 691.

11. Joseph B. Walther coined the concept of "hyperpersonal communication" to refer to the phenomenon reported by many online users that they find CMC to be more personal than regular face-to-face interpersonal communication. For instance, when communicating vie e-

mail there is a feeling of absolute dyadic privacy. "Computer-Mediated Communication: Impersonal, Interpersonal, and Hyperpersonal Interaction," *Communication Research, 23* (1996), 3–44.

12. Ibid.

13. William K. Rawlins, *Friendship Matters: Communication, Dialectics, and the Life Course.* (New York: Aldine De Gruyter, 1992).

14. Paulo Freire, *Pedagogy of the Oppressed* (New York: Continuum, 1984), 52.

15. Ibid., 54.

16. Nancy F. Burroughs, "A Reinvestigation of Teacher Nonverbal Immediacy and Student Compliance-Resistance With Learning," *Communication Education, 56* (2007), 453–477.

17. Ibid., 455.

18. A noteworthy exception occurred in January, 2008, a day before the important New Hampshire primary when Senator Hillary Clinton, who was campaigning in the highly competitive democratic primary, made good use of emotion when she grew visibly emotional after a supporter asked, "How do you do it? How do you keep up… How do you, how do you keep upbeat and so wonderful?" With tears forming in her eyes, she replied "It's not easy, and I couldn't do it if I didn't passionately believe it was the right thing to do. You know, I have so many opportunities from this country I just don't want to see us fall backwards." Maureen Dowd, "Can Hillary Cry Her Way Back to the White House?" *New York Times* (January 9, 2008), retrieved from http://www.nytimes.com/2008/01/09/opinion/08dowd.html.

19. Elisabeth Goodridge, "'72 Front-Runner's Tears Hurt," *U.S. News & World Report* (January 28, 2008), 50.

20. See Jim Rutenberg, "The 2004 Campaign: Rhetoric; A Concession Rattles the Rafters (and Some Dean Supporters), *New York Times* (January 21, 2004). Retrieved from http://query.nytimes.com/gst/fullpage.html?res=9B01E0D71239F932A15752C0A9629C8B6 3&sec=&spon=&pagewanted=print. For a general discussion of nonverbal communication in political discourse, see Maria A. Kopacz, "Nonverbal Communication as a Persuasion Tool: Current Status and Future Directions," *Rocky Mountain Communication Reviiew, 3* (2006), 1–19.

21. The social science literature calls these kinds of relationships *parasocial*. In a humanistic language, this is an example of what Richard Schickel calls the "illusion of intimacy." *The Culture of Celebrity* (Garden City, NY: Doubleday, 1985), 29.

22. Maria Sifianou, "Silence and Politeness," in Adam Jaworsky, ed., *Silence: Interdisciplinary Perspectives* (New York: Mouton de Gruyter, 1997), 63–84.

23. Adam Jaworsky, *The Power of Silence: Social and Pragmatic Perspectives* (Thousand Oaks, Sage, 1992) and Adam Jaworsky, ed., *Silence: Interdisciplinary Perspectives* (New York: Mouton de Gruyter, 1997).

24. *People Skills: How to Assert Yourself, Listen to Others, and Resolve Conflicts* (Englewood Cliffs, NJ: Prentice Hall, 1979), 30.

25. "A Perspective of Listening Skills," in Andrew D. Wolvin and Carolyn Gwynn Coakley, eds., *Perspectives on Listening* (Norwood, NJ: Ablex Publishing, 1993), 7.

26. Bolton*, People Skills*, 33.

27. See Arthur C. Graesser, Keith K. Millis, and Debra L. Long, "The Construction of Knowledge-Based Inferences During Story Comprehension," in Noel E. Sharkey (ed.), *Advances in Cognitive Science*, (New York: John Wiley, 1986), 125–157).

28. "Taking the Terror out of Talk," *Psychology Today* (January, 1988), 49.

29. *The Repression of Psychoanalysis* (Chicago: University of Chicago Press, 1983), 22.

30. *The Will to Power*, trans. Walter Kaufmann (New York: Vintage, 1967), 267.

31. See Hayden White, *The Content of the Form: Narrative Discourse and Historical Representation* (Baltimore: Johns Hopkins University Press, 1987) and Thomas S. Kuhn, *The Structure of Scientific Revolutions* 3rd ed. (Chicago: University of Chicago Press, 1996).

32. "The 'Ideograph': A Link Between Rhetoric and Ideology," *Quarterly Journal of Speech*, *66* (1980), 15.

33. Ideographs will be discussed in more detail in Chapter 9.

34. *The Skills of Communicating* (New York: Nichols Publishing Co., 1986), 46.

35. Sonja K. Foss & Karen A. Foss, *Inviting Transformation: Presentational Speaking for a Changing World* 2nd ed. (Prospect Heights, IL: Waveland Press, 2003).

36. "The Decay of Political Eloquence," *USA Today* (March, 1992), 87.

37. Heracles' Bow: *Essays on the Rhetoric and Poetics of the Law* (Madison: University of Wisconsin Press, 1985), 24.

38. Maureen P. Keeley & Allan J. Hart, "Nonverbal Behavior in Dyadic Interactions," in Steve W. Duck (ed.), Understanding Relationship Processes (Thousand Oaks, CA: Sage, 1994), 135–179.

39. See William W. Wilmot and Joyce L. Hocker, *Interpersonal Conflict* (New York: McGraw Hill, 2005).

40. Michael Monsour, "Similarities and Dissimilarities: Constructing Meaning and Building Intimacy Through Communication, in Steve W. Duck (ed.), *Understanding Relationship Processes* Thousand Oaks, CA: Sage, 1994), 112–134.

41. *Heracles' Bow*, 128.

42. Kenneth Burke, *Language as Symbolic Action: Essays on Life, Literature, and Method* (Berkeley: University of California Press, 1966), 44–62.

43. "Effects of Group Pressure Upon the Modification and Distortion of Judgments," in Eleanor E. Maccoby, Theodore M. Newcomb, and Eugene L. Hartley, eds., *Readings in Social Psychology* 3rd ed. (New York: Holt, Rinehart, and Winston, 1958), 174–183.

44. Ibid., 175.

45. Ibid., 177.

46. Ibid., 178.

47. Ibid., 179.

48. Ibid.

49. Ibid.

50. Maxwell McCombs and Donald Shaw, "The Agenda-Setting Function of Mass Media," *The Public Opinion Quarterly*, *36* (1972), 176–187.

51. *The Press and Foreign Policy* (Princeton, NJ: Princeton University Press, 1963), 120.

PART TWO

CHAPTER 6

Contemporary Theories of Persuasion

This chapter explores some of the more important contemporary theories of persuasion that ground the construction of many of the ads and influences to which we are exposed every day (recall the plethora of influences discussed in Chapter 3). Specifically, we will cover learning theory, perception theory, balance and consistency theory, enthymematic and self-persuasion theory, psychological reactance theory, inoculation theory, and identification theory. Knowledge of these theories and their basic assumptions is an important component of a critical awareness, as it helps us to understand better the psychological predispositions of audiences and how they are influenced or motivated. Such understanding is practical as it helps us to appreciate our own considerable conceptual resources and vulnerabilities in this age of pervasive (and invasive) mass persuasion. Simply put, this chapter may have significant implications for students, since the theories that it contains play important roles in many of the decisions that we make as consumers and as citizens. Remember, persuaders use these theories to create persuasion *against* us. While this is not necessarily bad, students who practice persuasion as a critical activity will appreciate knowing how these theories work in order to learn to *resist* them when the persuader, as is often the case, does not have our best interests at heart. For better or for worse, we, for the most part, live in a *laisser-faire* communication environment where the principle of *caveat emptor* holds sway.[1]

I begin this chapter by emphasizing the above point. In this way, I contrast my pedagogy from that of Professor Robert E. Denton, Jr., a well respected persuasion teacher and scholar in the communication discipline who did his doctoral work at Purdue University, studying under Charles J. Stewart as I did. In graduate school I heard stories about Dr. Denton, how he helped develop the highly successful *Army Be All You Can Be* campaign for the U.S. military. I smile when I contemplate him teaching his course from the perspective of how to use these theories to recruit soldiers, consumers, etc., while I use the *same* theories and perspectives to teach students how to *resist* such appeals. Rhetoric, Aristotle noted many centuries ago, is amoral; we bring to its study and practice our own ethical and political commitments.

✲ Learning Theories ✣

The first set of theories we are going to discuss are the *learning theories.* Common to the learning theories, as the name implies, is a desire to describe the process of how people learn. By understanding the learning process, we become, in effect, better "teachers"; that is, better at influencing others. Studies in this area have been carried out by two important research traditions: behaviorism and cognitivism. As we will explore below, research grounded in the paradigm of *behaviorism* focuses exclusively on the objectively observable aspects of learning, discounting the internal processing that might be associated with an activity. Behaviorism rejects the abstraction that is known popularly as "the mind." For behaviorism, learning is the acquisition of new behavior through material conditioning—the common example being the child who burns her or his hand on a hot stove. The *cognitive* paradigm, on the other hand, looks *beyond* behavior to explain brain-based learning through understanding mental complexes and schemata, such as emotions, values, and attitudes. In other words, while our bodies recognize and respond to stimuli, we also process stimuli in our minds—that is, we consciously *think* about the stimulus and decide the best way to respond. Specifically, the two learning theories we are going to discuss are stimulus-response conditioning (S-R) and stimulus-organism-response (S-O-R).

Stimulus-Response Conditioning

The most basic way to approach the learning theories is to begin with the most simplistic model available, that of *stimulus-response* conditioning. Persuaders who utilize the stimulus-response model of persuasion assume that, at some basic level, their audiences consist of people who are passive entities, unable, or at least hesitant, to engage in critical thought. According to this model, *ex-*

posure equals, in some way, *effect*. Take sexual symbols, for example. If a product can be associated with sexual arousal—by being photographed with a model in a seductive pose—it may be the case that the appearance of the product alone will provoke a positive or aroused feeling in the mind of the potential consumer. When such a relationship between a product and a particular desire is established, the consumer does not have to be engaged rationally in the persuasive appeal. Furthermore, we can even forget the particular ad that established the relationship between, say, sports cars and sexual prowess or between diamonds and love. The more that we are exposed to the product, or are exposed to the association through general cultural disseminations, the more "natural" the relationship becomes, and the more we internalize the "appropriate," sexualized, and desired response. Through such associations, sex, as in this example, becomes commodified and commodities become sexualized as "…the human becomes thing and the mutual becomes one-sided and the given becomes stolen and sold…"[2]

Certainly few of us like to think of ourselves as being open to manipulation in this way—that is, as pigeons or rats in some scientist's laboratory; our psyches and pride recoil at such a thought (one could say that it "ruffles our feathers!"). From the first days of our lives, we learn that we are free-thinking, free-willed, individuals, responsible for our actions, and able to make rational choices. We believe in our *intent*—the assumption that we *cause* or otherwise *author* our own actions. Yet, just as the stimulus-response model is reductionist (people are not pigeons or rats), and just as human behavior can be traced to a whole *other* range of psychological phenomena not found elsewhere in the animal kingdom, it *is* the case that stimulus-response types of behaviors are manifested at *some* level in human beings. There is, for instance, an association between the amount of money put into advertising and our consumptive habits.

The stimulus-response perspective of persuasion originated with Russian psychologist Ivan P. Pavlov in the early part of the twentieth-century, also with American theorists such as John B. Watson and Clark L. Hull. This was a popular way of approaching persuasion through the early 1960s, as typified by the so-called "Yale" school of research.[3] Stimulus-response theory comes out of a behaviorist epistemology or world view; the rationale behind this theory is that it is possible to predict human behavior by accounting for, and scrutinizing, the stimulus variables of constructed messages and their corresponding relationship with overt action. This view is summarized by Watson in an important 1913 essay:

> Psychology as the behaviorist views it is a purely objective experimental branch of natural science. Its theoretical goal is the prediction and control of behavior. Introspection forms no essential part of its methods, nor is the scientific value of its data dependent upon the readiness with which they lend themselves to interpretation in terms of consciousness. The behaviorist, in his efforts to get a unitary scheme of animal response, recognizes no dividing line between man and brute.[4]

As suggested in the excerpt from Watson's essay, an important assumption behind this theory is that internal thought processes are unimportant. As Watson notes, persuasion, "as the behaviorist views it, is a purely objective, experimental branch of natural science which needs introspection as little as do the sciences of chemistry and physics."[5] In the example of classical conditioning in Pavlov's dog, the poor animal had its face cut open so observers could measure the secretions of its salivary glands as it heard the ringing of a bell, having associated the sound with food. The saliva secretion is a conditioned response to the primary association. Presumably, the dog does not think about food and no food has to be present in order for the response to occur.

Applications of this theory are varied and range from the controversial to the mundane; some of which will be discussed below. These are: subliminal perception, neuromarketing, prestige suggestion, and product placement.

Subliminal Perception: The theory of subliminal perception has generated much skepticism and support throughout the years. Clearly, we are exposed every day to stimuli of which we are unaware—if nothing else, we selectively perceive only a small amount of the sensory information to which we are exposed each and every day. The question, basically, is whether or not we have to be conscious of the stimulus to be affected by it. If we are susceptible to unconscious stimuli, the question remains in what *ways* does it affect us?[6]

A subliminal message is the intentional dissemination of a message designed to affect a target below or outside the physiological limits of normal perception. For example, the message might be inaudible to the conscious mind as a dog whistle is inaudible to humans, but perhaps perceived unconsciously by some other part of our brain. Alternatively, the message might be an image transmitted so briefly that the vision part of our brain does not have time to process the image, although, again, the image was received by the brain to a certain extent. The example here being an image inserted into a few frames of a film. While the image does appear on the screen, it does not stay visible long enough for us to be consciously aware of it.

Subliminal persuasion is a controversial application of the stimulus-response theory in two senses. First, subliminal persuasion is, as a genre of influence, highly manipulative and widely considered to be unethical. Second, it is not entirely clear that it works in the way that many in popular culture fear that it works.[7] The theory became popular in the early 1970s due to a series of books by Wilson Brian Key, who argued that advertisers craft images that evoke primal emotions through crass and often morbid ways without our being aware of this influence.[8] The idea is that consumers, subconsciously, are able to transfer these feelings to the product in question. Key based his work on the assumption that humans can perceive things without consciously noticing them, which somehow "prime" us for action. Around the same time that Key was doing his research, religious and right wing critics of popular music (this was, after all, the Golden Age of Rock & Roll) were claiming that records were recorded with hidden lyrics or messages that were causing young people to engage in dysfunctional or anti-social behavior. This negative publicity, while grounded in some modicum of fact, was clearly overstated, although instances of subliminal advertising and back masking have been documented.[9] Horror films have been known to use this practice, and there is a multi-billion-dollar-a-year industry of self-help materials that deliver what are intended to be beneficial subliminal messages to help people lose weight, have better self-esteem, manage pain, be free from guilt, and enjoy a better sex life.[10]

Neuromarketing: In many ways, neuromarketing is the cutting edge of the industry in terms of the stimulus-response perspective. It is also the most intrusive and, arguably, the most unethical. Neuromarketing is an emerging field within marketing that explores how consumers respond to marketing stimuli at the subconscious level. Marketers use the technologies of neuroscience—not to help people—but to learn how to manipulate them better. These technologies include functional Magnetic Resonance Imaging (fMRI) which measures changes in activity in parts of the brain and electroencephalography (EEG) which measures activity in specific regional spectra of the brain response, and/or sensors to measure changes in a person's physiological state (i.e., heart rate, respiratory rate, galvanic skin response) as they are exposed to an advertisement.[11] Employing one or more of these technologies helps advertisers to learn why consumers make the decisions they do, and what part of the brain is telling them to do it. The idea is to bypass the cognitive decision making elements of our thinking to understand why consumers have certain emotional attachments to a product. For example, while Coke and Pepsi are near-identical products, brain scans show that Coke ads and not Pepsi ads register strongly in the part of the brain associated with pleasure. This might help explain the market edge that Coke has over Pepsi.[12]

Prestige Suggestion: The most prevalent use of stimulus-response conditioning in advertising is prestige suggestion.[13] This tactic works by associating products with prestigious sources—such as movie stars or athletes—so that consumers are encouraged to purchase items. While much of stimulus-response theory has been severely questioned, as in the case of subliminal persuasion, or in its early infancy in the case of neuromarketing, the associational aspects of the theory continue to be widely used in contemporary advertising.[14] While we may not be rats tugging levers for pellets of food, we, nevertheless, respond unthinkingly to various stimuli in ways colored at least by prestigious persuaders. Golf giant Tiger Woods, for example, is anticipated to earn one *billion* dollars in endorsements by the time he is 40.[15] Clearly, advertisers spend a great deal of money to associate their products with prestigious names and people.[16] Christian Dior is one high-priced brand name that often advertises its products without any written description. The name of Christian Dior becomes attached to the image of a product, and the product becomes elevated into an object of status. Gucci often does the same thing with its line of products. One ad has a series of ties against a white backdrop with the word "Gucci" written in large letters across the top.

Godiva chocolate advertises a product called "Gold Bullion." The advertisers are a little more honest about not wanting to give us any rational information that we can evaluate in our minds. We are told, "You don't have to say a word." What the advertisers are trying to suggest in the context of the ad is that the product speaks for itself. The candies come in a gold box and the backdrop of the photograph is gold-tinted. The value of the gold qualifies the "value" of the chocolate. If we feel this connection between the value of gold and the "value" of the product, then, suddenly, what would otherwise be merely candy becomes something for which it is worth paying more money.

One interesting development in this area of product promotion involves advertisers who co-opt pictures of famous people from the past and use them to sell their products. In a recent ad for Apple computers, Mahatma Gandhi is featured sitting and conscientiously writing. The only words on the page are "Think Different" and the Apple logo. (Other people, all dead, who have appeared in this campaign, are Albert Einstein, Pablo Picasso, Frank Lloyd Wright, Martin Luther King, Jr., and Franklin Roosevelt.) In the same vein, the Gap clothing company has had a long-running ad campaign starting in the early 1990s that featured famous (dead) people from all aspects of culture and asserts that they "wore khakis." John Wayne, Amelia Earhart, Steve McQueen, James Dean, Marilyn Monroe, Andy Warhol, and Jack Kerouac are long-deceased personalities that have appeared unwillingly in these ads.

Sometimes these types of prestige suggestions are done in the public interest, particularly when the audiences tend to be children or teenagers. Public libraries, for instance, are filled with posters that prominently display famous athletes and actresses/actors, pictured reading. When children see Harrison Ford (for example) reading a book, they may think "that's cool, reading is cool."

The best example of prestige suggestion can be found in the charismatic face of Magic Johnson, perhaps the quintessential endorser. Before him was O. J. Simpson, who was frequently shown in television ads running through airports (before running from the law), and since him Michael Jordan and now Tiger Woods have become the familiar, comforting faces that reassure us that consumption will fulfill our lives and bring us greatness. But there is something about Magic Johnson smiling in his Lakers' uniform with a can of 7-Up that seems to represent best the prestige suggestion as well as its problems. Is it really the case that drinking 7-Up will give us the "magic"? Will it make us better basketball players? Will it make us rich and famous?

Will it give us AIDS? This is where the magic of celebrity endorsement has the potential to fade fast.[17] Just as the prestige of a source elevates the product with which it is associated, the corruption of the source will contaminate the same product, a point all celebrity endorsers recognize if they wish to remain wealthy.[18] If celebrity endorsers wish to maintain their relationship with corporate sponsors, the celebrities have to maintain a sanitized public image. Derelictions here may mean the loss of lucrative contracts.[19] Sponsors can even protect themselves from the misdeeds of their endorsers by purchasing what is called "disgrace insurance." Lloyds of London—the British insurance institution which underwrites these type of claims—defines *disgrace* as any "offense against public taste or decency . . . which degrades or brings that person into disrepute or provokes insult or shock to the community."[20]

A good modern example of a disgraced endorser can be found in the December 2007, Mitchell Report on the use of steroids in Major League Baseball (MLB). When former Senator George J. Mitchell released his report on anabolic steroids and human growth hormone (HGH) in MLB, the athlete with the most to lose was pitcher Roger Clemens who was mentioned 82 times. As one reporter noted, given Clemens' phenomenal success as a player, given how recognizable he is throughout the United States, and given that he will have a lengthy retirement, Clemens is likely to lose many millions of dollars in endorsement opportunities.[21] Moreover, the reporter notes, sports memorabilia associated with Clemens is also likely to decline in value.[22] Clemens is in good company as a plethora of famous athletes in recent years, including National Football League quarterback Michael Vick and baseball slugger Barry Bonds have seen the value of their endorsements decline or evaporate as a result of their illegal or immoral activities.

Product Placement: product placement is an approach that is related to prestige suggestion. This approach involves promotional ads placed by ad companies using real commercial products and services in media, including gaming and virtual worlds, where the presence of a particular brand is the result of an economic exchange. This practice is common. James Bond films, for example, serve as platforms for many corporate/product sponsors, such as Smirnoff, Omega, Sony, Ford, BMW, and Sony Ericsson. If we are willing to watch movies that are, in effect, advertisements, I suppose this practice is fine; as intelligent consumers we get that for which we pay. But where this practice becomes particularly problematic involves the product placement of cigarettes.[23] Cigarettes companies are not supposed to advertise to children and teenagers. Yet, movies which are popular with teenagers may feature prominent characters smoking. This is no accident. The cinema has long been an important advertising venue for tobacco companies.[24] An example of this tactic is a 1983 agreement between Sylvester Stallone and Williamson Tobacco products to use their tobacco products in five films for half a million dollars. This agreement surfaced in the 1990s, as a result of the well-publicized litigation between many states and the tobacco industry.[25]

Stimulus-Organism-Response

A second, more sophisticated form of the learning theory is known as stimulus-organism-response. This theory assumes that we act (response) because of a message (stimulus) and its connection with mediating forces within us (the organism) that are triggered by drives and motives (i.e., our psyche). In other words, we act because we *think*, not because we lack thought, as is the case with the often-crude stimulus-response model. The focus of this perspective is on the *cognitive* capabilities of human beings. Theorists who articulate this theory start from the same basic assumptions that the stimulus-response theorists hold, but focus their attention on the cognitive capabilities of the individual to assimilate information and to mediate mentally between the stimulus and the response. The focus here is on the *mental* processes that make behavior possible. This theory grapples with the cognitive system (i.e., perceptions of our human-based values, beliefs, and attitudes) that helps individuals organize and understand information, and act by choosing among their various behavioral options. With one word, *organism*, we skip from being pigeons and rats to human beings with complex personalities, wants, desires, and motivations. In other words, we escape from behaviorism into cognitivism.[26]

A good way to start our discussion here is with psychologist Abraham Maslow. In his book, *Motivation and Personality*, Maslow discusses his famous "hierarchy" of human motivations.[27] According to him, all human beings, regardless of cultural experience, have certain motivations which unite them within a common species. Hence, humans have certain response mechanisms and motivational systems that can be understood, classified, and used to ground persuasive appeals. According to Maslow:

> Man is a wanting animal and rarely reaches a state of complete satisfaction except for a short time. As one desire is satisfied, another pops up to take its place. When this is satisfied, still another comes into the foreground, etc. It is a characteristic of the human being throughout his whole life that he is practically always desiring [i.e., needing] something.[28]

The most basic human needs (or wants) are air, food, water, and procreation. Without these, individual and collective life would perish. Human motivation, then, at its most fundamental level, can be understood as the mechanistic desire we have for satisfying our basic survival needs. The more that these needs are threatened, the less able we become to focus on other things. Once these needs are met, however, then we can struggle to attain the *next* level of concerns, those that involve *security*. As immediate threats to our survival become met, we have to secure our advantages so we do not lose them. In other words, we have to maximize them and protect them. As we perceive threats to our air, food, water, and to our survival, we experience a strong motivation to resolve these. Survival motives concern our immediate needs (i.e., find food for *today*); while social motives concern helps guarantee that we have food to eat *tomorrow*.

To have bread and the means to protect it is, however, not enough. While we may enclose ourselves securely in our homes, behind fences with elaborate security systems, and armed with high-tech automatic assault rifles and other military paraphernalia, we risk being lonely (assault rifles do not make for conversationalists). According to Maslow, basic needs and security needs are only at the beginning of our quest (our *telos*) to become fully human.[29] These base material concerns may have to be the grounding upon which we construct our higher sense of self, but construct that higher self we must. Implicit within us are higher needs that we have a drive to satisfy. A life lived at the security level alone is not a life worth living. To a certain extent we need struggle and uncertainty in our lives to propel us toward art and transcendence.

Being social creatures, we have *belonging needs*. We feel the drive to be a member of something, a part of something. We experience a desire to identify with a transcendence, what American philosopher William James classified as the "more."[30] Simultaneously, we belong to families, to jobs, to religions, to communities, to nations, and to the human species. Some of these belonging relationships may be more strongly felt than others. Yet, without these connections, at whatever level we wish to experience them, our lives would be substanceless. While we could feed our bodies, our spirits and our souls would starve. Well-nourished people become insane and even die without companionship. Merely touching one another has powerful psychological, physiological, and communicative effects on the body; studies on humans, primates, and rats indicate that mammals suffer psychologically when deprived of nurturing and touch.[31]

As an extension of belonging needs, we also experience *esteem* needs. We need to be wanted, valued, and needed. We do not just want to be in a group; at some level, we want to feel like that group needs us and that it will somehow be different or not exist at all if we were to withdraw our energy from the group. Esteem needs are an important part of our maturing ego needs, which are more firmly manifested at the next level of Maslow's hierarchy, the *self-actualization* needs. We all have potential that we try to live up to in our own eyes. We need to feel good about ourselves, to have self-respect, and to feel like we are accomplishing important and meaningful things in our life.

Then we have *knowledge/understanding* needs. Such needs involve the innate curiosity that we have for the unknown. This curiosity drive is an important part of the human condition and seems to be a characteristic that is unique to our species. We seem to be preoccupied with creating knowledge and with trying to understand our position in the world.

Finally, we have, according to Maslow, *aesthetic* needs. Humans intuitively seek representations or expressions of beauty, balance, and form in their lives. We desire these things in our surroundings and take satisfaction in creating works of art that exemplify them. Images that are beautiful or aesthetically pleasing aid us in our quest for self-actualization. Where they do not exist, we create them. While it may not be obvious to most of us, we live our lives poetically, or at least with a strong poetic or artistic element. Kenneth Burke went so far as to observe that while we are all poets in the construction of our lives, "some people write their poems on paper, and others carve theirs out of jugular veins."[32] In the art and poetry of life we find degrees of peace and violence, liberation and oppression, and health and disease. Human history reveals this need that we possess to observe aesthetically our surroundings and to take in and *improve upon*, in our own terms, the beauty the world has to offer.

Let us explore how stimulus-organism-response works in advertising. A generic ad for a weekly business magazine heralds itself as an authoritative voice on business and politics. For visual evidence, it provides a reassuring and towering picture of the Capitol building in Washington, D.C. The persona of some business executive announces that his business confidence is grounded or accentuated by his reading of the magazine. We are told that the magazine provides us with the information we need to feel powerful. The power of the Capitol and all that it represents is co-opted by the ad and presented to us for the price of a subscription. For the low price of the magazine, we can be assured of our confidence in our business dealings with others.

Notice how the "organism" is centrally appealed to in the above ad. It is not enough, in this case, for the advertisers to associate their product with power; there has to be a sense in which we *feel* this association, that we recognize and understand that we have a *need* for this magazine.

Need is a central component with the stimulus-organism-response theory, as evident in an encounter I had with a home water purification system salesman a few years ago. I had invited this person to my house for a two-hour demonstration of his product. When he arrived, I immediately asked him how much the product cost, and he politely refused to tell me, assuring me that it was in my best interest to not know the price until after I had seen what his product could do to save me money. He then launched into an impressive delivery where he meticulously documented how, in fact, the water purification system paid for itself in ten years. Apparently, having purified water running through the pipes in my house reduced the need for repairs on the pipes, resulted in a decreased need for laundry detergent, made moisturizing creams less necessary, and inflicted less wear-and-tear on our clothes, etc. As he proceeded through his demonstration, I agreed with each and every point he made. Yes, the product was of superior space-shuttle technology, yes it had a good warranty, yes it saved money over time. I agreed, enthusiastically, with everything he said—he was selling an impressive product. I would be proud to have it in my home. Yet, when it came time for me to sign the purchasing contract, I politely refused. The salesman was flabbergasted. "But you agreed..." he protested. "Yes," I replied, "I think you gave a wonderful presentation and I would stand by your product. But I simply do not *need* this water purification system. I am quite content bringing my empty water bottles to the market once a week to refill my *drinking* water." While he had mentioned during his presentation the horrors of drinking tap water, and while I perceive tap water as a threat to my health and to the health of my family, I easily remove the threat by taking empty water jugs to the market where I purchase purified water for 39 cents a gallon. All the other things he talked about, while true, were not perceived by me as needs. A $4,500 water purification system that had to be maintained did not seem a good substitute for my weekly water ritual in which I go to the market anyway to purchase food.

In an important sense, we have to feel like we are threatened, that we are not competitive, that we are at some disadvantage if we do not heed the persuader's appeal (i.e., that our needs are not met). So, to return to the example of the business magazine ad, if we do not subscribe to it we have to be made to feel that we are being somehow hurt, in this case, financially, which may or may not be the case. Finally, we have to feel relieved, or justified in spending the money on the product (if I purchased the water purifier, I would need to feel relieved that I was somehow protecting my health or something similar, which was not an issue in my case). To be persuaded, the benefits of a subscription or of the water purifier would have to clearly outweigh the costs, as they may do in the business magazine appeal. An important implication of this ad is that the low price of the subscription (as opposed to the high price of the water purifier) is more than compensated for by the "power" we will command with the knowledge that the magazine gives us.

Even if the business magazine ad does not get us "ahead," which would be a hard claim for the advertisers to make and impossible to guarantee, there is a clearly implied premise in this ad that states that reading this magazine will help prevent us from *falling behind*. This is a variation of the classic "Keeping up with the Joneses" appeal promulgated by the mass media in our society. This phenomenon refers to the desire to be seen as being as good as our neighbors or peers as measured by the accumulation of material goods. In our society, to fail to "Keep up with the Joneses" is often perceived as demonstrating socio-economic or cultural inferiority and may be experienced as a source of embarrassment or shame. Thus, the fear in losing to our "competitors" in the business or social realms is a motivating force behind much advertising. In our society, however, it is often not enough to succeed; there is also a sense in which *my* success has to come at *your* expense. One ad for diamond rings, for example, features a close-up of a large diamond ring with the text, "Make her ex-boyfriend hate you even more."

Another ad, this one from Allstate Insurance Company, shows a house engulfed in flames. Through the fire we can see the skeleton of the house as it is collapsing. As viewers, we can almost feel the heat radiating from the pages —as the flames cast a dangerous, eerie orange. Standing in front of the burning house, back to the camera, is a man in his pajamas. He stands as if he were us, watching the destruction of our home. This point is heightened by the camera angle which makes us the subject of the visual appeal. The grim question that

Allstate wants us to consider is: where are *our* children? We know where this man's children are; they are burning—their cries muffled by the roaring of the flames as their father has let them down. With this positioning, the advertiser now has our attention. Taking advantage of our awareness, Allstate now provides us with some instructions. They tell us that we need to have a family meeting place to gather when there is an emergency. We need to practice our escape. For more information about fire precaution and safety we should contact Allstate. Readers are already familiar with the general slogan of the company which is, "Allstate —You're in good hands." What is being evoked in this ad is our security and safety needs in particular, our needs to protect our family and our children.

A closer study of this ad reveals that it is not the fire we fear, but our own failure to prepare for it, our own inaction which results in the death of our children. After all, rhetorically speaking, we cannot blame fire for anything—it is a material condition of existence. We cannot banish fire, legislate against fire, or prevent fire from occurring in the sense of eradicating it like the polio virus. We cannot *blame* fire when it takes our loved ones from us. In other words, we cannot command any agency over fire. The fire has an agency and logic all its own. What we *can* do is to be prepared for the *contingency* of fire, and here is where the appeal to persuasion can work. The father in the ad was clearly unprepared. For the rest of his life, he will have to live with the memory of that night and his own inadequacy, his act of involuntary infanticide. It is that image of guilt, of remorse, of powerlessness, the irrationality of infanticide—the most horrendous crime a parent can accuse her or himself of, no matter how accidental—that may convince us to act so that we can escape *his* fate. We would rather die than to see harm come to *our* children. Recall, for instance, the guilt felt by the main character, Sophie, in William Styron's 1979 novel, *Sophie's Choice*, of having to chose between which of her two children to save and which to condemn to the gas chambers at Auschwitz. After trying throughout the novel (and subsequent film) to escape this guilt, she, in the end, commits suicide.

So while there is clearly a stimulus-response mechanism occurring in the just-explained fear appeal, the fact that Allstate claims that certain precautions "could save lives," and the fact that Allstate makes it clear that *it* is the source of those precautions, stimulates our thought and helps us to focus our concern on Allstate. We may even overlook the fact that Allstate is not the only source of information on fire safety or that its primary motive is to sell us insurance, which is *not* the same thing as protecting us from actual physical threats to our lives. Fire insurance is no magic talisman to protect against fire, just as life insurance does nothing to keep us alive.

The ad clearly encourages us to think. In the picture, the father's hands are powerless. His right hand is gripping his head with frustration, his left hand is held in front of his body in inaction. We look back to the ad's slogan, "Being in good hands is the only place to be." We think, clearly, this father's hands are *not* good hands. The failure that can be seen in the expression of the man's hands accentuate the security of the *other* pair of hands, the one personified by Allstate, an American institution that has woven its products into the seams of American culture. And what about our own hands? Should we accept that there is something wrong with us? We do not know, and cannot know for sure until it is possibly too late. To be safe, we may decide to rely on the products that Allstate has to offer.

A final example of stimulus-organism-response theory deals also with the next set of theories we will discuss, the *perception theories*. In a generic ad for an instant camera, the viewer is presented with a picture of a small boy, roughly five years old, sitting in the living room of his middle-class home. The child is smiling, has cute eyes, and is an intimate distance from the person taking the photograph. The photograph takes up five-sixths of the magazine's page. In the white space beneath the picture we read, in a child's scrawl, his gleeful greetings to his father. We realize that the child is supposed to be *our* child, that he is actually looking at us, and that we are holding this picture, and that his message is to *us*. To make sure that we are making these visual connections, the ad provides us with a brief narrative on the top of the page. It is early in the morning and the father is having a conversation with his son. The son asks if the father if he is going on yet another business trip. The father, with a discernable sense of guilt, admits that he is. His son then asks if he is going to take him on the trip. The father, reluctantly, confesses that he is unable to comply with his son's request. Then comes the crux of the exchange: the son asks if his father *would* take him if his father *could* take him.

And here we are, sitting on our plane or in our hotel room, holding the picture of the boy that we managed to "take" with us. But some of us did not have the foresight to purchase the camera, which is why the little boy we are looking at is not our own.

This only accentuates our inadequacy as parents, our disappointment in ourselves for letting down, yet again, our child. For, as the ad reminds us, we have left a disappointed little boy at home, as we probably have at times in real life, and will probably do again. The advertiser knows that most of us do not have the chance to watch closely as our children grow up. The ad forces us to confront and lament this fact and points out that an action so simple as taking a picture with their camera would be an important symbolic gesture to this child and would have solved, in part, the dilemma that most of us face between having to go to work in order to earn a living and wanting to play a more active role in our children's upbringing. The child in the photograph is smiling—a conscientious father saved *his* day. When was the last time that *our* child smiled in such a way?

Clearly, in the dialogue between the father and the child, the father answered "yes" to the all-important final question: "will you take me?" To prove the sincerity of his affection for his child, the father, presumably, pulled out the camera and said, "Yes, Eric, I will take you with me. I'll look at this photograph every chance I get." This works in placating the child because we know that what is important to the young boy is not that he is allowed to go on adult business trips, but that he is not abandoned by his father, that he is reminded constantly of his father's love for him. In a vital way, the photograph in the ad accentuates the father's affection for his son; it becomes a testimony to his love for his child. In so doing, the advertiser has gone a long way toward making its product indispensable for many of its customers.

ഔ Perception Theories ര

Perception theories highlight our attempt to understand how others order their perceptions based upon the messages they receive and their internal needs and values. As suggested earlier in the examples of stimulus-organism-response, our perceptions are important to the way we see and feel. Perceptions are the ways that our hierarchical motivations become triggered. In a sense, all theories of persuasion are perception theories. As we are discussing in this chapter, and indeed, throughout this textbook and course, persuasion involves little more than *perceived* relationships. Ethos, for example, is the *perceived* credibility of a source. Threats that persuaders construct for us in order to motivate us have to be *perceived* as such by the audience. We only believe what we can "see," and what we "see" involves our language (our "final vocabulary" or "terministic screens" discussed in the Conclusion of this book), our interpretations of the world and the judgments we make about its various "truths."

The first specific theory discussed in this section is attribution theory. *Attribution theory*, first articulated by Fritz Heider, involves the ways that we assign causation to the actions of others.[33] This theory tries to understand the way that people make inferences about what other people do. The assumptions behind attribution theory are threefold. First, people are afraid of uncertainty.[34] Part of our genetic heritage is our survival impulse, and the most archetypal (i.e., primordial) threat to the survival of any individual is the unknown. This is why, archetypally speaking, high places are better than low places and light is valued over darkness. The more we can see, and the further we can see, the more prepared we can be, and the better we can understand and deal with potential threats to our security. Part of this survival technique is the creation of order. The more order, predictability, and structure we build into our lives, the more comfortable we are when we walk down the street and see a stranger walking toward us. At the primordial survival level, we do not appreciate surprises.[35]

The second assumption behind attribution theory, extending from the first, is that people act systematically and assign causes systematically. What we see in other people when we look at them is simply the most visual part of a long series of internal processes. We intuitively realize this, and thus we constantly try to recreate or understand the other person's thought processes in our own minds.

The third assumption behind this theory is that the attributed cause affects our own internal states. That is, when we see somebody acting in a way that we perceive as strange, we immediately grow concerned. We mentally try to discern why this odd person is doing what she or he is doing. We try to come up with the most plausible explanations for the behaviors of others. We do this, ultimately, to justify *to ourselves* our actions. After all, we have to *respond* to this person. Our response is based upon our judgments. We run away, call the police, excuse the person's behavior, or reinterpret the behavior as "normal" based upon the attributions we make of her or his mental states.

A related perceptional theory is *self-perception theory*. Besides creating order in the world by attempting to understand the behaviors of others, we try to explain our own selves and our own actions. Since Sigmund Freud in the late nineteenth- and early twentieth-centuries, we know that human beings are complicated animals with complex psyches. We have many selves and many motivations and drives of which we are not aware, but which affect us greatly. We have a subconscious. And even when we are aware of ourselves as thinking human beings, most of us are not as self-reflective as we can be; while we may recognize ourselves in the mirror, we often do not appreciate ourselves as historical beings. Most of us do not understand fully why we think, feel, and act in the ways that we do. We tend to naturalize our condition and make excuses for our shortcomings.

Self-perception theory is important because it recognizes that we have a multiplicity of often-conflicting selves, and the theory encourages us to recognize that we are not always who we think we are. For example, how truly or honestly can we answer the question, "I give to charities because …?" Or, "I go to church or temple or mosque because…?" Do we give money because it makes us feel good or because it is nice, or do we give money for the tax advantages? Sometimes when we give money to organizations, they place our names on plaques or buildings, adding another motivation to encourage generosity (i.e., pride, social recognition, or status). Sometimes we give because in giving it is possible to gain power over another.[36] How honest are we, really, about the sources of our generosity?

Do we go to church because we love God, or do we go to church because it is socially acceptable? Church attendance is considered in some communities as the "right" thing to do, and may help us to achieve many of the rewards that society has to offer. Or do we go to church because we fear divine punishment if we do not go? Perhaps we attend church for other reasons, as well. For example, we may be looking for a spouse, or, more simply, for a way to be sociable, to have friends. None of these reasons are mutually exclusive of the others, although for any individual one may appear to be the more dominant motivation for attending church or any other religious institution.

Our self-perceptions affect us in other ways. Do we talk about ourselves in affirming, positive terms, or do we denigrate ourselves? Have we internalized our "Blackness," our "Jewishness," our "gayness," our "obesity" and use these traits to define ourselves? Have we used these marginalized identities as a whip to beat ourselves in self-fulfilling prophesies of failure? Do we recreate our negative self-perceptions in our children? A wonderful rhetorical question articulated by psychologist Catherine Steiner-Adair in the documentary film *The Strength to Resist*: *The Media's Impact on Women and Girls* challenges us to stop participating in what she calls the "rhetoric of body loathing."[37] We all do it; we look in the mirror and judge what we see against unreasonable and unattainable standards: we are too fat, tall, short, dumpy, etc. Our children watch and listen to us as we do this and they learn this rhetoric. Even people who know better—critical media scholars for example—often get caught up in this negative behavior; it is easy to do because none of us can live up to the images dangled before us. I am just as susceptible to this rhetoric as anyone, although I have developed resources, such as this textbook, to help mediate its negative effects on both myself and my family.

Say you bring home an "A" in a class and show it to your parents. Do you tell them that you cheated? Do you tell them that it was an easy, "blow-off" class? Most of us would probably not say either of these things, even if either of these two conditions happened to be true. In fact, we would probably tell our parents that the class was difficult and that we worked very hard for our "A." In classes in which we earn significantly lower grades than an "A," the reverse often becomes true. We seldom tell our parents that we did poorly in a class because we slacked off, drank too much, or otherwise did not care about our education. Rather, we tell them that the class was hard, the teacher biased, or that other people cheated and upset the curve.

The final perception theory, or perspective, discussed in this section is the *world-view theory*. The first two perception theories explore the actions of others and of our own behaviors. World-view theory, on the other hand, involves a larger explanation, or meta-narrative, for how we view and explain the world around us.

Meta-narratives are grand, explanatory "reasons" that are situated within a persuader's ideology as well as in the ideology of the persuadee. They are the large stories we tell about our culture: what it is, where it came from, where it is going. In addition, meta-narratives are the ideologies we use to constitute ourselves vis-à-vis the larger narratives of our society. Any religion is a meta-narrative. So are many political positions (e.g., liberalism, conservatism). We may not, in our daily lives, think in terms of religion or politics; nevertheless, we are guided by the principles of some meta-narrative at a fundamental level. Our questions of "justice," "community," and "purpose" are usually posed or colored in terms of meta-narratives.

Another way of seeing the influence of meta-narratives on our lives is to look closely at the terms we use to describe our daily activities. Do we describe the world as a *jungle*? If so, what types of interpretations are we likely to take from current national and international events? What sort of politics are we likely to support? What policies will we endorse? More than likely, if this is our world view, we are apt to support stricter laws, longer prison sentences, and the construction of more prisons—positions typically attributed to *political conservativism*. If, on the other hand, we see that the world is a fascinating place, we may reach out to embrace strangers, see in multiculturalism an expression of our democratic sensitivities and potentials as a nation, and be motivated to explore ideas that are different from our own. These positions tend to reflect more of a *liberal perspective*. Thus, we can see that from the narratives we use to frame our lives derives the order that we project on ourselves and on the world.

A good example of how attribution theory can be used in a persuasive campaign can be found in a well-known study of schoolchildren and littering.[38] The goal of the experimenters was to induce behavioral change in elementary school children, encouraging the children to become more conscientious in picking up after themselves in the classroom. They took a class of students and established a baseline reading of the amount of trash they generated each day. Then, over a period of 8 days, the researchers exposed the students to either a direct persuasive appeal ("You should pick up the trash because..." and another to attribution ("Wow, you are really clean and conscientious students."). The researchers found that the command "should" was less effective in getting the students to change, for it implied to the children that they were *not* tidy and made them dependent upon an external source, while labeling the children as "tidy" encouraged the students to internalize the attitude and to act accordingly. In the same article, the researchers reported similar results with inspiring students to improve their math scores. While the study was framed as distinguishing between "persuasion" and "attribution" in terms of the communication style of the message giver, what was taking place was, in fact, persuasion in the sense that we are studying it in this course. As the researchers conclude:

> Attribution can, of course, involve elements of persuasion. As we have seen, the statement "You are a neat person" may be a most effective means of persuading someone to be neat. Nonetheless, such attribution statements need not involve persuasive intent but may instead be sim-

ple statements of fact. Indeed, their guise as truth statements may be thought of as their most effective advantage. Not only does this enable them to work directly on a person's self concept, as noted, but it may also enable them to slip by the defenses a person ordinarily employs against persuasive attempts that are recognized as such. Attribution as persuasion may be further effective because it is less easily recognized as persuasion, and hence less likely to arouse resistance, counter arguing, or reactance.[39]

As we have discussed in this section, perception theories play an important role in how we interpret our own behavior as well as the behavior of others and the world around us. Because we do not see the world objectively, and because we often do not realize this limitation, a consequential way of influencing others is to color or shade their appraisals of their own behavior, or of the behavior of others, so as to direct the target's perception in ways that lead to the desired behavioral action that we seek from them.

ༀ Balance and Consistency Theories ༀ

Our understanding of *balance* and *consistency theories* can extend from our earlier discussion of learning theories and perception theories. As we are exposed to stimuli in the world around us, we respond by making sense of it. In the process, we may react emotionally to the stimuli. If this emotional reaction is acceptance, then it is relatively easy to process the information. However, if our emotional reactions are marked with *dissonance*, that is, by discord and hostility, then we are faced with a potentially uncomfortable scenario. What should we do? What we hear and what we feel have been placed at odds with each other. How are we going to react?

The assumption grounding our reactions in this case is that we strive to maintain a harmonious existence between our self and others and between our self and our self. In a sense, our civilization and personal lives depend upon some sort of harmonious relationships. Unchecked disharmony leads to the disintegration of community; it may also lead to personal failure and to loneliness. War and mutual annihilation are the extreme ends of disharmony.

In this section, I will discuss three perspectives on balance and consistency theory and then focus specifically on one theory, that of *cognitive disso-*

nance. Following this section, I present a sample analysis of a persuasive text which is used to illustrate many of the various theories we have been discussing thus far in this textbook and course.

The major assumption behind the balance/consistency approaches to understanding persuasion is that people are more comfortable with consistency in their lives than with inconsistency. Because of this, inconsistent information has to be dealt with. In most cases, it is simply discarded (that is, ignored). At other times, however, it forces us to reconsider our previous standards of consistency. The pursuit of consistency, therefore, can be considered a fundamental principle that organizes our cognitive processing. In other words, attitude change can result from information that disrupts the balance that we have created for ourselves, or otherwise points out that we were living under the illusion of balance.

The first dimension of the balance theories of persuasion is the idea that we want our attitudes to be in harmony with our relationships.[40] In order to understand this, we have to examine briefly the ideas of psychologist Milton Rokeach.[41] According to Rokeach, people's sense of self consists of highly organized systems of beliefs, attitudes, and values. Collectively, these guide our behavior. These phenomena combine to form self-concepts and are ultimately projected into overt expressions known as action, discussed more specifically in Chapter 8. For now, the point is that, as individuals, we want our attitudes, values, and beliefs to be in harmony with each other. So, for example, we find ourselves facing a "source-proposition" conflict when we detest the president of the United States as a person but support his position on crime. George W. Bush may strike me as a mean, arrogant, deceitful, and self-serving politician whose policies I find appalling, hence someone who cannot be trusted. I find, however, that his view on education may be closely aligned to my own view which wishes to see more responsibility placed on schools for the academic success of their students. Once I realize that I hold these two views, and realize that they are, in a sense, incompatible, I will be "unbalanced" (not to mention embarrassed). How can I distrust or dislike the president, yet agree with him on a particular occasion when I find that he and I think alike on an issue? If we agree on an issue, then we may have something in common, and then he cannot be as bad as I originally thought, I may think. Or, I can think the other way, although I probably will not: "If I like him and he is a bad person, I guess that means that I'm a bad person as well." I recently rejected a book that I was thinking of purchasing when I noticed that former president Bush endorsed it. Why did I do that? I would have purchased the book only if I thought I would enjoy it and learn from it. What if I did? How would that force me to reevaluate my feeling for Bush?

To take another example of an unbalanced position, a person may have revered President Bush as a moral manifestation of this country, but opposed the president's position on Iraq. "If war is murder," this person may reason, "how can the president support its practice? I'm not going to compromise on my principle—murder is wrong. Therefore, I have to conclude, something is really wrong with this country, and its leadership has lost its moral sanction to lead."

In both of the above cases, a person is forced to hold irreconcilable views, and that is unacceptable from the point of view of balance and consistency theories. Of course, there is a third option; the person simply may not care about the discrepancy in her or his life. While this may be true at times, the important point is that this theory assumes that it is easy for us to become unbalanced. Without at least the semblance of a commitment to balance in our lives, we run into the danger of becoming schizophrenic—unable to maintain the facade of being a civilized, well-adjusted citizen-participant in our communities.

When we think about it, it is difficult to hold a negative view toward a person and, simultaneously, like what that person is doing. The more we like what that person is doing, the more we will like that person. If I like the president and I like you, and if you do not like the president, I have either to stop liking you or reconsider the reasons why I like the president, at least according to this theory. To the extent that I like you and trust you, I will start to trust your reasons for not liking the president and my view may be susceptible to change.

As a law student, I experienced this unbalanced state not infrequently. For instance, to vary my study techniques, I would read U.S. Supreme Court decisions (the "meat and potatoes" of legal study) and avoid looking at which justice authored it. I would read the case and try to determine the author based upon the ideology I detected and the style in which it was written. I was horrified when, on occasion, I identified strongly with a decision and the Court's reasoning and then later discovered that it was authored by a justice whom I loathed. Conversely, I remember reading a Court decision that I strenuously *disagreed* with, only to discover it was written by Justice Thurgood Marshall, my all-time favorite justice. In each case, I was faced with an unpleasant feeling that I had to repress in order to keep my interpretive schema intact. While no schema is perfect, they help us to organize our world. When a particular schema ceases to do that consistently enough, we must cast it aside in a reorganized world. The casting aside of a schema is a drastic event, and is not one we consider lightly. To a large degree, when we change interpretative schemas we become slightly different people.

With congruency, another dimension of this theory, we want our different attitudes to be in harmony with each other. So, for example, we can have what is called an "attitude-attitude" conflict. We may believe that we must reduce government spending, but, simultaneously, demand more government spending on highways, prisons, police, and the military. Likewise, we may oppose government involvement in our lives, but demand legislation making abortion illegal, forcing the government to regulate same-sex unions more stringently, or endorse laws that invade our privacy, such as the USA PATRIOT Act of 2001. Anti-abortion activists who call themselves "pro-life" often act inconsistently when they support the death penalty or the war in Iraq. Or we may experience "perception-perception" conflicts. We may perceive big cities like Miami as dangerous, but also as good places to vacation. Or we may experience a "behavior-attitude" conflict. We may believe in law and order, but cheat on our taxes, or speed on the highway. Or we may, if we are underage, devise ways to acquire and consume alcohol, and still maintain our allegiance, generally, to the principle of "law and order."

Again, the assumption that the persuader makes with this theory is that people cannot tolerate imbalance or inconsistency because such a condition is unpleasant and causes the person to be uncomfortable. However, as practical experience shows, we may not necessarily *perceive* an inconsistency or an imbalance in our lives. In such a case, it is up to the persuader to point it out to us. This, however, may be difficult, as people utilize an enormous amount of psychological energy to repress the inconsistency of their behaviors. It is all too easy to deceive ourselves into seeing consistency where it does not exist or into excusing its absence. In addition, we may differ, considerably, in the amount of tolerance we have for inconsistent and unbalanced behavior. We are quick to hold other people accountable for their attitudinal indiscretions, but slow to realize our own, as when the parent tells the confrontational child, "Do as I say, not as I do."

The theory of *cognitive dissonance*, the capstone of the balance theory perspective, involves all the limitations and assumptions discussed above. This theory was first articulated by psychologist Leon Festinger.[42] The theory of cognitive dissonance is a useful heuristic and it is fundamental to most persuasion (e.g., it has many connections with the enthymeme and self-persuasion, as discussed later in this chapter).

Basically, as this theory and others illustrate, we are persuaded best when we, ourselves, feel the need to change. Persuaders who utilize the theory of cognitive dissonance in the structure of their persuasive appeals exploit this condition. If the persuader can point to imbalance, or to dissonance in the audience, or if she/he can create imbalance with her/his presentation, then the audience will have the motivation to change. In other words, dissonance produces tension and that tension acts as a stress that pressures the individual to change so that the dissonance is reduced.

Let us examine some examples from our common experiences. Whenever we purchase an expensive product—a car, a house, or anything that we cannot quite afford, or can barely afford—we experience dissonance. The more that we value the money, and the more money that is involved in comparison to the amount of money we have, the more we think twice about exchanging it for some product. The less force that is involved in our decision, the higher our subsequent dissonance. To the extent that we have *no choice*, then there is little dissonance, as when we spend a small fortune on a costly car or home repair. In such a case, while we may lament the expenditure, and perhaps the sacrifice we have to make to pay the bill, we rationalize that the expense was necessary to protect our investment in our house, to have a reliable means of transportation to work, etc. In other words, there is an *external* reason for why we did what we did and we do not need to justify our actions to ourselves or to the world.[43]

What we are really afraid of is some anticipated ridicule from our family and friends: "You paid how much for *that*? How can you be so stupid!" In order to feel better about what we purchased, we seek to find all sorts of evidence to justify our action. If we bought a car, we will collect literature to show just how good that car is. We may tell other people to buy the same model car and take pleasure in their so doing. We may even start to notice that other people, lots of them, have done the same thing; suddenly, it would appear to us, the roads are filled with Honda Civics or whatever car we happened to buy.

For example, in 2005, my wife and I purchased a new car. It was surprisingly painless, at least at first. We went to the Automobile Association of America (AAA), where part of our benefits as members included a service where a consultant helped us decide what kind of car to buy. The consultant took our requirements and secured the car for us. When we arrived to pick up the car from his office, it was an ugly gray. (The only information about car color we gave the agent was that we did not want the color red, as red cars, according to popular myth, tend to collect more speeding tickets than other color cars, and we had been burned more than once on a previous vehicle my wife owned that was red. Whether or not this claim about red cars is true empirically is beside the point; what matters as consumers is our *comfort level* regarding our consumptive habits.)

Needless to say, I hated the color, was actually fairly repulsed by it (our agent called it a "respectable, distinguished color"—meaning it is the color that old people prefer). Yet, we ended up purchasing the car. Why? All told, it was a good car. It had all the safety features we required and the price made it an excellent deal. But, mostly, my wife and I discussed how superficial it was to judge the car by its color. We are both educated people (my wife is a biology professor) who take a certain pride in not getting distracted by superficialities (at least, we like to think that, as intellectuals, our lives are contextualized by our quest for the authentic, although we may only be fooling ourselves). I thought that, after we bought the car my opinion of the color would change. It did, but after almost *two* years. Meanwhile, every time we drove in the car I searched for *other* cars with the same color—and found them. They appeared everywhere and I used them to train myself to like the color of our car. It worked, and now I find myself very pleased with the color. I have a difficult time imagining what I did not like about it then.

The classic example of cognitive dissonance, and an illustration of its limitations, is smoking. On the one hand, we smoke and we know that smoking kills us, and, on the other, we value our health. So why do we still smoke? There may be many reasons for this. One reason is the fact that cigarette smoking is an addiction. Some people simply *cannot* stop smoking, even though they know that it kills them, which strikes me as a good reason to make cigarettes illegal and to ban their production. Another reason why people smoke is habit or peer pressure, in which case it becomes psychologically difficult to stop.

What is important, if we want to stop smoking, is that we recognize that the behavior of smoking is incompatible with our desire to lead a long healthy life. Make no mistake about it, *smoking is antagonistic to our health; the single most important thing we can do for our health is to not smoke or, if we do smoke, to quit immediately.* We know this, yet we make excuses for our behaviors, and mislead ourselves to think that smoking really does not harm us. We may know people who smoke and do not get sick, or we may feel that we will die anyway, so why bother worrying about something that will happen in the future? Or maybe we just suppress the information, pretend that it does not exist. We may do many things. The point is, however, that in order for us to stop smoking we must confront clearly the health risk and declare to ourselves that it is unacceptable. It is the job of the persuader, in any context involving this theory, to get the persuadee to confront this contradiction, to feel and not shirk the dissonance, and to utilize that discomfort as a resource for change. Yet that perception, itself, will become clear only because of the cognitive dissonance that we experience.

ℬ Sample Analysis Illustrating Learning, Perception, and Balance/Consistency Theories ◯

Before going on to discuss enthymematic and self-persuasion, reactance theory, inoculation theory, and the theory of identification, I want to illustrate further the theories we just discussed (i.e., learning theory, perception theory, and balance/consistency theory). The text I have chosen to analyze is from a 1986 video production of the United Farm Workers of America, called *The Wrath of Grapes*, borrowing from the title of John Steinbeck's *The Grapes of Wrath* in their effort to end unfair labor practices and to better the lives of migrant workers in this country. This video is a classical persuasive artifact that illustrates clearly many of the theoretical ideas discussed above.

The video depicts the position of the United Farm Workers (UFW), a union started in the 1960s by the late César Chávez to improve the working conditions of California's large population of migrant farm workers and their families.[44] The half-hour video reviews the history of the union, highlights some of its important victories, and chronicles its major defeats. Throughout the film, the UFW is attempting to revitalize its concerns for working conditions, for food safety, and for the right of labor to organize. The film comprises a narrator, historical footage, reviews of newspaper articles, and testimony from people involved with issues relating to pesticide use and the commercial growing of grapes.

The film starts with, and extends from, a simple stimulus-response appeal to its viewers. From this, it builds a more sophisticated form of persuasion.

As discussed earlier in this chapter, the stimulus-response theory assumes that humans are basically passive entities without the capacity for free thought. Although humans clearly have the *capacity* to think freely at times, it is not true that we always so do. Sometimes we *do* react to graphic pictures and to emotional appeals in a way that is devoid of critical contemplation.

The UFW video attempts this type of influence in a direct manner. The producers flash dissonance-arousing pictures on the screen, accompanied by dramatic, suspenseful music. The effect of these appeals is to heighten a negative aura around the product that is being denounced in the film. The product, of course, is the grapes. One of these pictures is a skull and crossbones, which appears on the pesticide package. We are then shown farm workers who reach into this package to take out the pesticides that are sprayed on the grapes. In addition, there is a repetitive use of a military-style helicopter that evokes images of the assault helicopters in Vietnam during the American war (during the 1980s, such images became iconic through Vietnam War movies such as *Apocalypse Now* where similar helicopters were depicted dropping napalm on Vietnamese villages).

In one concrete associative scene from the UFW video, we watch as a helicopter, spreading pesticides, swoops down on the grape fields. Flashed on the screen at this time is the title of the film—*The Wrath of Grapes*—thus linking the violence of the Vietnam War to the "violence" of the grapes. Later this linkage is made overt through attribution when a migrant farm worker, the mother of a little boy who was born without arms and legs, remarks, with regard to the farm owners: "They never tell you when they spray pesticides because they don't care about people's health."

In addition to the previously mentioned images of death and violence (many more appear throughout the film), the producers appeal to the sympathy and sadness we feel for the children affected by these cancer- and deformity-causing pesticides. They do this with pictures of sad, sick children, accompanied by depressing music. These pictures are an attempt to encourage the viewers to react emotionally and without much thought, as the experience, watching the video, is gut-wrenching. Prestige suggestion is also manifest in the film in the guise of Mike Farrell, the actor who played B. J. Hunnicutt on the popular television show, *M.A.S.H.* (1972–1983). The popularity of this TV show, and Farrell's centrality to it, makes him a familiar voice, particularly in the mid-1980s when the show's popularity was near its peak. While we never see Farrell in the video, his voice—its very familiarity—lends a degree of credibility to the project that he is endorsing.

A more overt use of persuasion is utilized by the filmmakers in the form of the stimulus-organism-response strategy. It does not take long in the development of the film to see that it is loaded with information—in fact, it is easy to mistake this film for a documentary if we are not paying attention. The persuasion, while clear from the point of view of the eye trained by theory, conceals itself, like all good persuasion—the film assumes the air of a documentary. The text and the narration walk us through a series of issues and conflicts, complete with a dramatic history, demons (the Republican Governor of California, George Deukmejian, and the propertied growers that he represents), and heroes (the martyrs of the union). The images shown throughout the video are contextualized by a linguistic argument. That is to say, the bulk of the film provides us with reasons and evidence as to why the status quo cannot remain unchanged. Only the most unfeeling of us can remain unmoved by the *logos*, as well as by the *pathos* of the message.[45]

In the relationship between "image" (or stimulus) on the one hand, and the "response" the filmmakers are trying to cultivate, on the other, we find that the organism, or us, is centrally appealed to in this film. The producers act as if they are convinced that humans (meaning us, the viewers) actually do take what messages are given to them and are motivated by the stimulus (internally) to react in a certain way. Certain information will, according to stimulus-organism-response theory, trigger our internal needs for health, justice, etc.

For example, one of the most basic needs according to Maslow's hierarchy is for safe food and water. This video suggests that the grapes and other farm products we eat and feed to our children have dangerous and deadly pesticides on them that *cannot* be washed off. The ending sequence of the film is particularly illustrative of this point. This scene, in slow motion to emphasize the relationship being established, emphasizes the way in which the pesticides are sprayed on the grapes. From here we watch as the grapes are picked and placed in wood crates for shipping. In the next immediate scene, we watch as a mother stands with her young child in a supermarket aisle. The mother picks up a bunch of grapes and places them in her shopping cart. We then watch as this same mother is standing in her kitchen at home, carefully washing the grapes which will remain contaminated. A few minutes before this scene we were authoritatively told that the pesticides do not wash off! Finally, at the climax of this persuasive appeal, we watch as the mother takes a single wet grape and hands it to the child who innocently brings it to his mouth.

In short, by extrapolating from the danger posed to the farm workers to the dangers posed to consumers, by suggesting that the water in areas surrounding the farming fields is not safe to drink, and that the food has been contaminated by a "chemical time bomb," the producers of the video are involving our cognitive capacities in an effort to stimulate change. It is hoped that this information we take in and process will convince us not to buy conventionally grown grapes—since they could be deadly for us and for our children. In this way, the video is successful in getting our attention, at least, and of educating us. This is, however, a one-sided education, as nothing in the film suggests that there are any rational or justifiable reasons for the continued or judicious *use* of pesticides. The film flatly *denies* that they are needed at all. The UFW video presents us with a radically divided and hostile world, in which one side is all good and the other side is entirely evil and irrational, sacrificing people's health and lives in order to make an obscene profit. This point is driven home when the video points out that warning signs in fields, while required by law to be posted after a spraying, are not enforced by the governor who claims that the "multibillion-dollar-a-year agribusiness cannot *afford* the signs." This comment is coupled with footage from a funeral of a worker who collapsed in the field and died shortly after it was sprayed. No warning signs were posted.

In the end, if we are persuaded, we have decided for ourselves not to buy the grapes. If we are swayed by the presentation, we have reached that decision based on the information that the persuaders in the film have provided for us. This is why these theories are called "learning" theories and why most persuasion is education.

In addition to the two learning theories discussed earlier, the producers of this film also use balance and consistency theories to appeal to the viewers to change their behaviors and to boycott conventionally grown table grapes. What these theories assume is that human beings have an inherent desire for balance and consistency in their lives. As we walk around in our daily environment, most of us try to maintain some consistent image of ourselves. Unless we are narcissistic, we feel the need to be accepted within our communities.[46] While this involves the belonging needs that Maslow discussed, its practical manifestation is obvious we have to appear to be kind, conscientious, and considerate as human beings.

In terms of the *Wrath of Grapes* video, the cognitive dissonance that is created involves our notions of community and compassion. The farm workers, as noted above, are alien to most of us, so the film does a good job of associating the problem of pesticides in terms of things we can relate to—mainly our children. Building from this, the producers of the film create dissonance (or conflict and unrest) in us by problematizing our world, by personalizing the violence, by putting us in the position of having to feel the pain of others. Once our world becomes unsettled a bit, the producers can offer us a solution to the problems that they articulate. They aim to help us regain our balance and sense of self-consistency. The producers realize that as human beings we need to be able to look at ourselves in the mirror in the morning with a good conscience, and we need to present ourselves as respectable to other people, to our families, and to our friends. Life always gives us problems, and we cannot avoid that, but we have a range of solutions available to us, and we usually want to pick the ones that put us, our ideas, or our needs in the best possible light.

In other words, the producers of this video attempt to create this psychological unrest in viewers so that they/we will be forced to reevaluate our previous choices, beliefs, and perhaps choose a new way of doing things—a way that will benefit the persuader. We are, after all, presented with a win-win situation by the UFW. Boycotting the grapes helps us in terms of benefitting our health and the health of our children, and it helps the UFW attain power as a union.

In its effort to unbalance us, the UFW engages in a plethora of high-fear appeals.[47] They offer many examples to illustrate the harmful effects of pesticides on humans, the most graphic being the above-mentioned little boy born without arms and legs. Even though most of the examples of tragedies they show happen to people in and around the actual fields, they also tell us that these deadly pesticides stay on the grapes and could be fed to our children in other parts of the country. In fact, the last example of a sick child that we see is of a little *White* girl with clearly *middle-class* parents.

This threat to our health and to our children's health should be enough to create dissonance within us, the viewers. This could cause a conflict such as a perception-perception conflict in which case our perception that grapes are healthy and desirable conflicts with our perception that the harmful pesticide residues on grapes are deadly. The dissonance created by the filmmakers is enough to disrupt our need for balance, harmony, and consistency—they assume, after all, that we are buying and eating grapes on a regular basis. When confronted with our own personal histories, which come to the forefront of our minds when we see the video, we rethink our previous beliefs and, to restore our emotional comfort, change our actions accordingly. At least, this is what the producers of the film hope.

In conclusion, both learning theories and balance theories are created in this film to persuade viewers to boycott conventionally grown grapes. This desired action is predicated on our reactions to information given to us, as well as on our desire to find balance and emotional harmony in our lives.

ഔ Enthymematic and Self-Persuasion ര

In this section, we are going to discuss in more detail the concept of *self-persuasion*. As highlighted earlier, there is a sense in which all persuasion is "self" persuasion. Recall from Chapter 4 that the definition of persuasion itself implies "choice," at least at some level. Although we may do things that we do not like to do, to the extent that we can convince ourselves that we have a good reason to do them, we may start to form more positive attitudes toward the behavior, thus enhancing the possibility that the behavior will become permanent. As suggested early in this chapter, it is relatively easy to get someone to do a simple behavior, such as picking up and placing in a trash receptor a piece of trash that lies ignored by her or his feet. Encouraging an individual to form an attitude about the necessity of cleaning up the environment or being a conscientious member of the campus community is much more difficult.

Self-persuasion can be understood in at least the following three ways. The first and most important is the enthymeme. The other two are learning hypothesis and forced-compliance hypothesis.

To begin, we start with the *enthymeme*. The enthymeme is the essential principle that explains how persuasion works. Aristotle, in the first and most influential book on rhetoric ever written, calls the enthymeme "the 'body' of persuasion."[48] The function of the enthymeme, or, rather, of enthymematic reasoning, is to involve the audience in the construction of the argument, to attain agreement during the presentation by getting the audience to persuade itself, so that when the persuader arrives at the conclusion of an argument, she or he does not have to make the conclusion overt. The audience completes from within what the persuader intended from without. One clear discussion of the enthymeme is offered by organizational communication scholar George Cheney:

> Today we find corporate rhetors of many types vying to persuade mass audiences by supporting particular organizational value premises which may or may not coincide with others held in the wider society. If many people share the premise that government is too big, they will likely vote for candidates who vow to shrink it. If many share the premise that youth is beautiful, they will be likely to buy products which help them to look young. If many share the premise that owning a gun is a fundamental right, they will be likely to support pro-gun lobbies. And, of course, a particular message—say, one for cosmetics designed to emphasize youthfulness—may not need to state the major premise, "Looking youthful is good," because that audience already accepts it as a cultural "fact." These are types of rhetorical connections that various corporate rhetors hope their audiences will make.[49]

Here is an example of an enthymeme: "Iraq is Arabic For Vietnam." This slogan appeared on bumper stickers in the months and years following the U.S. invasion of Iraq in 2003. Taken literally, the statement is absurd. If you look up the word "Iraq" in an Arabic dictionary, it does *not* mean "Vietnam." The word "Iraq" denotes a country located in the Middle East. Vietnam is in Southeast Asia. Ostensibly, there is no relationship between the two nations. In order for this statement to make sense, it has to be placed in its historical/political/ideological context, which is the resource of enthymematic reasoning. Seen in context, what we have is a complex *argument* grounded in the tragedy of the American war in Vietnam and concludes with the statement that the war in Iraq is a colossal mistake and should be ended immediately. Unpacking the argument a bit, the reasoning goes that the United States was wrong to attack Vietnam, that we wasted tremendous amounts of life and treasure (i.e., money and other resources) to fight a war that was ill-conceived and immoral. We know this. The American people largely regret their country's misadventure in Vietnam, and the assertion here by the slogan is that we are going to repeat that experience in Iraq. Some viewers may think that this is a very bad argument; they will either disagree with the premise that the Vietnam War was regrettable or that a parallel exists between that conflict and the one in Iraq. Others may consider it a good argument and use the slogan as part of their anti-war effort. Still others may not understand the slogan at all because they are not part of the discourse community evoked by the argument. What we make of this statement depends upon our past understandings and political views.

With the learning hypothesis and the forced-compliance hypothesis, as with the enthymeme, persuaders pressure or otherwise encourage audiences to engage in counter-attitudinal activities to change their attitudes, and they do so by "inviting" them to be involved in a personal, direct fashion. So, for example, if we can get another to debate both sides of an issue, we are well on our way toward getting that person to change her or his mind. If we can get another to assume the role of a superior or a subordinate for a short time, then that person can learn how it feels to be on the "other" side of a position or perspective. In short, we learn by doing, and by encouraging others to *do*, we inadvertently encourage them to *know*. In the end, the persuader and the persuadee reach the same conclusion, in what appears to be a mutually independent act.

Many advertisers and product manufacturers use these principles of self-persuasion theory by getting us to use their product, to take it home, and to try it without feeling as if we are obligated to keep it. The more they can get our hands on their product, the less likely we are to let go, and the more likely we will rationalize away our objections to the product. "Don't decide now, sleep on it!" proclaims an ad for Tempur-Pedic. "Try the Tempur-Pedic mattress in your house for 60 nights. Complete 2-month guarantee." This strategy is widely used by car salespeople. As quickly as possible, they will try to get us behind the wheel of their car, even to take it home for the weekend (perhaps so our neighbors can see it). In test-driving the car, we start to imagine that we own the car, and we start to rationalize away the reservations we might have about price and the "extras" that are often included at an added cost.

A great example of self-persuasion occurs in many high schools across the country in courses designed to discourage teen pregnancy or smoking. A product, "Real Care Baby" is available as part of a teen pregnancy lesson plan. The doll must be fed, burped, rocked, and have its diapers changed, just like an actual baby, and it records all positive and negative care it receives, which can then be used to assign a grade to the student. These baby surrogates are extremely life-like and simulate well the energy involved in parenting young infants. St. Ambrose University psychologist Carol DeVolder describes an incident with a "Real Care Baby" involving a high school athletic coach:

> One of his girls brought her "baby" to practice and asked him to watch it for her. It started to rain and he tossed the "baby" in his trunk. A neighbor saw him and called the police. Shortly after he got home, the police arrived on his doorstep to investigate the report.[50]

Programs have students take care of these computerized babies for some extended time. This means that the "baby" must be fed, changed, burped, comforted, etc. Similarly, in anti-smoking programs, students are given a "pack" of cigarettes which they have to keep with them at all times. The pack is programmed to beep loudly at regular intervals to stimulate the need for a nicotine fix. Students then must stop what they are doing and go outside— perhaps in the cold and the rain—for six minutes, the average time it takes to smoke a cigarette. Students then realize how inconvenient it is to have a cigarette addiction, how the cigarettes control them, place them in uncomfortable situations, and waste their time.

To take another example of forced compliance, when I was attending Purdue University in the early 1990s there was a good deal of pressure on the university administration, and on universities throughout the United States, to comply with the unfunded mandates of the *Americans with Disability Act* (ADA). Passed in 1990, the ADA requires, among other things, all universities to be accessible to students with physical disabilities. An example of this would be having buildings and classrooms made wheelchair accessible. This necessitates installing elevators and ramps, as well as shaving curbs for people in wheelchairs. All of this cost money, which administers were reluctant to spend.

On our campus, disability activists created a day-long event entitled "Disability Awareness Day." As part of the public events, the organizers invited the campus leadership to attend and make speeches. This is easy, as it is in the self-interest of administrators to appear sympathetic to the needs of their students. They get the free publicity without having to do much. Then the organization challenged publically the university president to spend a few hours riding in a wheelchair. Again, this is an easy request to fulfill and a great photo-op for the administrator. Once he did this, however, he could see for himself how important the needed changes were, how compliance with the law was not a "nicety" but a fundamental responsibility on behalf of the university. As he "strolled" around campus, the president discovered that he could not get to the library, could not enter many buildings, and could not use the restroom. The abstraction of being disabled was brought home to an important person who had the power to enact the change desired by the persuader.

ೞ Psychological Reactance Theory ೞ

Psychological reactance theory was first discussed by psychologist Jack W. Brehm, who predicted that reactions of arousal, resentment, and anger occur when a person or agency threatens to restrict a free behavior in which we want to engage.[51] The theory assumes that we are autonomous, self-governing beings who make our own choices. Control, in fact, is often limited; the structure of language, the constraints of the economic realm, ethical narratives, and our history all limit us in substantial ways. Nevertheless, we need to feel *as if* we are in control. When people feel that their freedom to choose an action is threatened, they get an unpleasant feeling or psychological arousal called *reactance*. Similar to dissonance, reactance is an intense motivational state. A person with reactance is emotional, single-minded, and somewhat irrational. This arousal motivates people to engage or to perform the threatened behavior, thus proving to themselves that their free will has not been compromised. This state of arousal has other effects as well. For instance, the apparent loss of freedom makes us value more that which is restricted and to devalue the alternatives that we are "struck with." Further, we grow to resent and/or devalue the person/agency who is the source of the restriction.[52]

The experience of psychological arousal takes place in a three-step process. First, an individual perceives what she/he considers to be an *unfair* or unjustifiable restriction on her/his actions. This *perception* of wrongness is important; each of us consider ourselves authorities on what is good for us. Of course, we may be wrong—we may be immature or we may simply not have all the relevant facts to make good decisions. But as with all persuasion, the facts do not matter; what matters is how those facts are received by a persuadee. Take, for instance, the example of teenage dating. Most people have been in this situation either as the teenager or as the parent. In a generic scenario, a teenage daughter brings home a young man (perhaps older) who is totally unacceptable to her parents. If the parents were to "ban" dating that young man, they would run the risk of eliciting reactance from the daughter—that is, she will likely find the young man even more desirable.[53] No doubt, the daughter will perceive her parents as being unreasonable and mean-spirited. She does not have the maturity or the experience to understand her parents' point of view and will likely attempt to assert her independence by doing the opposite of what her parents want.

Second, as a result of this perceived unfair restriction, a state of reactance is activated in the individual. We can thus expect that the restricted teenage daughter will grow angry, and, having no creative place to displace that anger, turn it into resentment toward her parents as well as into an increased affinity for her boyfriend. Third, the person must act to remove the reactance. Here the daughter moves to reject her parents and to assert what she perceives to be her own individuality, neither knowing nor caring about probable and perhaps deleterious consequences.

Many things can be the cause or source of reactance. Censorship is one example. Censorship is often associated with elevated interest in and greater support for the position of the censored communication (e.g., students report more interest in hearing a message and greater agreement with the position of the message in conditions when they were told that the communication had been censored by an external agent compared to when no such censorship was believed to have occurred).[54] Warning labels on music and films indicating that it is only appropriate for "mature" audiences may be associated with increased interest among young people for the music or film. Restrictive parental mediating of television programming may be associated with a child's enhanced positive attitude about the restricted programming.

Another source of reactance is *limited editions*, such as books, coins, guns, or cars. The rarity of the object increases its value. A related source is *scarcity*—such as a natural disaster that destroys the Florida orange orchards, driving up the cost of orange juice—and sporting/concert tickets. When something becomes less accessible, we feel that the freedom to have it may be lost. Otherwise stated, things difficult to attain are often believed to be more valuable. In marketing, we see this as ads claiming a "limited number" now available or a "deadline" for a set offer. Such tactics attempt to convince people that restrictions to access to a product is a shortcut clue or cue to its quality and/or desirability.

It is important to note that scarcity can be *manipulated*—persuaders often increase the value of their product/message by creating the illusion of scarcity.[55] The classic example here is diamonds.[55] The price of diamonds depends on the perception of scarcity. If diamonds are perceived as being rare, then diamond prices will remain high. If new diamonds flood the market, prices will plummet. Until the 1870s, diamonds had been found only in riverbeds in India and Brazil. In the 1870s, however, large diamond deposits were discovered in South Africa, allowing unprecedented numbers of diamonds to enter the open market. Through its enormous wealth, power, and influence, the De Beers Consolidated Mines, a major world cartel, is able to buy large amounts of diamonds whenever countries attempt to flood the market. Because of De Beers, the price of diamonds has remained steady despite civil wars and conflict. The average diamond ring, for example, is marked up 100% to 200%.[56]

A related concept is called *psychological pricing*. In using psychological pricing, sellers consider the psychology of prices and not simply the economics. Price, many people tend to assume, says something about a product. That is, many consumers use price to judge quality. For example, "a $100 bottle of perfume may contain only $3 worth of scent, but people are willing to pay the $100 because this price indicates something special."[57] Consumers also tend to perceive high-priced cars or other durable goods as having higher quality than their lower-priced competitors. Recently, in a book called *The Wine Trials*, food critic Robin Goldstein studied the marketing and manipulation found in the wine industry. She reports a study from the California Institute of Technology and Stanford Business School that demonstrated that the more expensive a consumer thinks a wine is, the more pleasure they are apt to take in consuming it.[58]

As with everything else we have been discussing in this book and course, *perception* matters. What matters most is not what something *is* but what people think it is that determines how people respond to a stimulus. Further, people assign more value to opportunities when they are less available. For example, we know that we tend to value a group more if it is difficult to join.[59] The opposite is also true; if a group will take *anyone* as a member, some people will be discouraged from joining.

℘ Inoculation Theory ℚ

Inoculation theory is a perspective on persuasion which involves the process of supplying information ("refutational pretreatments") to receivers *before* an anticipated communication takes place in hope that the pre-supplied information would make the receiver more resistant to *future* counter-persuasion. Using a biological metaphor, inoculation aims to construct a defense (i.e., to immunize) against persuasion that challenges an individual's beliefs, attitudes, or values. The theory stems from the experience of captured American soldiers during the Korean War. During the war, many Americans troops were captured and taken to China as prisoners of war. There they were subjected to both coercive and non-coercive persuasion. After the war, a sizable number of these soldiers refused to be repatriated to the United States. In other words, they chose to remain in China or North Korea when given the chance to return to the United States. As a result of this embarrassment for our country—we were, after all, fighting "evil communists"—social scientists searched for way to explain what happened to these prisoners. In the popular media, we claimed that they were "brainwashed," but, as we will discuss in Chapter 7, that metaphor is not at all accurate to describe what occurred.

What researchers discovered is that, previous to the Korean War, army officials made an important (and false) assumption that it was unnecessary to train soldiers to argue for the correctness of their assumed attitudes or values. Thus, the soldiers had *no practice* in counter-arguing or defending their beliefs. There was, and continues to be, unfortunately, a widespread belief in our society that what we believe is right (i.e., *correct*) and what others believe is wrong (i.e., *incorrect*). That attitude works fine when we are surrounded by people who think like us. However, if we do not know the strengths or weaknesses of our opponent's arguments, as well as the strengths and weaknesses of our own, we become confused or lost when exposed to different ways of thinking and acting. This is what happened to captured POWs in China. They were separated from the resources of their community, they knew little about the weaknesses or fair criticism of American society, and their view of the enemy was excessively demonized. When captured, they were exposed to the human side of Korean and Chinese society and educated about pervasive problems in the United States, such as racism and poverty. Over time, the Americans felt lied to and betrayed by the U.S. government and embraced the ideology of their captors. This is similar to how religious cults operate, as we will discuss in Chapter 7.

Practical contemporary applications of inoculation theory include protecting children from unhealthy peer pressure. As children grow older, they increasingly become exposed to situations for which they have no experience to use as a resource for making a good decision. Peer pressure is very strong for children, and some of it can be extremely harmful to them. For example, peer pressure to smoke. I remember being in seventh grade, waiting for the bus to take me to school, when the smoking crowd came up to me to encourage me to smoke. In this situation, without having any training, I was defenseless. It was only the fear of being beaten by my mother who I knew was nearby that kept me from accepting their cigarette. A much more scientific way of approaching this all-too-common scenario is to educate carefully young children about the inevitability of these types of interactions so that they know how to respond. I was terrified and did not learn from my experience. Yet, if I had known they were coming, if I had been armed with a response, if I had role-played this very scene, I would have responded more appropriately or gracefully than I did (fearing my mother's wrath, I screamed and ran away). Cigarette resistance starts in the younger grades and is reinforced ("booster shots") at appropriate ages. In sum, youth can better resist social pressure when they are exposed to the pressure (e.g., in role plays), learn how to recognize it, and learn and practice skills to resist the pressures.

To take another example, an astute car salesperson might suggest that a customer go to a competitor and ask about their cars. The first salesperson will outline the arguments she or he expects from the competitor and offer counter arguments. Then when the customer actually hears the competitor's comments,

the counter arguments will already be in place and the second dealer will
pear to be the source of manipulation.

I experienced the above tactic personally a few years ago when I
switched martial arts schools. When I started training in 2004, I had no experience with any martial art system. My first instructor made it a point to repeatedly emphasize what he claimed were the strengths of his system and the
weaknesses of other systems. He did this to the point of arrogance, which I
thought was inappropriate, but it did make it difficult to change schools. While
studying at this first school I found it difficult to even *imagine* studying a different martial art style. Even as I grew increasingly disenchanted with my instructor (in particular, his arrogance), I could not contemplate switching
schools. When things finally came to a head and I had no choice but to leave, I
found it difficult, intellectually, to accept the value of my new system as I was
measuring it against the standards set by the old. As I write this book, more
than three years later, I still experience a small degree of dissonance in my decision to switch schools.

℘ Theory of Identification ℘

Kenneth Burke's theory of identification is the final contemporary theory of
communication discussed in this chapter. In many ways, it is the most important theory, because without identification, few of the psychological mechanisms discussed in this chapter can take place. Since our reactions to the world
are largely modeled on the behaviors of others, it is important to realize that we
become influenced by an ad, or by an appeal, only when we can see the person
depicted in that ad or appeal in a way similar to how we see ourselves. This, in
essence, is what we mean by identification—the ability to see a bit of ourselves
in the relative strangeness of others.[60] When we react well to what others say
and do, we are really reacting to that part of us that we see in them, the part that
is familiar to us and is reassuring. The more different people are from us, the
less likely we are to react favorably to them, and the less we will be able to see
that what they are and what they want and need concern us.

The concept of "identification" is a key term in Burke's system of persuasion, one that involves the entire realm of culture. As Burke explains, "Implicit in the powers of symbolicity are the resources of identification; the sim-

munication made possible by the sharing of a tribal
etry, drama, narrative, oratory, etc."[61] To this we
lly its emphasis on advertising. With a more spe-
on between identification and advertising, commu-
Messaris elaborates on this concept:

> In our real-world social interactions, our psychological capacity to
> identify with other people enhances our ability to predict their actions
> toward us, and it also allows us to learn through observation. By identi-
> fying with someone else, we turn the observed consequences of her or
> his actions into lessons for our own lives. Much advertising is patterned
> directly on this aspect of our real-world experiences. By presenting us
> with models whose sexual or financial or other types of success we
> may wish to emulate, advertising images draw upon our tendencies for
> identification in order to strengthen our emotional involvement with
> ads.[62]

It should be clear now that persuasion is very much tied up with identification. In fact, it should be clear that most of our lives are spent in the negotiation of our identifications, whether we are conscious of it or not. This is another sense in which we can see that persuasion is pervasive in our lives (which
was the subject of Chapter 3). Burke, in fact, makes the linkage overt when he
underscores the difference between what is often distinguished as the "old" and
the "new" rhetoric:

> If I had to sum up in one word the difference between the "old" rhetoric
> and the "new"… I would reduce it to this: the key term for the "old"
> rhetoric was "persuasion" and its stress upon deliberate design. The key
> term of the "new" rhetoric would be "identification" which can include
> a partially unconscious factor appeal.[63]

For Burke, identification is an "instrument" that can be used to show "how a
rhetorical motive is often present where it is not usually recognized or thought
to belong."[64]

In an important sense, Burke is calling attention to the ways that rhetoric permeates all areas of human inquiry. Thus, one of Burke's more lasting
contributions to our understanding of persuasion involves his ferreting out of
rhetoric from where it tries to deny itself or where it has been hidden. As he

explains, "In accordance with the rhetorical principle of identification, whenever you find a doctrine of 'nonpolitical' aesthetics affirmed with fervor, look for its politics."[65] When people react emotionally to something that seems innocuous, we should be on our guard, that this may be a clue that something more substantial is occurring.

๛ Three Types of Identification ๙

Burke explains how the concept of identification can be understood in terms of three "types." The first type of identification is the establishment of an *overt* connection between the persuader and the audience. The archetypal example that he gives is "that of a politician who, though rich, tells his humble constituents of his humble origins."[66] Dressed in blue jeans, plaid shirt, boots and a straw hat, our generic politician says, "Don't let the trappings of power and money fool you, I'm still the same old farmer that I used to be." *A*, in such cases, claims to be consubstantial with *B*. In Burkean rhetorical theory, *consubstantiality* is a strategic compensation that the persuader makes for the division inherent in being human (e.g., we all have different nervous systems). Burke maintains that the doctrine of consubstantiality, "either explicit or implicit, may be necessary to any way of life. For substance, in the old philosophies, was an *act*; and way of life is an *acting-together*; and in acting-together, men have common sensations, concepts, images, ideas, attitudes that make them *consubstantial*."[67]

Closely related to this is the tactic of *dissociation*. With dissociation, the opposite appeal is enacted. "I'm not like those other politicians in Washington," our imaginary politician might say, "I'm not a Washington insider." In the first case, we identify with those things that we respect. In the second case, we dissociate from the things that we distrust. In one 1990 campaign ad for reelection, North Carolina Republican Senator Jesse Helms attacked his opponent, Charlotte mayor Harvey Gantt this way: the announcer, at the end of the video depicting the problem of drug dealing and the murder of law enforcement officers, offers viewers a choice between "extreme liberal values" and what the ad calls "North Carolina values." The message in this appeal is clear: Jesse Helms reflects our interests and Harvey Gantt represents all the things that a good Southerner finds distasteful.

To take a further example, consider an ad for a generic congressperson that suggests we can judge a candidate for congress by the enemies she or he makes. It goes on to claim that Democrats/Republicans should be proud of Senator Jane/John Smith because she/he is one of a handful of leaders that Big Oil/Big Business is angry at. Further, Big Oil/Big Business has good reason to be angry, as our senator has championed legislation that has cost Big Oil/Big Business billions of dollars and has saved working families hundreds of dollars. By dissociating from the things we do not like, such as Big Oil/Big Business, our generic public servant hopes to enlist our loyalty. She/he is, after all, our protector and we have a common enemy.

Both of these appeals are used in a single ad by beer magnate and Republican Pete Coors in his 2004 bid against Democrat Ken Salazar for the Senate in the state of Colorado. Coors begins his ad by denouncing professional politicians. He denies being one or aspiring to become one. He has no interest in government careerism or in working up through the ranks from position to position, as Ken Salazar has done successfully. Presumably, professional politicians are bad. Coors goes on to identify himself as a *businessman* and distinguishes that class of people from *bureaucrats*, which he associates with his opponent. As a businessman, Coors *creates* jobs. He contrasts his job creation credentials with Salazar the *litigator*, a class of people responsible for interfering with the healthy prerogatives of business. In the morality play evoked by Coors, businessmen are the good, honest people, folks who *accomplish* things, while lawyers are the *opposite*. Moreover, Coors, a very wealthy man, identifies overtly with the *average* people whose vote he covets; he says, in effect, that the Senate has too many people in it who represent *elitist* institutions and that he will represent *main street*. Overall, Coors claims that there are too many lawyers in Congress and that he will provide a needed fresh perspective and be the voice of people like you and me, honest and hardworking taxpayers.

In the above cases, the function of identification is to imply that there is a relationship between the two distinct entities (the speaker and her or his audience). The best example I have seen of this is an ad from Betty Crocker that presents us with a computer-generated image of a middle-aged middle-class woman, a composite of 75 real women. The ad provides a narrative in which all of us are positioned as being a part of the Betty Crocker experience, an experience indistinguishable from our lives. Betty Crocker is in us, part of our cultural DNA. *We* are Betty Crocker.

In many cases, identification takes place almost on an unconscious level. The effect is greatly emphasized with the subtle use of the pronoun "we" which enthralls the non-reflective mind. As Burke writes, the use of "we" best represents "the vagaries and vagueness of identification."[68] So, for instance, as we listen to a presidential address and we hear the omnipresent "we" spoken, we feel as if we were willing participants within a larger political or social narrative. In other words, it is difficult for any one of us to escape from the president's command when he says that "we all have to make sacrifices," as if the "sacrifice" of the millionaire is the same as the sacrifice of a person who works in a grocery store.[69] Or, in a particularly famous passage, Burke writes that "whenever 'we' fight a war, the range of identifications under the one head extends from men in combat to Wall Street gamblers who make a killing in war stocks."[70] One Second World War propaganda message from President Franklin Delano Roosevelt reads:

> We are now in this war. We are all in it all the way. Every single man, woman, and child is a partner in the most tremendous undertaking of our American history. We must share together the bad news and the good news, the defeats and the victories—the changing fortunes of war.

At first glance, this appeal seems reasonable, as war between two or more nations tend to accentuate an "us" and "them" mentality. But if we look further we understand that such thinking is not necessarily to our advantage. America, at the time, was much more divided than Roosevelt suggests. It is not clear why African-Americans or minority groups in general should support the war effort or why the working class should fight. Even recently, when former president George W. Bush talked about how *we* are at war against terrorism, it is not at all clear to many people that *we* consented to the terms and narratives offered by the Bush Administration, or that *we* are really fighting for the things that Bush says we are, or that *we* will benefit in any way from "victory" or even suffer from "defeat." Outside of jingoistic platitudes repeated on television, it is not obvious to many Americans that they have a stake in this war. But when the president authoritatively states that "we are at war" or commands that we must "support our troops" we are disinclined to think critically and become accused of being "anti-American," unpatriotic, or worse.[71]

Similarly, at the second level of identification, that of *mistaken identification*, the connections we make are completely unconscious, or at least subtle to the point of becoming natural. Mistaken identification, Burke tells us, occurs when we confuse the qualities of something else for qualities of our own. He gives the example of the automobile:

> [T]o walk faster, or run faster, one works harder. Similarly, to drive faster on a bicycle, one works harder. But when I learned to drive a car, I suddenly found myself confronting a quite different realm of motives. For I needed but press down the gas pedal the slightest bit more, and the car could pick up terrific speed, with no more work at all on my part. Here was a fantastic coefficient of power. And surely, I thought, here is a fundamental *moral* problem. It seemed to me that we, as individuals, are easily tempted to mistake these mechanical powers for our very own... . Such thoughts concern man's *identification* with his machines in ways whereby he mistakes *their* powers for *his*, and lives himself accordingly.[72]

Burke's assumption is that we are susceptible to the allure of this identification. Only a few of us do not feel any better when the power of some machine becomes an extension of our own desires. This type of identification also occurs when people come to associate some product as exemplifying a particular lifestyle. Is there anyone reading this who is not guilty of purchasing some product—a big screen TV, an expensive piece of art, a faster or more complex computer—in an attempt to purchase the lifestyle that the product represents? I am as guilty of this behavior as anyone. For years I made a conscious decision to avoid Nike products because of their hyped commercialism and for their poor treatment of their workers, but found myself attracted to them once I started practicing martial arts and began perceiving myself as "athletic." Now the brand seems a "natural" fit to me.

The third type of identification is *antithesis*. Antithesis involves the pairing of mutually antagonistic or contradictory statements and positions to achieve a psychological effect. The effect of the juxtaposition is that the audience is jarred into thinking differently about something. Identification by antithesis is an example of how style affects thought and helps the mind to perceive things differently. For instance, under the conditions of a well-positioned antithesis, two previously unaligned parties can set aside some of their more fundamental differences and develop a consubstantial relationship that is based on a mutual alignment against a third party. Burke calls this "the most urgent form of congregation by segregation."[73] In more popular terms, this is known as *scapegoating*. When a community practices scapegoating, it unifies its ranks by symbolically purging the differences that divide its people. To do this, these differences are placed on a third party. Historically, the community places its sins on a goat and then sacrifices it, thereby "cleansing" the community. As Burke notes, "It may well be that people, in their human frailty, require an enemy as well as a goal."[74]

An inspiring example of communication as this type of misidentification and its correction is the remarkable personal transformation of C. P. Ellis, an uneducated, onetime Ku Klux Klan leader who became a preeminent civil rights and labor activist.[75] Ellis was born into poverty within a racist Southern culture that held faith in the virtues of being a God-fearing, law-abiding citizen and working hard for a better life. He married at 17 years of age and soon had a family of four to support. Ellis worked two jobs, as much overtime as he could, was an honest citizen, and yet was unable to provide a better life for his children than he had. No matter how hard he worked, his family subsisted on the edge of a perpetual poverty—a condition that relegated his children to the status of "poor White trash." Alienated, embarrassed, and angry, Ellis was drawn to the Ku Klux Klan, as was his father, because of the community and sense of power and belonging that membership in that organization offered. The Klan's targeting of Blacks as the problem for poor Whites offered a scapegoat for the injustice that he was experiencing, providing him with a significant degree of psychological comfort. As Ellis explains:

> All my life, I had work, never a day without work, worked all the overtime I could get and still could not survive financially. I began to say there's something wrong with this country. I worked my butt off and just never seemed to break even... . I really began to get bitter. I didn't know who to blame. I tried to find somebody. I began to blame it on black people... . I was led into a large meeting room, and this was the time of my life! It was thrilling. Here's a guy who's worked all his life and struggled all his life to be something, and here's the moment to be something... . It disturbs me when people who do not really know what it's all about are so very critical of individual Klansmen. The majority of 'em are low-income whites, people who really don't have a part in something.[76]

As a member of the Klan, Ellis was elected by the city of Durham, North Carolina, to serve on a citizen committee to address emerging issues related to school desegregation. He was soon asked to co-chair the school committee with a Black civil rights activist named Ann Atwater—a proposition that he nearly was unwilling to do because of his hatred for Black people. However, through his tumultuous work relationship with Ann and their many yelling matches, arguments, and, later on, discussions and conversations, Ellis began to realize that Atwater and other Black people were experiencing the same problems as he and other poor Whites faced. He saw that their differences were less significant than he had assumed previously and that they both wanted the same thing: a better life for themselves and their families. He began to see that the problems that he and others were facing were systemic, a result of institutionalized and protected privilege for a small powerful group of people rather than the fault of Blacks who shared the experience of disenfranchisement with him. As Ellis explains:

> I met a black person and talked with him, eyeball to eyeball, and met a Jewish person and talked to him, eyeball to eyeball. I found out they're people just like me. They cried, they cussed, they prayed, they had desires. Just like myself... I'd look at a black person walkin' down the street, and the guy'd have ragged shoes or his clothes would be worn. That began to do somethin' to me inside.[77]

Ellis and Atwater became close friends, and Ellis became a dedicated civil rights activist and a labor organizer. The communication between Ellis and Atwater, thus, allowed them to create new realizations together that they shared many of the same struggles and hopes, and is illustrative of the potential for communication to provide liberatory, transformative experiences for people, allowing them to transcend their previously "fixed" understandings of reality and their acceptance of ideas as "given" truths.

ဆ Extended Example of Identification in Advertising ര

To conclude our discussion of identification in this chapter, I want to analyze briefly an extended example of identification as it is clearly utilized in a multi-paged advertisement. As we will see in this ad, the advertiser tries to "normalize" her or his product by placing it squarely within the identifications that situate our lives.

This eight-page ad for General Motors (GM) begins with a picture of a little baby in diapers, sitting in the grass with three apple scattered around him from the tree whose shadow is cast against the baby and the grass. The baby's mouth is agape and he is looking straight at the camera, one hand on his check, looking somewhat perplexed. We have arrived in the world and into the comforting arms of GM

On the facing page are some progressively older toddlers and we are told that, as young children, we are soothed by the gentle rolling of the tires and the soft hum of the engine. Who cannot relate to this? All of us grew up as infants driven around in the backseats of an automobile. The dominant photograph on this page is the arch of a bridge as seen from somebody sitting low in the backset through the side or back window. Text on the bottom of the page informs us that GM vehicles have special seats designed to protect small children from harm in the case of an accident.

On the next page, this same child has now metamorphosed into a sixteen-year-old boy who is triumphantly holding his driver's license. Again, most of us can relate to this cultural rite-of-passage. We are told that, at this age, we want fast cars, plenty of gas, and freedom from the prying eyes of our parents. However, we also need good brakes and other safety features to help keep us alive in the case of a wreck, which the ad reminds us comes with the GM vehicle. As parents, we would be foolish to not ensure our child has the safest car possible.

Turning the page in this ad, we find that we have now reached young adulthood. The dominant figure is of a young woman who appears to be someone in the middle of her college experience. At the top of the page is a photo of a highway sign announcing that an onramp is a few miles away, a not-so-subtle reminder of the busy lives we will soon lead. The implication in this scene is that our college years are the time to enjoy ourselves before we are burdened by responsibility, and that means driving places and exploring the world in a carefree fashion. The two accompanying smaller pictures on this page are of a neon blur that a passenger might see looking out the side window as a car speeds down the main drag on a Friday evening. The second picture, right next to it, is of the people in that very car—all young adults of both sexes. The box to the side of the narrative informs us that all GM vehicles offer 24-hour roadside assistance programs. We are not fully independent yet; help is there, if we need it.

Turning the page, we find out that the "freeway" suggested in the previous page is much closer than we thought. The top photograph is of a marriage. The bride and groom are greeted as they leave the church by the crowd of smiling, waving friends and relatives. The closest figure to us is a young girl, freckled and smiling. She is the only figure turned away from the wedding scene and is looking into the camera. This girl and her smile remind us that the distance between carefree adolescence/college and the responsibility of young adulthood is very short.

The bottom photograph is of a young couple shopping for houses in a developing suburb. We are told that it is time to settle down and have children. The next picture is of a father throwing his two-year-old son in the air; the kid is laughing with his hands outstretched. The accompanying narrative evokes an expectant mother who wonders how she can lead a normal life with a baby between her and the steering wheel. The ad goes on to tell us that there are more than two and a half million pregnant drivers in America and that GM is developing special crash dummies to learn how to protect such expectant mothers and their unborn children. We are left with the impression that GM cars are safer than other cars for pregnant mothers.

Turning to the seventh page of this ad, we find that we have progressed further down life's road. The picture is of a middle-aged woman, her figure not quite so youthful. Another picture is of a late-middle-aged couple leaving a fancy restaurant. As in the other images, there is a car pictured here, and the perspective is from a person sitting in the driver's seat looking out the side view mirror, monitoring the car behind her or him. We are told that we change, but that is okay. While our eyes get worse, our wisdom grows. We get cold easily and we do not like rock music, but we can still have a good time out on the road. The final page of the ad presents us with a blurred image of a car driving into the sunset on a long stretch of desert road.

Clearly, the above ad is an attempt by GM to normalize our relationship with automobiles. The automobile is positioned as a natural, healthy extension of the human life cycle. To do this, GM individualizes our experience with its product. Every stage of our idealized life is situated vis-à-vis the GM product.

❧ Conclusion ❧

Students are often afraid of theory. To them, theory seems obtuse or impenetrable, disconnected from the things that we do every day. This reticence to engage theory is unfortunate, as an understanding of persuasion theory is important for communication students, and for consumers of the mass media. Learning specific persuasive tactics, as important as those are, is not enough. Rather, we have to begin to understand *why* those tactics work. Toward this end, a study of contemporary theories of persuasion helps illustrate the psychological predispositions of people that make them susceptible to manipulation. In this chapter, we have discussed some of the more important contemporary theories of persuasion that lie behind the construction of many of the ads and appeals that we see every day. As such, the chapter has emphasized that an awareness of these theories, of what they assume and how they work, is an important step in the creation of a critical consciousness.

ɞ Notes ɕ

1. *Laisser–Faire* is a philosophical perspective that deemphasizes government oversight, regulation, or interference with an individual choice in the marketplace. It means "hands off" and, in practice, means that people are left to fend for themselves as best they can under whatever circumstances they are in. The corresponding term *caveat emptor* means "let the buyer beware" and denotes an ethic wherein buyers bear responsibility for the integrity of the products they consume.

2. Catharine A. MacKinnon, *Only Words* (Cambridge, MA: Harvard University Press, 1993), 26.

3. For a review of this program, see Mary John Smith, *Persuasion and Human Action* (Belmont, CA: Wadsworth, 1982), 213–240.

4. "Psychology as the Behaviorist Views It," reprinted in *Psychological Review, 101* (1994), 248.

5. Ibid., 253. Notice the reference to chemistry and physics. This is an example of what humanists call "scientism," the inappropriate application of the methods of natural science to the study of human beings.

6. For a critique of this theory, and a review of the literature concerning it, see Timothy E. Moore, "Subliminal Perception: Facts and Fallacies," *Skeptical Inquirer, 16* (1992), 273–281.

7. In Burkean terms, the stimulus-response theory is suspect because it reduces human "action" to the realm of "motion." For his important distinction between these two concepts, see Kenneth Burke, "(Nonsymbolic) Motion/(Symbolic) Action," *Critical Inquiry, 4*(1978), 809–838.

8. *Subliminal Seduction* (New York: Signet, 1974); *The Clam Plate Orgy* (New York: Signet, 1981); and *The Age of Manipulation: The Con in Confidence, The Sin in Sincere* (New York: Henry Holt: Madison Books, 1989).

9. August Bullock, *The Secret Sales Pitch: An Overview of Subliminal Advertising* (San Jose, CA: Norwich Publishers, 2004).

10. Lawsuits by plaintiffs who claim to have been hurt due to subliminal messages in both music and film have generally lost—for example, *McCollum v. CBS Inc.*, 249 *Cal. Rpter* 187 (1988) against Ozzy Osbourne for the song "Suicide Solution"—although director Oliver

Stone came close to liability in such a suit after his film *Natural Born Killers* (1994) was reputed to have inspired many copycat murders. Stone, himself, admitted (with hyperbole no doubt) that he hoped that the movie would inspire people to go out and kill people.

11. The technique is discussed in Hilke Plassmann, Tim Ambler, Sven Braeutigam, and Peter Kenning, "What Can Advertisers Learn From Neuroscience?" *International Journal of Advertising, 26* (2007), 154–157.

12. Douglas L. Fugate, "Neuromarketing: A Layman's Look at Neuroscience and its Potential Application to Marketing Practice," *Journal of Consumer Marketing, 24* (2007), 385–394.

13. See Brian D. Till, Sarah M. Stanley, and Randi Priluck, "Classical Conditioning and Celebrity Endorsers: An Examination of Belongingness and Resistance to Extinction," *Psychology & Marketing, 25* (2008), 179–196.

14. For example, Till, Stanley, and Priluck report that an estimated billion or more dollars was paid to celebrity endorsers in 2005.

15. Robert H. Ruxin, *An Athlete's Guide to Agents* 4th ed. (Sudbury, MA: Jones and Bartlett Publishers, 2003), 29.

16. Nike, for example, spent nearly 1 and ½ billion dollars on celebrity endorsers—such as Tiger Woods and Michael Jordan—in 2003. Diana Seno and Bryan A. Lukas, "The Equity Effect of Product Endorsement By Celebrities," *European   Journal of Marketing, 41* (2007), 121.

17. Magic Johnson (his real first name is Earvin) was diagnosed in 1991 as having HIV, the virus that leads to the AIDS disease. While there was initial hostility toward him by some NBA players, he escaped, for the most part, the stigma of the disease and has been an out spoken advocate for AIDS research. The fact that Johnson, worth many tens of millions of dollars, can survive more than 30 years with HIV offers hope for treating AIDS as a chronic manageable disease. On the other hand, Magic Johnson *also* exemplifies that vast moral gulf between the wealthy and the poor with regard to access to life-extending AIDS medicine.

18. Brian D. Till and Terence A. Shimp, "Endorsers in Advertising: The Case of Negative Celebrity Information," *Journal of Advertising, 27* (1998), 67–82.

19. To their shame, many endorsers allow themselves to be silenced by their sponsors. For instance, when asked why he did not take a public stance against the race-baiting tactics of his home state Senator, North Carolina Republican Jesse Helms, as Helms successfully fought off African-American challenger Harvey Gantt for reelection, basketball superstar Michael Jordan replied that "Republicans buy sneakers, too." Jordan has since expressed

regret at his actions. After Helms died in July 2008, Jordan said "What I said was true—Republicans buy sneakers. And usually full retail. But I've since realized that there are more important things than money, or market share or the Jordan brand." "Jesse Helms' Death Prompts Michael Jordan to Issue Belated Endorsement of Harvey Gantt," *The Sportsman Daily* (July 4, 2008), retrieved from http://www.236.com/blog/w/the_sportsmans_daily/jesse_helms_death_prompts_mich_7535.php.

20. B. Zafer Erdogan and Tanya Drollinger, "Death and Disgrace Insurance for Celebrity Endorsers: A Luxury or Necessity?" *Journal of Current Issues and Research in Advertising, 30* (2008), 72.

21. David Sweet, "Clemens Can Kiss Endorsements Goodbye," *MSNBC.com* (December 26, 2007), located at http://www.msnbc.msn.com/id/22398390/.

22. Ibid.

23. Bryan Gibson and John Maurer, "Cigarette Smoking in the Movies: The Influence of Product Placement on Attitudes Toward Smoking and Smokers," *Journal of Applied Social Psychology*, 30 (2000), 1457–1473; Annemarie Charlesworth and Stanton A. Glantz, "Smoking in the Movies Increases Adolescent Smoking: A Review," *Pediatrics,* 116 (2005), 1516–1528.

24. Curt Mekemson**,** Stanton A. Glantz, "How the Tobacco Industry Built its Relationship With Hollywood," *Tobacco Control, 11* (2002), 81–91

25. A photocopy of Stallone's agreement can be found in Stanton A. Glantz, John Slade, Lisa A. Bero, Peter Hanauer, and Deborah E. Barnes, eds., *The Cigarette Papers* (Berkeley: University of California Press, 1996), 366.

26. As exemplified by the earlier Watson quote, *behaviorism* is the school of psychology that maintains human behaviors can be described scientifically and without recourse to internal physiological events. *Cognitivism*, on the other hand, is the school of psychology that maintains that internal mental functions can be studied and understood.

27. 2nd ed. (New York: Harper & Row, 1970).

28. Ibid., 24.

29. *Telos* is an Aristotelian notion in which all objects are created or born with a predetermined end. This is not determinism in a crass philosophical or religious sense, but in a biological or existential one. Take the seed of a rose plant, for example. Implicit in the seed is the beautiful flower that people have come to love. The *entelechy* of the seed or plant, its potential and its goal, is to produce the flower. Many philosophers and theologians stipulate

a particular *telos* for human beings. The ones that I find most believable are those that see human freedom and creativity as being the ultimate embodiment of our humanity.

30. *Varieties of the Religious Experience: A Study in Human Nature* (Middlesex, England: Penguin Books, 1982).

31. Matthew J. Hertenstein, Julie M. Verkamp, Alyssa M. Kerestes, Rachel M. Holmes, "The Communicative Functions of Touch in Humans, Nonhuman Primates, and Rats: A Review and Synthesis of the Empirical Research," *Genetic, Social, and General Psychology Monographs, 132* (2006), 5–94.

32. *Permanence and Change* (Berkeley, CA: University of California Press, 1984), 76.

33. *The Psychology of Interpersonal Relations* (New York: Wiley, 1959).

34. For a discussion of a related perspective, "uncertainty reduction theory," see Charles R. Berger and James J. Bradac, *Language and Social Knowledge: Uncertainty in Interpersonal Relations* (London: Arnold, 1982).

35. I have once experienced this state of undiluted fear—the result of an unwelcomed surprise—at the primordial-animalist level that helps illustrate this point. I had graduated from high school and was living with my grandmother, waiting to start college. I was asleep one night alone on the couch in my grandmother's living room. I heard the door open where there should not have been a door and heard/felt someone (not my grandmother) walk across the room. Every muscle in my body tensed and I experienced the heightened sense of adrenalin associated with the "flight or fight" response. My fear then morphed into terror as I felt the sheets lift from the bed and somebody climb in beside me. The terror then exploded into something even more extreme as I felt a hand touch my shoulder. At this point, I ceased, in my mind, being recognizably human. It felt like the hair on my body was standing on end, I felt my hands seize up like I had claws, and my teeth were bared like a wolf. I felt like a wolf. Snarling, I leaped over to attack the intruder, intending to rip her/him to shreds with my hands and teeth, only to smack hard against the back of the couch. I was alone. My grandmother slept soundly two rooms away. The entire experience had been some kind of weird dream. Besides feeling a little foolish, I was left with, and still retain, a sense of awe at the connection I felt toward my base animality. In a strange sense, I was never so fully alive as in that moment.

36. In Chapter 7, we will discuss how corporations donate large sums of money to popular causes as an apologetic tactic—an effort to improve their image with the public. The U.S. government does this also, using international aid as a way of expanding its influence around the world.

37. This is an award-winning 2000 film, produced by Margaret Lazarus and Renner Wunderlich and distributed by Cambridge Documentary Films.

38. Richard L. Miller, Philip Brickman, and Diana Bolen, "Attribution Versus Persuasion as a Means for Modifying Behaviour," *Journal of Personality and Social Psychology, 31* (19–75), 430–441.

39. Ibid, 438.

40. Fritz Heider, *The Psychology of Interpersonal Relations* (New York: John Wiley & Sons, 1958).

41. *Beliefs, Attitudes, and Values: A Theory of Organization and Change* (San Francisco: Jossey-Bass, 1969).

42. *A Theory of Cognitive Dissonance* (Palo Alto, CA: Stanford University Press, 1957).

43. Leon Festinger and James M. Carlsmith, "Cognitive Consequences of Forced Compliance," *Journal of Abnormal and Social Psychology, 58* (1959), 203–210. Festinger and Carlsmith document that inducing a person to say something contrary to her or his private opinion will encourage attitude change. They note, however, that the greater the outside pressure, the less likely the attitude change. In their study, subjects were subjected to boring tasks and paid to lie about it. The greater the material reward, the less subjects experienced attitude change as the more they interpreted their actions as being caused by the external reward as opposed to being an uncomfortable intrapersonal conflict.

44. For a historical/rhetorical discussion of Chávez and the UFW, see John C. Hammerback and Richard J. Jensen, *The Rhetorical Career of César Chávez* (College Station, TX: Texas A&M University Press, 1998).

45. And yet, some remain without feeling. When I was at Purdue University, located in rural Indiana and surrounded by farming communities, I had a student write a paper in which he identified as being from a farming family. He had watched the UFW film and argued that the migrant workers were "animals" and deserved what they got.

46. Narcissism is psychological condition in which someone is so self-centered, they are unable to conceptualize or recognize the needs of others.

47. Fear appeals will be discussed in Chapter 8.

48. *On Rhetoric: A Theory of Civic Discourse*, trans. George A. Kennedy (New York: Oxford University Press, 1991), 30.

49. *Rhetoric in an Organizational Society: Managing Multiple Identities* (Columbia: University of South Carolina Press, 1991), 8.

50. The quote can be found at: http://improbable.com/2006/11/11/experiment-baby/.

51. *A Theory of Psychological Reactance* (New York: Academic Press, 1966).

52. Michael Burgoon, Eusebio Alvaro, Joseph Grandpre, and Michael Voulodakis, "Revisiting the Theory of Psychological Reactance," in James Price Dillard and Michael Pfau, eds., *The Persuasion Handbook: Developments in Theory and Practice* (Thousand Oaks, CA: Sage, 2002), 216.

53. Reactance becomes particularly salient when a subject is *ordered* to do or not do something. In one study, two signs were placed on a college bathroom walls. The first read: "Do *not* write on these walls under any circumstances." The other: "*Please* do not write on these walls." The sign that can be perceived as an order or command elicited the most graffiti. James W. Pennebaker and Debra Y. Sanders, "American Graffiti: Effects of Authority and Reactance Arousal," *Personality and Social Psychology Bulletin*," 2 (1976), 264–267.

54. Stephen Worchel and Susan E. Arnold, "The Effects of Censorship and Attractiveness of the Censor on Attitude Change," *Journal of Experimental Social Psychology*, 9 (1973), 227–239; and Stephen Worchel, Susan E. Arnold, and Michael Baker, "The Effect of Censorship on Attitude Change: The Influence of Censor and Communication Characteristics," *Journal of Applied Social Psychology*, 5 (1975), 227-239.

55. Donna J. Bergenstock and James M. Maskulka, "The De Beers Story: Are Diamonds Forever?" *Business Horizons* (May-June, 2001), 37–44.

56. "From Military Engagements to Engagement Rings: Tracing The Path of Conflict Diamonds," on-line lecture retrieved from http://www.pbs.org/newshour/extra/teachers/lesson plans/world/From%20Military%20Engagements%20to%20Engagement%20Rings.ppt

57. Philip Kotler, Marketing Management: *Analyis, Planning, Implementation, and Control* 6th ed. Revised (Englewood Cliffs, NJ: Prentice-Hall, 1988, 510).

58. Reported by Eric Asimov, "Wine's Pleasures: Are They All in Your Head?" *New York Times* (May 7, 2008, ¶10), retrieved from http://www.nytimes.com/2008/05/07/dining/07pour.html

59. Elliot Aronson and Judson Mills, "Effects of Severity of Initiation on Liking for a Group," *Journal of Abnormal Social Psychology*, 59 (1959), 177–181.

60. A good exegesis of this theory can be found in Gary C. Woodward, *The Idea of Identification* (Albany: State University of New York Press, 2003).

61. "The Rhetorical Situation," in Lee Thayer, ed., *Communication: Ethical and Moral Issues* (New York: Gordon and Breach Science Publishers, 1973), 267.

62. *Visual Persuasion: The Role of Images in Advertising* (Thousand Oaks, CA: Sage, 1997), 44.

63. "Rhetoric—Old and New," *Journal of General Education*, 5 (1951), 203.

64. *Rhetoric of Motives*, xiii.

65. Ibid., 28.

66. *Dramatism and Development* (Barre, MA: Clark University Press), 28.

67. *Rhetoric of Motives*, 21.

68. "The Rhetorical Situation," 271.

69. When the president of the United States addresses the American people as "my fellow Americans," or when a general tells her/his troops that "we have got to take   that hill," an explicit relationship is being constructed by the speaker. The same thing happens when a politician kisses a baby or wraps herself or himself in the American flag. The purpose of each appeal is to involve the audience emotionally in the moral argument or position that the persuader is offering.

70. "The Rhetorical Situation," 272.

71. I had an argument with a co-worker a few years into the war about the need to "support our troops" in Iraq. She told me that they were "dying for me." No, I replied; they are dying, for sure, more than 4,329 as I write this in July 2009 with tens of thousands wounded, but they are dying and being crippled for a multitude of *other* reasons that have nothing to do with me, my "freedoms," or my security. This is not to say that I do not want the troops to come home safely; I do. "Support The Troops" means bringing them back to the United States, and perhaps giving them the opportunity to go to college and take courses such as this one.

72. "The Rhetorical Situation," 270.

73. Ibid., 268.

74. *The Philosophy of Literary Form* (Berkeley, CA: University of California Press, 1967), 219.

75. Studs Terkel, *American Dreams: Lost and Found* (New York: Pantheon Books, 1980).

76. Ibid. 201–203.

77. Ibid., 205.

CHAPTER 7

The Persuader

My son and I are comic strip junkies. We collect and read as many different comic strips as we can. In addition to being a resource for mirth and enjoyment, much wisdom can be found in this art form. There is often a universality or transcendence in these strips as the characters struggle with issues of identity, morality, and imagination. One particularly enjoyable comic strip is *Calvin and Hobbes* by Bill Watterson. Most students in this class are familiar with the basic storyline. Calvin is a young boy with a large ego who has created an imaginary friend in his stuffed tiger named Hobbes. The two roam their universe in an effort to master adult problems and situations. This is, of course, impossible for such a young child, but Calvin's struggle opens up for the rest of us glimpses of how a life examined can, indeed, be a life worth living. The genius, I think, of cultural artifacts such as *Calvin and Hobbes* is to remind us, on a daily basis, that we are not as wise, smart, or secure as we think. We always have room to grow.

In one *Calvin and Hobbes* cartoon, Calvin, the child with the prodigious imagination, runs enthusiastically up to Hobbes with a small object in his hand. He cries out with great excitement that he has a box that a bar of soap came in. Putting down the small hand soap box, Calvin stands on it as if it were a real box—or a tree stump, in the American tradition—one that allows him to tower over the heads of his listeners and be heard. With great optimism and a little bit of pride, Calvin declares that, according to tradition, if you want to pontificate to the masses, you need to stand on a soap box. In his face we can see that the young Calvin is clearly looking forward to offering a good pontification. Like the rest of us, Calvin struggles to have an influence on the world around him.

In the final frame of this example, Calvin grows disappointed. He is clearly *not* towering over anyone. His hope and elaborate posturing have returned no fruit. Besides Hobbes, Calvin has no audience. In fact, Calvin simply appears to be a little boy with an inflated self-image standing on a pathetic and smashed paper box. With his classical oratorical gesture, Calvin has failed to gain any audience or to increase his own stature or influence. The world has taken no notice of him. Perhaps these things take time.

What Calvin fails to realize is that persuasion is not just about standing up in front of a group of people and "haranguing" them. Calvin clearly wants to be a persuader—more specifically he wants to have power *over* people. However, Calvin is unaware of what exactly that entails. He wants to carry forth to the "masses" because that is what he thinks a person is supposed to do when she/he has command of a forum. In creating this cartoon, Bill Watterson evokes part of our rhetorical past. In both the American and the British cultural traditions, the popular speaker or orator would stand on a soap box or tree stump and command a rhetorical and often a political situation. This image goes back, in Western culture, all the way to Demosthenes and to the Greek rhetor system in Athenian legal and judicial practice.[1]

What Calvin has not taken the time to appreciate, understandably for a five year old, is that being a persuader involves a multitude of variables and sensibilities—including his own motivations—and he would undoubtedly benefit from a textbook and course such as ours. To be an effective persuader involves much more than simply having access to a podium, although having access to a "podium" is essential in this age of the consolidated and privatized mass media. In fact, one First Amendment theory is known as "access theory." The idea is that under the U.S. Constitution, people have, or should have, a right of access to the mass media, particularly as the media have become more concentrated in the hands of conglomerates and wealthy broadcasters and pub-lishers, excluding the vast majority of us.[2] Without an opportunity for our voices to be at least somewhat audible in the din of a crowded marketplace dominated with established and well-financed corporate speakers, how do we fulfill our democratic obligations to speak our minds on behalf of the public good?

No matter what his motivation, we should not besmirch Calvin for his single-minded quest for a podium, since podiums are at a premium these days. Personally, I wish him well, as Calvin's tyrannical impulses will, over time, likely temper into practical cosmopolitan problem-solving skills. We have much to learn from his optimism, energy, and creativity. I would, however, caution Calvin, and point out to him that some of the communication variables that Calvin has to learn, particularly those concerning speaker credibility, or *ethos*, which are the subject of this chapter. Specifically, in this chapter we will study what we mean by *ethos* (or source credibility), the places where the resources of credibility can be found, ways persuaders try to control credibility, specific principles of credibility gleaned from the social scientific study of persuasion, and ways to enhance credibility when a source comes under attack—prominent here will be the apologetic tactics.

℘ *Ethos* (or Source Credibility) ℜ

The concept of *ethos* was first codified by Aristotle in circa 326 BCE in his book on rhetoric.[3] In his book, Aristotle outlines a three-fold conceptualization of rhetoric—what he characterizes as the *artful* use of persuasion. Artful persuasion is distinguished by Aristotle from things like torture and bribery, both of which may "persuade," but neither of which, properly speaking, extends from the intellectual *skill* of the persuader; these are known as *inartistic* persuasion. The three dimensions of persuasion, according to Aristotle, are the perceived credibility of the source in the minds of the audience (*ethos*), the emotional appeals that move an audience (*pathos*, see Chapter 7), and the logical appeals, or the use of reasoning and logic to convince an audience (*logos*). For Aristotle, rhetorical persuasion occurs through logical demonstration or through an emotional appeal. However, and this is what is most important to understand, the extent to which either appeal is successful is dependent upon the speaker's credibility, upon how well the speaker *appears* to be believable and trustworthy. Because of this, *ethos* may be considered the most important of the three major proofs in rhetorical persuasion. This is certainly Aristotle's position:

> [There is persuasion] through character wherever the speech is spoken in such a way as to make the speaker worthy of credence; for we believe fair-minded people to a greater extent and more quickly [than we do others] on all subjects in general and completely so in cases where there is not exact knowledge but room for doubt. And this should result from the speech, not from a previous opinion that the speaker is a certain kind of person, for it is not the case, as some of the technical writers propose in their treatment of the art, that fair-mindedness on the part

of the speaker makes no contribution to persuasiveness, rather, character is almost, so to speak, the controlling factor in persuasion.[4]

Credibility involves the *judgment* that we make of a speaker by com-
paring all that the speaker is, in our view, with everything that we are, or think
that we are.[5] In other words, our understanding of another's *ethos* is extremely
subjective. This is why perception is so important when we talk about persuasion. In dealing with persuasion, we are dealing with *negotiated* relationships,
and what is being negotiated are our perceptions of ourselves and of others.

What this means is that *ethos* is primarily an interpretation of a relationship and interaction that occur between a speaker and an audience. This
interpretation takes place at two different levels. The first level involves the
mode of influence that extends from the internal virtues of the persuader (i.e.,
who the persuader *is* and what the persuader *represents*). This level of *ethos*
extends from Platonic rhetorical theory, particularly as reiterated by St.
Augustine and the Christian rhetorical tradition. Such a view sees internal virtue as a prerequisite for persuasion, as well as for an understanding of Truth. In
Plato's sense of *ethos*, articulated most clearly in his *Gorgias*, internal virtue
corresponds to a persuader's proximity to the ontological conditions of Truth:
the closer the persuader is to the Truth, the greater is her or his understanding,
the more convincing is her/his exposition, and the more she/he can claim moral
leadership and responsibility.[6]

A similar position was held by St. Augustine. For him, piety was more
important than anything else in a persuasive context. Augustine believed that
the example set by the preacher was more important than the beauty of her or
his words. While words and style were certainly relevant, one's ability to use
them to persuade was limited by the extent to which she/he appeared pious to
her or his Christian audience. In demonstrating piety, a speaker could demon-
strate that she or he had something important to say, particularly as far as sav-
ing souls was concerned, and could only then use the appropriate language or
choose from the three types of classical style (i.e., grand, middle, and plain) to
instruct or to move an audience. In other words, one assumed a degree of
credibility by showing how well one adapted to the Christian norms of her/his
audience. As Augustine explains:

> For one who wishes to speak wisely, therefore, even though he cannot
> speak eloquently, it is above all necessary to remember the words of

Scripture. The poorer he sees himself to be in his own speech, the more he should make use of Scripture so that what he says in his own words he may support with the words of Scripture. In this way he who is inferior in his own words may grow in a certain sense through the testimony of the great.[7]

The upshot of both Plato's and Augustine's notions of credibility is that communication must be, above all else, *clear*—the purpose of credibility is to put the Truth into sharp relief. Thus, Augustine counsels, "The speaker should not consider the eloquence of his teaching but the clarity of it."[8] The second way in which *ethos* has been characterized historically is as a mode of persuasion that the speaker uses by creating a character in relationship to a specific historical context. This comes out of Aristotle's conceptualization, and is well reflected in the earlier quote by him.

Under Aristotle's conception, we get a sense of the contingency of rhetoric, and of the volatility and fragility of *ethos*. Because *ethos* is based upon contingences such as the inner perception of the receiver and the strategy of the persuader, audience interpretations are constantly changing. *Ethos* is dynamic in the sense that a speaker makes choices about what to say and what images to present, and these choices have to be made in the process of the presentation itself—it is part of the dialogic nature of persuasion. While Plato and Augustine, and the communication traditions that reflect their schools of thought (namely those found in science and in religion), reject this view of credibility, and while they tend to see credibility as static, something a person has or does not have, existing in relationship to some external standard or foundation of Truth, it is very difficult to find objective standards for credibility in the actual messy world of human affairs.

❧ Sources of Credibility ☙

The credibility of a speaker comes from many places, and not just from what the person says. In general, the wellspring of credibility is located in what the persuader is conceived of being by her/his audience. *Ethos* comes from a communicator's lifestyle—from the tone of her/his talk and from the idiosyncrasies of her/his gestures. In many respects, credibility is who we are. Our messages, our policies, our ideas, cannot be separated from us, the subjectivities that utter them, and, in uttering them, grant them significance and substance. Identification, as we discussed in the previous chapter, also has an important role to play. The more we see others as we see ourselves, and the better we think of ourselves, the more we are going to interpret others as being credible.

In the classical literatures, the dimensions of credibility were defined by Aristotle and Cicero. In the following, for example, Aristotle describes what he considers to be the dimensions of credibility in a speaker or source:

> There are three reasons why speakers themselves are persuasive; for there are three things we trust other than logical demonstration. These are *practical wisdom* and *virtue* and *good will*; for speakers make mistakes in what they say or advise through [failure to exhibit] either all or one of these; for either through lack of practical sense they do not form opinions rightly; or through forming opinions rightly they do not say what they think because of a bad character; or they are prudent and fairminded but lack good will, so that it is possible for people not to give the best advice although they know [what] it [is].[9]

Aristotle also writes:

> But since rhetoric is concerned with making a judgment (people judge what is said in deliberation, and judicial proceedings are also a judgment), it is necessary not only to look to the argument, that it may be demonstrative and persuasive but also [for the speaker] to construct a view of himself as a certain kind of person and to prepare the judge; for it makes much difference in regard to persuasion (especially in deliberations but also in trials) that the speaker seem to be a certain kind of person and that his hearers suppose him to be disposed toward them in a certain way.[10]

Cicero wrote that in order for an orator to be credible, she or he must have a virtually universal knowledge as well as skill. As he explains:

> In my opinion, indeed, no man can be an orator possessed of every praise worthy accomplishment, unless he has attained the knowledge of every thing important, and of all liberal arts, for his language must be ornate and copious from knowledge, since, unless there be beneath the

surface matter understood and felt by the speaker, oratory becomes an empty and almost puerile flow of words.[11]

Later in the same dialogue, Cicero writes, "I, indeed, shall never deny that there are some sciences peculiarly well understood by those who have applied their whole study to the knowledge and consideration of them; but the accomplished and complete orator I shall call him who can speak on all subjects with variety and copiousness."[12] The ideal orator is contrasted by Cicero with those who are "nothing but a set of mechanics with glib and well-practiced tongues."[13]

Modern theorists have isolated three general areas of speaker credibility. The first area involves an audience's perception of a speaker's *competence* and *authoritativeness*. This includes perceptions of intelligence, confidence, poise, knowledge, reasoning, judgment, and mental alertness. What we call "authority" is fundamentally an interpretation, a judgment we make based on our assessment of a person's ability to lead or otherwise pass judgment in some fashion. In the words of rhetorical scholar Gerard A. Hauser:

> We trust people who speak with integrity, who show themselves to make virtuous decisions, and who inspire confidence that they know what is right and have the courage of their convictions. We trust these people to be truthful with us and to offer advice that will not bring us to shame or unjustly harm others.[14]

The second dimension of speaker competence to which audiences are sensitive involves issues of *trustworthiness* and *safety*. This includes such characteristics as honesty, sincerity, reliability, fairness, justness, loyalty, ethics, restraint, even-temperedness, maturity, rationality, democratic values, sensitivity, and sympathy. As Hauser writes, "These virtues should be present in the way the rhetor argues a cause. In other words, virtue is not demonstrated by arguing that we are morally upright. It is demonstrated by arguing in a morally responsible way."[15]

The internalized "correct" action, or moral habit, that Hauser mentions above is a sentiment that originates in Aristotle's discussion of the term. George A. Kennedy, translator of what is widely recognized to be the best English translation of Aristotle's *Rhetoric*, writes, "The predominant meaning of *ethos* in Aristotle is "moral character" as reflected in deliberate choice of actions and as developed into a habit of mind."[16]

The third dimension of perceived competence involves the element of *dynamism*. The persuader in this case must come across as being forceful, decisive, energetic, vigorous, active, enterprising, industrious, and creative. Rightly or wrongly, such physical strength is often interpreted as outward manifestation of inner moral strength. It is no accident that the American public is inundated by pictures of their politicians jogging, cutting wood, windsurfing, commanding speed boats, and appearing in other vigorous poses.

Consider how perceptions influence our ideas of a person. Imagine a series of photographs in which the same man appears, but in each photograph there is a progressive change in his appearance. Without knowing anything else about him, we react to his image. In the first photograph, the man has long hair and a thick beard. In the next picture, the same man appears, but with his hair cut and his beard neatly trimmed. Then we see the man presented in an even neater fashion. The beard is gone; the hair appears in a crew-cut style.

What does each picture evoke in us? What change in each picture corresponds to which changes in our perceptions? Or, to make this exercise more concrete, imagine a series of faces taken from all walks of life. Maybe these faces belong to people we saw today as we were walking to class or taking care of our lives outside of campus. What do we feel when we see these people on the street? What sorts of people evoke what sorts of reactions in us? Why do we feel like we do when we encounter people we have never before met? What happens after we meet them, talk to them, and get to know them? What changes? Thinking about our responses to these questions, we will get some clue as to how our perceptions of a person's credibility fundamentally position us vis-à-vis that person.

As we learned from our discussion of Aristotle, or at least from the Aristotelian tradition, *ethos* exists in a negotiated relationship between an audience and a speaker at the time of the speaker's appeal. But what happens *prior* to the appeal and *after* the appeal are also of crucial importance. These events involve associations, prior reputation, endorsements, previous behaviors, and the introduction of the speaker by a host or other welcoming agents. Sometimes the persuader can control these elements, and sometimes the persuader cannot control these elements. Below we will explore some examples of each instance.

❧ Controlling Credibility Prior, During, and After the Message ❧

All persuaders must be sensitive to the need for controlling credibility prior, during, and after the message. Sometimes this is something that can be done easily, and at other times persuaders must react to how others position them. At no time, however, can a persuader deceive her/himself into thinking that image management is unimportant—without careful attention placed here, a person's message, no matter how valuable, is vulnerable to attack or even diminution over time. The "sleeper effect," for example, is the tendency for highly credible sources or messages to lose credibility as a result of the passing of time and low-credibility sources or messages to gain credibility over time.[17]

Credibility Prior to the Message

Associations, prior reputation, endorsements, previous behavior, introductions and the like serve as the backdrop upon which a person speaks. As mentioned above, politicians need to convey that they are dynamic, energetic people. Even Ronald Reagan, who was physically too old to jog, would be photographed cutting wood, clad in a cowboy uniform. Other presidents, such as Carter, Bush, and Clinton, and George W. Bush were able to jog, although Carter and the elder Bush both compromised their image by collapsing, in public, during mid-stride. In each case, the president (and in some cases, the vice-president—Al Gore, for example) makes a public display of his physical fitness so that the press can take and circulate photographs of him looking fit and energetic. This manipulation is wholly controlled by the persuader and has become part of the style and media spin that surround the American presidency.

The president's agents make sure that every picture that circulates is one that positions the president in favorable ways. Granted, this is getting more difficult to control now, and unwanted images do circulate. As a practical matter, years ago presidential handlers had a much easier time hiding from the public images of the president that would hurt his ability to appear charismatic. Noteworthy, for example, is the fact that there are few photographs featuring President Franklin Delano Roosevelt (FDR) in a wheelchair or on crutches. Most Americans at the time that FDR was in office did not realize that he was disabled.[18] In each publically circulated photograph of President Roosevelt, he is sitting behind a desk, waving from a car, or propped up behind a podium. If someone from the public happened to be in a position to take an unauthorized photograph of the president in his wheelchair or on crutches, the film would be confiscated by secret service agents.[19]

A noteworthy example of how persuaders control and often manipulate the way their credibility is manifested prior to a particular engagement is that of George H. W. Bush at the 1992 Republican National Convention in Houston as he was running for reelection against Bill Clinton. That election was noteworthy for the videos that both candidates produced and presented to the audiences at their respective conventions and to the television-viewing population. Before we discuss the Bush video, however, a few words must be said about the more reserved Clinton video to help frame the aggressiveness of the Bush appeal.

The Clinton video—entitled "The Man From Hope"—was presented in a subdued, sublime style in which Clinton is positioned as the heir of the Kennedy legacy. This identification is made overt by film footage of the young Bill Clinton meeting and shaking President Kennedy's hand.[20] Besides this, however, the images, for the most part, are of Clinton's hometown and of his family and friends, and are colored by a collage of gentle reminiscence. We learn, for instance, that Clinton once stood up to his alcoholic stepfather when the stepfather struck Clinton's mother, and that he disagreed with the racial segregation of his home town.

The more striking video was Bush's aggressive appeal. This video, narrated by Robert Mitchum, whose patriotic voice is instantly recognizable and reassuring to many Americans, provides a collage of images spanning the last two hundred years of American history. We are told that "America needs" a number of traits in a leader which happen to read as Aristotelian *topoi* of credibility-evoking terms. According to Jon Hesk, "An Aristotelian *topos* can be a pattern of argument which one would expect to be able to deploy again and again in different contexts and in relationship to different political, forensic, or epideictic contexts."[21] *Topoi*, or topics, are otherwise known as "seats" of arguments. They are locations where ideas can be found—heuristic and inventional resources. *Topoi* are usually presented as lists of standardized concepts that cover the range of a subject and lead to further thought in a particular direction.[22] In the case of the Bush video, the *ethos*-creating *topoi* contributed to much of the good will that many Americans felt toward Bush.

Evoked in the film is the "integrity" and "character" of George Washington, an "honest man." The "fairness" of Thomas Jefferson is highlighted. We are told that Abraham Lincoln had the "courage" to preserve the Union and that Teddy Roosevelt had the "grit" to lead us into the glorious age of industrialization as America became a world power. From there, the narrative accentuates the "resolve" of FDR to face down tyrants, such as Adolf Hitler, whose ranting image appears on the screen. The "wisdom" of Dwight D. Eisenhower is held up to us, and we are told that the problems the president is faced with are "difficult" and only the best of men can excel at the job.

The film explains that the "imagination" of John F. Kennedy took America and human kind to the moon, and that the "determination" of Richard Nixon brought us peace with China after decades of hostility, war, and fear (Watergate is not mentioned). Finally, the film explains how the "leadership" of Ronald Reagan led to the collapse of communism. "The Cold War is over," declares Mitchum as we are shown images of cheering crowds toppling a statue of Vladimir Lenin (the founder of the Soviet Union), and because of America's efforts, "more of the world enjoys the sweet taste of freedom."

After reminding us of these important traits (i.e., credibility *topoi*): "integrity," "fairness," "courage," "grit," "resolve," "wisdom," "imagination," "determination," and "leadership," the short film ends with George H. W. Bush swiftly climbing the steps of his plane as the narrative voice concludes that only one man can be trusted to assume the mantle of leadership: "George Bush, he is that man." This narrative does what the Clinton video does not do: it arouses the audience so that, by the time Bush walks out, literally from between the two television screens to deliver his nomination address, it is as if destiny has descended, personified, from the sky. Even critical viewers of the film and of the elder Bush himself find it easy to become swept away, overpowered by the tempo of the music and the images. Simply, the film is awe inspiring in the way that *Triumph of the Will* was mesmerizing to German audiences in 1935.

Students in any persuasion course ought to be at least aware of *Triumph of the Will*, as it is a paradigmatic persuasive document. I would go as far as to say that it is a remarkable film in the same manner in which the Bush film was intended to be remarkable; that is, politically expedient. Made by the famous Leni Riefenstahl, *Triumph of the Will* is widely considered to be among the best examples of cinematic propaganda ever produced.[23] It is a brilliant, path-breaking film that, unfortunately, had an utterly despicable subject— Adolf Hitler and the Nazi Party. Impassioned by the renaissance many perceived as taking place in Germany in the early years of the Nazi rule, Riefenstahl united history and philosophy and the longings of the German people for self-respect and prosperity after many years of deprivation and neglect. By combining aerial photography of Hitler descending from the clouds in his plane, Wagnerian music, iconographic architecture, and religious references, Riefenstahl succeeds, at least for the purposes of the film, to deify Hitler and to unite the German people and his leadership.

Sometimes, however, the persuader cannot control how her/his credibility is being manipulated by others. In such a case, a person's character becomes defined by an outside source—which can serve as a significant impediment to a person's persuasiveness. One notable example in recent years is the case of Dan Quayle, vice-president of the United States under the first George Bush. Quayle was lifted from his relative obscurity in the Senate by the then vice-president George Bush who was running for the presidency against Michael Dukakis.

Rightly or wrongly, Quayle was quickly positioned as the "state joke" by many political cartoonists and commentators who spent four years assaulting Quayle's credibility. To take only a few examples: during the first Gulf War, Quayle was portrayed as more concerned about playing golf than in following the progress of the war; he was portrayed as not knowing how the American Civil War ended; he was portrayed as being an unacceptable replacement for Bush in the event of Bush's death in office; and, in general, he was positioned as a buffoon. In most images in these political cartoons he is presented as a child or as child-like.

Quayle, however, had a law degree, had been a U.S. senator, and had been elected vice-president of the United States. Surely, he was not as inept as he was portrayed by his many detractors. He must have had some strengths and good qualities. Yet these hardly came across in the media. While Quayle had his supporters, and while he was photogenic as a person, the persona of his public image was that of a spoiled, privileged, and not altogether bright person. Quayle, for his part, did not help matters much, with his many erroneous, incomprehensible, and wanton admissions of cultural ignorance, as in thinking that the language spoken in Latin America was Latin, in his misspelling of the word "potato," and in his garbling of the slogan for the United Negro College Fund (UNCF).[24]

At one point, in Quayle's home state of Indiana, a local radio station played a song—a parody of the state's anthem "Back Home Again In Indiana"—on its "Bob and Tom" show, written by Tom Griswald and Ricky Ridel, that provoked controversy. The song, "I Spent The War in Indiana" by the "group" "Danny and the Quails," portrays a squeaky-voiced Danny, clearly an adolescent, who opens the song by saying, "Hi, my name is Danny, and this is my band, uh, 'Danny and the Quails.' We had to pull some strings to get this recording contract but we did and this, ah, this is our first song. Ah, Thanks Dad." The song lampoons Quayle's avoidance of active military duty in the Vietnam War, made possible by his wealthy father's influence. Quayle was reassigned to the National Guard, what the song identified as a "summer camp platoon."

What could Dan Quayle have done in response to this or to any of the frequent attacks on his character? It was clear to him that he had an image problem. But how do we respond to attacks such as this? Do we deny them? Do we refute them? Anything that Quayle could have done would just have made matters worse. Thus, Quayle tended to ignore these assaults on his character, but such assaults hurt him politically. After leaving office, and a lackluster run for the Republican presidential nomination, he has all but disappeared from public life.

Credibility During the Message

Important here are things such as topic selection, lines of argument, language, evidence, identification, delivery, dress and physical appearance, and attitude.[25] Does the speaker express care and concern for the audience? We have all seen speakers who were present in body but not in mind, who expressed indifference or worse to the audience.

Credibility After the Message

Almost as important as the message itself is the *interpretation* and *reporting* of the message, fulfillment of promises, alteration of audience behavior, and endorsements. Perhaps the best example of this is Abraham Lincoln's famous Gettysburg oration. At the time of his death, Lincoln was not a respected figure and his presence at the memorial service for the Union and Confederate dead was not particularly desired. We forget today that the main speaker at the Gettysburg memorial service was not Lincoln, but a man named Edward Everett, a famous orator and president of Harvard University. The press at the time reported on Everett's 2-hour, 13,607-word address and largely ignored Lincoln's. Around this time, the first transatlantic telegraph cables were laid and copies of American papers were sent to England. It was the British who first recognized the importance of the speech and wrote about it in their papers. Not until the English papers were sent back to the United States did people in this country become aware of the historic significance and artistic excellence of President Lincoln's remarks. Even then, it was not until the 1880s, when the North and South were attempting reconciliation, that Lincoln's speech assumed the national renown that it now represents.[26]

❧ What We Know About Credibility ☙

One of the most important things we know about credibility is that we tend to trust people who are similar to us and who share our beliefs, attitudes, and values.[27] If the persuader shares certain beliefs, attitudes, and values with us as members of an audience, there is a good chance that we may come to exaggerate the similarities and assume that the persuader shares all of them. Conversely, if the persuader does not share certain beliefs, attitudes, and behaviors, we may judge the persuader as being different from us. As a result, unscrupulous persuaders will often try to create the image or appearance of similarity in order to cultivate in us a sincere feeling of identification. The more the persuader appears to be like us in appearance and in surface attitudes, the more likely we are to over-attribute similarity, and, indeed, affinity.[28] The more that the persuader is, in fact, different from us, or is advocating ideas that, in the end, will hurt us, the more that persuader has to appear to be like us. In its extreme form, these are the tactics of the demagogue, a leader who gains and maintains power by appealing to popular prejudices in order to exploit those prejudices.

Another way of addressing what can be called the "problem of the demagogue" is that credibility should be *earned*, at least ideally, and some persuaders manage to avoid the arduous task of earning our respect by appealing to those apparently similar traits that evoke, psychologically, our respect and sense of unity. Such persuasion seldom comes to any good, because the persuader is manipulating the audience by creating a trust that is not grounded in any material or interpersonal commitment; in such a case, it is the words that get us excited and our imagination of what these words may mean or how they become exemplified in practice.

As suggested throughout this chapter and course, identification is clearly an important variable in determining a person's credibility. However, in some cases, we do not want our identifications to be *too* complete. *More* identification is not necessarily *better*, although a persuader always has to have *some*. Things that are too familiar often lose their mystique, and mystery is an important part of all relationships.[29]

For example, in some sense we want the people who persuade us to be different from us in important ways. In order for us to respect them they must be a bit wiser, braver, more knowledgeable, and more insightful. This is especially true when we turn to people for help and seek "expert" advise or testimony on "facts." If we could do the job ourselves, we would not need the assistance of these professionals. But what makes a professional a "professional" is the fact that she or he has some sort of training or skill and knowledge that the rest of us do not have. Acquiring these skills and knowledge usually requires that the person engage in certain lifestyle choices that separate her or himself from the rest of society, such as years of academic study and disciplinization. Thus, there is a relationship between knowledge and behavior and, by extension, between knowledge, morals, and motivation.

If the people we sought to help us were just like us, they would be just as lacking as we are in terms of the experience necessary to succeed in their jobs. Thus, when we go to visit the doctor we expect the doctor to look different than us, talk different than us, and, in effect, *be* different than us. In her or his personal life, a doctor may, in effect, engage in some of the behaviors that we do, such as going to the movies, drinking beer, or sporting a tattoo. But if we were to trust that doctor, she/he would, in some respect, have to be mysterious. As Burke notes, in any order "there will be the mysteries of hierarchy, since such a principle is grounded in the very nature of language, and reinforced by the resultant diversity of occupational classes."[30] In other words, mystery, for Burke, "is a major resource of persuasion. Endow a person, an institution, a thing with the glow or resonance of the Mystical, and you have set up a motivational appeal to which people spontaneously... respond."[31] As society is structured hierarchically, a sense of cohesion will have to be fostered. We all have to think we have an equal stake in our social order. We are complacent, in part, because we do not know how the "other half" lives. It works both ways. We do not fully understand the privileges and prerogatives of the rich nor do we fully understand the suffering of the poor. In our ignorance, we accept the social order as given and, thus, natural.

This mystery is implicit in professionalization. People of different professions are alien to each other. While the doctor may be able to relate to us on our level, we cannot relate to the doctor on her or his level. We do not have the technical language or the experience that comes from professional practice to understand what it means to be a doctor. However, when one doctor talks to another doctor, there is nothing mysterious about the interaction. The conversation is between two equals, two people who discern things on a similar level, and who can appeal to common experiences and knowledge bases. They both have an investment in their status as doctors.

To understand better the relationship between mystery and authority and what happens to someone who violates audience expectations, let us now turn to the historical example of President Jimmy Carter, our nation's 39th president. Jimmy Carter came to the presidency amidst an unusual set of political circumstances.

Carter was succeeding President Gerald Ford. Ford had been in office for two years and had replaced Richard Nixon who resigned the presidency after facing a probable impeachment trial for his involvement in the Watergate break-in and for other abuses of presidential power. Ford himself was never elected to the vice-presidency, but had been handpicked by Nixon to replace Spiro Agnew, who had resigned from office because of corruption charges that stemmed from when he was governor of New Jersey. Because of this, President Ford became the first president of the United States who had not been elected to an office higher than the House of Representatives. To make matters worse, Ford outraged the nation by pardoning Nixon. Public confidence in government was at an all-time low.

Similar to Senator Barack Obama in the 2008 presidential campaign, Carter rose to assume the presidency by speaking to the need for change in the workings of what many Americans considered to be a less than fully honest government. He spoke of the need for accountability. Carter presented himself as a Washington "outsider," and made an effort to simplify government, or at least the image of government. He wanted to make the government more humane, trustworthy, and comprehensible to the American people. In other words, he wanted to dispel some of the mystery surrounding the presidency. To this end, Carter was often photographed, early in his administration, in work shoes and blue jeans—rather than in the traditional suit and tie. Much publicity was made of Carter hanging out and drinking beer with his brother Billy at Billy's countryside gas station. Carter walked, rather than drove in a limousine, to the White House from his inauguration. He downsized the fleet of government limousines. A disastrous interview with him even appeared in *Playboy* magazine, in which he admitted to lusting after women in his heart.[32]

This type of behavior resulted in, or contributed to, his low popularity as a president. When Carter left office he had the lowest popularity rating of any president in recent history.[33]

Since leaving office, however, his credibility has improved. People tended to forget about the Iranian hostage crisis and Carter's inability to resolve it, including his botched attempt to rescue the hostages by military force.[34] In addition, Carter has become an "elder statesmen," and has had a high profile negotiating better political relationships with leaders of foreign countries, most notably those in North Korea. He also spent time building houses for Habitat for Humanity. For all of this work, Carter was awarded the Nobel Peace Prize in 2002.

Ronald Reagan, on the other hand, who left office with the highest approval rating in modern history, saw his credibility plummet when his connection with the Iran-Contra scandal was revealed.[35] In addition, Reagan accepted a two-million-dollar house in Bel Air (a wealthy suburb in Southern California) from wealthy businessmen and a multi-million-dollar speaking tour of Japan. This hurt Reagan's credibility with the American public, as it appeared that Reagan was being rewarded for helping special interest groups at the expense of the nation. Further, people were beginning to understand that the effects of the Reagan Administration's economic, racial, and environmental policies were deleterious to the lives of average Americans.

The examples of both Carter and Reagan illustrate that credibility or image is subject to change over time and situation.[36] The perception of credibility fluctuates, and there is a constant need for reinforcement. A more detailed example of this is evident in the career of President Richard Nixon.

Nixon began his political career as an obscure junior senator from California in the 1950s. His obscurity changed, however, when Nixon played second fiddle to Senator Joseph McCarthy, the man who lent his name to "McCarthyism."[37] Nixon gained so much, politically, from his notoriety, particularly from his persecution of U.S. State Department official Alger Hiss as a Soviet spy, that he was asked by Eisenhower to serve as Eisenhower's vice-presidential running mate in the 1952 elections.[38] However, a few months into the campaign a scandal broke out. The press revealed that Nixon was collecting money from rich investors in California in a so-called "secret slush fund." While Nixon had done nothing illegal in accepting this money, and while the Democratic vice-presidential candidate had also accepted money from similar sources, popular sentiment quickly turned against him, with the aid of the sensationalist newspapers and the encouragement of Nixon's growing list of personal enemies. Eisenhower, sensing Nixon's declining popularity, was prepared to drop him from the ticket. Nixon, however, was given an unprecedented chance to redeem himself when he was granted television time to mount his defense. He was to speak to the American people and to explain to them what had happened:

> "My only hope to win," Nixon remembers, "rested with millions of people I would never meet, sitting in groups of two or three or four in their living rooms, watching and listening to me on television. Getting their support required that the broadcast must not be just good. It had to be a smash hit—one that really moved people, that was designed not simply to explain the complicated and dull facts about the fund to the people, but one that would inspire them to enthusiastic positive support."[39]

Nixon was successful in this task, largely by using the credibility enhancing tactics that will be discussed in the next section of this chapter.

Already we can see that by 1952, Nixon's credibility waxed and waned and was dependent upon public perceptions of him. But this was just the beginning of his credibility challenges and successes. After Nixon left the vice-presidency he ran for the presidency and lost in 1960 to John F. Kennedy, largely because he looked sinister on television, particularly when compared to the youthful Kennedy. Nixon then ran for governor of California in 1962, lost to Edmund G. Brown, and "gave up" politics, after angrily denouncing the media at a press conference where he emphatically stated that "You won't have Nixon to kick around any more because, gentlemen, this is my last press conference."[40]

Later, after Nixon had been elected president in 1968, he was surprisingly popular, even during the tremendous anti-war period when he was considered to be the primary demon of the age by young protesters. In 1972, Nixon easily won reelection against George McGovern, the liberal anti-war candidate. The high point of Nixon's presidency was his 1972 trip to China, where he initiated the normalization of relations with that powerful nation. The close ties between the two nations that we take for granted today are the result of Nixon's efforts.[41]

In the midst of his success, however, the Watergate story broke and, within a short time, led to his undoing. Nixon left the presidency in disgrace, resigning the office to avoid facing impeachment charges. In retirement, Nixon wrote books and remained quiet for the most part, offering advice on occasion to certain presidents, until his death in 1996, at which time he was hailed by the media and treated with national honor, although bitterly hated by millions of Americans who remember his "secret" wars against Laos and Cambodia and the destruction he, along with President Lyndon Johnson, wrought on the people of Vietnam.

❧ Ways Persuaders Can Enhance Credibility ☙

Because the audience's perceptions of a persuader's credibility change over time, and because credibility has to be constantly reinforced to be effective, persuaders are always looking for ways to improve and to rebuild their credibility. The longer a person stays in the public view, and is dependent upon pub-

lic support, the more likely she or he will experience swings in public perception.

There are several ways that persuaders, when they perceive their popularity to be lacking, can improve their credibility in the minds of their supporters. These include identification/association, and dissociation tactics; arguing
against one's own best interests; identifying self or organization late in the
presentation; grounding in *logos*; endorsements; careful introduction; dress and
appearance; and apologetic tactics. In the paragraphs to follow, I will discuss
each in turn.

Identification/Association and Dissociation Tactics

First, the persuader can engage in identification, association, and dissociation
tactics. By "wrapping themselves in the flag," by associating with the church
or the state, or by enthusiastically attacking what the public perceives to be
their "enemy," persuaders can often skirt important issues surrounding their
moral misconduct. This tactic involves dimensions of balance theory (as discussed in Chapter 6). "You do not like me, but you like America, so if I can
associate myself with things that are 'American,' you may come to think of me
as a patriot and change your appraisal of me."

Arguing Against One's Own Interest

Second, the persuader can argue against her or his own best interests. A persuader can construct a case for her or his sincerity by demonstrating that there
is no conflict of interest, and that, in fact, the pursuance of a policy actually has
detrimental consequences for the persuader. Sincerity and sacrifice, it should
be emphasized, are essential dimensions of a persuader's credibility. For example, when Mike Gilbert, sports agent, business advisor, and trusted confidant of
disgraced football star O.J. Simpson published his book, *How I Helped O.J.
Get Away With Murder: The Shocking Inside Story of Violence, Loyalty, Regret, and Remorse*,[42] he anticipated attacks on his character, that the book was
pandering and self-serving. To help deflect some of that criticism, Gilbert
makes it clear that the proceeds from the book are to be donated to charity. By

this move, Gilbert is helping to prove the sincerity of his book by renouncing any possible financial gain from writing it.

Identifying Self or Organization Late in the Presentation

Third, if the persuader and/or her/his organization are objects of contempt for an audience, the persuader can identify self or organization late in the presentation, and thus slowly build goodwill with the audience. This tactic is particularly effective if the persuader can express, early, some of the positive views held by the audience. Remember, as mentioned earlier, audiences tend to overcompensate for perceived similarities.

A strong extended example of how unpopular persuaders withhold information about their organization is seen in cult persuasion. As I have had some experience with this, I would like to draw out my example in the form of a personal narrative.

I was raised in a middle-class Jewish community in West Los Angeles during the 1970s and 1980s, a period of time in which cult recruitment was particularly high in this country.[43] Several times a week in the afternoon my friends and I would walk or ride our bikes to the local temple (synagogue) for high school youth group activities. Within this group we were exposed to a fair amount of cult-training awareness.[44] Middle and upper class Jewish youth make up a large proportion of the people who become inducted into cults—as much as 10 to 12 percent in the case of the Unification Church (i.e., the Moonies).[45] In response to this threat, the Jewish community, in the 1980s, made a concerted effort to inoculate their children against cult appeals and to raise awareness of how cults operate. This cult training serves as a backdrop for the following story.

One day, I found myself confronted by members of a cult. At the time this experience took place, I was sitting in Southern California at the Santa Monica Pier. I had just returned from Israel, where I had lived for eight months, and I had a few months to wait until the beginning of my freshman year in college. The public schools had not yet let out for the summer; thus, it was unusual for a teenager to be sitting alone at the beach on a weekday (I was eighteen at the time). Judging by my appearance, my age, and by my lackadaisical persona (I was "hanging out"), an onlooker could conclude that I was clearly not employed or in school. I was approached by two fairly attractive young women. They struck up a conversation with me and introduced themselves as being members of C.A.R.P. (Collegiate Association on the Research of Principles), a student organization affiliated with the University of California Los Angeles (UCLA). They invited me to have dinner with them and with others that evening.

While I had not heard of their organization at the time, I had a strong suspicion that this "organization" was a front for the "Moonies," one of the largest of the religious cults that were active in the country at the time. In fact, I had been shown a movie at temple which specified how the Moonie cult operated. The movie was so exact in detailing the experience of a young man who was abducted and went though the process of becoming a Moonie, that I was able to recognize what was happening to me that evening as I went through the beginning of the Moonies' induction phase.

I went home and called the student center at UCLA and inquired as to whether or not C.A.R.P. was a registered student organization. It was not.[46] I was not sure, at this point, if this was the Moonies I was dealing with, but I was sure that it was a cult. I decided to find out for myself what this group was. I wanted to test my cult training skills. I had, after all, survived for eight months on my own in Israel, much of that time among the *Yeshivot* (fundamentalist theology communities) in the old Jewish Quarter of Jerusalem, which itself was a cult-like experience.[47]

Before I left my apartment that evening, I wrote a long detailed letter to my grandmother, with whom I was staying, explaining what I had done, and instructing her to find me and to bring me back home if something were to happen to me, even if it were against my later wishes. I did this because after being inducted in a cult, people frequently resist the efforts of family and friends to help free them from their dependency on the cult. I placed the letter where my grandmother would find it if I did not return home, but in a location where I could safely retrieve it when I made it back (the junior James Bond that I was, I placed the white letter among the napkins in the napkin holder).

I met the two women at the place were they told me to wait (i.e., at the local mall), and we were soon joined by a van and some other people. With some trepidation, I stepped into the van.

Once in the van, I had become an instant celebrity. Everyone was so eager to know me, to talk to me, to ask me questions. Everyone smiled. The people were well-dressed and happy. They wanted me to feel happy, too. As we drove, I noticed that we were going deeper and deeper into L.A., making it harder for me to explain myself if I were to require help in getting back home.

We finally came to the house that the organization was using as its meeting place. Inside was a group of about 25 people. The attention that I had received in the van was now magnified. As a group we sang as somebody played guitar, and we ate international food as was promised by the two women I met at the beach. It appeared as if we were having a wonderful time, and I could have easily given myself to the moment. If I had genuinely felt alienated with my life, this would have been the start of a good antidote— young people, especially women, were providing me with a significant amount of warmth and attention. Could this be the start of something wonderful, perhaps a feeling of inclusion, of family?

While keeping the appearance of an enthusiastic participant, I surveyed the situation. It did not take me long to realize that, of the twenty-five people in the room, there were, in fact, only two of us who were not a part of the cult. In other words, 23 of the 25 were "plants" whose job was to give the "party" the appearance of verisimilitude.

In fact, this was no "party." It was clear I and one woman were being "worked upon" by the group; this cult was trying to *recruit* us. This other woman was about my age and was across the room from me. Both of us were surrounded by our hosts. She seemed to have given in to their attention. I remembered that the cults structured their indoctrinations to make the potential recruit feel warm and welcomed, and often kept her or him from talking with other people who were not a part of the organization. I felt the urge to talk to the other woman, to warn her, to let her know what was going on. However, I knew that our hosts were not going to let me approach her. Part of their job was to keep us isolated from each other, so we could not use each other to ground our perceptions of what was happening.

I tried, casually, to work myself across the room so that I could strike up a conversation with this woman. But I could not. Every time that I tried to reach out to this woman, I found myself repositioned by the group. It was as if there was an invisible ball of energy around both of us that repelled us every time that we got close. It was subtle the way our hosts kept us apart. One moment I would seem to get close, and the next moment I would find myself standing across the room again. This was extremely disconcerting and I began to appreciate the manipulative power the group wielded.

After dinner, talking, and the group activities, someone announced that it was time for the "presentation." Apparently, the group had a "philosophy" they wanted to share with everyone (meaning, in effect, the two of us). This was the first time that my hosts had let on that there was a "philosophy" or teaching behind this group, although because of my training, I was expecting something of the sort. The group was then led to a large room that had been converted into a small lecture hall. The existence of such a room had been concealed, as the small auditorium was clearly out of place in a residential house. Everyone sat in rows of seats. There was a speaker and a slide show. Both were innocuous. The presentation was vague enough so that people could read into it what they wanted.

At this point, however, there still was no mention of what the group was, what they represented, and whose teaching they followed. Every time I asked questions about this my attention was redirected by my hosts. No one would give me a direct answer. Clearly, and this is the point of my story, the group was *not* prepared to reveal itself until as *late* in the presentation as possible.[48] To approach me at the beach and announce, "Hi, we are Moonies," would have been to give the game away before it even started. Even without cult awareness training, it was clear to me, and to most people at the time, that the Moonies were a bad group with which to be associated.

In fact, it was not until *after* the lecture, and *after* the subsequent slide show on the "camp" they had in the San Bernardino Mountains, and it was not until *after* they asked me to go to the camp, and *after* they made it clear how fun it would be, and *after* they pointed to the van outside, waiting to take me right now, that a small sentence appeared at the bottom of one of the slides indicating that the guidelines of the camp were premised on the principles of the Rev. Sun Myung Moon.

So at last, more than three hours into the event, I knew that they were, in fact, Moonies. But had I not been so careful, during the previous three hours, in keeping my mental and emotional distance from these people, I might have, when confronted with the incongruence between my positive feeling for them and my negative but second-hand feelings for the Unification Church (what Moon's cult was officially called), rationalized away my previous negative feelings about the church. If I felt so good among these people, how could they be so bad?

Knowing that people, at this point in the presentation, would feel uncertain of what was going on and what they should do (after all, it was a fairly significant action that the persuader was requesting), the cult members turned up the pressure they had been exerting all evening. Even with my training and preparation, I was surprised at how determined my hosts were to whisk me off to camp. The appeal was immediate. The action requested was *now*. They knew that if I went home and talked with my family and friends, I would be discouraged from coming. So they wanted me to make a commitment right *then* and *there*, before I could be exposed to counter-persuasion. They wanted me to give myself completely into them before I had the chance to entertain any doubts about them.

What was chilling was the fact that I could have disappeared at that moment. By assenting at that point, I would have slipped silently out of this world. Moreover, if I was as aimless and as disconnected as I appeared on the beach, nobody would have known, and nobody would have come looking for me. I would have "vanished," only to appear months later on the streets of New York City with a new identity, personality, and a new frame of mind selling candy or flowers. In addition, I would be subject to their intense surveillance and coercion. If I had been weak-willed, the Moonies may have had their grasp over me for years.

I knew also that the Moonies could not be accused of "kidnapping," that my journey to their camp would be entirely legal. I knew that once at camp it would have been harder and harder for me to leave. Even if they would not force me to stay, I would have been in the middle of the mountains, far away from family and friends, with no way to contact them and no way to get home. I would have been surrounded by the attention, the supervision, and the gaze that is so powerful and transformative. I would have been denied adequate sleep, fed no protein, bombarded by "love" and "affection" in massive group hugging sessions, kept out of contact from the outside world, and relentlessly fed their propaganda. In time I would have become one of them.[49]

This, in a nutshell, is how brainwashing works. As discussed in Chapter 6, brainwashing is never literal, as it is portrayed in movies such as *The Manchurian Candidate* (1962), its 2004 remake, or *Conspiracy Theory* (1997). Rather, brainwashing involves the slow breaking down of our past identifications, the discrediting of our past knowledge, and isolation from the sources of our past mental nourishment. These persuaders break our connections to the past and, in their place, give us new dependencies, new vocabularies, and new idols to worship. Since personality is largely the result of community identifications, we find that we accept our new persona within cults because that is what we see in the faces of the people who reflect the cult's ideology back at us.

Needless to say, I did not go on that trip. My hosts were adamant about learning the reasons why I did not want to go; they would not take "no" for an answer. To appease them, I told them that I was enthusiastic about going to their camp and that their philosophy was that for which I had been searching. I said that I was just about ready to get in the van. In fact, I told them that I wanted to go tomorrow evening. People were expecting me tonight to do some things, so it was imperative that I got home, but once I took care of this business, no one would be expecting anything from me, and I would be free to go to their camp for a couple of weeks.

I asked them if they could drive me to my house so that they could know where to pick me up tomorrow, and they were pleased to do that. When we got to my general neighborhood, I asked them to stop at the Safeway supermarket and wait for me while I got some groceries to bring home to my grandmother. I then went through the back door of the store and lost them on Wilshire Boulevard.

That is the story of me and the Moonies. What happened to the young woman, I cannot say. I suspect she was inducted. She was a new student at the University of Southern California and seemed rather insecure. Cults have a long history of having a particular effectiveness with first-year college students or other young people who suffer from a lack of experience in decision making, low self-esteem, a strong desire for peer acceptance, emotional vulnerabilities, under stressful situations, and have emotional distance from family support systems.[50] Freshmen beware; the first year of college is the most difficult for students, and is the time in which they are at the greatest risk of dropping out and of having other bad things happen to them.

As this story illustrates, persuaders with something to hide often take significant measures to refrain from identifying themselves. The longer they can conceal their true identity from us, the longer we have to listen to them, and perhaps be affected by what they have to say, without measuring their message against what we already know about them. With this in mind, when people we do not know want things from us, it is a good idea to ask who they are and what they represent. If these strangers balk at offering the requested information, or otherwise attempt to weasel their way out of answering clearly, it is a strong indication that they have less-than-honorable objectives (Amway, for instance, or other "pyramid" marketing schemes).

Grounding in Logos

A fourth way that a controversial persuader can improve her or his credibility is to couch controversial claims within logic—the framework of solid content, a well reasoned argument, and a competently organized structure. The less likely that an audience will take for granted the premises of a controversial appeal, the more careful that persuader has to be in establishing clearly those premises and in defending them. The more ethical the persuader, the more that person will be able to ground her/his appeals within the context of evidence. The less evidence that a person has to support her or his position, the harder that person has to work to get the rest of us to overlook that fact. This is especially important because the persuader wants to speak outside of her/his immediate followers that do not need convincing about the rationale grounding certain taken-for-granted premises.

Simply put, in attempting to convince outside people about the importance of a cause, the unpopular persuader will have to provide a logical argument. If a persuader cannot do this, that persuader is bound to have limited influence. For example, take a speaker who is critical of the United States for, say, the invasion and occupation of Iraq. To argue that the United States is a "imperialistic nation" trading "blood for oil" invites the labeling of that person as belonging to the so-called "loony left." Now imagine the same speaker who, instead of using emotive and extreme rhetoric, argues from a set of principles grounded in the claim that invading sovereign nations under false pretext to advance a leader's personal policy goals is wrong morally. She/he may argue that no credible evidence existed to link Iraq with the September 11 attacks on the United States and that no credible evidence links Iraq to weapons of mass destruction (which, at-any-rate, as a sovereign nation, Iraq is entitled to have). Further, that person may argue, evidence suggests that not only was evidence for these claims non-existent, the Bush Administration knew that and actively misled the American public to push for war. To the extent that these sentences are demonstrably provable, which I believe is pretty much beyond doubt, an individual has provided an argument based on sound reasoning.

Endorsements

Fifth, to the extent that a persuader can find others who will endorse her or his credibility, it is beneficial to make this endorsement public, as it is a way of attracting further support. The credibility of an endorser (a third, independent party) often acts as an intermediary between the unknown or negligible credibility of a source and the general disposition of most audiences to assume, or seek, a good-willed relationship with a speaker. In most cases—particularly in the realm of politics—we do not know personally the persuader, but when someone familiar to us knows her or him, or has some significant second-hand involvement or familiarity with the persuader and her/his ideas, we tend to view that endorser as a sanctioning agent. So, for example, when former Secretary of State Colin L. Powell, himself a Republican and an early member of the Bush Administration, endorsed democratic presidential candidate Barack Obama instead of Obama's Republican rival John McCain on October 19, 2008, a few weeks before the presidential election, many understood it to be, in the language of the *New York Times*, "a powerful reassurance to voters about Mr. Obama's national security credentials."[51] This was a crucial endorsement for Senator Obama, whose biggest weakness as a candidate was on national security.

Employ a Careful Introduction

Sixth, the use of a careful introduction is also important in helping the persuader to negotiate difficult credibility issues. The use of a careful introduction involves reading one's audience well enough so as to negotiate skillfully the parameters of the intended discourse with them. It is important for controversial speakers to set strategically the conditions for the morality play of a particular persuasive effort. A related goal of the careful introduction is to lift up major emphases, interrelationships, and the possibility of a coherence that is not self-evident. In other words, with this tactic the persuader suggests a *frame* or an *order* with which to contextualize the communication.

In my experience, a careful introduction is commonly employed in academic writing when care must be given when editing a journal or book to show how the authors of a series of discrete essays fit into the larger context of the published volume. In such circumstances, the editor must carefully write an introductory essay interpreting the writing of the individual authors and placing it within a larger context that would not be self-evident to a reader. Even when the product is the result of a highly planned and collaborative engagement among the authors, the editor's ability to say what has finally come forth often may lead readers to an understanding of how the work, collectively, fits together. The idea is to provide the audience with a path that aids comprehension which would otherwise be difficult if the material is obtuse.

A good example of a careful introduction in political discourse comes from Malcolm X's *The Ballot or The Bullet* speech. Delivered first in April 1964, the speech is Malcolm's most well-known and widely discussed.[52] African-Americans, he counseled, must start voting in numbers to hold White politicians accountable for civil rights. Voting, however, might not be enough; in which case, African-Americans have a human right to defend themselves with weapons. This commonsensical notion was controversial and terrifying for Blacks and Whites in the early 1960s, a time in which the mainstream Civil Rights Movement was eschewing such forceful rhetoric, as would become popularized a few years later with the formation of the Black Panther Party for Self Defense. In addition to the message being controversial, Malcolm, himself, was a controversial person. Malcolm was associated with Black Nationalism, hatred of White people, and violence.[53] Further, he was Muslim in a society that was, and continues to be, suspicious of Muslims. This in mind, Malcolm began his speech by "clarifying" for his audience his personal religious beliefs. He acknowledges that he is a Muslim and that he follows the teaching of Islam. His audience already knows this; as suggested above, his identity as a Muslim leader is an important source of their suspicion of him. To challenge that suspicion and to normalize his identity, Malcolm points to other well-known religious leaders working for civil rights such as Adam Clayton Powell and Martin Luther King, Jr. Malcolm X goes out of his way to emphasize how they and *he* work for civil rights, and that *he* is just like *them*. What matters is that they are all *ministers*.

In so doing, Malcolm acknowledges what his audience perceives as his weakness and situates or explains his weakness in terms the audience understands. We understand Christian leaders who work for civil rights and respect them for that work, even if we ourselves are not Christian. What is important is the work they do, not their personal beliefs. Malcolm explains that he is no different in kind from these respected people: differences between Christianity and Islam are reduced to expressions of personal, even *private*, style and are deemed irrelevant to the tumultuous *public* context of the Civil Rights Movement. Malcolm accentuates this point in the next part of his careful introduction by dissociating his religion from the issue upon which he wishes to speak—that of civil rights for Black people. Emphatically, he asserts that he is not holding forth on the podium to promulgate his beliefs about Islam or to criticize people for their Christian beliefs. He makes it clear that while religion may divide him from his audience, it would be a mistake to allow this to happen. Rather, he insists, his Black audience needs to overcome their differences and recognize that they have a common problem, and that is racist America. He concludes that all Black people are caught up in and victimized by racism and that the common enemy is White supremacy. Divisions among Black people only serve the powers that benefit from Black sectarianism.

What we see clearly in this passage is that Malcolm X understands that his audience has reservations about him. He does not take for granted that his audience sees him as he sees himself, but that he must carefully introduce himself—that is, define himself for his audience, to redefine the terms of their relationship with him. In other words, he must educate his audience so that the things they at first thought were strange about Malcolm become demystified and repositioned more favorably into their schemas of understanding. By working with the predispositions of his audience, rather than ignoring them, he coaxes them to accept him on his own terms.

Dress and Appearance

Seventh, how one looks is an important factor in helping a person establish her or his credibility. While dress and appearance obviously should not be the most important thing to consider when analyzing a persuasive appeal, we should remember that our dress and appearance often position us in society in significant ways. We ignore this only to our discredit as persuaders, and we are influenced by it only to the extent that we are not careful consumers of persuasion. While some people look "sharp," it should be the integrity of their ideas that move us. Whatever their conditions, however, people try to look their best when they strive to be influential, and it is this intent, more than anything else, that carries some weight in how audiences judge people. If a persuader really cares about her/his message, she/he will usually take the time to present it, and its vessel, the speaker, in the most positive light possible.

Apologetic Tactics

The eighth and final way to improve one's credibility discussed in this chapter involves the use of *apologetic tactics*. Apologetics is the study and practice of the intellectual defense of a belief system, ideology, event, policy, or person. An apologist is someone who speaks or writes in defense of a person, cause, faith (or ideology), or an institution. The early Christian leader Tertullian was an apologist for a church persecuted by the Romans. Secretary of State Condoleezza Rice was an apologist for the Bush Administration's unpopular foreign policies. Anytime someone's or something's credibility is under attack, an apologist has an opportunity to step in to try to improve the popular perception. Such an attack against a person's credibility typically involves two components: the accused is held responsible for an action and that action is considered to be offensive. In other words, apologetic tactics are ways that unpopular or "damaged" persuaders redeem themselves.

The first apologetic tactic is *denial*. By denying participation in, or relationship to, that which repels the audience, the persuader attempts to encourage the audience to see her or him as she or he was prior to the accusation of wrongdoing. Another way of conceptualizing denial is the idea that the persuader can take her or himself out of the locus of control in a bad or degenerate situation. In relinquishing control, the persuader tries to relinquish blame. As rhetorical scholars B. L. Ware and Wil A. Linkugel explain, "The person who is charged with some despicable action often finds a disclaimer of *intent* as an attractive means of escaping stigma if the denial of the existence of the action itself is too great a reformation of reality to gain acceptance."[54] Fundamentally, denial "consists of simple disavowal by the speaker of any participation in, relationship to, or positive sentiment toward whatever it is that repulses the audience."[55]

For example, Senator Ted Kennedy, in July of 1969, was involved in the infamous "Chappaquiddick Affair." Kennedy was driving home from a party late at night, drunk. He was accompanied by Mary Jo Kopechne, a young woman who was not his wife. Kennedy lost control of the car and drove off a bridge. Kennedy managed to escape, but the woman did not—she sank with the car and drowned. While there is some debate on the issue, Kennedy apparently made little effort to save Ms. Kopechne. What is clear, however, is that Kennedy did not report the accident until the next day, presumably after sobering up and securing legal and political advice. There was a public outcry, and Kennedy, like Nixon before him, was about to lose his political career—and Kennedy, like Nixon, had presidential aspirations. In the most immediate sense, Kennedy was being asked to step down from his Senate seat.

In his speech of self-defense, Kennedy succeeds at removing himself from the locus of control and, thus, from moral responsibility. He argues that it was late. It was dark. He was confused. He had a concussion. The water was murky. The pond was cold and deep. He was in shock. In general, he positions himself as the *victim* of circumstances that were beyond his power of control. Such a defense is not unreasonable. People commonly appeal to such reasoning all the time. In fact, it is largely because we do so that Kennedy was successful in his immediate task of remaining a U.S. Senator from Massachusetts. While Kennedy does not deny that the events surrounding the accident were true (i.e., he was driving the car, he had been drinking, he was with a woman not his wife, the woman had died, etc.), he does *deny* that he did anything wrong—he was simply at the wrong place at the wrong time, as, unfortunately, any of us could be. As David Ling explains, "These statements function rhetorically to minimize [Kennedy's] role as agent in this situation. That is, the statements suggest an agent whose actions were both moral and rational prior to the accident... It suggests the scene as the controlling agent."[56]

While he ultimately saved his Senate seat by convincing people to feel sorry for him and to empathize with him for his bad luck, and while his career as a Senator would continue for four more decades, Kennedy, in the process of achieving his short-term goal, sacrificed his long-term presidential goals. For in admitting that he was not the agent responsible for the events at Chappaquiddick, he admitted his own inability to be in control of the situation—a definite disadvantage for the president of the United States. As Ling concludes, the "myth that has always surrounded the office of the President is that it must be held by an agent who can make clear, rational decisions in an extraordinary scene. Kennedy, in this speech was, at least in part, conceding that he may not be able to handle such situations."[57]

The second way that persuaders can improve their credibility through apologetic tactics involves the use of *bolstering* or *identification*. Bolstering or identification is the opposite of denial and "refers to any rhetorical strategy which reinforces the existence of a fact, sentiment, object, or relationship. When he bolsters, a speaker attempts to identify himself with something viewed favorably by the audience."[58] With this tactic, a persuader associates with things that the audience reveres and dissociates from things that the audience does not like. This tactic plays upon those characteristics of the speaker or situation that have a strong base relevance in the audience and that help them to experience the persuader in a more human fashion. A good example of this tactic is Richard Nixon's "My Side of the Story" address, the speech referred to earlier in this chapter in which Nixon defends himself against charges of accepting money in return for granting political favors. In his defense, Nixon gives the television audience a detailed account of everything he owes and owns. At the climax of this narrative, Nixon discusses a dog that was given to his children by one of his supporters:

> One other thing I probably should tell you because if we don't they'll probably be saying this about me too, we did get something—a gift— after the election. A man down in Texas heard Pat on the radio mention the fact that our two youngsters would like to have a dog. And, believe it or not, the day before we left on this campaign trip we got a message from Union Station in Baltimore saying that they had a package for us. We went down to get it. You know what it was? It was a little cocker spaniel dog in a crate that he sent all the way from Texas. Black and white spotted. And our little girl—Tricia, the six-year-old—named it Checkers. And you know, the kids love the dog and I just want to say this right now, that regardless of what they say about it, we're gonna keep it.[59]

By standing up for his children, and by demonstrating his love for them, Nixon reveals a "human" side that was otherwise irrelevant to the situation that created the need for the speech. As funny as this passage appears now, it was an important part of his presentation. After all, Nixon, in this case, was not guilty of anything. While it was alleged that Nixon had been accepting bribes, an independent audit by the prestigious law firm of Gibson, Dunn, and Crutcher had guaranteed the legality of Nixon's "secret" fund which, as Nixon points out, was never "secret." The issue, therefore, was not Nixon's "guilt," but Nixon's *character*. Thus, throughout the speech we find that Nixon emphasizes his fight against communism, his humble lower-middle-class origins, and his dedication to his family.

The next apologetic tactic, one that is progressively more sophisticated than the previous two, involves *differentiation*. This tactic renames or redefines whatever repels the audience so that it is seen in a new and favorable light. Further, differentiation, note Ware and Linkugel, subsumes those strategies which serve the purpose of separating some fact, sentiment, object, or relationship from some larger context within which the audience presently views that attribute. The division of the old context into two or more new constructions of reality is accompanied by a change in the audience's meaning. At least one of the new constructs takes on a meaning distinctively different from that which it possessed when viewed as a part of the old, homogenous context.[60]

In other words, "strategies which place whatever it is about him that repels the audience into a new perspective can often benefit him in his self-defense."[61] Another way of saying this is that the controversial persuader renames her or his controversy so that it does not seem so bad. In the 1980s, for instance, the Chrysler Corporation was caught disconnecting odometers on cars that they were testing and then later selling the test cars as new. In one ad that was intended to rebuild Chrysler's credibility after this news broke to the public, President and CEO Lee Iacocca admitted that Chrysler had made a "mistake." He said, in effect, that while testing cars is worthy practice, disconnecting odometers to make the cars appear new was a "lousy idea." He went on to characterize that practice as a "mistake" that Chrysler would never do again. That sounds reasonable; unless we are paying attention, we will miss the fact that what Iacocca calls a "lousy idea" and a "mistake" others call "breaking the law" and "fraud."

The next and most sophisticated form of apologetic tactic is *transcendence*. Transcendence is the opposite of differentiation. The goal here is to cognitively join "some fact, sentiment, object, or relationship with some larger context within which the audience does not presently view that attribute."[62]

Transcendental strategies "psychologically move the audience away from the particulars of the charge at hand in a direction toward some more abstract, general view of this charter."[63] When utilizing this tactic, the persuader places the issue that is adversely affecting her or his credibility in a larger or higher context in order to improve her or his image. For example, disgraced NFL quarterback Michael Vick stated that his fall from grace brought him to Christianity; after pleading guilty to dog-fighting charges in 2007, he said "Through this situation I found Jesus and asked him for forgiveness and turned my life over to the Lord."[64]

The final apologetic tactic is *counterattack*. Counterattack is what persuaders sometimes do when all else fails to justify or otherwise explain away an action that people are judging as bad. Specifically, the practice of counterattacking occurs when the persuader turns around the issue hurting her or his credibility by charging or challenging the opposition to defend her or himself on an unrelated, sensationalist issue. In biological terms, it is what the octopus does to protect itself—in squirting the black ink, it can escape in the momentary confusion that it creates. A recent example of this can be found in an ad from The Presidential Coalition, a Republican 527 political organization. 527 groups are tax-exempt political organizations created under federal law to allow partisan groups to raise money in order to influence elections. These groups are unregulated by federal or state elections commissions and are not subject to the same contribution limits as political action committees. The ad at issue here features a picture of Jimmy Carter and reads "Worst President Ever!" Continuing, the ad states: "Former President Jimmy Carter continues to criticize President Bush's courageous War on Terror, and, most recently, the Terrorist Surveillance Program administered by the National Security Agency." The ad then proceeds to remind readers of the negative traits of the Carter Presidency, including hyperinflation, high unemployment, high interest rates, gasoline rationing, the return of the Panama Canal to Panamanian authority, and the Iranian hostage crisis. The ad concludes by stating that President Carter "should continue his work with charities like Habitat for Humanity—not needlessly criticizing the Commander-In-Chief in a time of war." In other words, Carter broke from precedent and was openly critical of the sitting President. The ad, then, is an attempt to neutralize this criticism.

As an extended example of apologetic tactics, consider the following ad from the much-maligned Tobacco giant, the Philip Morris Company. It is a two-page ad that appeared in *Vanity Fair* in December 1996. There are five pictures on these two pages. The first is of a man baking food. The caption identifies this scene as a part of Project Angel Food. The next photograph is of two dancers who are with the Alvin Ailey American Dance Theater, an influential performance company. The third picture is of an old lady standing in her kitchen, representing a program called Citymeals On Wheels. The next photograph is of a smiling African-American teacher in his classroom, representing the Multicultural Alliance. The final picture is of an American farmer in his corn field, representing the American Farmland Trust.

What unites all these organizations is Philip Morris, best known for its Marlboro cigarettes. In this ad, however, Philip Morris is not selling us its cigarettes, but its credibility. The mid-1990s saw the tobacco industry on the defensive. For the first time in its long history, the tobacco industry started to suffer serious political and legal setbacks. Provoked by the negative publicity surrounding the tobacco industry, Philip Morris positions itself as having the courage and moral foresightedness to inspire all sorts of civic/community organizations to help people realize their potential. In so doing, Philip Morris, corporate villain extraordinaire, positions itself as a courageous company with bold vision and leadership and a genuine compassion for the human community.

Their ad goes on to inform readers that this courage of leadership is what has defined the company for more than 40 years. As contemporary examples of their claim, the ad points out that Philip Morris sponsors initiatives against hunger; that it develops nutritional programs for your children; and that it supports education, the arts, the environment, and the fight against AIDS. The ad ends by reaffirming the company's commitment for further support of these worthy organizations/goals so that humanity can be uplifted in body and soul.

What is being denied in this ad is that Phillip Morris is primarily a *cigarette* company. Tobacco does not appear in the ad. The one crop we see is corn. The message implied in this ad is clear: do not attack us. We are good people and we contribute something important to society. With ads such as these, Philip Morris is trying to encourage the American people to think of it as a beneficent company.[65] Such image control is not a new phenomenon for Philip Morris. Between 1924 and 1955, Marlboro cigarettes were marketed as a woman's brand under the slogan "Mild As May." One ad features a young baby admonishing his mother to smoke a cigarette so as to control her temper and avoid scolding the child. At least two other ads in that series used babies, encouraging their mothers to smoke. By the later 1950s concern about the health effects of smoking started to surface and Philip Morris decided to masculinize Marlborough, which featured a feminine filter ("ivory tips protect the lips"). The result was the iconic Marlborough Man and a very different experience with the Marlborough brand, which suddenly became a blockbuster item.

ഏ Conclusion ര

In this chapter we discussed *credibility* or *ethos*, one of the four artistic proofs that Aristotle and other classical rhetoricians argued constituted the parameters of persuasion as the art of influencing others. As discussed in previous chapters of this textbook and course, these artistic proofs are known as *ethos*, *pathos*, *logos*, and *mythos*. Of these methods of reasoning, Aristotle argued that *ethos*, which he conceptualized as involving *good sense*, *moral character*, and *good will*, was the most important. Aristotle's insights have been verified by modern researchers who approach credibility as *competence*, *trustworthiness*, and *dynamism*. In each case, what matters is not actual competence or trustworthiness, but *perceived* competence or trustworthiness. Credibility, we have seen, is a *perception* that audiences hold toward a source which changes over time. Credibility must never be assumed and it must be reinforced constantly. Finally, we have defined credibility as a negotiated relationship between a speaker and her or his audience. In so doing, we discussed what credibility is, where it comes from, and how it can be improved upon. In the next chapter, we will focus on the element of the communication interaction that receives the persuader and her/his message—the audience.

❧ Notes ❧

1. For a description of the legal and civil court systems in Ancient Athens, and of the centrality of the citizen-orator in that context, see Mogens Herman Hansen, *The Athenian Democracy in the Age of Demosthenes* (Oxford: Blackwell, 1991). For a discussion of Demosthenes, the tradition of oratory he exemplifies, and for a translation of the most exemplary speech from the classical world, see James J. Murphy, ed., *Demosthenes' on the Crown* (New York: Random House, 1967).

2. Although legal scholars continue to fight for a democratic right of media access, this idea suffered a setback by the U.S. Supreme Court in *Miami Herald v. Tornillo* (1974). There, the Court held that under the First Amendment, government had no right to force newspapers to publish views or ideas of citizens in the interest of fairness or democracy. In language I find regrettable, the Court reasoned that a "responsible press is an undoubtedly desirable goal, but press responsibility is not mandated by the Constitution and like many other virtues it cannot be legislated." In other words, a person running for political office in a market served by limited media cannot demand space to respond to negative coverage of his campaign. Freedom of the press means freedom for the person *owning* the press.

3. *On Rhetoric: A Theory of Civic Discourse*, trans. George A. Kennedy (New York: Oxford University Press, 1990).

4. Ibid., 38. In a technical sense, Aristotle considered previous credibility to be inartistic, rather than artistic.

5. David K. Berlo, James B. Lemert, and Robert J. Mertz, "Dimensions for Evaluating the Acceptability of Message Sources," *Public Opinion Quarterly*, *33* (1969), 563–576.

6. Trans. W.C. Helmbold (New York: Bobbs-Merrill Company, 1952).

7. *On Christian Doctrine*, trans. D. W. Robertson, Jr. (New York: Macmillan Publishing Company, 1958), 122.

8. Ibid., 132.

9. *On Rhetoric*, italics added.

10. Ibid. 121.

11. *Cicero on Oratory and Orators*, trans. J. S. Watson (Carbondale: Southern Illinois University Press, 1970), 11.

12. Ibid., 21

13. Ibid., 26.

14. *Introduction to Rhetorical Theory* (Prospect Heights, IL: Waveland Press, 1991), 98.

15. Ibid., 98.

16. *On Rhetoric*, annotation, 163.

17. G. Tarcan Kumkale and Dolores Albarracín, "The Sleeper Effect in Persuasion: A Meta-Analytic Review," *Psychological Bulletin, 130* (2004), 143-172.

18. In 1921, when he was 39 years old, FDR contracted either paralytic poliomyelitis or Guillain-Barré syndrome, causing paralysis from his waist down for the remainder of his life. See Armond S. Goldman, Elisabeth J. Schmalstieg, Daniel H. Freeman, Jr., Daniel A. Goldman, and Frank C. Schmalstieg, Jr., "What Was the Cause of Franklin Delano Roosevelt's Paralytic Illness?" *Journal of Medical Biography*, *11* (2003), 232–240.

19. Davis W. Houck, "Reading the Body in the Text: FDR's 1932 Speech to the Democratic National Convention," *Southern Communication Journal, 63* (1997), 20–36. Houck reports that only three such photographs are known to exist.

20. A still from this scene and a brief review of the film appears in Kathleen Hall Jamieson, *Packaging the Presidency: A History and Criticism of Presidential Campaign Advertising*, 3rd ed. (New York: Oxford University Press, 1996), 495.

21. "'Despisers of the Commonplace': Meta-*Topoi* and Para-*Topoi* in Attic Oratory," *Rhetorica*, *25* (2007), 363.

22. Robert C. Dick, "*Topoi*: An Approach to Inventing Arguments," *Speech Teacher*, *13* (1964), 313–319. For example, journalists use the *topoi* list of *who, what, when, where, why*, and *how* in order to be able to write any news story.

23. Susan Sontag, "Fascinating Fascism," in Brandon Taylor and Wilfried van der Will, eds., *The Nazification of Art: Art, Design, Music, Architecture and Film in the Third Reich* (Hampshire, UK: Winchester Press, 1990), 204–218.

24. The UNCF's "A mind is a terrible thing to waste" became in Quayle's mouth, "You take the United Negro College Fund model that what a waste it is to lose one's mind or not to have a mind is being very wasteful. How true that is."

25. See my discussion of Senator Edmund Muskie and Governor Howard Dean in Chapter 5.

---

26. Gabor Boritt, *The Gettysburg Gospel: The Lincoln Speech that Nobody Knows* (New York: Simon and Schuster, 2006).

27. Michael Monsour, "Similarities and Dissimilarities: Constructing Meaning and Building Intimacy Through Communication," in Steve W. Duck, ed., *Dynamics of Relationships* (Thousand Oaks, CA: Sage, 1994), 112–134.

28. Michael Monsour, Sam Betty, and Nancy Kurzweil, "Levels of Perspectives and the Perception of Intimacy in Cross-Sex Friendships: A Balance Theory Perception of Shared Perceptual Reality," *Journal of Social and Personal Relationships*, *10* (1993), 539–550.

29. Charles R. Snyder and Howard L. Fromkin, *Uniqueness: The Human Pursuit of Difference* (New York: Plenum, 1980).

30. *A Rhetoric of Motives* (Berkeley: University of California Press, 1969), 279.

31. "Mysticism as a Solution to the Poets' Dilemma: Addendum," in Stanley Romaine Hopper, ed., *Spiritual Problems in Contemporary Literature: A Series of Addresses and Discussion* (New York: Institute for Religious and Social Studies, 1952), 105.

32. G. Barry Golson, ed., *The Playboy Interview* (New York: Wideview Books, 1981), 456–457.

33. Carter's satisfaction rating of 22% in July 1980 can be compared with George W. Bush's rating of 27% in May 2007. "Bush's Lowest Rating Tops Worst Marks for Nixon, Carter," *Wall Street Journal* (May 30, 2007), retrieved from http://wsj.com/article/SB118047452890-317616.html.

34. The Iranian Hostage Crisis occurred between November 4, 1979 and January 20, 1981. During this time (444 days), 52 U.S. diplomats were held hostage by Iranian militants under the protection of the new revolutionary government of that country which had overthrown the U.S.-backed Shaw. On April 24, 1980, a special U.S. commando unit, ordered by Carter, attempted to penetrate Iran and rescue the hostages. The mission failed and eight U.S. soldiers died in a helicopter crash.

35. The Iran-Contra affair revealed to the American public how manipulative and deceitful was the Reagan Administration. It involved illegally selling arms to Iran (which, as suggested in the previous footnote, was our enemy) and illegally using the proceeds to fund a secret war against the revolutionary government of Nicaragua. When news of the exchanges broke, the Reagan Administration engaged in a tactic of obstructing justice by destroying documents. Eventually, eleven high-ranking members of the Reagan Administration were convicted of crimes related to this activity, including the Secretary of Defense.

36. Recently, I had a personal experience with the fluctuation of my credibility here on campus in the Plaza Building where I have worked for five or six days a week for more than seven years. During these seven years, the only time I have been approached by campus police and asked to produce my school identification card occurred on a day in which I was not dressed wearing my typical tie, dress shirt, and slacks. Instead, I was dressed rather shabbily with sweatpants and ragged t-shirt. It was a Sunday afternoon, the Plaza Building was open and weekend classes were in session. There was no discernable reason for campus security to approach me and demand identification, yet approached I was. The officer had some suspicion of me. The interaction was all the more strange because I recognized the officer as someone I routinely pass in the halls.

37. Joseph McCarthy, a Republican Senator from Wisconsin, was the central figure in a dark part of American history in which an intense fear of communism, coupled with run-away paranoia cultivated by the government, resulted in unaccountable power grabs by unscrupulous politicians and the loss of many civil liberties. From just after the Second World War until the late 1950s, thousands of law-abiding citizens were condemned as communists and suffered humiliation, loss of their jobs, and even imprisonment.

38. Hess, it turns out, was probably innocent, but such distinctions were not important when McCarthyism was in full swing.

39. Quoted in Edwin Diamond and Stephen Bates, *The Spot: The Rise of Political Advertising on Television,* Rev. ed. (Cambridge: The MIT Press, 1988), 69.

40. Quoted in Diamond and Bates, *The Spot,* 122.

41. On a personal note, without Nixon, I never would have met my wife, whose opportunity to study in the United Sates was made possibly by that trip, and my son never would have been born. Everything is somehow connected when it comes to human beings and the truism is becoming increasingly more salient as we stumble, still blindly it seems, into the thick of the 21st century.

42. (Washington, DC: Regnery Publishing, 2008).

43. Lita Linzer Schwartz and Florence W. Kaslow estimate that during this period there were as many as 3,000 organizations that had cult-like qualities. "The Cult Phenomenon: A Turn of the Century Update," *The American Journal of Family Therapy, 29* (2001), 13.

44. The case for this training was laid out in Lita Linzer Schwartz, "Cults and the Vulnerability of Jewish Youth," *Journal of Jewish Education, 46* (1978), 23–42. See also Saul Levine, "Alienated Jewish Youth and Religious Seminaries—An Alternative to Cults?" *Adolescence, 19* (1984), 183–199.

45. Ibid., 23. What I and others call "Moonies" are followers of Korean religious leader Sun Myung Moon, who is considered by his followers to be the Messiah. This organization is formally known as the Unification Church, a wealthy organization founded in 1954. Moon is a prosperous business man known for his weapons factories and fanatical anticommunism. He is actively involved in politics, education, and the media—owning, for example, the *Washington Times* and the University of Bridgeport.

46. Such a group indeed exists; it is a non-profit, collegiate organization that fronts for the Unification Church. I found out later that there had been a UCLA chapter, but it was expelled from campus some years earlier. An active branch can be found at the University of Minnesota.

47. While researching for this textbook I read Saul Levine's "Alienated Jewish Youth and Religious Seminaries" which brought back strong memories of this time. This article, published the year before I went to Israel, highlights the similarities between the Yeshiva and cult experiences. Because of the cult training I had in high school, I felt very comfortable allowing myself to be "invited" to spend time in various *Yeshivot* without feeling threatened. Levine's description of how young Jewish men travel to Israel for secular reasons and then become lost to these fundamentalist communities parallels my experience, but with one major difference. I used to joke to myself that my "religion" (secular/cultural Judaism) protected me from my religion (fundamentalist Judaism). Ultimately, I would reject these types of identifications entirely. See my "On Becoming a Featherless Biped," in Andrea R. Patterson, Regina Silverthorn, and Myra M. Shird, eds., *The Quilt: Cultural Voices* (Dubuque, IA: Kendall/Hunt, 2007), 134–143.

48. This point is accentuated by ex-Moonie, K. Gordon Neufeld, "Where Have All the Moonies Gone?" *First Things: A Monthly Journal of Religion & Public Life* (March, 2008), 16–18. For a review of Reverend Moon's continuing influence in American society, see Anna Kaplan, "The Moon's the Limit," *The Humanist* (September/October 2004), 14–17; 44.

49. Common tactics of cult persuasion include isolating recruits from normal society (i.e., family and friends), peer group pressure, loving bombing (e.g., flattery, touching, hugging), sleep deprivation and fatigue, removal of privacy, poor nutrition, frequent chanting, and fear/intimidation.

50. John M. Curtis and Mimi J. Curtis, "Factors Related to Susceptibility and Recruitment by Cults," *Psychological Reports*, 73 (1993), 451–460.

51. Retrieved from http://thecaucus.blogs.nytimes.com/2008/10/19/powell-endorses-obama/?hp.

52. Malcolm X gave many versions of this speech in which the wording is changed subtlety, although the argument structure remains the same. A copy can be found reprinted in *The Portable Sixties Reader*, ed., Ann Charters (New York: Penguin Classics, 2003), 72–80.

53. These were somewhat misrepresentations. One thing clear is that Malcolm was a complex person who was ever recreating himself, continuously learning and applying what he learned in service of benefiting his community. See his classic *The Autobiography of Malcolm X* (New York: Ballatine Books, 1987).

54. "They Spoke in Defense of Themselves: On the Generic Criticism of Apologia," *Quarterly Journal of Speech*, *59* (1973), 276.

55. Ibid.

56. "A Pentadic Analysis of Senator Edward Kennedy's Address to the People of Massachusetts, July 25, 1969," *Central States Speech Journal*, 21 (1970), 80–86.

57. Ibid., 86.

58. "They Spoke in Defense of Themselves," 277.

59. "My Side of the Story," in *The Senate: 1789–1989: Classic Speeches: 1930–1993*, ed. Robert C. Byrd (Washington, D.C.: U.S. Government Printing Office, 1994), 659.

60. "They Spoke in Defense of Themselves," 278.

61. Ibid.

62. Ibid., 280

63. Ibid.

64. Text of Michael Vick's Statement (August 27, 2007). *CBSSports.com Wire Reports.* Retrieved from http://www.sportsline.com/nfl/story/10319802.

65. John Koten, "The Strategic Uses of Corporate Philanthropy," in *The Handbook of Strategic Public Relations and Integrated Communications*, ed., Clarke L. Caywood. New York: McGraw-Hill, 1997), 159–161.

CHAPTER 8

The Centrality of the Audience
in Persuasive Discourse

The next component of the persuasion process that we will discuss in this textbook and course is that of the *audience*. The most important point to make with regard to the audience is that persuasion is *audience centered*. Without a strong understanding of a *particular* audience, a persuader has little chance of being successful: in a fundamental sense, audiences "write" the persuasion. By this I mean that persuasion, to be successful, must "fit" the needs and constraints of the people that a persuader is trying to influence. Besides theory, as discussed in this chapter, the ability to produce a "fitting" message requires on-the-ground research to discover an actual audience's needs. Such practice is called *demographic research* which explores the characteristics of a population to identify a market appeal. Common variables in demographic research include race, age, gender, socioeconomic status, physical ability, and geographic location. Just as we saw with Calvin in the previous chapter on the persuader, simply having a message and communicating that message is no guarantee of one's effectiveness. Not only must we focus on ourselves as sources of persuasion, but we must be fluent with the language and psychology of those we hope to influence.

As is obvious, audiences come in all shapes, sizes, and ideological configurations. They can be as small as a dyad. Or, as is increasingly the case, they may be global in scope and significance. For instance, during the 2008 presidential campaign season I was listening on National Public Radio (NPR) to a reporter interviewing people on a street in London, England. The interviewer was asking people he met what they thought of the U.S. presidential candidates Barack Obama and John McCain. While each person responded differently, the interviewer ended by asking each for which candidate she or her would vote. This was an awkward question; it was clearly puzzling for each British person asked, as it was for me listening, because, being British, none of the interviewees was able to vote in the U.S. presidential election. This seemed like an obvious mistake on behalf of the interviewer. But it was *not* a mistake, as the reporter replied to one puzzled Briton, "Well, don't you think you *should* be able to vote in this election? After all, the outcome clearly *impacts* people in Britain and throughout the world."

Upon hearing the reporter say this, I thought to myself, "ahh, here is a person articulating publically what others throughout the world understand intuitively. What happens in the United States impacts the world, and the world, therefore, might justly argue that it has a say in what we as Americans do." While this statement may sound controversial to my U.S. audience, it is grounded in an element of reality. As the world grows increasingly interdependent, and as problems become global, we are each caught up in and affected by the policies and actions of others. This makes all of us interested parties in a globalized conversation rooted, disproportionately, in American terms. This makes us responsible to constituencies outside of our borders. If nothing else, when American business, political, and cultural leaders talk, the world *listens*. Thus, we have to be very careful in what we say and what we do. The world may have more of a claim on us than we think.

In many ways, the audience is the most important component of the persuasion process, as it determines, at least in the Aristotelian model, the objective or ontological conditions under which persuaders have to work in order to be successful. Remember, as was discussed in Chapter 2, Aristotle defined rhetoric as "an ability, in each [particular] case, to see the available means of persuasion." [1] These *means* exist within the context and perspective of the people receiving the communication. Persuasion, it must always be remembered, is an art, and the audience establishes the parameters within which the process can be initiated and maintained. As I suggested above, all persuasion starts with the audience, with the things that it *believes* and *feels*, with who and what it *is*. To be effective, all communication must be audience centered. While it is the case that intrapersonal persuasion is *self-centered*—the persuader wants to make her or himself feel better, she/he remains the audience for her/his persuasion. This paradox, if indeed it is one, is easily resolved when we recall that an important assumption that I have been making in this course and textbook is that our sense of a unified singular self is an illusion which persuaders exploit, consciously or unconsciously. Inevitably, persuaders, according to this perspective, must know and understand the people they are seeking to influence and must design their specific efforts to fit that community. Evidence, for example, is neither "good" nor "bad," but is dependent upon what a particular audience is willing to accept.[2] To ignore the importance of audience is to invite irrelevance and failure.[3]

The traditional conceptualization of the importance of audience, while often accurate enough, also has some problems in terms of our understanding of communication. In reality, while we like to think in terms of a specific "audience" in order to hone and perfect our strategy, audiences, themselves, often have no idea what they are and most often are created and maintained by the speaker. In one sense, audiences are an abstraction, as in Chaim Perelman's concept of the "universal audience"[4] or in Michel McGee's description of "the people."[5] In another sense, audiences consist of flesh and blood individuals; but even here we cannot assume that the mere existence of a group of people constitutes an organic or conscious whole. The mere existence of warm bodies is insufficient to constitute an audience. Status as an "audience" is an internalized phenomenon that takes place in a person's mind.

Discussing what he terms "the audience problem," communication scholar Dennis McQuail explains how the "audience... is not usually observable, except in fragmentary ways. Hence the term audience has an abstract and debatable character... [and] can thus be defined in different and overlapping ways."[6] We should not think of an audience in binary terms: this group of people *is* or is *not* an audience. Rather, people belong to different audiences at different times and in different ways. So in thinking about audience, then, the responsibility is on the persuader to decide for her or himself the goals of a particular persuasive effort and identify or create an audience for it. By this I mean, the persuader must figure out who or what group has the power to make her/his vision a reality and to identify and situate this policy within the specific needs of these people. To do this we need to at least begin to understand the psychology behind human motivation, which is my goal in this chapter. Specifically, I will begin by discussing the influence of values and motives on persuasion, then move on to discuss the persuasiveness of emotional appeals, and end with a consideration of emotional intensity and persuasion, focusing on the example of fear appeals.

❧ Influence of Attitudes, Values, and Motives on Persuasion ❧

For the most part, persuaders, particularly advertisers, want audiences to *do* something—typically to purchase a product or service or vote for a candidate. Thus, the loadstar of most persuasion is an overt act of some sort, some measurable change in the target's *behavior* that brings some advantage to the persuader (e.g., money or political support). This makes it important to understand people's behavioral motivation—why people act like they do.

To begin, we know that every behavior (thinking, feeling, acting) is the product of two or more *attitudes*. An influential definition of an attitude is that it is "a learned predisposition to respond in a consistently favorable or unfavorable manner with respect to an object."[7] Attitudes are easy to see, as people project intentionally their attitudes regarding a range of things in order to attract similar people and discourage interaction with others. This is how we navigate our social lives. From the clothes we wear to our jewelry, to our cars and speech idioms, we project preferred images of ourselves for others to see and we are quite astute at reading the projections of others. Sometimes this projection is crude, as in stereotypical high school cliques (e.g., the punk rocker, the head banger, the stoner, jock, geek, and the like) but become more nuanced as we grow older and more sophisticated socially (e.g., become spouses, bankers, doctors, or thrift store cashiers).

Attitudes, in turn, derive from our *values* and our *beliefs*, from the fundamental things that we feel, often intuitively, about our world. *Values* are fundamental and deeply rooted beliefs that we have regarding ideal states of existence and ways of acting that motivate us to think, feel, and/or express ourselves in particular ways. According to psychologist Milton Rokeach, these values can be classified as "terminal" or as "instrumental."[8] *Terminal values* are things such as "comfort," "security," "freedom," and "beauty," the end states we hope to achieve in our lives. *Instrumental values* are the traits of our character that help us to achieve those conditions. "Ambition," "imagination," "reasonability," and "self-control" are examples of such instrumental values. These terminal and instrumental values exist at both the survival and the social levels. In addition to survival and social motives, we also have survival and social *emotions*. Emotions, social scientists tell us, are psychological and often physiological reactions to salient stimuli that we experience in the form of powerful feelings. From the point of view of persuasion, they are important because they help prepare or prime us for action. Be astute and watch how your emotions are strategically targeted by persuaders. They do this because our perceptions are triggered by appeals to our emotions, and our perceptions are what link together our values, beliefs, attitudes, and behaviors.

In order to motivate us to act, astute persuaders often play upon these values and emotions, which serve as psychic "triggers." In many cases, advertisers view their efforts as "button pushing." While it is not that simple, there is almost a stimulus-response rationale behind many of the assumptions of advertising, particularly when it appeals to some of our basic values and motives. While we are more complicated psychological beings, cognitively speaking, than rats or pigeons, we are, physiologically speaking, very similar to other animals in how our bodies respond to pleasures and threats. While, in general, humans take great pains to justify their belief that they are *not* animals, we do ourselves a disservice in trying to make this distinction and one place where this is manifested is in our attitude toward the effect of advertising on us. The following paragraphs present some survival and social values and examples taken from ads to illustrate their appeal.

Safety and Security. An ad may appeal to our desire or need for safety and security. "Fire can kill you," one ad for a smoke detector informs us. Our desire for the product, in this case, derives from our motivation to preserve our health and to provide for the safety of our family. An ad for Bayer aspirin offers as a warrant for its appeal that "no one makes or *purifies* children's aspirin like Bayer." Or another ad that pictures a young boy being battered reads, "The scars of an abused child can stay with *us* all his life." In this case, it is not our pity that is being aroused, but our *fear*—this child pictured in the ad may grow up and harm *us*; we are vulnerable to being robbed or attacked by abused children who grow up to be thugs. So we are motivated to stop child abuse because of the cycle of violence that it spawns, perhaps engulfing us. But security does not have to be defined specifically as physical safety alone. An ad for Mutual of America, an investment firm, talks about "security," and pictures a young couple in the rain, being kept dry by a protective rain jacket that is being held up as an umbrella over both their heads. In each of these examples, we consume the appeal and we have an emotional response. We do so because we are motivated to seek a safe existence. By reminding us that threats to our safety and security exist—that is, by *problematizing* our world as all persuasion does in some fashion, persuaders hope to unsettle us, and thus motivate us to change. This process will be discussed in more detail when we discuss fear appeals later in this chapter.

Youth and Vanity. Few things are as important to us as our desire to appear young and look our best. Who among us can resist the alluring and mythic "Fountain of Youth" promised in so many advertisements? So, for example, an ad for skin cream promises that users will "get ten years back." Even though we know, rationally, that this is not true, that age and death are indelible parts of life, we may feel emotionally attracted to the product. An ad for a retirement community pictures a late-middle-aged man with a dog. The text reads: "Add years to your life, starting now. Studies show people who live in retirement communities live longer, healthier lives." As we fear getting old and dying, these type of claims attract our attention. Maybe, just maybe, they are true, as this ad probably is. An ad does not have to lie to be calculatedly manipulative.

Appeals to youth and vanity are some of the most powerful appeals that exist and they are difficult to resist, even among people who ought to know better. To take a personal example, my wife (recall that she is a scientist here at UCD) came home one day from work excited. She had seen a seminar in which a well-established scientist was discussing his research on preventing the deleterious effects of aging. His results were promising and published in peer-reviewed science journals. My wife found him to be a dynamic speaker and was intrigued by what he said. After his talk, she met with him and discovered that he had started a company to market a supplement product based on his research—having to do with concentrated amounts of red grape skin. After hearing my wife describe what she had seen and heard, and with her endorsement, I went out and purchased a sizeable quantity of this product, only to be sickened by the supplement. I knew better and she knew better—we are talking basic science where medical breakthroughs, while often significant in-and-of-themselves for advancing scientific *theory*, do not translate necessarily into *practical* applications until many years or decades down the road, if ever. While we both understood this rationally our emotions prevailed—well, we thought, why not give it a try anyway? It cannot hurt. As it turned out, I had wasted a hundred dollars and spent one miserable day nauseous and with the worst headache I have had in my life. The remaining supplements went into the trashcan.

Generosity, Considerateness, and Equality. Most of us want to feel that we are nice, considerate, and "reasonable" people who are sensitive to the needs of others, and we receive social capital for sharing and being concerned with those in our community. Generosity is a virtue, we are often reminded and urged to give. Thus, consumers of the mass media frequently view pictures of sick or poor children, accompanied with appeals such as, "A little girl should not have to beg for food" or "Protecting one precious life at a time."

Sometimes these appeals can be very sophisticated. For example, I received a thick envelope one day from an organization called the National Campaign For Tolerance. The ad consisted of eight pages of appeal plus a certificate stating that my name has been placed on a "Wall of Tolerance" in Montgomery, Alabama. The wall, I was told, honors "those who are leading the way toward a more tolerant America as Founding Members of the National Campaign For Tolerance." Two signatures appeared on the certificate—one of which was Rosa Parks, the great civil rights icon. According to the letter, the wall is intended to honor people like myself who fight daily for the cause of tolerance in the struggle for human rights in the United States. Of course, I have to make sure they spell my name correctly, and there is an envelope available to confirm the spelling of my name and enclose my check. Although for the most part baseless (I was on a mailing list because I had donated money previously to a related charitable organization), this was a flattering letter. But with its flattery came a predicament. I either send in my money confirming the good judgment of this selfless and upstanding organization or I admit to myself that I am *not* the great person they thought I was. Do I want to let down Rosa Parks and the wonderful movement for civil rights and equality that she represents?

Popularity and Belonging. When we are told to "Be a Pepper" or to "Join the Pepsi Generation," advertisers are playing upon an important motivation in our lives—the need to belong to something (i.e., the need for inclusion). Now most of us would look at those slogans and laugh. After all, they are empty. What is the Pepsi Generation? Objectively, it is nothing. But subjectively, it is an attitude, one that we and our children internalize if we are heavy consumers of the media. Belonging to the Pepsi Generation is a learned behavior. Yes, we think such appeals are superficial, but, in spite of ourselves, they work. By consuming products, we often come to feel included in a particular world view. In turn, we invest ourselves in that world. Through consumption, we experience vicariously the psychological rewards of belonging to something larger than ourselves.

Pride and Material Success. People have ambition to be the best, to succeed, to achieve the higher stages of Maslow's hierarchy (as discussed in Chapter 6). We want happiness, pride, prestige, material comfort, and convenience. "You've earned it. Now enjoy it" says one ad for Buick's Park Avenue automobile. Buick adds, "You've worked hard. Put in the extra hours. Now it is time to take a little time off for good behavior." "Because you deserve to be rewarded" states Visa alongside a picture of a deserving middle-class couple. "Have a vision. Be demanding" is one message that the U.S. armed forces promotes. In each of these cases, audiences are inclined to accept the persuader's basic premise—that we are special, deserving people whose turn it is to be rewarded for what we do. Who will disagree with that? Few people are honest enough with themselves to say, "No, I'm not, I don't, I'm a lazy, no good shiftless slacker who cheats people whenever I can. What I deserve is a swift kick in the behind!" In this highly competitive world where many of us are often underappreciated for what we do at work, it feels good to be recognized and flattered, even if it is only self-flattery.

These types of appeals remind me of an anecdote from when I took my first teaching position at another university. One of the faculty members had purchased a new car. While she was eager to tell us this fact, she refused to tell us the *type* of car she bought. One day after work two other faculty members and I were leaning against our cars (mine was a Honda Civic, another was a station wagon, and the third was a similar type of modest, practical car), chatting in the parking lot before going home. The door to the building opened and out walked the faculty member who would not tell us what car she had just purchased. As she saw the three of us standing in the parking lot she turned bright red (she clearly had not expected us to be there looking at her). We watched as she walked awkwardly across the parking lot toward a new BMW. Nobody said a word. As she was about to enter her car, she turned to us and said, apologetically, "Well, I thought I deserved it." This woman was clearly uncomfortable with her purchase. On the one hand, she coveted the car; on the other hand, she felt dissonance about either the price or the incongruity between the luxury car and the academic persona which tends to frown on such extravagance and superficiality. She was also an insecure person and was using her consumption of the car as a gage of her accomplishments and her self-esteem. Purchasing the car was her way of announcing that she had "arrived," that she was "somebody." We found this spectacle pathetic and felt sorry for this person who was, in general, petty and mean to others, being held hostage by her need for such an extreme outside affirmation of her worth as a human being.

The dangers of such lack of self-esteem are most evident in appeals for cigarettes. For instance, a Merit cigarette ad presents a picture of a respectable, accomplished woman and declares that "you can do it!" An encouraging message, yes, but lung cancer is nothing to brag about. Nor is it particularly an accomplishment when Virginia Slims cigarettes urges women to "find your voice" only to lose it to a tracheotomy. We can, and should, be better than this, but it is sometimes difficult to find affirming messages in our society and we turn, frequently, to products to fill this need.

Love. As differentiated from sex appeals (discussed next), love appeals attempt to capitalize on what can be the best in all of us—our desire or need to nurture and watch over those we care about deeply. So, for example, an ad for Toyota Previa reads, "We know how precious your cargo can be" and it features four little children and a cute dog. "You know what makes children so special! Everything. We feel the same way about our new Previa."

Other ads try to commercialize or commoditize the emotion of love itself. An ad for diamond rings declares that this is "what extraordinary love looks like." An ad for a cologne reads, "Your love should be so strong." It is precisely because love appeals are so effective in getting our attention, and so defining of human character, that politicians attempt to appear loveable and loving. A good way to do this is to be pictured with their families. The best way, however, is to be pictured holding a baby. The more the merrier, and politicians can always be found with babies nearby, especially during elections.

Sexual Attraction. One easily and often manipulated survival emotion is sexual attraction. While the intensity of appeals to sexual attraction ranges variously from context to context, the appeals are unmistakably present in many of our magazines and billboards. The appeal may involve, innocently enough, the picture of a woman lying on a raft in crystal clear waters, advertising Hawaii, the Bahamas, or the Virgin Islands. Or the appeal may involve a man, who happens to be selling cologne, looking as if he were the "ideal" lover. Ads such as these probably do not cross the border into what we understand socially as pornography, and there is certainly nothing wrong with reminding us that we are passionate, romantic, even sexual creatures. Honest expression of healthy sexuality is nothing for which to be ashamed and may be among our greatest resources as a species. The shame people feel toward sexuality is *added* to the experience of sex by us; it is not found in nature. Worldviews or ideologies that defile sexuality and interpret it as something alien to ourselves and "dirty" are themselves alienating and potentially calamitous to human psychological health.

But sometimes, combined with innuendo, or even with photogenic flair, the sexual connections become more overt, increasingly imitating the images found in mainstream pornography—these range from silly to insulting. In an ad for cigarettes, two women are having lunch together. One woman, grinning with a naughty expression on her face, says to the other that "length doesn't matter." She is holding in her hand a long cigarette, but it does not take much of an imagination to reposition the pose and the object of admiration. An ad for Southern Comfort whiskey boldly declares that its product is a "liquid panty remover." In an ad for Robert Lee Morris watches, the viewer is confronted with a black and white picture of a naked woman, featuring her abdominal and pelvic regions. Her hand is covering her reproductive organ. The pubic hairs have been removed. She is wearing the advertised watch. In consuming the product, we are encouraged, in a sense, to "consume" something else. Similarly, in Paris Hilton's soft-core pornography television ad for Carl's Jr. she sexualizes the consumption of a hamburger.[9]

A commercial for a candy bar draws the connections in an even more overt way. The commercial is a parody of commercials for phone sex. In the thirty-second spot, we are presented with three women in sexy, seductive clothing and poses. Striking a prurient ethos, the women whisper about hot peanuts and creamy chocolate. One of the women lusciously informs the audience that we know this is what we want, that consuming the product is our desire. Another devilishly asks us about the size of our appetite. This example, presented in a tongue-in-cheek fashion, is intended less to sexualize the candy bar in question than it is to co-opt the critique of sex in advertising. Indeed, I would agree that many sex appeals are funny or foolish, but many are consequential. The ad only works as a parody because there is something substantial to begin with. Likewise, an ad for a company that sells men's deodorant, cologne, and aftershave cream products pictures a beautiful blond women licking, with determined interest and prurient appeal, an ice cream cone. In contrast to the sexuality suggested, the text tells us that this is merely an attractive woman enjoying an afternoon indulgence of ice cream. We are told that the ice cream is enjoyable and the sun is hot. Shame on us for having dirty thoughts; the ad concludes by telling us that we should be clean!

That substantial "thing" that I was alluding to above and which is the backdrop to both these parody sex appeals for real products is the deleterious depictions of women in our society. These depictions are pervasive and what these two ads do is to belittle the harm that they cause. Criticism of the advertising industry for being sexist is undermined at the same time its harm is reinforced. Again, the harm is not sex or sexuality per se. Rather, the harm is relational. Pornographic images, no matter what intensity, help train us to view each other and ourselves in stereotypical and limited ways. They are, in essence, educational. Such "education" is stated clearly in an ad from Estée Lauder which features a beautiful (and well-tanned) woman. The caption reads: "Defining beauty." That, in a nutshell, is the problem. Depictions of beauty and sexuality impose upon women and men an unhealthy view of each other, one that fails to recognize authentic human needs for mutual nurturing at both the physiological and psychological levels.

One place where depictions of women and sexuality are particularly harmful involves body image. There is a pressure to be thin, to "weigh our self-worth," to define ourselves in unrealistic and unachievable corporate terms. As an ad from The Body Shop, a cosmetic company, reminds us, "There are three billion women who don't look like supermodels and only eight who do." We must, as feminists have long reminded us, reconnect with the notion of beauty and sexuality. A popular sentiment from second wave feminism holds that our notion of beauty needs to be refigured and defined anew. It must stem from what we are as individuals and what we need as feeling, emotional creatures. Failure to do this means that the concept of "beauty" is alien to us, an enemy, something that hurts us rather than brings us joy. We must learn to see beauty as the special language that gives our lives meaning and brings meaning and happiness to others. It is to rejoice in what one *is*. Feminist leader Gloria Steinem said it best when she remarked that "every body makes sense on its own terms." [10]

We are who we are and products cannot change our bodies on a fundamental level; it is a form of social disease to even want to try. The best we can hope for, or should expect, are products that accentuate the parts of ourselves that we want to celebrate. When expressed from an internal sense of joy, cosmetics, perfume, or clothing can accentuate life and our relationships with others. However, as women, we often feel pressure to conform socially or sexually in ways that are counter to what we are, and as men, we invest in women a false sense of what we can be together. Besides the advertisers themselves, no one is well-served by these depictions. Men are just as trapped in debilitating sex norms as are women. Women, however, more so than men, are vulnerable to sexual abuse which masquerades as normal because "sexual" has become often synonymous with "abuse." For men in this class, this statement may not make sense, but for women, I would be surprised if what I just wrote did not resonate strongly with many of their experiences. And these women are our wives, sisters, daughters, and friends. What concerns them should concern all of us. In the end, sexuality is only liberating when it is liberated from the false images of what women and men can be and can be together.

Fear, Anger, and Indignation. When preachers evoke "the devil," "hell," or some other metaphor for pain and punishment, they are trying to get us emotionally involved with some position which, henceforth, becomes a *moral* position. Take any objective condition and associate it with something to be hated and feared and it becomes a moral issue. The Temperance Movement was one historical example of making moral issues out of social ones. In this case, a morally neutral object—alcohol—became associated with evil, corruption, and decay. The result was vivid rhetoric that lead to prohibition for a time, but which ultimately did nothing to deal with the problem of alcoholism. A similar dynamic is at work with regard to the "war on drugs." While alcohol and drug abuse are social problems, and while the dangers of substance abuse are all-too-real, attaching moral stigma to people who abuse drugs, and throwing them in jail, confuses the issue. Moralization and criminalization in this area create the wrong sort of energy needed to confront the social problem. We should use our power to moralize judiciously, as the emotion itself causes us to be overly judgmental and such people are like children with hammers—every problem becomes a nail to be "hammered."

In one copy of *Awake*, a propaganda tool for the "Jehovah's Witnesses," there is a depiction of the Earth heading down a powerful river, about to float over the top of a large waterfall. The caption reads, "Moral bankruptcy—where is it leading?" The waves of the water are labeled "drug abuse," "dishonesty," "venereal disease," "bribery," and "murder." With this cover, the

Jehovah's Witnesses are trying to instill a fear, or at least appeal to our prior fearfulness. If they are successful then we may open the magazine and read. If they, or any persuader, can be successful in getting us to feel fearful, or any other emotion, they are in an excellent position to alleviate such fear or otherwise fulfill an important need that they have identified in us.

One particularly interesting ad that plays upon the notion of indignation is from Sentry Insurance. The picture in the ad is of a small boy hugging his teddy bear and looking despondent. We are told that his parents had died when they were struck by a drunk driver one evening when they went out to dinner. The ad goes on to discuss the devastation caused by drunken drivers and to explain how we, the careful, considerate, and law-abiding drivers, have to pay the price with higher insurance premiums. Now that we are angry at this injustice, we learn that Sentry Insurance has a special program that will save us money. As a result of this appeal, we may consider purchasing insurance from this company since it provides us with an outlet for our indignation.

Guilt. Unlike the other emotions we have discussed previously, guilt is unique to human motivations. Guilt does not exist in nature; rather, it is grounded in our ability to use and misuse symbols. We produce guilt for ourselves. According to Kenneth Burke, guilt is the end of order, since the negative "thou shall not" is imposed on the world through human communication and our tendency to moralize our environment. Because we live in an intensely moralized environment, every action or non-action with which we engage has the potential to produce guilt. Burke writes, "out of the negative, *guilt* will arise. For the negative makes the law; and in the possibility of saying no to the law, there is guilt."[11] We feel guilty when we succeed (someone else failed or we left someone from our previous community behind), and we feel guilty when we fail for we have proven ourselves unworthy. In Burke's terms: "Those 'Up' are guilty of not being 'Down,' those 'Down' are certainly guilty of not being 'Up.'"[12] No matter where we are in the social hierarchy, there is something we could have done better, differently. The fine balance between conflicting loyalties, needs, and desires is impossible to strike and maintain for very long. In fulfilling one need, we inherently violate another.

An important motivation behind communication is to purge ourselves of this guilt. In this sense, guilt is generative and persuaders take advantage of this susceptibility in people: "Haven't you missed enough of your child's games?" reads a flier presenting the opportunity to work at home along with a picture of a smiling dad and son after a soccer match. "Help stop a different type of child abuse," is an appeal from Save The Children, depicting an African child who is about to die of starvation with a vulture standing by to feast on the child's carcass. "These babies miss their mother. Is she on your back?" is accompanied by a photo of three small minks looking forlorn in an appeal to get us to stop wearing fur. "What did you do today... for freedom?" is one World War II era poster accompanied by a drawing of dead soldier. The appeal continues: "Today at the front he died... Today what did *you* do? Next time you see a list of dead and wounded, ask yourself: 'What have I done today for freedom?'" The ad encourages people to join the Citizens Service Corps. In each of these cases, the audience is forced to defend her or himself and her/his decisions from the vantage point of a *different* moral point than the one she or he occupied when making a decision in the first place. Few of us are moral monsters, but *all* of our choices are open to criticism by some standard or perspective. Good persuaders come to us armed with such alternative standards or perspectives.

In this section we have covered some of the more common values and motives that advertisements frequently target. We have learned that we are all vulnerable to manipulation when persuaders appeal to our deep-seated values in order to motivate us. This influence is not necessarily wrong, but it is consequential. Awareness of this process may make us better able to evaluate such appeals as we encounter them in the future. In the next section, we will discuss some of what we know about the persuasiveness of emotional appeals.

ೞ The Persuasiveness of Emotional Appeals ☙

What do we know about the persuasiveness of emotional appeals? The most important thing we know is that audiences cannot easily tell whether an appeal is emotional or logical—it is highly dependent upon the idiosyncrasy of an individual person.[13] Logical and emotional appeals are not exclusive of one another. If we agree with what the persuader is saying, then we tend to interpret the appeal as logical; if we disagree, then we tend to see it as emotional.[14] This initially might sound strange, particularly because the words "emotional" and "logical" are, themselves, heavily laden with ideological assumptions we have inherited about the world. Ever since Plato, we in the West tend to separate "truth" from "appearance" (privileging one and disparaging the other), and one repercussion of that bifurcation is that we have separated the emotional from the logical.[15] *Logic*, in the sense that it has been popularly and operationally defined, involves the analytical pursuit and refinement of some knowledge that exists outside of ourselves. *Emotions*, on the other hand, are little more than feelings we have with regard to the world. Often they are "irrational" and interfere with our perceptions of "Truth." Only by purging such emotions, Plato counsels, can we transcend our baseness and act "correctly" in relation to the Good or the Just.

While the earlier characterizations of logic and emotion are meaningful to some extent, they are inadequate for a more full explanation of the relationships that human beings have with the world. For example, logic, in its Aristotelian sense, is nothing more than a *system* of relationships, a structure or *frame* we place on the world.[16] Another way of seeing logic is as a grammar. Within its rules and system of authority we define, systematically, what we consider to be true. Thus, there is no inherent ontological relationship between "truth" and "logic." There are, however, epistemological and axiological relationships, which is why persuasion is such an important part of human understanding.

Once we give up the idea that there is an inherent correspondence between "logic" and "truth," then we start to realize how difficult it may be for an audience member to discern between logic and emotions. The "end" of a logical argument is not moral or conceptual certainty, but *procedural* certainty. In other words, logical arguments work only *within* the confines of the system that it, itself, offers. Another way of saying this is that all logical systems are, in some sense, tautological—they justify themselves to themselves; one is either a part of or not a part of such a system. To write this is not to disparage logic or rationality: both are essential for human communities to flourish. Rather, my aim is to raise the status of emotions in human reasoning and to recognize, on an equal basis, the role of emotionality in human relationships. In other words, the credibility of a logical argument, and even its structure, is dependent upon the emotional commitments we have with regard to its construction and character. As long as we are within a particular logic structure, the boundaries between "logic" and "emotions" will seem clear, but that is only because our emotional commitments tend to conceal themselves.

To bring our emotional commitments to the fore of our consciousness, we have to step outside our logical frameworks and look back at ourselves. Or, more easily, we have to look at another society's logical construction. The more *dissimilar* the society to ours, the more *illogical* their social customs appear to us. But if we take the time to study that culture, and if we can bracket our own tendencies to be ethnocentric, we may find that what we mistake as "illogical" by or own standards, makes sense from within the standards of that society. From this experience we may self-reflexively explore our own culture and realize that what we mistook to be self-evidently "logical" was nothing more than our emotional commitments and beliefs that became fossilized as "truth."

The point of the above is that there exists a dialectical relationship between "logic" and "emotion," and that basic to all structures of communication is the perceptual element, which we have discussed in prior chapters of this textbook and throughout our course. What we have discussed when we talked about perception is how emotional commitments and "sight" itself is highly dependent upon the individual and her/his ideological or subjective dispositions. Variables such as mood, past experiences, needs, the situation, and informational levels all affect people's emotional constitution, and position them uniquely in the communication fabric.

Another thing that we know about the success of emotional appeals is that we must *display* some of the emotions that we want audiences to experience (i.e., *pathos*).[17] One of President Ronald Reagan's strengths as a leader involved his ability to do this well. Millions trusted Reagan, in part, because he was effective at matching his oral arguments with expressive facial gestures and emotive telegraphing. When Reagan wanted us to be mad, he was mad and we could feel his anger. When Reagan wanted us to be afraid, he appeared to personify the proximity of these fears. In this respect, Reagan appeared sincere and to be "above" politics—he seemed actually to believe in what he said. Reagan was just a guy, like any of us, and he seemed to speak in a language that made us want to listen. For this reason and others, Reagan was known as the "Great Communicator." Commentators often said that Reagan wore a Teflon coat—even people who disagreed with his policies or recognized his faults continued to like and trust him.[18]

❧ Emotional Intensity and Persuasion: The Example of Fear ☙

Our understanding of the persuasiveness of emotional appeals is complemented by our understanding of emotional intensity. Understood somewhat sterilely, emotional intensity can be defined as "the quality of language which indicates the degree to which the speaker's attitude deviates from neutrality."[19] While emotional intensity is relevant to a range of different emotions, this section will illustrate the importance of variance by discussing fear appeals. Perhaps no other variable in persuasion research has been studied as much as fear. As far back as Aristotle, theorists have recognized the political uses of fear. In his treatise on politics, Aristotle observed:

> Regimes are preserved not only through the things that destroy them being far away, but sometimes also through their being nearby; for when [men] are afraid, they get a better grip on the regime. Thus those who take thought for the regime should promote fears–so that they will defend and not overturn the regime, keeping watch on it like a nocturnal guard–and make the far away near.[20]

Or, consider the following statement from Hermann Goering, second in command of Nazi Germany under Adolf Hitler. In a jailhouse interview shortly before his suicide during the Nuremberg Trials where he and other top-ranking Nazis were being tried for war crimes against humanity, Goering responded to an interviewer who implied that democracies were better than dictatorships because the people living in democracies would make better decisions when it came to issues of war and peace:

> Naturally the common people don't want war neither in Russia, nor in England, nor for that matter in Germany. That is understood. But, after all, it is the leaders of the country who determine the policy and it is always a simple matter to drag the people along, whether it is a democracy, or a fascist dictatorship, or a parliament, or a communist dictatorship. Voice or no voice, the people can always be brought to the bidding of the leaders. That is easy. All you have to do is tell them they are being attacked, and denounce the peacemakers for lack of patriotism and exposing the country to danger. It works the same in any country.[21]

Aristotle's and Goering's observations should concern us, particularly in light of current events, meaning, at least in part, our government's response to the September 11, 2001 terrorist attacks. As disruptive and consequential as those attacks were, they were dwarfed in scope by the *fear* stoked by the Bush Administration and its proxies which led directly to the invasion and occupation of a nation that had nothing to do with those attacks. Clearly, fear appeals work and no society is immune to the manipulations of its leaders. Our society, however, is more consequential than many others in this regard and our fellow citizens would do well to pay more attention to how fear appeals are used to influence us.

What are fear appeals? When a persuader warns an audience of some negative result if they do not follow a particular course of action, that persuader is using the fear appeal. By playing on the audience's deep-seated fears, practitioners of this technique hope to redirect attention away from the merits of a particular proposal and toward steps that can be taken to reduce the fear. Fear appeals thus involve the following variables: threatening stimulus; recommendation from a persuader for alleviating or mediating that threat; perception by the audience that both the threat and its alleviation are believable and workable; the perceived vulnerability of the audience and specificity of recommendations by the persuader; and capability of the audience in carrying out the action.[22]

Some common examples of this tactic include the portrayal of a gruesome accident involving an automobile and an overt reminder to wear safety belts. In this case, the bloody accident is the fear-arousing trigger and the solution "seat belts" is the mechanism for alleviating the fear. Another might be literature from an insurance company that prominently features homes destroyed by natural disasters along with information about insurance plans. A third occurs when a politician flashes images of violent crime on law-abiding citizens and then suggests that she/he is "tough on crime."[23]

The point I make here is that we must design and use fear appeals carefully. We must vary the intensity of our appeals to satisfy a number of communication variables.

The *first* variable involves the amount of exposure to an appeal that an audience has. The more recent the appeal for a particular audience, the more possibility there is for intense fear to be cultivated. Conversely, the older the appeal, the more we have to temper it with regard to the experiences of the audience.

The *second* variable involves the degree of vulnerability that an audience feels with regard to the "threat" that the persuader is trying to make the audience feel. The more invulnerable an audience feels to the concerns raised by the speaker, the higher the emotional intensity needs to be in order for the speaker to create a significant degree of dissonance in her or his audience. The more vulnerable the audience already feels, the less intense the persuader's message has to be. Audience sensitivity is of extreme importance because audiences who already perceive a high level of threat to their safety before the appeal may actually become panicked during and after the message if their high level of arousal is combined with an intense emotional presentation. For instance, on October 30, 1938, millions of Americans panicked when they heard a radio broadcast by Orson Welles, couched in the form of a realistic sounding news bulletin that purported to announce an invasion of Earth by Martians. Coming on the heels of the Great Depression and in the run up to the Second World War, people were already living on edge, psychologically. The show's emotional realism and the sense of despair people felt upon being overwhelmed by superior Martian forces, contributed to a temporary state of mayhem.[24]

A *third* variable involves the degree of relevance an audience might feel. If the audience sees no relevance in what the persuader is trying to highlight, more graphic and intense appeals may be necessary in order to help the audience gain the "correct" perspective. For many decades, Americans have resisted the effort of the federal government to demonize the recreational use of *Cannabis sativa* (i.e., marijuana). Since early in the twentieth century, the U.S. government has attempted to associate marijuana with the devil, insanity, and death. And while the government has succeed in putting millions of recreational drug users in prison for long periods of time, marijuana remains the most popular illegal drug in the United States. Simply, young people are disinclined to believe the claims found in *Reefer Madness* and other propaganda/education efforts that casual use of marijuana leads to "harder drugs" or to the standard litany of evils (devil worship, prostitution, etc.). Switching tactics after the terrorist attacks of September 11, 2001, government propaganda has tried connecting recreational drug use to terrorism. For instance, Bush's Office of National Drug Control Policy ran advertisements which argued that buying drugs was financing terrorists—"whether you're shooting heroin, snorting cocaine, taking Ecstasy or sharing a joint in your friend's backyard." As Bush declared: "If you quit drugs, you join the fight against terror in America."[25]

A *fourth* variable involves the perceived credibility of the persuader. Language intensity corresponds to speaker credibility—more credible persuaders can use more intense types of language. Obviously, the more intense the language is, the more intense the appeal to fear becomes, and the more graphic the scenario that can be drawn, and the more the issues become bifurcated into black and white terms. With increased bifurcation, the believability of the presentation will be dependent upon the perceived good will or credibility of the persuader. After all, few things in the world are as grave, as timely, or as clear cut as most of us make them out to be. This is not to say that, on occasion, we do not have good reasons to be alarmed. Yet there is often a gap between events/consequences, on the one hand, and our characterization of them, on the other.

A *fifth* important variable that influences the emotional intensity we use to arouse our audiences is the type of action required. To arouse people emotionally without justifying that arousal does two things: first, it makes the persuader look bad; second, and more significantly, it may cause some people who cannot manage their anxiety to transfer it to areas unintended by the persuader. Consider what it is like when you watch a scary movie at home, alone, late at night. As you watch, your arousal levels go up and up. At first, this level is unperceivable. Your heart begins to beat faster, your perspiration flows a little more quickly, but it takes a while to sense these subtle changes in your physiology. You may even find yourself looking over our shoulder at times, and being unsure why you do it. Then, at a certain point, it hits you—you realize you are scared. In a conscious way, you notice the more intense heartbeat and increased perspiration that you are experiencing. In addition, you may notice that you have become sensitive to sounds far away; you may see things in your familiar environment that you did not notice before.

Then gradually, as the show winds down and the tension is resolved, you start to notice that your anxiety and fear levels have gone down, and, eventually, you cannot perceive them anymore. So now you feel fine and you step into the kitchen to get a bite to eat. As you do this your cat jumps in front of you from behind the door, and you shriek and jump in the air. How is it that your kind cat can frighten you so severely?

The reason why you overreacted to an everyday non-arousing situation is because you were already aroused without being aware of your condition. Inside of you a spring had been coiled and was waiting for the moment to burst forward. This idea also explains why, after a long, difficult day at work, you sometimes snap at your family members for no reason and cannot understand why you lost our temper.[26] This is also why there tends to be an increase in domestic violence after popularly watched television shows that emphasize themes of fear or violence.[27] It is not that the shows themselves cause violence, but they do cause *arousal*, and if you are aroused and not sensitive to that arousal, it is only natural that it will express itself in certain unexpected and perhaps deleterious ways. This is why persuaders have a moral responsibility to realize that it is not just the *act* of communication that matters, but the *effects* of communication as well.

Now that we have gone over some of the important variables that influence the type of intensity persuaders can use in emotional appeals, let us explore some specific examples. We will begin with examples of *high fear appeals*. One public service announcement has two pictures. On the left is a black and white picture of a coffin. On the right are people playing football. The large print at the top of the page reads, "It's quite simple, either you do drugs… or you don't." The part that reads "do drugs" appears over the coffin, and the "you don't" appears over the football players. A second example features a young man progressively wasting away in three pictures that depict a year of his life. We are told that "This could happen to you in one year… the toll of Pep Drug." A final example from the drug genre reads, "Smokeless tobacco can do for you what it did for Sean Marsee." Marsee was a popular high school track star in the 1980s who began chewing tobacco at age 12 and died at age 19 of mouth and throat cancer. Two pictures accompany the appeal. In the first, a young and handsome Marsee is pictured looking like any healthy person. In the second picture, taken a year later, he is shown decked out with his athletic medals and the most valuable player plaque that he had been awarded. He is lying in his hospital bed, face bloated and contorted from the cancer that is killing him, an oxygen tube sticking out of his nose.

A final example of a high fear appeal comes from The Coalition To Stop Gun Violence. The appeal begins by warning readers that without our immediate attention and financial support, 19 assault rifles that have been banned previously will become legally available again on the open market.

One of the guns listed, and pictured, is the UZI. We are informed that the UZI can kill 130 people a minute. It is "as tough as your toughest customer." Another gun, the TEC-9, has the same kill rate as the UZI and it is the "weapon of choice for youth gangs and drug dealers." A third gun, the AK-47, has a slightly lower kill rate and is the preferred weapon of youthful thugs and drug cartels. In each of the above three examples we are presented with a terribly bifurcated world, one of extreme causation. One mistake on our part can lead to horrible consequences.

While in a sense the above may be true—our actions *do* have consequences (although in most cases, our actions do *not* have the accentuated consequences that extreme fear appears often imply). This is why high fear appeals work best when audiences have had only a limited exposure to the message. For example, many people who use drugs never suffer the dire consequences that intense fear appeals frequently portray (i.e., we may be recreational consumers of marijuana and not experience the parade of horrors prophesied by the 1936 film *Reefer Madness*). The same is true with anti-smoking ads. It is difficult to convince people who are healthy in the present that their future will be as bleak as anti-smoking ads commonly portray it. Such audience members may expect that our warnings are motivated by something other than our concern for their well-being, that we are perhaps imposing a moralistic agenda on them which they may resent.

An example of a *moderate fear appeal* is a public service announcement that shows a man walking the yellow line in front of a police officer and a police car with bright red lights. The man is wobbling and is clearly drunk. The caption reads, "Don't worry about getting caught, count on it." The strength of this ad is predicated on the likely event that we will be caught if we engage in the crime of driving while intoxicated. The fear of the arrest, the fines, the embarrassment, the possible jail term, and the loss of our driver's licenses are often more pressing than the fear of a dreadful accident, which we often dismiss.

To illustrate better the difference between high and moderate fear appeals in the case of drunk-driving prevention, compare the above ad with a story that circulated in the 1980s regarding a man who came home drunk late one evening, and then went to bed without suspecting that anything was wrong. In the morning, however, he was in for a ghastly surprise. He got into his car, which was in the garage, and started to pull away. He stopped when his wife had come out of the house to bring him the lunch that he had forgotten. When she saw the front of the car she fainted. Concerned, the husband came over to the wife to help her. When he did, he "saw an eight-year-old girl imbedded in the grill of his car."[28]

With this high fear example we are again faced with the dire repercussions of our actions. In these cases, the more dire the better because, if we believe them, they lead to strong emotional dissonance (i.e., such examples are extremely upsetting). However, as suggested previously, we frequently discount such messages, particularly upon repeated exposure.

A good example of how repeated exposure desensitizes us to the seriousness of a persuasive message can be found in our experiences with dentists. For years, dentists and other oral hygiene professionals used high fear appeals in their effort to get us to fight plaque. To motivate the American populace to have routine checkups and to be diligent about flossing and brushing our teeth, the dental profession inundated us with pictures of decaying, bleeding, and diseased gums. The effect of such dissonance-arousing images would frequently last for as long as the active memory of the image persisted in our minds. However, people have the propensity to forget unpleasant things, such as pictures of decaying, unhealthy gums. As we put the unpleasant pictures out of our minds, we lose the health and hygiene messages that are associated with them.

Because of this, dentists and advertisers for dental products have begun to use more moderate fear appeals in their efforts to win the war on plaque. If the audience has had prior exposure to the message, and if the audience only feels somewhat vulnerable, and if we are exposed to counter-persuasion (say an older sibling or friend who does not floss and still has healthy gums), then we need to have a more realistic picture drawn for us, one that is believable, one that cultivates a fear of a *plausible* outcome. So, for example, an ad for dental floss pictures a glass of water with a pair of dentures in it. The print on the top of the picture reads, "One alternative to flossing daily." No blood. No threats. The ad presents us with two options and encourages us to make the reasonable choice, as does a similar ad which concludes, "You don't have to floss all your teeth, just the ones you want to keep." We engage in the requested behavior (perhaps) because we have internalized the choice and assumed responsibility for it. The options become real, because, unlike the implausible choice between the coffin and playing football discussed above, it is quite possible that we have seen our grandparents cleaning their dentures and how awkward that made us feel.

Another example from this genre can be found in an ad for toothpaste. Against a white background is the mirrored instrument that dentists use to look inside their patients' mouths. The camera angle is such that we, the agents enacting the gaze, are positioned as being the patient. Reflected in the mirror is the metal hook that dentists use to scrape the plaque off our teeth. The image of the ad suggests that their product may keep us from having to suffer in the dentist chair like this person. The success of this ad is dependent upon how we respond to the image of the hook; while we might have to wait years for acute gingivitis to set in, we may find ourselves in the dentist's chair much sooner than we would like.

Let us turn now to some examples of *low fear appeals*. As implied from our above discussion, low fear appeals are necessary when the audience has had a great deal of prior exposure to the message or if the audience feels exceedingly vulnerable. Also, persuaders with questionable credibility must be restrained in the types of claims they can assert reasonably. Finally, low fear appeals are most effective when the action required is more simple and easy to accomplish.

As an example of a low fear appeal, we turn now to an ad for a calcium supplement that asks the following rhetorical question: "When you lose weight do your bones get skinnier?" While this sounds preposterous, there is a sense in which it is true, as the ad illustrates. The picture included with the ad shows a woman, presumably dieting, weighing herself on a scale. She is obviously concerned about her weight and probably has not given a thought to the relationship between dieting and her bones (i.e., the risk of osteoporosis). In essence, the model in the photograph is ourselves. The people creating this ad know that women frequently go on diets and so they carefully explain that when women diet they often starve their bones of calcium which leads to problems when they are older. The solution to this problem is simple: chew on the advertiser's calcium supplements.

A second example of low fear appeals can be found at the beginning of a Richard Simmons video. Simmons, a popular personal fitness guru, was a flamboyant and goofy television personality in the 1980s and 1990s. In addition to television shows, he had a series of aerobic workout videos. In the video I am discussing here, Simmons asks people not to duplicate (i.e., pirate) his tape illegally. Although he may be a popular television character, Simmons is not normally thought of as a highly credible figure. While he may be, in some sense, an authority on exercise, the public image that he cultivates is that of a buffoon. Also, Simmons' self-interest is clearly being evoked in his appeal, further detracting from his credibility; he is not endorsing some common beneficent cause, he is trying to protect his own product (and profit).

Simmons is also aware that traditional means of copyright protection are insufficient to guard his intellectual property. As viewers of any commercial videotape are well aware, the federal government ensures that all commercial video cassettes and DVDs display the following warning: "The unauthorized reproduction or distribution of this copyrighted work is illegal. Criminal copyright infringement, including infringement without monetary gain, is investigated by the FBI and is punishable by up to five years in federal prison and a fine of $250,000." We have all seen this warning thousands of times, and few people take the warning seriously. Part of the reason why it has become invisible, aside from the sheer repetition of the exposure, is that it does not appear appropriate for the context. The FBI warning is too harsh. It threatens us with a stiff prison sentence and an excessive fine for illegally duplicating commercial videos, even if we are not duplicating for monetary gain. The incongruence between the "crime" and the punishment heightens our disrespect for what appears to be an intrusive government policy. After all, we bought the tape, so why should we not be able to make a copy to give to our friends?[29]

Another way to read the FBI warning is that it is directed at commercial pirating, which is not exclusively the case. Either way we look at it, the warning seems excessive or irrelevant, not to mention unenforceable when copying is done for private consumption, and thus people tend not to comply. The harshness of the FBI warning reminds me of another instance, of the warning that appeared for decades on pillows and mattresses that read, "Do not remove under penalty of law." While the warning was there for the *manufacturer*, it looked as if it were speaking to *us*. Playing off of this confusion, a cartoon displayed a house surrounded by police, the army, and a SWAT team. A surprised man is poking his head through the door and is being confronted by a detective who says, "We have been informed that you removed the little tag from your mattress."[30] It is within this environment of discounting threats that are perceived as being unbelievable or unenforceable due to audience familiarity and viewer rejection, as in the FBI warning for individual duplications, that Simmons seeks to persuade us.

Simmons wants a simple action—what amounts, in effect, to a non-action: He pleads with us to not duplicate his tapes. To get us to see this as an important message, Simmons presents us with a 90-second skit. The video opens with Simmons and a small group of police officers standing in front of a warehouse. He tells us that someone is inside the warehouse illegally duplicating copies of his "Sweating to the Oldies" exercise tapes. As the police burst into the operation, they find many rooms filled with Simmons' video material and scores of duplicating machines. Simmons is beside himself with disbelief and anger that somebody would do such a mean thing to him.

After a few moments, the police announce that they have captured the ring leader. Simmons races to confront this criminal and is shocked to find that the culprit is his little white-haired mother. "Mother! What are you doing here?" he exclaims. His mother replies in her grandmother voice, "I'm making tapes… for my friends." Simmons shakes his head in disbelief and asks a police officer how many pirated tapes there were. The officer replies, "There must be fifty thousand tapes here." The scene inside the warehouse ends with Simmons ordering the police to cart her off to jail.

The final scene of this skit returns us to the police gathered outside the warehouse. Inside a police car is Simmons' mother. She is handcuffed and beats the handcuffs against the window of the car as she cries, "Let me out." Simmons, choking back tears, watches as the police car pulls away. Looking straight into the camera, he says, "Please don't duplicate tapes. This may happen to you . . . or to your mother." He calls out, "Bye, Shirley . . . write."

After the skit fades away, we see the traditional FBI warning. While we may have ignored the FBI warning, we were drawn in by the "drama" or humor of Simmons' skit and we became active consumers of his message. Whether or not Simmons' skit keeps us from duplicating his tapes is another issue. The skit was successful, at least, in getting its point across and that by itself is an accomplishment, given the cultural limitations of the message.

A final, more extended, example of fear appeals and of emotional manipulation comes from the efforts of officials in Nazi Germany to justify their extermination policies of the sick and the mentally ill in the years immediately preceding the "Final Solution" (i.e., the genocide) of the Jews. In their test run for their larger efforts against the Jews, the Germans, in a program called Aktion T4—the Nazi code for their murder campaign against the disabled—attempted to rid systematically their country of their sick and invalid.[31]

To promote their policies, the Nazis made a number of "informational" films and feature pictures that attempted to depict their actions in a "moral" light. In one such film, the viewer is presented with an extended scene; a classroom with healthy "Aryan" children and their handsome professor, a man described as being "close to life's experiences."[32] These Aryan images are contrasted with what John J. Michalczyk calls "frequent staged scenes of degradation"; that is, images of sickly human beings, who are presented as mentally, morally, and spiritually incapable of comprehending human existence.[33] Many of the people are healthy, but they are shown in dark rooms with stark underneath lighting to make them appear grotesque and fearsome. As Michalczyk notes, "These films expose the apparent tragic state of the hereditarily ill by deliberately stigmatizing their situation."[34] Such efforts by the Germans were early examples of visual deception used to manipulate emotional arousal. (Visual deception is discussed in Chapter 10.)

In the speech that the Nazi professor gives to his class, he makes us fear the hopeless invalids that he describes, and whose images are interspersed throughout the film. He emotionally builds the case that any rational person would want to die rather than to be like them. Of course we, as audience members, can make that sort of decision now, particularly when it is *other* people that we are condemning to death. But it is a fallacy to assume that we would feel the same way if *we* were in similar conditions. The actual experience of these patients may, in fact, be quite different from the images we are encouraged by the Nazis to digest.

What is mystified further is the questionable premise that the State should involve itself in systematic "mercy" killings. Such issues are obfuscated because of the images we see. What we are given is an image of something fearful, which tends to override critical, rational thought. To enforce our emotional, rather than our critical, responses, the victims are described as "mad" and "incredibly idiotic." We are told that they live an "existence without life" and are "life unworthy of life." The professor further portrays the patients as "innocent victims" of circumstance who would choose their own deaths if they had the mental capacity to be aware of their conditions: "Is this not the sacred demand of charity," he implores, "that we alleviate their suffering?"

As mentioned above, paraded before the gaze of the viewer are scores of "monsters," the most grotesque and obscene of the physically and mentally deformed. The film implies that these cases are typical, the standard by which all patients should be judged. In other words, because of the monstrosity of these creatures we can reach the conclusion that the mentally ill, *en masse*, should be condemned to a "merciful" death. From here, it is easy to extend this conclusion to a wide range of conditions that we define as "mentally ill," such as political or religious dissent. The standard for the most extreme cases becomes the standard to judge all cases.

The professor ends his appeal with a personal gesture. In light of the horror to which we have been exposed, he admits that he, too, would want to die in order to avoid those conditions. In so doing, the professor speaks all of our fears. Any of us, he warns, can be stricken down by some crippling disease and made dependent upon the mercy of others. Would we not, then, want to be relieved of our pain? The professor ends his speech with a quote from a mother who wrote to him. She implores him, "Don't ask, just do it!" which is, of course, the very message that the Nazi government wanted its citizens to internalize with regard to its social and political policies.

ஐ Conclusion ଔ

In dealing with audiences, particularly in this mass-mediated culture in which we live, we have to be aware of how we are positioned and how our emotions are constantly being manipulated. Advertisers, not to mention the people we interact with every day, know that we have hopes, fears, needs, and desires and they attempt—either innocently or not—to use these emotions to encourage us to do things. The goal may be to sell a product, sell a candidate or an idea, or to increase one's intimacy with another, but the process is the same. This is wholly human and normal. This chapter, and, in a wider sense, this textbook and course, has been about heightening our awareness of this positioning and manipulation, and about empowering individuals who make up the audience to be more engaged and discerning citizens. With a little bit of critical awareness and some practice, we may find our lives to be a little less physically and emotionally cluttered. We may find that we can breathe a bit easier and experience life in a more human and humane fashion.

൭ Notes ൖ

1. *On Rhetoric: A Theory of Civic Discourse,* trans. George A. Kennedy (New York: Oxford University Press, 1991), 36.

2. This point is reflected in several essays in J. Jeffery Auer, ed., *The Rhetoric of Our Times* (New York: Meredith Corporation, 1969).

3. Interestingly, audiences may exist in the future; that is, they may come into existence long after the speaker has died. For example, Friedrich Nietzsche was ignored during his lifetime and his work, to the extent it was read, was ridiculed. Yet Nietzsche expected this and self-consciously wrote for a future audience where his arguments would be appreciated. Throughout his writings he acknowledged how premature his thinking was in the context of his time. As he noted in his autobiography, "The time for me hasn't come yet: some are born posthumously." *Basic Writings of Nietzsche* (New York: Modern Library, 2000), 715.

4. See John W. Ray, "Perelman's Universal Audience," *Quarterly Journal of Speech, 64* (1978), 361–375.

5. Michael Calvin McGee, "The 'Ideograph': A Link Between Rhetoric and Ideology," *Quarterly Journal of Speech, 66* (1980), 1–16.

6. *Audience Analysis* (Thousand Oaks, CA: Sage Publications, 1997), 2.

7. Martin Fishbein and Icek Ajzen, *Belief, Attitude, Intention and Behavior: An Introduction to Theory and Research* (Reading, MA: Addison-Wesley, 1975), 6.

8. Milton Rokeach, *Beliefs, Attitudes, and Values: A Theory of Organization and Change* (San Francisco: Jossey-Bass, 1968).

9. The ad can be viewed at http://www.spike.com/video/paris-hiltons-carls/2671016.

10. *The Strength to Resist: The Media's Impact on Woman and Girls*, produced and directed by Margaret Lazarus and Renner Wunderlich (Cambridge, MA: Cambridge Documentary Films, 2005).

11. *The Rhetoric of Religion* (Berkeley: University of California Press, 1970), 294.

12. *Language As Symbolic Action* (Berkeley, CA: University of California Press, 1966), 15.

13. Richard L. Johannesen, *Ethics in Human Communication* 4th ed. (Prospect Heights, IL:

Waveland Press, 1996), 127. See Samuel L. Becker, "Research on Emotional and Logical Proofs," *Southern Speech Journal, 28* (1963), 198–207.

14. Ali Lefford, "The Influence of Emotional Subject Matter on Logical Reasoning," *Journal of General Psychology, 34* (1946), 127–151; and Randall C. Reuchelle, "An Experimental Study of Audience Recognition of Logical and Intellectual Appeals in Persuasion," *Speech Monographs, 25* (1958), 49–58.

15. See my chapter on Plato in *The Rise of Rhetoric and Its Intersection With Modern Critical Thought* (Boulder, CO: Westview Press, 1998), 118–153.

16. Frames are discussed in Chapter 9.

17. Stephen Lucas, *The Art of Public Speaking 7th ed.* (New York: McGraw, 2001), 423.

18. The term "Teflon coat" was coined by Democratic congresswoman Pat Schroeder. John Algeo and Adele Algeo, "Among the New Words," *American Speech, 64* (1989), 248.

19. John W. Bowers, "Some Correlates of Language Intensity," *Quarterly Journal of Speech, 50* (1964), 416.

20. *The Politics*, trans. Carnes Lord (Chicago: University of Chicago Press, 1985), 163.

21. Quoted in Gustave Gilbert, *Nuremberg Diary* (New York: Farrar, Straus & Co, 1947), 278–279.

22. This information is adapted from The Institute for Propaganda Analysis and can be found on their webpage at http://www.propagandacritic.com/articles/ct.sa.fear.html. See also Franklin Boster and Paul Mongeau, "Fear-Arousing Persuasive Messages," in Robert N. Bostrom, ed., *Communication Yearbook, 8* (Newbury Park, CA: Sage, 1984), 330–375.

23. Ibid.

24. Howard Koch, *The Panic Broadcast: Portrait of an Event* (Boston: Little, Brown, 1970).

25. For a sample video, "America's Drug Habit Funds Terrorism & Terrorists," see http://www.youtube.com/watch?v=AVQnbNspHsk

26. An alternative explanation for this type of situation can be found in the Freudian notion of displacement.

27. Or violent sports such as football. See Walter Gantz, Samuel D. Bradley, and Zheng Wang, "Televised NFL Games, the Family, and Domestic Violence: A 15-city Study," in Arthur A.

Raney and Jennings Bryant, eds., *Handbook of sports and media* Mahwah, NJ: Lawrence Erlbaum Associates, 2006), 365–381.

28. From an Ann Landers syndicated column published in the 1986. The example was widely circulated and later debunked as an urban myth. See http://www.snopes.com/horrors/gruesome/bargrill.asp.

29. Intellectual resources, arguably, are meant to be shared. As Thomas Jefferson famously noted, "He who receives an idea from me, receives instruction himself without lessening mine; as he who lights his taper at mine, receives light without darkening me. That ideas should freely spread from one to another over the globe, for moral and mutual instruction of man, and improvement of his condition, seem to have been peculiarly and benevolently designed by nature, when she made them, like fire, expansible over all space, without lessening their density at any point, and like the air in which we breath, move, and have our physical being, incapable of confinement or exclusive appropriation." Letter to Isaac McPherson, August 13, 1813, in John P. Foley, ed., *The Jeffersonian Cyclopedia* (New York: Funk & Wagnalls, 1900), 433.

30. Responding to the confusion caused to consumers, the wording was changed in recent years to "This tag may not be removed except by the consumer."

31. This was the abbreviation for Tiergartenstrasse 4, the address of Reich Health Office in Berlin.

32. The Nazi film footage is included in an American documentary, *Selling Murder: The Killing Films of the Third Reich* (Discovery Channel, 1993), written by Michael Burleigh and directed by Joanna Mack.

33. "Euthanasia in Nazi Propaganda Films: Selling Murder," in John J. Michalczyk, ed., *Medicine, Ethics, and the Third Reich* (Kansas City, MO: Sheed & Ward, 1994), 65.

34. Ibid.

CHAPTER 9

Persuasion and the Transformative
Power of Language

Language, the subject of this chapter, is perhaps the most exciting and intellectually satisfying aspect in our study of persuasion. It is certainly the most *substantial*. As philosopher Susanne K. Langer notes, language "is the highest and most amazing achievement of the symbolic human mind. The power it bestows is almost inestimable, for without it anything called 'thought' is impossible. The birth of language is the dawn of humanity."[1] Such sentiment is not hyperbole, nor is Langer alone in her appraisal of language. Kenneth Burke talked proudly of being a "word-smith," that is, a coconstructor of meaning along with fellow word-smiths. Philosopher Martin Heidegger argued that we live in the house of language. Other philosophers such as Ralph Waldo Emerson, Friedrich Nietzsche, Michel Foucault, and Richard Rorty took note of, and celebrated, the influence of language in defining and grounding the human experience. From this observation, they constructed their philosophical humanisms—philosophies that liberate people from the stultification of custom and dogmatism, reinvesting in humans responsibility for their actions. All of them maintain that what counts as "truth" is the socially appropriate manipulation of rhetorical tropes and figures, and that the use of such tropes and figures are morally, socially, and politically consequential, demanding our great attention as critical students, consumers, and citizens—recall our discussion in Chapter 1 of Nietzsche's definition of truth as a "mobile army of metaphors, metonyms, and anthropomorphisms."

On a more practical level, many scholars and students who have become involved with the communication discipline were first attracted to it by an intuitive love of language. Either through high school or college debate, a profound experience that we might have had with popular music or literature, or the everyday love of being and sharing with family and friends, we are drawn to the study of communication because of the power and beauty of *words*—words that bring us together in friendships and communities or words that take us apart. Almost without exception, we love to talk, joke, argue, socialize, and be entertained. We take pleasure in the sound of our voice and in the voices of others. Words matter to us in profound ways, and we often sense this even when we do not have the theoretical language to describe it. We are humans *first* and theorists or students of communication *second*. The study of communication is, from a humanist point of view, the study of our humanity. In studying language, we are, in many ways, studying ourselves, and what could be more interesting and important than that?

In my situation, it was Beat author Jack Kerouac's 1957 novel *On The Road* that initiated me into the study of communication. The chord that it struck with me sensitized me to the power of language to inspire and transform people.[2] When I read and reread the novel in high school and college, I experienced its profound power over me, and I could see its exciting influence on other people and on society in general. The novel both spoke to me and transformed me; I wanted to be like Kerouac and the other Beat writers and help instigate a new literary revolution and inspire a counterculture. I longed for the world Kerouac described and to be a member of the counterculture that grew up around it. As a young man I found Kerouac's book and its aura captivating, but did not understand the book's power over me and society—I felt it intimately but could not name it. Later, in my first semester of graduate school, in my Introduction to Graduate Studies course, I discovered that rhetorical theory helped me to understand Kerouac's influence and to view communication as a resource for personal and social change. I could be *different* than I was. I did not have to accept the world offered to me by my parents, an un-theorized world they bequeathed to me by default. I learned that I could pursue my *own* vision and author my own destiny—I understood that I had within me an important agency for the construction and reconstruction of my life.

Rhetorical and communication theory, in short, helped me to intellectualize and thus gain a degree of control over the power of language in my life and to redirect my literary interests into academic expression, culminating in a book of mine on Kerouac that I characterize as an act of love, a giving back to the person who gave so much to me.[3] This intellectual flowering allowed me to move cognitively from literature to politics, from fiction to history, from poetry to philosophy, and from reaction to action in my everyday experience of living. Everything I have written since that time—and my approach to teaching as well—has been an extension of my power *over* myself to reach *beyond* myself to confront and engage, in whatever small way I can, the larger forces in society. This textbook and course in persuasion is one prominent example of this confrontation and engagement and my growth as a scholar, thinker, and human being. Many of my students have had similar experiences, or *will*, if they allow their education to touch, and thus, *change* them. Pedagogy, in my view, has no higher aim than to aid students in such self-transformation.

In this chapter, I want to explore the persuasive uses of language and various important language strategies that persuaders use every day in their attempts to influence us. These strategies involve a range of intensity and importance—from mere spice, some flavor we add to what we say for aesthetic reasons, on the one hand, to something that I call *monster production*, on the other. Monsters do not exist; they are created out of human fears and in relation to human needs. They are embodiments of our collective insecurities, the manifestation of the *Other* personified, the anti-being to our being. In other words, "monsters" are ideological constructions and the tools for their creation are the resources of language, as discussed below.

Specially, in this chapter, I am going to discuss the following concepts. We begin with the sermonic nature of language and the rhetorical source of meaning. By this I mean that language is *moralistic*; it encourages or discourages a point of view. Language *names* and, in so doing, it *blesses* and *condemns*. We then discuss the *exigence*, a concept in persuasion in which a rhetorical situation is created by the confluence of some dissonant event, the characteristics of an audience, and the constraints imposed on the speaker. From there we explore the political and potentially propagandistic uses of language, which include framing, jargon, god words/devil words (or ideographs), slanting, euphemism, ambiguities, qualifiers/weasel words, puffery, naming/renaming, ridicule, imagery, rhetorical questions, unusual uses of language, and metaphor. I conclude this chapter with a brief discussion of impact of gender on language and credibility.

ℬ Language Is Sermonic ℛ

As should be clear from the lecture and readings up until now, language is a powerful resource for the construction of our communities and our lives. At all levels (intrapersonal, interpersonal, group, public, and mass), how we talk and the things we say matter. Meaning is created through language; further, with "meaning" we introduce morality and value into the world. Through language, we are communicating constantly our likes, dislikes, enthusiasm, and commitments, among other things, placing ourselves and others into hierarchies or, at other times, challenging these hierarchies. Through language, we fall in love, fight, kill, invent, create, destroy, entertain, and take our leisure. No part of our lives exists untouched by language. All of our activities—or inactivity—reflect motives, preferences, and stances we have taken vis-à-vis the world. All conscious action is a reflection or articulation of those preferences.

In a foundational sense, we are all born persuaders; our capacity for symbol use ensures as much. As Richard Weaver notes, we "are all of us preachers in private or public capacities. We have no sooner uttered words than we have given impulse to other people to look at the world, or some part of it, in our way."[4] By this, Weaver means that communication involves the presentation of the values we use to create and sustain our moral and ideological universe. We exude these values through everything we do and are. He notes:

> No person can live a life of direction and purpose without some scheme of values. As rhetoric confronts us with choices invoking values, the rhetorician is a preacher to us, noble if he tries to direct our passion toward noble ends and base if he uses our passion to confuse and degrade us.[5]

The question, therefore, is not whether we should or should not check our values at the proverbial door, but, rather, *whose* values do we apply and to *what ends* do we apply them.

Rhetoric, as Weaver notes, is the art of emphasis, an ordering and embodiment of our desires, hopes, and fears. As such, rhetoric is advisory, "it has the office of advising men with reference to an independent order of goods and with reference to their particular situation as it relates to these."[6] Weaver goes on to note that rhetoric, or what we have been throughout this textbook and course calling persuasion more generally, "inevitably impinges upon morality and politics; and if it is one of the means by which we endeavor to improve the charter and the lot of men, we have to think of its methods and sources in relation to a scheme of values."[7] Weaver states this position elegantly:

> Men are such because they are born into history, with an endowment of passion and a sense of the ought. There is ever some discrepancy, however slight, between the situation man is in and the situation he would like to realize. His life is therefore characterized by movement toward goals. It is largely the power of rhetoric which influences and governs that movement.[8]

As Weaver and others have noted, every use of language, every attempt to communicate "exhibits an attitude, and an attitude implies an act. 'Thy speech bewrayeth thee'; is aphoristically true if we take it as saying, 'Your speech reveals your disposition,' first by what you choose to say, then by the amount you decide to say, and so on down through the resources of linguistic elaboration and intonation."[9] Weaver concludes that, "as long as man is a creature responding to purpose, his linguistic expression will be a carrier of tendency."[10]

Weaver's ideas overlap in many ways with those of Kenneth Burke who also emphasizes that "speech in its essence is not neutral. Far from aiming at suspended judgment, the spontaneous speech of a people is loaded with judgment. It is intensely moral—its names for objects contain the emotional overtones which give us the cues as to how we should act toward these objects."[11] For example, to "call a man a friend or an enemy is *per se* to suggest a program of action with regard to him."[12] Weaver and Burke's notions on the sermonic nature of language pan out empirically, since we have known for some time that the public *labeling* of a person elicits behavior consistent with that label—for example, as "deviant."[13] Language often contributes to a self-fulfilling prophecy—the more we talk in a certain way, the more we become what we speak and the more the world around us is transformed into our image.

ଚ The Exigence ଈ

Against the backdrop of the sermonic nature of language, a persuader establishes, through various stylistic and rhetorical methods, that the argument being made is vital to an outcome, that the ideas/arguments being expressed are necessary, and are urgently needed and compelling. In rhetorical theory, we call this the *exigence*. An exigence involves the way a persuader communicates a sense of urgency to the audience that is appropriate to the context and other constraints. The exigence is part of the *rhetorical situation*, first described in a provocative 1969 article by rhetorical scholar Lloyd Bitzer.[14] Bitzer defined an exigence as an "imperfection marked by urgency. A defect, an obstacle, something waiting to be done, a thing which is other than it should be."[15] An exigence is a situational urgency. It is something waiting to be done that discourse needs to address. An exigence consists of the circumstances that necessitate communication. An exigence is a problem, a defect, a challenge out there in the world that compels people to communicate. Exigencies come and go, have increased or lessened potency, and are more or less consequential for a community. For example, in the United States, the most pressing exigencies of current times include health care reform, national security, and environmental threats to the planet. These issues have no objective morally neutral solution. They are solely human problems that must be addressed, no matter how imperfectly, through coordinated rhetorical effort that will emphasize or deemphasize particular options. None of the options will be *a priori* self-evident. Rather, they all exist in a specific political and moral economy which becomes important resources for the persuader.

Otherwise stated, an exigence stems from the fact that things happen in the world—floods, disease, disaster. In few cases can human beings control these things. However, we can characterize and be responsible for our response to their threat, and it is the persuader who can make real this threat, and direct us toward the most correct forms of preparedness. The persuader, in a sense, makes "a mountain out of a mole hill" if she/he can convince us that a little mole hill has a power over us that we cannot perceive. Helping us perceive that power changes our perception toward the phenomenon. This, in short, is the magic of persuasion, but it is dependent upon the good will that must be attributed, at least at first, to the person who presents us with such implausible ideas.

Paradigmatic examples of an exigence are the terrorist attacks on the United States of September 11, 2001. These attacks on the Pentagon and the World Trade Center were consequential, but not necessarily in the way that most people think. Certainly, the loss of life was significant and reason to mourn (the death toll from the attacks was 2,974 individuals), but each year approximately 40,000 Americans die in car accidents and perhaps 195,000 due to hospital errors and this, collectively speaking, does not bother us.[16] We have already lost more American lives with our invasion of Iraq (4,329 and more than 31,431 wounded as of July, 2009), a nation that we attacked ostensibly, but falsely, for its connections to 9/11.[17] In a fundamental sense, it is not the loss of life that matters, but what this loss of life *means* in terms of our world view. Lives lost on the road driving are not a threat to our world view, nor are the American or Iraqi lives lost in Iraq. The attacks of September 11, on the other hand, *did* constitute such a threat and are important because they created an exigence, a threat to our coherent narrative about what *should be*. What the attacks managed to do was to "shake things up"; that is, they radically unsettled our world and provided an opportunity for seismic and paradigmatic change to occur to our world view. The attacks precipitated a "crisis," which, as illustrated beautifully by the Chinese character *weiji*, involves both a "danger" and an "opportunity." We must not fear crises in our lives, since that would be foolish; rather, we must be able to deal with crises in ways that help us weather them and come out of the experiences stronger.

The metaphor I like to use to illustrate exigence is of an ant colony in an ant hill. The ant hill is the defining element for that community. The ant hill exists where it exists across a landscape; it has no meaning, yet the ants work persistently and diligently so the colony can grow and thrive. What happens to the ants, however, when a mean child comes and kicks over the ant hill or floods it with a hose? The ants become a swarming mass of chaos and anarchy until, gradually, a new ant hill, a new order, takes form. Only then does the frenzy of dishevelment that characterizes the ants subsequent to the attack on the ant hill give way once more to ordered diligence and the normal bustling of collective life. Humans experience the world no differently. Normally, we, like the ants, do not exist in a frenzied state. Rather, we exist in an ordered, structured environment and work diligently in millions of small ways to support and nurture that system. As we build, we take solace in our construction. We are, or strive to be, good ants.

Yet, like the ant hill, the particular structure of our society is without inherent meaning. Meaning, to the extent that it exists, must be created within the context of a specific community. We give structure meaning through our work and play. When that meaning is shattered, as with the case of the September 11 attacks, we are propelled into a frenzied state of dissonance and uncertainty in which we search frantically for a new grounding. This state is what

I mean by the exigence. The exigence provokes in people a creative, liminal state (an in-between what *was* and what *can be*).[18] The liminal state is uncomfortable and is one from which order needs to be re-imposed—and re-imposed it will be. As spiders weave webs to catch their food, humans weave webs of meaning to gain their substance. The exigence, in short, is a junction, and decisions made here represent the foundations for a new order. The possibilities are wide open and *somebody* will step up to impose order on her/his terms. President Bush's response was only one of *many* possible responses. How Bush characterized the event is not the same as what another person would (say, for example, Barack Obama). This is what leadership means—the ability to imprint one's will on a group so that the group comes to see itself in the vision the persuader wants it to have. If Bush had not acted, someone else would have—*meaning*, like *power*, abhors a vacuum. In the hands of a different rhetor, perhaps one wiser than President Bush, the exigence created by the 9/11 attacks would have committed us toward a very different world than the one that now exists.

ಐ Political Uses of Language ಆ

Any modern discussion of the political uses of language must begin with the famed British writer George Orwell. Most students recognize Orwell as the author of the novels *1984* and *Animal Farm*. What people may not realize is that Orwell was a lifelong student of political language and the author of many other important political novels and essays on political/social commentary (unfortunately, Orwell died of tuberculosis in 1950 at the young age of 46). In 1946, he published his classic essay "Politics and The English Language."[19] In this essay Orwell argued famously that, in modern times, "political speech and writing are largely the *defense of the indefensible*."[20] By this he meant that the atrocities of the early-to-middle twentieth century—things such as British Imperialism, the Soviet purges and executions of the 1930s, the annihilation of Hiroshima and Nagasaki through atomic holocaust, the Allied firebombing of Dresden, Hitler's extermination of three-quarters of all European Jewry—were and *are* indefensible to the typical individual, the normally kind, even compassionate, woman or man who goes about life managing her/his own business, ostensibly harming no one. Yet these are *exactly* the people responsible for the planning and execution of such horrendous events—not the masterminds, but the everyday worker ants, the people who labor every day to an order that they do not question.[21] Reflecting on the horrendous destruction unleashed on Vietnam during the U.S. attack on that country, Kenneth Burke notes that an "overwhelming amount of the damage done by our ingenious, spendthrift modern weaponry in Vietnam was made possible by humble, orderly, obedient, peacefully behaving job-holders, who raise their families in the quiet suburbs and perhaps do not even spank their children."[22] The sentiment behind Burke's comment is not unique. Evil, notes philosopher Hannah Arendt, is banal—it is produced by the good intentions of sane, everyday people who are part of a terrible social system.[23]

The vast majority of people are good. Unless an individual is psychotic or has some other physiological condition affecting her/his brain structure, she/he wakes up in the morning and looks in the mirror and sees a nice person. For the most part, our self-images as civilized human beings preclude the types of barbarism that is frequently unleashed upon the world, such as those mentioned by Orwell. The magnitude and depravity of these acts preclude rational contemplation or understanding. Most people would reject any of them or their related practices. As a result, in order to make such practices possible among a community, "political language has to consist largely of euphemism, question-begging and sheer cloudy vagueness."[24] Orwell proceeds to give an iconic example of such political manipulation through language:

> Defenseless villages are bombarded from the air, the inhabitants driven out into the countryside, the cattle machine-gunned, the huts set on fire with incendiary bullets: this is called *pacification*. Millions of peasants are robbed of their farms and sent trudging along the roads with no more than what they can carry: this is called *transfer of population* or *rectification of frontiers*. People are imprisoned for years without trial, or shot in the back of the neck or sent to die of scurvy in Arctic lumber camps: this is called *elimination of unreliable elements*. Such phraseology is needed if one wants to name things without calling up mental pictures of them.[25]

In this passage we see the power of framing, naming, and dehumanization which allows for normal everyday people to do things that their consciences and sense of empathy for others would never allow; thus, they have to be circumvented by crafty and unscrupulous politicians. In the harshest terms possible, Orwell concludes that "Political language . . . is designed to make lies sound truthful and murder respectable, and to give an appearance of solidity to pure wind."[26] Students should keep this in mind when listening to our nation's leaders, for many of them serve themselves, not justice (or the public), and engaged citizens such as ourselves must listen to the words of our leaders with more than a little suspicion. This chapter will help us to accomplish this.

Our understanding of the political uses of persuasive language has developed over the past sixty years since Orwell wrote. Some of the more common ones are discussed below.

Framing. A frame is a persuasive device used to fix meanings and organize experience for an audience. Frames are conceptual "boundaries" that are constructed for us by a persuader and from within which we form our understandings of the world. Concepts "outside" the fame are not considered, usually not even recognized by us—they are, literally, non-sense—they make no sense to us at all. It is the frame or context that situates meaning. In this way, frames are norm-building and prescriptive; they provide a singular interpretation of a particular situation and then indicate appropriate behavior for that context.

The act of framing involves two parts: *selection* and *salience.* As communication scholar Robert M. Entman notes, to frame is to emphasize a particular element of a reality people receive and to make that aspect of reality more present or relevant than other elements in order to promote/endorse that saliency "interpretation, moral evaluation, and/or treatment recommendation for the item described."[27] In other words, frames emphasize and moralize by punctuating and pointing. Furthermore, frames "diagnose, evaluate, and prescribe."[28] They propose solutions to ongoing problems. They help us to "digest" ideas. Metaphors are examples of frames (e.g., "the *war* on X.").[29] For instance, the "war on terror" positions us to be receptive to any type of violence that the president or other leaders claim is directed against something called "terrorists." The Bush Administration insisted that the invasion of Iraq was justified because it was the front line in the "war on terror," just as his father the first President Bush insisted that the U.S. invasion of Panama in 1991 was an important victory in the "war on drugs." Wars are to be won and nearly anything that advances that goal is to be considered acceptable by nature of the threat. In war, there is little room for dissent. Nor is there appreciation for in-dependent thought. But this is precisely when such thought is most necessary.

Reframing is also persuasion. Since meaning depends on context, we control meaning by controlling the context. A new frame (or metaphor) chang-es perceptions and, thus, how people understand and behave. Entman notes that framing involves the "selection of some aspects of a perceived reality in order to make them more salient, to promote a particular problem, definition, casual interpretation, moral evaluation, and/or treatment recommendation" for the object being discussed.[30]

As an example of framing, and other dehumanization tactics as well, consider the following example of an apparently routine government memo.[31] The situation being described is this: A government official has penned a memo to the manager of a factory that manufactures industrial vans. The gov-ernment has purchased a dozen or so of these vehicles, some of which have already been delivered and placed into operation. The government is generally satisfied with the use of their vans, but has requested that small changes be made to improve overall performance. The memo sets out to document these changes and is part of a request that they be made immediately on the vans yet to be delivered and retrofitted on the vans that are already in service when they are brought in for routine maintenance. There is nothing usual about this inter-action; millions of memos like this are produced each year by governments and business people throughout the world. Memos are the "blood" of organiza-tional life.

The first point, notes the memo writer, is that, as experienced users of the van, the government has noticed that, in practice, the design of the van can be improved to make it more efficient. For instance, the writer notes that "maximum use of space is impossible, not because of any possible overload, but because loading to full capacity would affect the vehicle's stability." No vehicle is much use if it is unstable. This is a structural problem, making a "re-duction of the load space... necessary." The memo writer explains that the government is forced to reduce "the number of pieces loaded." This is clearly inefficient and "extends the operating time, as the empty void must also be filled with carbon monoxide." Unstable vans are dangerous and compensating for such problems as they exist interferes with productivity. The next passage of the memo is worth quoting in its entirety:

On the other hand, if the load space is reduced, and the vehicle is pack-ed solid, the operating time can be considerably shortened. The man-ufacturers told us during a discussion that reducing the size of the van's rear would throw it badly off balance. The front axle, they claim, would be overloaded. In fact, the balance is automatically restored, because the merchandise aboard displays during the operation a natural ten-dency to rush to the rear doors, and is mainly found lying there at the end of the operation. So the front axle is not overloaded.

The memo writer goes on to explain that the lighting inside the cargo area of the van needs better protection. He wants the lamps to be enclosed by steel mesh to keep them from being smashed by the cargo. Presumably, the heavy grates of goods shift during travel and bang up the van's interior. He goes on to state that, in actuality, the manufacturer can dispense with the lights altogether because they are not really used. But he adds, however, that the darkness is alarming for the cargo: "it has been observed that when the doors are shut, the load always presses hard against them as soon as darkness sets in. This is because the load naturally rushes toward the light when darkness sets in, which makes closing the doors difficult." The writer thus counsels that it would "be useful to light the lamp before and during the first moments of the operation." Using the light apparently results in less "screaming" from the cargo hold.

The final request is that for "easy cleaning of the vehicle, there must be a sealed drain in the middle of the floor. The drainage hole's cover, eight to twelve inches in diameter, would be equipped with a slanting trap, so that fluid liquids can drain off during the operation. During cleaning, the drain can be used to evacuate large pieces of dirt." This request is certainly practical, as the proper cleaning of any vehicle is an important part of routine maintenance and serves to help protect the government's investment. As our parents' have no doubt reminded us, cleanliness is next to godliness.

With the sole exception of the word "screaming," it is impossible to determine what is being "processed" in these vans. Livestock does not scream. People scream. The people, in this case, are Jews, and the government writing this memo is Hitler's Nazi regime. The effect of this discourse is to keep from mind what exactly is being done here—the mass execution of people. These vehicles were, in essence, mobile gas chambers. Exhaust from the vehicle was captured and recycled back into the cargo hold where people were packed. The victims died from carbon monoxide poisoning as the van was driven to a disposal site.

Jargon. The specialized language, words, or terminology peculiar to a group or specific activity (i.e., the in group) which substitutes for common language (i.e., the out group) is called *jargon*.[32] Jargon is extremely useful for facilitating the communication of detailed or sophisticated information, often by the invention of shorthand or technical terms. In an important sense, knowledge is housed in jargon—as we learn new things we invent words for them. Further, as knowledge is becoming increasingly technical, our jargon will necessarily reflect such sophistication. Knowledge, in general, usually takes place in a disciplinary context or among a disciplinary discourse community. When such experts talk to one another, they reach consensus on what is or is not important. This is the practical use of jargon. Common examples of jargon found throughout society include: *cholecystectomy* (gall bladder surgery), *cardiac arrest* (heart attack), *involuntary conversion* (theft), *hygienic treatment* (preparation of a body for burial), and *drafting* (in cycling).

Jargon, however, serves additional functions in human communication. For instance, it has a *social* purpose. It can be used to effectuate inclusion or exclusion. Someone who utilizes a group's jargon is identified as a fellow member, while someone who does not understand the same jargon is marked as an outsider. Jargon also has an *alienation* function—that is, it can be used to marginalize by making things more difficult to understand. Such language serves to mystify. Another word for this function of jargon is *scientese*: "the use of scientific jargon to create the impression of a sound foundation in science for claims, without substantive empirical evidence to support the jargon used."[33] In using this tactic, persuaders "appropriate the credulity granted to science without relying on scientific evidence itself."[34]

A classic example of the power and misuse of jargon can be found in physicist Alan Sokal's great academic hoax, entitled "Transgressing the Boundaries: Toward a Transformative Hermeneutics of Quantum Gravity" published in 1996 in the journal *Social Text*.[35] This article, published in a prestigious humanities journal, was peer-reviewed by some of the best and most respected humanity scholars in the country. Writing as a respected physicist, Sokal argues in his essay that gravity is a relative concept and that scientific facts do not exist. This, of course, is hogwash, but it is what his postmodern reviewers wanted to hear from what they thought was a renegade scientist.[36] Upon publication, Sokal went public with his manipulation and used the opportunity to chastise members of the humanities for their postmodern theory fetish that often replaces common sense. A major crisis in the academy followed. All in all, it was quite amusing to watch this drama unfold.

The important question for us is how did this happen? How did this article survive the rigorous peer-review process? By all accounts, the article was a mishmash of incomprehensible rubbish that pandered to the biases and egos of its reviewers. The article was published, in large part, because of Sokal's master use of jargon which concealed or blunted the absurdity of his claims. He mixed and combined the disciplinary words of his audience, making his article sound impressive or, at least, important. In fact, the article is near unreadable. Here is a sample of the prose:

> Here my aim is to carry these deep analyses one step farther, by taking account of recent developments in quantum gravity: the emerging branch of physics in which Heisenberg's quantum mechanics and Einstein's general relativity are at once synthesized and superseded. In quantum gravity, as we shall see, the space-time manifold ceases to exist as an objective physical reality; geometry becomes relational and contextual; and the foundational conceptual categories of prior science—among them, existence itself—become problematized and relativized. This conceptual revolution, I will argue, has profound implications for the content of a future postmodern and liberatory science.[37]

At first glance, this is part of a structurally sound introductory passage. Sokal reviewed a problem in the field (a disconnect between the work of scientists and humanists) and proposed a solution that has great potential impact across the natural sciences. As a humanist scholar, it is easy to become excited by what Sokal is trying to do. But if we look more closely at his prose, what we see in this passage and others is a thick layer of jargon that is presented in an authoritative manner. In a well-organized fashion, Sokal proposes big ideas with the language of advanced postmodern theory. Yet, the words are self-referential—ultimately, the language Sokal uses connects with nothing but itself; in other words, to a discourse community removed from common sense.

God Words and Devil Words. Otherwise known as *ultimate* terms, these are words to which the highest or lowest respect is paid in a culture, words to which the populace appears to attribute the greatest sanction or the greatest abhorrence. The concept originates from Richard Weaver as part of his sermonic perspective on language. As discussed earlier in this chapter, Weaver argues that it is the nature of being human that "conscious life… revolve around some concept of value."[38] These values could be observed and studied; indeed, they are often the resources of cultural critique. According to Weaver, God terms are expressions "about which all other expressions are ranked as subordinate and serving dominations and powers. Its force imparts to the others their lesser degree of force, and fixes the scale by which degrees of comparison are understood."[39] These words are symbols of approval or derision, of group identification or disidentification and are similar to *ideographs* (discussed in Chapter 5) which are one-term summations of a group's ideology, words "pregnant" with ideological meaning and moral significance.

Weaver was a cultural critic and observes that "every culture manages to achieve some sort of relationship among the attractive and among the repulsive terms, enabling members of the culture to identify a hierarchy of value within a culture."[40] The examples Weaver provides are *progress*, *science*, and *fact*. To this we can add *free market*, *democracy*, and *entrepreneur*. To test whether a term has reached this lofty status: the "capacity to demand sacrifice is probably the surest indication of the 'god term,' for when a term is so sacrosanct that material goods of this life must be mysteriously rendered up for it, then we feel justified in saying that it is in some sense ultimate."[41] Devil terms are the opposite—"terms of repulsion"—and express negative values; they incline audiences toward repulsion and repudiation. *Communism, socialist, terrorist, welfare, dictator, Big Brother*, and *government regulation* (or *big government*) are words that fall into this category.

Slanting. This is the tactic wherein a persuader uses specific words to deliberately emphasize or de-emphasize an interpretation of a person or event. The tactic involves selecting moderate language to enhance what/who we like and negative language to denigrate/marginalize what we dislike. Typical examples of slanting pairs include: *stocky/fat, unattractive/ugly, associate/crony*, and *aids/ handlers*. In conflict, our people are *murdered,* their people are *killed.* Our "soldiers" are "sharpshooters" and their "elements" are "snipers." Government response to an economic crisis can be a "bailout" for banks that made risky investments or a "bipartisan rescue package." A noteworthy example of this tactic occurred during the Anita Hill/Clarence Thomas controversy in the early 1990s when the people helping Judge Thomas were described by the press as "aids" while the woman accusing him of sexual harassment had her people described as "handlers." While most viewers of television may not consciously note the difference and think to themselves, "hey, that's not fair," they will be conditioned to feel, collectively speaking, more negative to the target of the less attractive label and more positive toward the other.

　　Euphemisms. In the simplest of senses, a euphemism is the substitution of a better sounding word for a less appealing common word. A euphemism is an expression intended by the speaker to be less offensive, disturbing, or troubling to the listener than the word or phrase it replaces.[42] Some examples include *passed away* for *died*, *held back* instead of *failed*, *pre-owned* for *used*, and *mature* for *old*. As employees, we have learned to fear the words *restructuring* or *downsizing* which are substitutes for *laying off* or *firing*. In real estate, a *handyman special* is a house that needs a great deal of work and a house that is *convenient to the interstate* may be rather noisy.

　　The opposite of a euphemism is *dysphemism*, words or phrases that are substituted for better words or phrases to emphasize an item in a negative or repulsive light.[43] Examples of dysphemism include: *idiot box* for television, *bullshit* for lies, *worm food* for a dead person, *snail mail* for using the post office, *loony left* to undercut a supporter of progressive politics, and *fascist* to attack someone conservative or an authority figure you do not like. In addition, most racial or gendered slurs are dysphemisms (i.e., *coons* for African Americans, *slant-eyes* for Asians, *bitches* for women, *pricks* for men, and *fag* for gay).

　　Euphemisms may be used to hide or deemphasize unpleasant or disturbing ideas. We may want to do this to be polite or sensitive, as at the funeral of a relative, and there is certainly nothing wrong with that; doing so provides us and our loved ones with cognitive comfort. However, as communication scholar Neil Postman writes, euphemisms "are a means through which a culture may alter its imagery and by so doing subtly change its style, its priorities, and its values."[44] For example, the military uses the term *friendly fire* for instances when soldiers shoot their own troops or *collateral damage* for the "inadvertent" killing of civilians.[45] A *surgical strike* denotes a so-called *precision bombing* and gives it a health-related coloring, like removing a deadly tumor. A *forced retreat* becomes a *strategic withdrawal* or *strategic re-deployment.* Following Adolf Hitler's *final solution* of the *Jewish problem,* perpetrators of genocide—that is, the systematic mass murder of a people— prefer to use the phrase *ethnic cleansing* to describe their practices.[46] When used in public relations and politics, as in these examples, this type of euph-emism is sometimes called *doublespeak.* According to English scholar William Lutz:

> Doublespeak is language which pretends to communicate but doesn't. It is language which makes the bad seem good, the negative seem pos-itive, the unpleasant seem attractive, or at least tolerable. It is language which avoids, shifts or denies responsibility; language which is at var-iance with its real or purported meaning. It is language which conceals or prevents thought.[47]

Elsewhere, Lutz explains:

> Basic to doublespeak is incongruity, the incongruity between what is said or left unsaid, and what really is. It is the incongruity between the word and the referent, between seems and be, between the essential function of language—communication—and what doublespeak does: mislead, distort, deceive, inflate, circumvent, obfuscate.[48]

An important subcategory of doublespeak is called *nukespeak.* Accord-ing to rhetorical scholar Edward Schiappa, nukespeak involves the use of language strategies, such as euphemism, jargon, metaphor, and acronyms to portray nuclear weapons in a "neutral" or positive way.[49] Such language, according to Schiappa, domesticates nuclear weapons and makes them seem non-threatening or seem benign. Nukespeak also hinders the implications of nuclear concepts to insulate them from public inspection by the use of acronyms and sanitized jargon. In Nukespeak, for example, there is the term *city-bargaining.* This sounds like something a Mayor or town council would do, or perhaps a squabble between two cities over which gets to house a major sports franchise. Unfortunately, it is more serious than that. *City-bargaining* is a concept that people strategizing nuclear war use to denote the strategy by which a war is controlled after it has begun. Specially, we "bargain" by knock-ing out one of our enemy's cities in response to that nation's attack on our own country. In other words, cities become "bargaining chips" in an elaborate game of doomsday. Another concept is *mega-corpse*, which denotes a million dead people. The use of such language helps us to ignore or underestimate the horrors of nuclear war. Other examples include calling intercontinental ballistic missiles "peacekeepers" or calling the testing/detonation of a hydrogen bomb in the Pacific Ocean "Operation Sunshine."

Thankfully, this tactic works the other way as well, as illustrated by the following from Roger Fisher in the *Bulletin of the Atomic Scientists*, the journal of a group working diligently to prevent nuclear war. There is, we know, a person who accompanies the president of the United States. She or he has a thick briefcase popularly known as the *nuclear football* or *football* for short. Inside the briefcase are the codes and controls the president needs to order a nuclear strike (i.e., nuclear war). The idea is that the president has the potential to launch a nuclear attack at any moment, no matter where she/he is in the world. Nukespeak, or jargon more generally, helps the president to accomplish this. For instance, in an emergency s/he might say, "On SIOP Plan One, the decision is affirmative. Communicate the Alpha line XYZ."[50] This language keeps the president from contemplating the horror of what she/he is about to do, making it easier to *push the button*. Fisher, however, has another idea to encourage the president to think more carefully before ordering an attack:

> Put that needed code number in a little capsule, and then implant that capsule right next to the heart of a volunteer. The volunteer would carry with him a big, heavy butcher knife as he accompanied the President. If ever the President wanted to fire nuclear weapons, the only way he could do so would be for him first, with his own hands, to kill one human being. The President says, "George, I'm sorry but tens of millions must die." He has to look at someone and realize what death is—what an innocent death is. Blood on the White House carpet. It's reality brought home.[51]

This may sound very extreme, but is it? Why is it that the killing of one person by hand is a crime, but the mass killing of many thousands, tens of thousands, or millions by remote control is an acceptable policy choice? The difference may be that when an *individual* kills a person directly, with a knife or a gun, that person *scares* us. Such a person is "out of control," behaving in a way that is unpredictable and threatening. If that individual kills one person, we may reason, what is to stop that person from killing another? But a person who kills from a *distance*, by pushing buttons or creating conditions of warfare, is in *control*, her or his passions are not clouded by emotions or anger. Such a person is only "doing her/his job" and the ethical implications of the action belong to someone else, to the "policy makers." Perhaps, none of us are wise enough on our own to make judgments about the social utility of what we do—whether we engineer bridges or bombs, whether we use our knowledge of medicine to heal or to torture. Still, the fact that we have to *hide* the outcome of our behavior should be a strong indication that we are doing is, if not wrong, at least morally questionable. Fisher concludes his point by writing, "When I suggested this tactic to friends in the Pentagon they said, 'My God, that's terrible. Having to kill someone would distort the President's judgment. He might never push the button.'"[52]

Ambiguities, Ambiguous Language, and Equivocations. Ambiguous or equivocal language involves words with unclear, multiple, or indeterminate meanings. Anything that is said to be ambiguous or equivocal is open to a multitude of interpretation and understanding. Sentences and words that are ambiguous have more than one possible meaning.[53] There are, we know, a number of ways in which we may or may not mean the same thing by the same name or expression that we use. In the rough-and-tumble of everyday life, the meaning of words or phrases may shift as a result of inattention, or may be deliberately manipulated within the course of an argument.[54] A term may mean one thing when it appears, and mean something different when it appears in the conclusion of an argument.[55]

The use of ambiguous language may be ethically or strategically justified. For example, ambiguous language can be used to heighten receiver attention through puzzlement. Ambiguous language can be used to promote maximum receiver psychological participation in the communication transition by encouraging people to create their own relevant meanings. In so doing, ambiguous language may serve to preserve options, impression, and protect privilege. Ambiguous language is deniable.[56] As noted by communication scholar Richard L. Johannesen:

> We can itemize a number of specific purposes for which communicators might feel that intentional ambiguity is ethically justified: (1) to heighten receiver attention through puzzlement; (2) to allow flexibility in interpretation . . . (3) to use ambiguity on secondary issues to allow

for precise understating and agreement on the primary issue; (4) to promote maximum receiver psychological participation in the communication transaction by letting them create their own relevant meanings; (5) to promote maximum latitude for revision of a position in later dealings with opponents or with constituents by avoiding being "locked-in" to a single absolute stance.[57]

Examples of ambiguous language include: *large, small, old, young, middle aged, reasonably priced, very good, excellent, superior condition*, and *one of the best*. The application of this type of language is useful in political or organizational discourse, as it allows for a wide degree of identification and a greater number of people feel included (i.e., ambiguous language allows for unity and diversity by fostering multiple viewpoints). The larger the interpretations are, the more inclusive is the audience. For example, a powerfully ambiguous word in U.S. political rhetoric is *middle-class*. In the United States, the middle-class is normative; that is, our official discourse is keyed to the interest of this class and Americans gravitate to its image. Unless one is as rich as Bill Gates or living penniless on the streets, most Americans identify as belonging to the "middle class." For instance, when I was growing up, my mother was a single parent with a high school education who made $18,000 a year as a bookkeeper. Yet it was important for her to raise me in a "good" (albeit an expensive) part of Los Angeles. A kindly landlord gave us a reduced rent, I wore hand-me-downs from my older cousins, a friend each week brought us discarded vegetables and fruits from a local market where she worked, and our synagogue waived membership dues and activity fees so that we could participate in their community. Because we lived in a wealthy part of Los Angeles, I felt poor in comparison to all my friends who had expensive hobbies, tastes, and, later, cars. Yet my mother insisted we were "middle class" and she supported the same politicians and policies as my wealthy friends' parents. When I would confront her about this, she would say that poor people were those on *welfare*, and because she had never taken welfare (she was too proud, she told me), she belonged to the *middle class*. Politicians take advantage of this very sentiment; it helps foster agreement on abstractions. When a politician says, "my proposal will help the middle class," I do not think that she/he has people such as my mother in mind.[58]

The *rhetoric of ambiguity* (i.e., *strategic ambiguity*) involves the art of making a claim using language that avoids specifics. The goal, as suggested above, is for a person to be deliberately vague on a policy so as to preserve her or his options. For example, U.S. policy toward China, since Nixon's successful trip to normalize relations more than 30 years ago, has been to honor Beijing's "One China" stance. Basically, Beijing insists that Taiwan is a province of China, all evidence and common sense to the contrary. To non-diplomats, Taiwan looks, acts, and feels like a sovereign nation and the people who live in Taiwan certainly think of themselves as a sovereign nation, but we are all wrong. In the parts of the world where China exerts its significant influence, Taiwan *is* a part of China; there is no room for debate on this issue. In order to maintain warm ties and business relations with Beijing, the United States and most other nations in the world must go along with this fiction, no matter what the Taiwanese people have to say. As a result, Taiwan is isolated diplomatically from most of the world. The problem for the United States is that Taiwan is an important ally—we backed its government during the Chinese Civil War (1927–1949) and protected it from Mainland China in 1949 when the defeated Nationalist Party fled the mainland in defeat and retreated to Taiwan. Thus, the United States has an interest in being on good terms with both nations. This balance is aided by what analysts call "strategic ambiguity."[59]

Specifically, the United States recognizes that China and Taiwan are ultimately part of the same sovereign entity, but opposes any move to reunify them by force. While the United States undertakes to supply Taiwan with some military supplies against China's strenuous objections, it also continuously avoids sending signals that might encourage the island nation to declare formal independence— and thus provoking Beijing. The point is that *neither* China *nor* Taiwan would be able to predict if the United States would intervene in the event of Beijing's attack of the island. The idea is that the potential U.S. involvement in the war would discourage Beijing from initiating violence against Taiwan, and the possibility that the United States would *not* intervene to help Taiwan if it did provoke a war with China would discourage Taiwan from asserting its independence, such as pushing for formal independence—for example, insisting on regaining its United Nations seat after losing it to Beijing in 1971. Newly elected President George W. Bush violated this principle of strategic ambiguity in April 2001 when he told ABC News with his characteristic bravado that Beijing needs to understand that the United States would "do whatever it takes" to defend Taiwan. This raised international consternation on both sides of the Pacific Ocean and Bush was forced to retreat from his comments and reiterate his commitment against Taiwanese sovereignty and to the doctrine of strategic ambiguity.[60]

Qualifiers, Weasel Words, and Puffery. Within this context, qualifiers, weasel words, and puffery are very important, and are related to our earlier discussion of ambiguous language. A *qualifier* is a word or phrase that can change how absolute, certain, or generalized a statement or claim can be.[61] Qualifiers allow persuaders to modify statements, weakening or diluting any concrete meaning or force a statement may have. This allows persuaders to say anything without offending anyone or putting themselves into danger of being contradicted. It is a way to avoid accountability. For example, to claim that a product *helps* to accomplish something is not to say very much. The claim creates a positive feeling in the persuadee but it adds nothing of value. Likewise, to claim that a product is *improved* or *better* is empty. Verbs such as *acts*, *works*, *effective*, *efficient* suggest action but offer nothing of quantitative value. Impression, at the expense of substance, is created by the words *seems*, *appears*, *looks*, *is*, *like*. Words such as *many*, *most*, *virtually*, *almost all* are ways of talking about quantity without saying anything specific that can be held to account.

Related to this are what are known as *weasel words*. Weasel words are designed to give the appearance of truth while protecting the speaker from attack or legal redress.[62] They are very common in advertising and marketing, where the goal is to attract people emotionally rather than ask them to think deeply about something. The allusion is to the animal weasel, which sucks out the eggs of birds through a small hole, leaving the egg appearing intact, but of course not having any life within it—all that is left is literally an empty shell. To claim that Smith brand toothpaste *combats* bacteria that cause tooth decay is not to say very much—to combat something is not necessarily to succeed.[63] Located in the same category of language strategies is *puffery*, advertising which praises an item to be sold with subjective opinions, superlatives, or exaggerations, vaguely and generally, stating no specific facts. Examples of puffery include: *world famous burgers*, *best hotdogs in town*, and *incredible (or amazing) low price*. These words matter; people, it seems, are willing to pay more money for food labeled "natural," "healthy," and "organic."

Naming/Renaming. Otherwise known as *differentiation* or *labeling*, this tactic involves the use of words to define or redefine an "object" and to alter how we view it and reality. This tactic actually affects perception and the experience of marginalized groups, as rhetorical scholar Haig Bosmajian notes:

> The power which comes from names and naming is related directly to the power to define others -- individuals, races, sexes, ethnic groups. Our identities, who and what we are, how others see us, are greatly affected by the names we are called and the words with which we are labeled. The names, labels, and phrases employed to "identify" a people may in the end determine their survival.[64]

To name or rename something is, according to Weaver, to "define its nature—to describe the fixed features of its being. Definition is an attempt to capture essence. When we speak of the nature of a thing, we speak of something we expect to persist. Definitions accordingly deal with fundamental and unchanging properties."[65] Moreover, Weaver notes, "the listener is being asked not simply to follow a valid reasoning form but to respond to some presentation of reality. He is being asked to agree with the speaker's interpretation of the world that is."[66] Most social movement persuaders have a strong grasp on this concept. One such leader is Stokely Carmichael, the leader of the Student Nonviolent Coordinating Committee (SNCC), who popularized the slogan "Black Power" in the 1960s as part of the Civil Rights Movement. In his treatise, *Black Power*, which he co-wrote with Charles Hamilton, Carmichael explains that

> Black people in the United States must raise hard questions which challenge the very nature of the society itself: its long-standing values, beliefs, and institutions. To do this we must first redefine ourselves.... We shall have to struggle for the right to create our own terms through which to define ourselves and our relationship to the society, and to have those terms recognized. This is the first necessity of a free people, and the first right that any oppressor must suspend.[67]

Probably the best example of this tactic was the renaming after the Second World War of the "Department of *War*" as the "Department of *Defense*." Since 1947 politicians have funded "defense" rather than "war."[68]

Ridicule and Dehumanization. Persuaders use ridicule to mock, make fun of, or dismiss people or ideas. The goal with this tactic is to weaken a claim or undermine credibility by making an idea or person appear ridiculous and unworthy of respect. Ridicule is a form of discourse which does not aim to directly convince the target of something; instead, ridicule aims to prevent others from adopting the target's positions and/or to lower esteem for the target. Ridicule is an example of *verbal aggressiveness*—using symbols to express irritability, negativism, resentment, suspicion, and the like.[69] To ridicule someone is to portray them as inconsistent, self-contradictory, illogical, irrational, inept, stupid, silly, trivial, grotesque, inhumane, or monstrous.[70] For example, Tennessee State Representative Debra Young Maggart, speaking on pending legislation in Arizona to make it difficult for same-sex couples to adopt children, said: "Most homosexual couples have numerous emotional dysfunctions and psychological issues that may not be healthy for children" and that gay couples adopt young men for "unfettered access to subject them to a life of molestation and sexual abuse."[71] None of this is true; what we have is an example of bigoted, ignorant language that Representative Maggart is using to prey on the fear and hatred of her constituents for base political advantage. In this capacity, ridicule is a fundamental part of the *dehumanization process.*

Dehumanization is the process whereby opponents view each other as less than human and thus not deserving of humane treatment or what are generally accepted as fundamental human rights. Dehumanization plays a large role in the process of *moral exclusion*, a dire condition in which "individuals or groups are perceived as *outside the boundary in which moral values, rules, and considerations of fairness apply.* Those who are morally excluded are perceived as nonentities, expendable, or undeserving; consequently, harming them appears acceptable, appropriate, or just."[72] In other words, it is necessary, psychologically, to so categorize the enemy if it is to be possible to engage in warfare or otherwise violate the generally accepted norms of behavior regarding other humans. Dehumanization is actually an extension of a less intense process of developing an "enemy image" of the opponent. An enemy image is a stereotype—a negative oversimplification—which usually views the opposing group as evil, in contrast to one's own side, which is seen as entirely good. Enemy images are usually black and white. Shades of gray—meaning one's own faults or one's enemies' values—are usually discounted, denied, or ignored.

Dehumanization can be more subtle, as well, even "objective" or "scientific" with the infamous Tuskegee syphilis study being one such paradigmatic case.[73] That study, which began in 1932, was a 40-year research project conducted by the U.S. Public Health Service to trace the progression of syphilis in African-American men. The research targeted a study group of over 400 African-American men with the disease and a control group of more than 200 men who were not infected. As many as 100 men in the study group died from syphilis-related diseases and others (including partners and families of the infected men) suffered from blindness, insanity, and heart disease as a result of the researchers not only withholding clear information about their disease status and treatment from them but also discouraging and even preventing them from seeking outside treatment for syphilis. This occurred despite the fact that the health consequences were known and satisfactory treatment became available during the course of the study.[74]

In 1972, a reporter named Jean Heller published the details of the study and public outcry sparked an investigation that determined that the study would not even have met the standards for research ethics accepted in 1932, which were less stringent than they later became. This study was conceptualized, implemented, and continued over the course of *4 decades,* including the publishing of 13 progress reports—one of which detailed the dire health consequences incurred by the patients—in major medical journals, and yet only two objections to the study were documented during that time. This "moral astigmatism" was made possible by the normative communication mode of the objectivist paradigm—a mode that obscures questions of value and ethics and excludes "non-scientific" perspectives. By employing the communication conventions of objective science, socially, economically, and politically marginalized African-American men were redefined as merely sites for the gleaning of scientific knowledge and a "scene" for the "dynamic agent"—the disease—to unfold. As rhetorical scholar Martha Solomon explains:

> The consequence is dehumanization and a process of division (as opposed to identification) between patients and the scientific community… Although the doctors were withholding treatment which could alleviate the suffering of victims, they re-defined their activities as the observing of the consequences of the disease "uninfluenced" by treatment… Knowledge becomes an absolute value….[75]

In other words, through the careful use of such neutral "objective" language, the infected patients were intentionally targeted and dehumanized, and the dire ethical and moral dimensions and consequences of this project were rendered invisible or irrelevant to readers and medical research staff. As Solomon concludes:

> The reports encouraged readers to dissociate themselves from the sub-
> jects by highlighting the differences between the two groups and by de-
> humanizing the men involved. Rhetorically, the generic conventions of
> scientific writing not only encouraged neglect of ethical questions but
> also played an important role in the study's continuation.[76]

What we learn from this discussion is that dehumanization need not be drastic and intentional in the crass sense of a demagogue or politician attempt-ing to justify the moral exclusion of an enemy through crude propagandistic caricature. While it could involve this, as in the Nazi equation of the Jew with vampirism or parasitism, it is often found, in more "balanced" societies, such as in Western liberal democracies, in our daily professional or commonsensical assumptions about the way the world works. For instance, we, in the United States, do not often think of ourselves as heartless and cruel to the suffering of the poor, but, we are, in practice, largely callous and/or indifferent to the tens of millions of poor in our nation because we have internalized the sense of the poor as "undeserving," "lazy," or otherwise responsible for their own suffer-ing.[77]

Imagery. Imagistic language involves the use of word pictures contain-ing multi-sensory words to "color" and influence our experience, or even sub-stitute for an experience. This tactic draws on vivid sensory descriptions and figurative language to re-create or construct an experience for a reader. Such language is often used in trial situations in which attorneys use persuasive communication to elicit mental images in the minds of a jury.[78] As Weaver notes, "rhetoric always comes to us in well-fleshed words, and that is because it must deal with the world, the thickness, stubbornness, and power of it."[79] Imagery is embodied in descriptive writing that draws on vivid sensory de-scriptions and figurative language to recreate an experience for a reader. These types of language have the power to penetrate our consciousness and affect us on a deeply emotional level.[80] So, for example, the anti-abortion National Right to Life organization has used the testimony of Brenda Pratt Shafer, a nurse identified as "pro-choice" who had an ideological conversion as a result of a medical procedure she witnessed.

The appeal is called "What the Nurse Saw." Using highly emotive and prejudicial language, Nurse Shafer recalls how she helped a doctor perform a late-term (or so-called "partial-birth" abortion). She describes the baby's heart-beat, tiny arms, fingers, legs, and head. She reports that he had an "angelic face" that she will never forget. She testifies that the doctor took "a pair of scissors" and stuck them into the head of the baby, causing him to flinch his arms out, startled, "like a baby does when he thinks that he might fall." Continuing, the nurse narrates how the doctor opened the baby's skull with the scissors and inserted a suction device to "suck out the baby's brains."[81]

Such language is horrifying, which, of course, it is meant to be. Why, the ad encourages us to ask, do we allow such barbaric practices as abortion? They exist because, in part, this narrative is not the only narrative one could give—it is intensely political and emotive. The purpose of this language is to be persuasive. The goal of the persuader is to color our world in a profound way. Excluded are any interests of the mother for the integrity of her own wishes and control over her own body and reproductive decisions as well as considerations of the mother's physical health.

Rhetorical Questions. These are questions to which we do not expect overt answers but, rather, to encourage an audience to think for itself about a specific point. Rhetorical questions incline the target to say "yes" to preliminary questions in order to build agreement and trust before we hit them with the sales pitch. So, for example, an ad from Planned Parenthood asks, "Are you sleeping with someone to die for?" and "Who else has he charmed the pants off?" An ad from the Episcopal Church asks, "Is the Me Generation doing to Christianity what the lions failed to do?" With these examples, the target is being asked to contemplate whether her or his actions are in accordance with what she/he really believes about issues of health and religious sincerity. The goal is to invite the audience to spot an inconsistency or illogic between what one believes and what one does and to exploit that so that the person becomes impelled to change.

Unusual Uses of Language. Persuaders use this tactic to gain attention, create identification or distinction, or emphasize a specific point. The use of unusual language helps persuaders to break through the clutter of all the ads to which we are exposed so that *their* product or idea can stand out in people's minds. In 2006, for example, a restaurant in India called itself *Hitler's Cross*— it was an Adolf Hitler-themed restaurant, decorated by symbols of the German Third Reich (i.e., the Nazi period). According to the restaurant's manager, "We wanted to be different. This is one name that will stay in people's minds. We are not promoting Hitler. But we want to tell people we are different in the way he was different."[82] In this case, the tactic worked, only it worked too well.

The restaurant got noticed, of course, but international outrage caused the restaurant to later change its name to the Cross Cafe.[83]

Metaphor. Metaphors are extremely important to persuasion. A metaphor is an implied comparison denoting one kind of object or idea in place of another to suggest a likeness between them—to explain the unknown in terms of the known.[84] A metaphor involves the expression of an understanding of one concept in terms of another concept, emphasizing or creating similarity between the two. Metaphors are not merely decorative rhetorical devices; rather, they are a characteristic form of human communication. They are inherent in human thinking and communication, and are central to furthering the progress of human knowledge. In their influential book *Metaphors We Live By*, linguists George Lakoff and Mark Johnson argue that metaphors are "pervasive in everyday life, not just in language but in thought and action. Our ordinary conceptual system, in terms of which we both think and act, is fundamentally metaphoric in nature."[85] They go on to explain:

> The concepts that govern our thought are not just matters of intellect. They also govern our everyday functioning down to the most mundane details. Our concepts structure what we perceive, how we get around in the world, and how we relate to other people. Our conceptual system thus plays a central role in defining our everyday realities.[86]

Metaphor is inherent in human thinking, and its main function is to help us bridge the known and the unknown. Powerful metaphors both describe and explain and then go even further; they articulate new ideas, invite further exploration of similarities and differences, and generate new analogies which include features not yet fully understood and previously undiscovered. According to Burke, "It is precisely through metaphor that our perspectives, or analogical extensions, are made—a world without metaphor would be a world without purpose."[87]

The Persuasive Function of Metaphors. Persuaders may use metaphors as a resource in several fashions. First, she/he may find that they help to aid understanding by simplifying and making concrete. In other words, metaphors give substance to intangible ideas. Second, metaphors are useful to heighten emotions by making ideas more "in the flesh," making the experience of the idea more emotive. Third, metaphors help persuaders to reinforce beliefs and attitudes in an audience. Fourth, metaphors may be useful for altering perceptions of a phenomenon. In an important study, rhetorical scholar Edwin Black explored the "communism is a cancer" metaphor in political discourse of the radical right during the Cold War and concluded that "there are strong and multifarious links between a style and an outlook."[88] In other words, the repeated use of the metaphor makes the use of atomic weapons become acceptable.[89] After all, extreme diseases demand extreme interventions. For example, U.S. General Paul Donal Harkins in 1962 described U.S. operations in Vietnam as "doing all we can to support the South Vietnamese efforts to eradicate the cancer of Communism."[90] What does this mean? In practice, it may mean going village to village, house to house to terrorize a population, to depopulate a community, to defoliate a community's crops, and to annihilate all the people who disagree with you. Likewise, a 1964 editorial published in the United States reads: "The cancer of communism in this hemisphere has to be excised, but we have all seen how hard it is to make some governments grasp the surgeon's knife."[91] In this case, the "knife" represents potential death squads and the mass arrest of leftists, labor activists, and human rights workers, as was frequently the case during the so-called "dirty wars" of this period.

A special type of metaphor, more powerful than most, is *archetypal metaphors*. These are images rooted in deep, universal images relevant to humanity, involving primordial elements such as the sun, light, heat, earth, water, air, fire, birth, and death.[92] These metaphors are globally spread—that is, they transcend culture and context. Their symbolic meaning goes back to ancient times. All human beings understand the importance of light, water, health, etc. Because metaphors based on these things are so fundamental to who we are as organic beings, they easily trigger our emotions when utilized by a persuader. For example, in inspiring the British to resist German attacks during the Second World War, British leader Winston Churchill said:

> If we can stand up to [Hitler], all Europe may be free and the life of the world may move forward into broad, sunlit uplands. But if we fail, then the whole world, including the United States, including all that we have known and cared for, will sink into the abyss of a new Dark Age, made more sinister, and perhaps more protracted, by the lights of perverted science.[93]

In Churchill's passage, light (freedom) and darkness (tyranny), two intractable enemies, are clashing. The world watches as darkness falls. The British people are asked to push back against this darkness, to move the world toward the "uplands" and peace. Hitler and his army are positioned as regressive; they are the dark, corrupted and sickly forces, a threat to civilization. Churchill's language is severe because his situation is severe. The Germans, in this case, *are* these things, and their military might *is* aimed at Britain. The British must do their part if the Allies are to win the war. Now is the time for action, he urges. In this speech, Churchill's language and credibility combine to strengthen the resolve of a battered nation to urge them to their "finest hour."

೫ Biological Sex, Gender, and Language ೮೩

Both the biological sex and the sociological gender of the persuader are important factors in the use of the language strategies discussed in this chapter. Female and male persuaders each come to a communicative event with a set of certain perceived strengths and weaknesses. Before I describe these strengths and weaknesses, I should point out that that biological sex and gender do not mean the same things. According to communication scholar Julia Wood, "Gender is a social, symbolic construction that a society confers on biological sex."[94] This can be contrasted with biological sex which is a "personal quality determined by genetic and biological characteristics."[95] This distinction often escapes many audiences who typically expect consistency between these two categories; when they are violated this often translates into a loss of credibility.

Within this typography, for example, male persuaders can use more intense language and are often expected to do so; such language is considered masculine. Female persuaders are often hindered by language limitations; they often face what is called the *double bind*. Women must not only perform better than men to be considered equally competent, they are also perceived negatively when they try to be direct, assertive, and forceful. On the other hand, men who are direct, assertive, and forceful are congratulated for their persuasive abilities.[96]

A related trait of language that often cuts along gender lines is that it conveys power and powerlessness. *Powerful* speech forms, often associated with masculine speaking styles, are speech instances that convey authority and credibility and certainty.[97] Language that challenges, leading questions, metaphors, orders, verbal aggression (e.g., "Make my day!", "Read my lips!", and "Take your best shot!") are examples. *Powerless* speech forms, on the other hand, tend to be associated with feminine speaking styles and involve things such as apologies, hesitations, disclaimers, excuses, intensifiers, hedges (forms of uncertainty such as "I guess," "I think," "well, kinda"), indirect questions, influences ("I didn't mean to…", "I was forced into…", "Do you think maybe…", "Uh…", and "Uh… you know…ummmm"), the use of empty adjectives (words such as "cute," "sweet," or "divine"), and question forms at the end of sentences.[98]

Is this structural bias against women in our society fair? No, of course not, but these conditions remain an important constraint in not only how we utilize language and persuasion, but in how our world is ordered and structured. Such structure and order is not immutable and social conditions and equality for women in our society have been improving. Nevertheless, knowledge of both the tactics of persuasion and the limitations of things such as gender are important in order to continue challenging them. Seen in this light, Senator Hillary Rodham Clinton's campaign for the Democratic presidential nomination in 2008 was heroic; it represents a further step toward full gender equality in the world of public persuasion.

∞ Conclusion ∾

Language is a wonderful, joyful phenomenon that is, for good or ill, a uniquely human experience. I would go so far as to write that it *is* the human experience. In making this claim I do not mean to discount animal communication, empathy between animals, or culture within animal social communities to the extent that it exists in the animal kingdom outside of human beings. I honor and respect such experiences. Yet I do believe that, as human beings, we are more or less *unique* in the world to the extent that we live in a symbolic universe and draw our sustenance from our symbolic resources—that without language, we would not be recognizable as a species. We would be something different.

In this chapter, we have explored some of the common language strategies that persuaders use frequently not only to sell their selves, ideas, or products, but also to color our world. Such coloring is consequential, as I argue in Chapter 11, because such coloring is *inevitable*. The question is not to color or not to color, but *who* is going to do the coloring and toward what ends. While it is the individual who acts, our actions as individuals are aided or constrained by factors that we cannot control—our gender or race, for example, and the stories people tell about these traits.

ಬಿ Notes ೞ

1. "Language and Thought," in Gary Goshgarian, ed., *Exploring Language* 7th ed. (New York: Harper Collins College Publishers, 1995), 57.

2. "Beat literature" is a genre of writing associated with a core group of artists in the late 1940s through the 1960s. The most prominent member of this group was Jack Kerouac; others in this group include William Burroughs, Neal Cassady, Gregory Corso, Lawrence Ferlinghetti, and Allen Ginsberg. For more information on the Beats and their influence on American culture, see my two entries "Counterculture" and "Beats and Hippies" in Roger Chapman, ed., *Encyclopedia of the Culture Wars* (Armonk, NY: M. E. Sharpe, 2008).

3. Omar Swartz, *The View From* On The Road*: The Rhetorical Vision of Jack Kerouac.* (Cabondale, IL: Southern Illinois University Press, 1999).

4. *Language Is Sermonic*, edited by Richard L. Johannesen, Rennard Strickland, and Ralph T. Eubanks (Baton Rouge: Louisiana State University Press, 1970), 224.

5. Ibid., 225.

6. Ibid., 211.

7. Ibid., 213.

8. Ibid., 221.

9. Ibid., 221.

10. Ibid., 222.

11. *Permanence and Change* (Berkeley: University of California Press, 1969), 177.

12. Ibid.

13. Howard S. Becker, *Outsiders: Studies in the Sociology of Deviance* (New York: Free Press, 1963). A classic study by William J. Chambliss reports on two "gangs" of teenagers from the same school. Depending on which gang they were in, the children were treated differently by school officials and law enforcement. See, "The Saints and the Roughnecks," *Society, 11* (1973), 24–31.

14. "The Rhetorical Situation," *Philosophy and Rhetoric*, 1, (1968), 1–14.

15. Ibid., 6.

16. Sarah Loughran, "In Hospital Deaths from Medical Errors at 195,000 Per Year USA," *Medi cal News Today* (August 9, 2004), Retrieved from http://www.medicalnewstoday.com/art icles/11856.php.

17. These numbers come from Antiwar.Com. Updated statistics can be located on their webpage at http://www.antiwar.com/casualties/.

18. I discuss the power of liminality for social transformation in my book *The View From* On The Road, 94−102.

19. This essay is one of the most reprinted in the English language. The text that I used is from *Propaganda*, ed., Robert Jackall (London: Macmillan Press, 1995), 424−437.

20. Ibid., 432, italics added.

21. See, for example, Daniel Jonah Goldhagen, *Hitler's Willing Executioners: Ordinary Germans and the Holocaust* (New York: Vintage, 1997).

22. "Realisms, Occidental Style," in Guy Amirthanayagam, ed., *Asian and Western Writers in Dialogue: New Cultural Identities* (London: Macmillian, 1982), 41.

23. *Eichmann in Jerusalem: A Report on the Banality of Evil* (New York: Penguin Classics, 2006).

24. Orwell, "Politics and the English Language," 432.

25. Ibid.

26. Ibid., 436.

27. "Framing: Toward Clarification of a Fractured Paradigm," *Journal of Communication, 43* (1993), 52.

28. Ibid.

29. George Lakoff and Mark Johnson, *Metaphors We Live By* (Chicago: University of Chicago Press, 1980).

30. "Framing: Toward Clarification of a Fractured Paradigm," *Journal of Communication, 43* (1993), 52.

31. This memo has been analyzed by at least two scholars: Richard Kalfus, "Euphemisms of Death: Interpreting a Primary Source Document on the Holocaust," *The History Teacher*, *23* (1990), 87–93; and Stanley Katz, "The Ethic of Expediency: Classical Rhetoric, Technology, and the Holocaust," *College English*, 54 (1992), 255–275 and is reprinted in both.

32. Russell Hirst, "Scientific Jargon, Good and Bad," *Journal of Technical Writing and Communication*, *33* (2003), 201–229.

33. "Jenifer Haard, Michael D. Slter, and Marilee Long, "Scientese and Ambiguous Citations in the Selling of Unproven Medical Treatments," *Health Communication*, *16* (2004), 412.

34. Ibid.

35. The original essay, plus responses in both the academic and popular literatures, are reprinted in *The Sokal Hoax: The Sham That Shook the Academy* (Lincoln: University of Nebraska Press, 2000).

36. *Postmodernism* is a difficult topic to discuss here, but it stems from a broad philosophical tradition skeptical of the philosophy of science. This is *not* to say that postmodernists are disbelievers of scientific *practice*; rather, they disagree with modernists on what this practice *means*. Tensions exist throughout the academy between modernist and postmodernist paradigms, and the Sokal affair represents an example of how this has spilled over into popular culture.

37. *The Sokal Hoax*: *The Shame That Shook the Academy*, ed. *Lingua Franca* (University of Nebraska Press. 2000), 12. Sokal's copious footnotes have been omitted.

38. *The Ethics of Rhetoric* (Davis, CA: Hermagoras Press, 1985), 213.

39. Ibid., 212.

40. Ibid.

41. Ibid., 214.

42. Keith Allan and Kate Burridge, *Euphemism & Dyphemism: Language used as Shield and Weapon* (New York: Oxford University Press, 1991).

43. Ibid.

44. *Crazy Talk, Stupid Talk*: *How We Defeat Ourselves By The Way We Talk and What to Do About It* (New York: Dell Publishing, 1976), 212.

45. I place "inadvertent" in parenthesis to point out a further manipulation of language. There   is no such thing as "inadvertent" deaths when you bomb a target. Bombs are intended to kill indiscriminately whoever is in the area of the target. When you drop massive bombs on heavily populated areas the massive "collateral damage" is anything but inadvertent.

46. One such murderer was Dr. Radovan Karadzic, the ultranationalist leader of the Bosnian Serbs in the 1992–1995 civil war in the former Yugoslavia. Dr. Karadzic was indicted by a United Nations war crimes tribunal on charges of genocide and crimes against humanity for orchestrating the murder of civilians during the siege of Sarajevo and the massacre of an estimated 8,000 Bosnian Muslim men in Srebenica, in eastern Bosnia. As I was writing this chapter, Karadzic was captured in July 2008 after more than a decade as a fugitive.

47. "Doubts About Doublespeak," in Gary Goshgarian, ed., *Exploring Language* 7th ed. (New York: HarperCollins, 1995), 467.

48. Cited in "Frank Grazian, "How Much Do Words Really Matter?" *Public Relations Quarterly* (Summer 1998), 37.

49. Edward Schiappa, "The Rhetoric of Nukespeak," *Communication Monographs, 56* (1989), 251.

50. Fisher, "Preventing Nuclear War," *The Bulletin of the Atomic Scientists* (March 1981), 16.

51. Ibid.

52. Ibid.

53. John Hospers, *An Introduction to Philosophical Analysis* (New York: Routledge, 1989), 80.

54. Carl Cohen and Irving M. Copi, *Introduction to Logic* 13th ed. (Upper Saddle River, NJ: Pearson/Prentice Hall, 2009).

55. Ibid.

56. Eric M. Eisenberg, "Ambiguity as Strategy in Organizational Communication," *Communication Monographs*, *51* (1984), 227–242.

57. *Ethics in Human Communication* 4th ed. (Prospect Heights, IL: Waveland Press, 1996), 126.

58. As a side note, there is nothing wrong with welfare. It is what it is intended to be, a program to help people "fare well," a worthy goal for any democracy.

59. This policy is discussed in Roy Pinsker, "Drawing a Line in the Taiwan Strait: 'Strategic Ambiguity' and Its Discontents," *Australian Journal of International Affairs, 57* (2003), 353–368.

60. Tony Karon, "Why Bush Taiwan Comments Set Off a Diplomatic Scramble," *Time Magazine* (April 25, 2001), retrieved from http://www.time.com/time/printout/0,8816,10764 2,00.html.

61. Sharon Crowley and Debra Hawhee, *Ancient Rhetorics for Contemporary Students* (New York: Allyn and Bacon, 1999), 130.

62. See, Paul Wasserman and Don Hausrath, *Weasel Words: The Dictionary of American Doublespeak* (Sterling, VA: Capital Books, 2006).

63. Ralph Henry Johnson and J. Anthony Blair, *Logical Self-Defense* (New York: International Debate Education Association, 2006), 229–230.

64. *The Language of Oppression* (Lanham, NY: University Press of America, 1983), 5.

65. *Language is Sermonic*, 209.

66. Ibid., 210.

67. *Black Power: The Politics of Liberation* (New York: Vintage, 1992), 34.

68. William Lutz, *Doublespeak Defined* (New York: Harper Resource, 1999), 23.

69. Dominic Infante, *Arguing Constructively* (Prospect Heights, IL: Waveland Press, 1987), 7.

70. Charles J. Stewart, Craig Allen Smith, and Robert E. Denton, Jr., *Persuasion and Social Movements* 5th ed. (Long Grove, IL: Waveland Press, 2007), 172.

71. "Family Pride, Leaders Respond to Maggart, Upcoming Subcommittee Hearings," *Out & About,* April 1 2006, retrieved from http://outandaboutnewspaper.com/article.php? id=475.

72. Susan Opotow, "Moral Exclusion and Injustice: An Introduction," *Journal of Social Issues,* 46 (1990), 1.

73. Fred D. Gray, *The Tuskegee Syphilis Study: The Real Story and Beyond* (Montgomery, AL: New South Books, 2002).

74. Martha Solomon, "The Rhetoric of Dehumanization: An Analysis of Medical Reports of the Tuskegee Syphilis Project, *Western Journal of Speech Communication, 49* (1985), 233–247.

75. Ibid., 242–243.

76. Ibid., 234.

77. Michael B. Katz, *The Undeserving Poor: From the War on Poverty to the War on Welfare* (New York: Pantheon, 1990).

78. Stephanie L. Swanson and David Wenner, "Sensory Language in the Courtroom," *Trial Diplomacy Journal*, *14* (Winter, 1981/1982) 37–43.

79. *Language is Sermonic*, 207–208.

80. Rodney Jew and Martin Q. Peterson, "Envisioning Persuasion: Painting the Picture for the Jury," *Trial*, 31 (1995), 74–80.

81. The appeal can be found on the Right to Life home page, at http://www.nrlc.org/ABORTION/pba/pbacampaign.html.

82. The manager also said, "This place is not about wars or crimes, but where people come to relax and enjoy a meal." Quoted in Scott A. Lukas, "A Politics of Reverence and Irreverence: Social Discourse on Theming Controversies," in Scott A. Lukas, ed., *The Themed Space: Locating Culture, Nation, and Self* (Lanham, MD, Lexington Books, 2007), 271.

83. Ibid.

84. Max Black, "Metaphor," *Proceedings of the Aristotelian Society*, *55*, (1954), 273–294

85. (Chicago: University of Chicago Press, 1980), 3.

86. Ibid.

87. *Permanence and Change*, 194.

88. The Second Persona," *Quarterly Journal of Speech*, *56* (1970), 109-119.

89. Ibid.

90. *Time* (Feb. 23, 1962). Retrieved from http://www.time.com/time/magazine/article/0,9171,895898,00.html.

91. The publication is *The Record*, published by Marist College, March 25, 1964. The edition can be downloaded at http://library.marist.edu/archives/Circle/1964/1964_3_25.pdf.

92. Michael Osborn, "Archetypal Metaphor in Rhetoric: The Light-Dark Family," *Quarterly Journal of Speech*, 53 (1967), 115–126.

93. Cited in Martin Gilbert, *Churchill: A Life* (New York: Macmillan, 1992), 664.

94. *Gendered Lives: Communication, Culture, and Society* (Belmont, CA: Wadsworth, 2005), 310.

95. Ibid., 304.

96. See Kathleen Hall Jamieson, *Beyond The Double Bind: Women and Leadership* (New York: Oxford University Press, 1995).

97. Lawrence A. Hosman, "Language and Persuasion," in James Price Dillard and Michael W. Pfau, eds., *The Persuasion Handbook: Developments in Theory and Practice* (Thousand Oaks, CA: Sage, 2002), 379.

98. Nancy A. Burrell and Randal J. Koper, "The Efficacy of Powerful/Powerless Language on Attitudes and Source Credibility," in Mike Allen and Raymond W. Preiss, eds., *Persuasion: Advances Through Meta-analysis* (Cresskill, NH: Hampton Press, 1998), 204.

CHAPTER 10

Ethics and Persuasion

There is probably no more important subject to discuss in this textbook and course than ethics; indeed, everything we have studied in this course has been framed within an ethical or moral point of view. In an important respect, this course has been one of *applied* ethics, or what Aristotle calls *phronesis* (i.e., practical wisdom).[1] For example, throughout this course I have invited students to question actively the social construction of their commercial environments and I have provided tools or resources for that task. Moreover, this course explicitly exemplifies the *consumer protection model* of persuasion discussed in Chapter 3—the idea that the study of persuasion can help protect us from the unwanted or undesirable persuasion of others. My tone in this textbook and course also embodies a *human nature perspective* ethical code as discussed later in this chapter. According to this code, any persuasion that harms or takes advantage of another human is blameworthy and should be scrutinized rigorously.

Moreover, the title of this textbook—*Persuasion as a Critical Activity: Application & Engagement*—suggests that persuasion is an ethical activity and that it deals inherently with motivations, judgments, and effects and that the very practice of persuasion invites as a necessary correlate its critique and evaluation. Finally, as we saw in the previous chapter on language, to use rhetoric (or persuasion) is to be a type of public preacher and it is the job of all preachers, as theistic or secular guardians of a moral order, to *judge*—that is, to exalt or condemn. Most of the hubbub of human social life can be attributed to this important function of language and its manifestation in persuasive communication.

In this chapter, I will begin by first defining ethics. Then I will outline what I see as the scope of our ethical challenges that we face as individuals and as a nation. Following that discussion I will discuss the sources of a persuader's ethical responsibility, two of which—the persuader's status and the effects of a persuader's message on others—will be explored in depth. I will then discuss the ethical responsibility of the persuadee. From there, I discuss various ethical codes or what I am calling "argument forms" that persuaders use to justify an action. I then cover mythical and pseudo-events and conclude this chapter with a discussion of the art of deception and how to detect it.

❧ What Are Ethics? ☙

As the subsequent sections of this chapter make clear, students of persuasion need to have at least an introductory exposure to the vocabulary and main ideas contained in the ethics of persuasion. The quality of our political, social, and economic lives depends upon literacy if not competency in this area. As many testaments on the subject suggest, ethics can be understood as the systematic inquiry into the actions of individuals with the purpose of delineating the rules that underlie life in complex human society. Ethics involves the study of the origin of morals and the moral choices made by individuals in their relationships with others.[2] The word "relationship" is important since there are no ethics in the abstract. Whatever principles exist must be situated or actualized in functioning communities and in the daily practices of everyday life.

In a larger sense, ethics are the value systems by which people determine what is right or wrong, fair or unfair, just or unjust. Ethics may also involve the rules or standards governing the conduct of the members of a profession. Communication scholar Kenneth E. Anderson defines ethics as the "systemic study of value concepts such as good, bad, and right and the application of such terms to actions."[3] Another communication scholar, Richard Johannesen, writes that "Ethical issues focus on value judgments concerning degrees of right and wrong, goodness and badness, in human conduct."[4] In all cases, ethical decisions are *conclusions* we make to arguments put forward by others as to social arrangements. Ethical decisions themselves are neither "right" nor "wrong," "good" nor "bad," but *persuasive* or *unpersuasive*.

As many theorists in the discipline of communication note, persuasion, as human action, is inherently ethical because, in contrast to coercion as discussed in Chapter 4, free human choice is involved. As we have learned throughout this textbook and course, persuasion involves one person, or a group of people, attempting to influence other people by altering their beliefs, attitudes, values, and overt actions. As Johannesen notes, persuasion involves conscious choices among ends sought and rhetorical means used to achieve the ends.[5] Persuasion necessarily involves a potential judge which could be any or all of the receivers, the persuader, or an independent observer. Because there seems to be no absolutely and universally unethical acts, ethical judgments focus on *degrees* of rightness and wrongness. In sum, ethical judgments are, in themselves, ethical and political acts in addition to being acts of persuasion.

ଓ Scope of Our Ethical Challenges ଓ

In general, we are challenged, ethically, on at least two levels. First, we have *individual* responsibility for how we act and encourage others to act. We make hundreds of decisions each day (often without giving them much thought) many of which have significant impact upon others and upon the environment. Many of these decisions are unwise or less-than-ethical. We consume food that is unhealthy for us and bad for the environment, drive cars that contribute to global warming, or, perhaps, act manipulatively in our interpersonal relationships. Clearly it is important for all of us, myself included, to challenge ourselves to make small changes in our behavior to act more ethically and civilly in our dealings and interactions with others. Even the smallest of efforts here will contribute positively to countering the larger pervasive social attitude discussed by political scientist David Callahan in his book *The Cheating Culture: Why More Americans Are Doing Wrong to Get Ahead* (discussed below).[6] Second, we have a *collective* responsibility to make sure that our ability to perceive and exercise our agency is not unduly limited by institutional or bureaucratic obstacles that stress us, causing us emotional pain that distorts our sense of right and wrong. For instance, many of our institutional norms emphasize and reward short-term economic vitality over ecological sustainability or economic fairness. Restated, what I wrote is a fancy way of saying that institutionally and structurally, we are often abused and mistreated as workers and we are encouraged, in turn, to abuse and mistreat others. To resist such abuse is an organizational imperative.

It should come as no surprise to any of us that there is a growing concern over what is undoubtedly a dearth of ethics in our society at both the individual and collective levels. Much public perception believes that our nation is heading into ruin. The financial meltdown on Wall Street that began in September 2008 has exacerbated this perception. Average Americans (people like me and you) are working harder for less, the quality of life in the United States is declining, and the gap between the wealthy and the rest of us has never been greater.[7] People feel pressured and are afraid; they do not know who to trust. People are disillusioned with authority and have lost belief in our most fundamental institutions. Articles can be found in the paper every day about corporate and government fraud, scandals, and cover-ups, as well as information about falsified news articles that take the form of such things as political propaganda, pseudo-events (discussed later in this chapter), and Video News Releases (VNRs) which, collectively, betray the public trust. Sadly, our most cherished values as a nation no longer inspire us to improve our lives, communities, and world. If the excitement that surrounded the 2008 presidential election is any indication, Americans are thirsty for hope and for change.

VNRs are particularly perilous to our collective life as a democratic society. VNRs are visual press releases, created and disseminated by public relations (P.R.) firms, advertising agencies, marketing firms, corporations, or government agencies. While often costly to produce, VNRs are provided free to television news stations, which receive them gladly, for the purpose of informing; shaping public opinion; or promoting and publicizing individuals, commercial products and services, or other interests.[8] VNRs are a form of corporate or political propaganda that simulates a news production, actively or subtly misleading the viewing public. According to journalism scholar John V. Pavlik, the use of VNRs is widespread nationally with little or no attribution as to their source.[9] In this way, VNRs exploit the credibility that has in the past been associated with the broadcast news and with the integrity of people such as Walter Cronkite and Edward R. Murrow—two giants in the history of broadcasting whose ethics and moral integrity remain unquestioned.[10] What we increasingly see on television now is not the fruit of professional reporting with well-established ethical standards, but the substitution of P.R. for news— literally, propaganda disguised as something else (i.e., information, entertainment, etc.).

Where this has become particularly egregious and corrosive of the trust needed for self-government is in government practice. During the administration of George W. Bush, for example, VNRs were used unlawfully but frequently to advance Bush's political goals. According to the *New York Times*, nearly two dozen agencies of the federal government, including, most notably, the Department of Defense, disseminated hundreds of these documents, many of which were freely utilized by local broadcasters around the nation *without* acknowledging the source of the material.[11] Two of the examples from this article were of an Iraqi-American in Kansas City being shown jubilantly celebrating the 2003 fall of Baghdad: "Thank you Bush. Thank you USA" (the footage was actually produced by the State Department), and a report exalting "another success" in the Bush administration's "drive to strengthen aviation security" in which the reporter called it "one of the most remarkable campaigns in aviation history." In fact, this "reporter" was "a public relations professional working under a false name for the Transportation Security Administration."[12]

Students today probably do not remember the era of rampant corporate corruption of the 1980s, exemplified by people such as Charles Keating and Michael Milken, which led to the Savings and Loan Crisis, in which over 700 financial intuitions failed, billions of dollars were stolen, and the country's financial institutions had to be bailed out by the taxpayers.[13] At the time, this was the worst recorded fraud in this country. Against this background, *The Wall Street Journal* reported that "25% of 671 managers said that high ethics could hinder a successful career, and that bending the rules was necessary for survival."[14] Given the fact that the corruption of the 80s was dwarfed by the corruption scandals of the early twenty-first century—Enron, Quest, Tyco International, WorldCom, and Arthur Andersen, to name but a few[15]—one can expect that such numbers of people who express disdain for ethics and integrity in business have only grown. According to political scientist David Callahan, there is a "pattern of widespread cheating throughout U.S society." He argues that "not only are [people] cheating in more areas but are also feeling less guilty about it."[16] Callahan notes that attorneys lie to overstate their billable hours, students turn in canned papers and cheat on their exams, and athletes take banned performance-enhancing substances. Everyone, it seems, does what she/he can to get ahead—or, at least, to avoid the axes wielded by others.

As suggested above, it is not just people in high pressure or high powered occupations who are acting unethically.[17] Honesty tests are increasingly being used in run-of-the-mill employment interviews to uncover the propensity of employees to cheat, lie, or steal from their employers. According to the Congressional Office of Technology Assessment (OTA), an estimated 5,000 to

6,000 business establishments use honesty tests each year.[18] OTA has defined honesty tests as "written tests designed to identify individuals applying for work in such jobs who have relatively high propensities to steal money or property on the job, or who are likely to engage in behavior of a more generally 'counterproductive' nature."[19] "Counterproductive," in this context, means what the report calls "time theft"—"tardiness, sick leave abuse, and absenteeism."[20]

I suspect that Callahan is correct when he argues that in the cutthroat economic climate in which we exist people feel threatened and act accordingly; such behavior is understandable since our society is unkind to what it considers to be its failures. Not only that, but government deregulation has taken away important safety nets that insured, at some level, accountability and fairness in our dealings with one another. Added to this is the fact that white-collar criminals are seldom prosecuted and, if prosecuted, punished only lightly, which breeds the notion that "playing by the rules" is a ruse to help others succeed at our expense. From the Oval Office to our doctor's office, hypocrisy is endemic in our society and this provides people with a ready excuse for the practice of incivility and for social apathy regarding ethical misbehavior.

My intent here is not to condone the lack of ethical behavior evident in our society, but to recognize that much of it is caused by systemic problems in our political and economic structures. While individuals are, ultimately, responsible for their actions, much of who we are and how we act as individuals is culturally conditioned. We are creatures of our environment. A diseased and dysfunctional environment will breed diseased and dysfunctional people. Placing people whom we catch breaking the rules in jail does not solve the problem—the problem exists outside the cages and bars—in the inherent way we do business in this country.[21] Something has to change. Aside from the moral issue of our decision to "warehouse" the poor, we simply cannot afford to keep these mostly nonviolent people in prison.[22]

While politicians for the past two decades justified building more prisons by waving before the American people the bugaboo of violent crime, Americans have found the concern with ethics to be particularly salient during the two terms of the administration of George W. Bush (2001–2009). Starting from the "stolen election" of 2000, in which critics charge that Bush was "selected, not elected," Bush's closeness with Enron leaders such as CEO Kenneth Lay, the orchestration and manipulation leading up to the Iraq war, as well as the execution of the war itself, Bush repeatedly lied, cheated, and mis-used/abused the powers of his office. For instance, in their study of pre-war intelligence documents, communication scholars Stephen J. Hartnett and Laura A. Stengrim conclude that Bush's "arguments were fabrications spun from evidence that was shaky at best, outright nonsense at worst, and that the labyrinthine cover-ups following these initial fabrications amount to a second, equally dangerous series of lies."[23]

Still, these ethical issues are not limited to the Bush Administration and my comments here should not in any way be taken as partisan (i.e., either *for* or *against* the Democrats or the Republicans). Throughout American history, U.S. presidents—both Democratic and Republican—have lied repeatedly to the American public. In this context, I define "lie" as political scientist James P. Pfiffner does, as "an untruth communicated with the intent to deceive."[24] While this has been true, historically, most Americans were either unaware of this or took it in stride. As a result, the bar keeps being lowered. According to historian Eric Alterman, "In American politics today, the ability to lie convincingly has come to be considered an almost prima facie qualification for holding high office."[25] Such a condition is unacceptable; regardless of political affiliation and the delicate nature of international relations, citizens in our democracy "must trust the president because they do not have all the information that he has. If the president misrepresents the nature of crucial information, he undermines the democratic bonds between citizens and president upon which this polity is based."[26] With this in mind, it is important to review noteworthy examples of such lying from the executive office so that we can appreciate the larger context in which such lies occur. With one exception that I picked for its historical parallels to contemporary times, the examples I have picked are from the post-Second-World-War period, which have been most memorable and consequential to people now living.

James K. Polk: Polk was the 11th president of the United States (1845–1849). Most students probably do not know much about him. In an important sense, however, he prefigures our current situation, locked as we are in two wars in the Middle East, not to mention the saliency of the issue of illegal immigration (i.e., immigrants from Mexico). In 1846, Polk was looking for a pretext to invade and annex parts of Mexico. He ordered the U.S. military to make an incursion into Mexican territory. When the Mexican government attacked the invading troops, Polk went to Congress and claimed that the

Mexican army had invaded the U.S. and attacked U.S. troops *on our own soil*. Congress and the American people believed him and thus started the Mexican-American War, which culminated in our appropriating (i.e., stealing) nearly one-half of Mexico's territory.[27]

Harry Truman: When Truman announced to the world that the United States had dropped an atomic bomb on Japan during the Second World War, he said: "The world will note that the first atomic bomb was dropped on Hiroshima, a *military* base. That was because we wished in this first attack to *avoid*, insofar as possible, the killing of civilians."[28] In fact, nearly a quarter of a million people were in the city at the time, almost *all* of them civilians. Further, in studying the deliberation regarding the decision to drop the bomb, historian Barton Bernstein notes that its use was, in part, *intended* to "dramatize the killing of noncombatants."[29] It does not take much in the way of a moral imagination to realize that one does not drop an atomic bomb on a populated city if one wants to avoid the killing of civilians. Further, the American people were misled into thinking that the use of atomic weapons was necessary for winning the war against Japan, since Japan had already indicated its willingness to surrender.[30]

Lyndon Baines Johnson: Early in his administration, Johnson claimed that U.S. navel forces were attacked by North Vietnamese naval forces on August 2 and 4, 1964. This never happened. Nevertheless, Johnson appeared on television and told the American people that we had to respond and that they should support a Congressional resolution. Three days later, Congress approved the Tonkin Gulf Resolution, giving Johnson unilateral authorization for the use of military force in Southeast Asia which he used to escalate American involvement, leading to full-scale military operations and outright war between the United States and the people of Vietnam.

Richard Nixon: Even before the Watergate scandal brought down the Nixon presidency in 1974, Nixon was caught lying when he denied having illegally extended the Vietnam War into Cambodia. American fighter pilots were trained for missions in Vietnam and, once in the air, were redirected to targets in Cambodia. The official reports were that they had bombed targets in Vietnam. Later, in one of his memoirs, Nixon claimed that he hid this policy change from Congress and the American people because of his fear of domestic anti-war protest.[31]

Ronald Reagan: When Reagan became president in 1981, American power and prestige in the world had been waning. Reagan replaced the unpopular Jimmy Carter. Following the Watergate scandals that consumed Presidents Nixon and Ford, and following the massive distrust of the U.S. government by Americans and nations around the world brought on by the lies and manipulations associated with the war in Vietnam, Carter promoted a softer, open, and less aggressive government and foreign policy. Indeed, while Carter was in office, several highly sensitive political revolutions occurred around the world replacing repressive regimes friendly to the United States with ones distrustful of American intentions. In each case, Carter exercised restraint, as becoming of a mature nation. Particularly sensitive to Reagan were the civil wars in Central America, where, Carter aside, the United States had been replacing regimes it did not like for some time.[32] Reagan wanted to act militarily to prop up right-wing dictatorships and destroy left-wing political movements; the problem was that Congress, still smarting from the ordeal of Vietnam, did not want to go along, nor did the American people. Legislation passed between 1982 and 1984 (i.e., the Boland Amendment) explicitly forbid such direct military involvement.[33]

Reagan was not to be deterred. In order to get money to fund his "secret wars," that is, wars that did not have the approval or oversight of Congress and were hidden from the American public, Reagan became involved in an elaborate scheme of weapons, drugs, and covert operations with Iran.[34] All of this Reagan steadfastly denied until he was forced by the evidence to make the following non-apology, "A few months ago I told the American people I did not trade arms for hostages. My heart and my best intentions still tell me that's true, but the facts and evidence tell me it is not."[35]

In the end, eleven high-ranking members of the Reagan Administration, including National Security Advisors Robert McFarlane and John Poindexter and Secretary of Defense Caspar Weinberger, were convicted of severe felonies, including perjury and obstruction of justice. Everyone responsible was subsequently pardoned by President George H.W. Bush, who had been vice president at the time this wrongdoing was going on, and was himself implicated in the same illegal activity.[36] Many thousands of people died as a result of Reagan's bellicose, behind-the-scenes manipulations and lies that were against public policy, the public interest, and the law.

Bill Clinton: Well known to the current generation of college students, ethical and moral problems and accusations and illicit sexual escapades were hallmarks of the Clinton presidency. Simply, Clinton was a womanizer who lied, repeatedly, to the American public regarding this behavior. Most of us, for example, can recall Clinton's forceful denial he made on television: "I want you to listen to me. I'm going to say this again: I did not have sexual relations with that woman, Miss Lewinsky."[37] This was an outright lie and Clinton's efforts to weasel out of responsibility for his sexual indiscretions were nothing short of ludicrous. In his 1998 grand jury testimony on the Monica Lewinsky affair, for instance, President Clinton made statements such as "It depends on what the meaning of 'is' is" or "It depends on how you define 'alone.'" Or earlier in 1992 when he was first running for the presidency he addressed allegations of past marijuana use as saying that he "didn't inhale."

In sum, presidents, like all of us, are human, and the fact that they have their faults is not in itself blameworthy. But, as political scientist James P. Pfiffner observes, there is a *typology* of presidential lies, what he calls "justifiable lies," "lies to prevent embarrassment," and "lies of policy deception."[38] Some lies are justifiable, such as to protect bona fide state secrets serving legitimate public policy ends. These must be defined as limitedly as possible. The shibboleth of "national security" must be characterized by its rarity in political life. Other lies are justifiable when they protect the legitimate privacy interests of an individual; even presidents have protectable privacy interests with regard to their health and family. Indeed, two of the major areas where presidents tend to lie are with regard to their sex lives and health. As recorded by Rick Shenkman, the list of presidents who had and concealed sexual improprieties includes: George Washington, Thomas Jefferson, James Garfield, Woodrow Wilson, Warren Harding, Franklin Roosevelt, John Kennedy, and Lyndon Johnson. Presidents who lied regarding their health include: Chester Arthur, Grover Cleveland, Woodrow Wilson, Franklin Roosevelt, Dwight Eisenhower, John Kennedy, and Ronald Reagan.[39] However, lies that affect public deliberation about any substantial matter—for example, questions of war and peace—demand full disclosure of *any* and *all* relevant material as well as maximum deliberation among the widest possible audience. A lesser standard will only continue the types of harmful deceptions that have led the United States into many wars and conflicts, the wanton loss of human life, as well as to the depletion of the public treasury. Evaluated in these terms, the actions of the two administrations of President George W. Bush should be looked upon in the most unfavorable terms possible.

১ Sources of a Persuader's Ethical Responsibility ৫

As I have been suggesting in this chapter there are, in the abstract, no ethical or unethical acts. Ethical evaluations are moralizations and gain their salience against a backdrop of a specific set of values and cultural norms. Murder, for example, is a judgment not an action. While murder is universally condemned, *homicide* (i.e., the act of taking human life) is not. We "kill" people all the time for a variety of reasons—in war, in politics, in our policy decisions, with poverty and pollution, with indifference to the other, etc. Seen from this perspective, all ethical judgments are at the same time *persuasive* arguments with regard to our interpretation of how the world ought to be. Otherwise stated, "morals are fists."[40] In the end, all preaching, all sermons (religious, secular, political, etc.) are types of definitions that we force upon the material artifacts of the world.[41]

According to Johannesen, a persuader's ethical responsibilities may stem from several different sources. One is the *pledges* or *promises* made by the persuader. As in law more generally, we incur obligations to others with the commitments we make voluntarily. Absent these commitments (either stated or implied), others have little claim to us. Outside of our general tax obligations, for instance, we are excused by the law when we ignore the world around us when there is no duty-bound connection between our prosperity or health and the suffering of another.[42] However, if I say *X* and promise to do *Y*, others develop an expectation that allows them to rely on what I say I will do. In general, the stronger the reliance of others, the greater is my responsibility for following through with my pronouncements.

A second source of a persuader's ethical responsibility is being accountable to *agreed upon rules and regulations* found in some community. Every profession or association of people has an explicit or implicit set of rules and norms that its members must abide by in order to be a member. Such rules and norms guide medical and legal practice, for example. In order to benefit from membership, one has to adapt her/his behavior to the proscribed conventions; to depart from these norms is to invite censor from one's professional peers.

Next, I will discuss two of the more important sources of ethical responsibility articulated by Johannesen: the status of the persuader and the intended or unintended effects of the persuasion on others.

Status Earned or Granted: Political or religious leaders, chief-executive-officers, college professors, and sports and entertainment celebrities, for example, are all held to higher ethical standards than other people by virtue of the influence they wield over young people or society in general. Athletes who commit crimes or use illegal drugs are judged more harshly than the rest of us because these people are objects of respect and emulation. Their athletic prowess inspires us to be our best—they are, in a sense, moral spokespeople. When they betray their highest ideals, they betray us as well.

A more specific example of how status earned or granted applies to ethics is Dr. Jack Kevorkian, known in the press as "Dr. Death." In the 1980s and 1990s, Dr. Kevorkian was an outspoken activist for euthanasia or mercy killing. Unlike many activists for this cause, Kevorkian was a trained medical doctor and his practice of doctor-assisted suicide—he reportedly assisted in 130 deaths of terminally ill and suffering patients who requested his help—repulsed many people who felt that Kevorkian betrayed the fundamental trust implied in the doctor-patient relationship. Physicians, it is assumed, have the highest regard for the interests of their patients, which is *a priori* believed to be that of maintaining life. When doctors use their knowledge of disease and health to hurt, torture, or take away life, it goes against the grain of what we imagine physicians to be. When a physician acts this way, it makes us potentially fearful of *our* doctor and the power she or he wields.

In a different example, President Ronald Reagan, not realizing he was speaking before a "hot" microphone shortly before an August 11, 1984, weekly radio broadcast to the nation, made what he considered to be a joke. He leaned into the microphone and said, "My fellow Americans, I am pleased to tell you today that I've signed legislation that will outlaw Russia forever. We begin bombing in five minutes."[43] Reagan's "joke" quickly spread from the room and was heard around the world, greatly upsetting many people. Communication scholar Nancy Snow sums up the global implications of Reagan's bombshell:

[Reagan's] seeming insensitivity to real fears evoked during the Cold War created a global media stir and provided the USSR with appropriate propaganda fodder for the bipolar information and ideology war. Now the world can see that the presidential cowboy, like a reckless sheriff in a town gone scared, was ready to make a unilateral decision to fire on innocents… . For America's public diplomacy corps, it didn't help their efforts to win global hearts and minds to have the chief CEO of the USA to project an image of America as a country gone mad.[44]

What may have been a joke to Reagan, who fancied himself as "tough" on the Soviets, becomes something else entirely when the person making the joke has the power, like he did, to issue such an order and is expected to exercise restraint. The fact that Reagan would even *contemplate* giving such an order, much less make light of it, gave thoughtful Americans, and much of the rest of the world, pause. Nuclear holocaust is no laughing matter. Reagan's incautious and callous comments were a betrayal of the tremendous trust the American people invested in him. With this discussion in mind, it would be good to recall the worldwide condemnation of George W. Bush when he responded in June 2003 to the growing insurgency in Iraq with the challenge: "Bring it on!"[45] While such bravado may be excusable at a barbeque dinner with friends or over drinks at a party, it is incompatible with the measured, reasoned diplomatic activity that we expect from the president of the United States during a time of heightened global insecurity.

Subsequent Effects of Persuasion on Others: We are surrounded by persuasive messages that have direct or indirect negative consequences for individuals and for society. For example, alcohol ads promote drinking as fun, sexy, desirable, and harmless. We are told that drinking is a way to be sociable and have romance. Alcohol, however, is far from harmless, both individually and socially. Approximately 85,000 people die in the United States each year as a result of alcohol-related diseases and accidents with an estimated annual cost of $185 billion.[46] We also know that there is a strong association between drinking and a range of deleterious "secondary effects" such as domestic violence and child abuse.[47] We know that advertising stimulates alcohol consumption among underage youth and youth just above the legal drinking age.[48]

By far, the most consequential persuasion with dire effects on its intended audience is advertising for cigarettes. Among other things, cigarette advertising encourages the practice of cigarette smoking and mitigates against an individual's motivation to abstain.[49] Thus, advertising contributes to an environment in which quitting is difficult to maintain. Moreover, and perhaps most insidiously, cigarette advertising discourages full and open debate and understanding on the problems associated with smoking because much of the media depends on revenues gained from cigarette advertising.[50]

Historical claims in cigarette advertising have been egregious. A 1945 ad for the Kools brand of cigarettes portrays a weight lifter struggling with a dumbbell because of a cold who becomes rejuvenated with a cigarette. Spuds cigarettes claims that its brand of cigarettes is "good for colds, nose, and throat congestion." Lucky cigarettes promoted its brand by suggesting that it helped people lose weight: "Avoid that future shadow," warned one ad, "to maintain the modern figure of fashion." "Reach for a Lucky rather than a sweet" suggests another ad from 1928 with an image of a young, slim woman emerging from the shadow of an older, fatter self. An ad from Viceroy cigarettes has a woman asking, "What kind of cigarettes should I smoke, doctor?" More prominently, a campaign for Camel cigarettes boasted that their brand was the brand of choice by physicians.

Overall, cigarette ads, past and present (almost without exception), conjure up images of health, sexuality, attractiveness, success, and self-confidence. In such a context, it is almost unthinkable, although perhaps inevitable, that some cigarette company would appear to position itself uniquely (and ethically under this standard) against such practices: enter Death Cigarettes, produced by the short-lived Enlightened Cigarette Company. Death Cigarettes were produced from 1991 to 1999 in Great Britain and marketed there as well as in the United States.[51] Prominent on each box of Death Cigarettes was a skull and crossbones. Dispensing machines were designed to look like coffins. A panel on the side of the cigarette box advises clearly, emphatically even, that cigarette smoking is highly addictive and can lead to catastrophic health effects. We are told not to start smoking and to stop if we do smoke.

Death Cigarettes was the brainchild of B.J. Cunningham, himself a heavy smoker. One of his ads explained his unique marketing ploy.[52] The ad, from the early 1990s, begins with the common sense notion that cigarette smoking constitutes a health risk. It goes on to explain that no cigarette company has ever admitted the proven links between smoking and a host of adverse health effects, such as heart disease, emphysema, and lung cancer. Against such background, the ad states that it is time for a tobacco company to speak up, to fill the moral void left by the others. We are that company, they insist, "the only cigarette maker to tell it like it is." The ad goes on to criticize the practices of other companies whose ads evoke images of style, sex, and eroticism and contrasts that with their brand, *Death*: "The name alone leaves you in no doubt as to the risks you're taking. And neither does the pack" which is black with a prominent white skull and cross bones and the large words "Tobacco Seriously Damages Health" and "Smoking Kills" across the bottom. The ad specifically states that smoking *causes* lung cancer, heart disease, emphysema, and bronchitis and concludes with the challenge that we should be honest with ourselves. If we were honest, we would admit that we "already smoke death cigarettes. They just happened to be called something else."

Although I believe firmly that cigarettes should be banned throughout the world on public health grounds, I consider this ad campaign to be both interesting and ethical. It is upfront and honest, it positions its product well vis-à-vis its competition, and it allows consumers to make a conscious decision with full knowledge of the implications of that decision. I wish that all advertising was this open and direct about what it offered.

ഔ Ethical Responsibility of Persuadee ര

Earlier in this chapter and perhaps throughout this textbook and course, I have been critical of *persuaders* for the content and methods of what are often, I argue, manipulative and unethical practices. Our world would be a kinder, gentler place if persuaders of all stripes acted more conscientiously with regard to their efforts. Yet, as I have pointed out in numerous places, while systemic factors have a tremendous impact on personal decision making, consumers *also* have agency and responsibility over their own behaviors and lives. With a little education and self-confidence, most people can act to make better decisions in the marketplace. Nobody is forced to smoke. Nobody is forced to eat at McDonald's or to drink Coca-Cola. These are all choices we make. We make these and hundreds of other choices each day without giving them much thought. In this context, I want to make clear the ethical responsibilities of the *persuadee*—the individual whom advertisers and public relations professionals often call the "target."

The first responsibility that we all have is to use *reasoned (or intelligent) skepticism* when encountering a persuasive message.[53] That is, we should accept or reject a claim only after analyzing and evaluating both the claims and the motivations of the person or persons making them. Of course, this assumes we have the educational and conceptual tools to accomplish this, and these resources are often in short supply. Nevertheless, it is reasonable, as Johannesen observes, to nurture a healthy skepticism that "represents a balance between the undesirable extremes of being too opened-minded or gullible, on the one hand, and being too closed-minded or dogmatic, on the other."[54] As the saying goes, if something sounds too good to be true, it probably is. Remember that we often act on emotion and impulse, and try to justify our decisions after the fact.

The second responsibility that we all have is to *provide feedback* and to *ask for clarification.* According to Johannesen, "We should tolerate, even seek out, divergent and controversial viewpoints, the better to assess what is being presented."[55] In short, be proactive—take responsibility for being a consumer of persuasion. Be proactive in the construction of your life. Question authority throughout all aspects of your life, be the "friction in the machinery," as suggested by American philosopher Henry David Thoreau in his celebrated essay *On Civil Disobedience.*[56] One way to do this is to be aware of the various codes of ethics (i.e., ethical forms) and see how they work in persuasion as arguments for manufacturing or justifying consent.

℘ Codes of Ethics ℘

Before discussing specific ethical codes (or forms), I want to lay out what communication scholars often consider to be the ideal ethical framework. Often called the *dialogical perspective*, this is the code (or idealized practice) most worthy of participation in a democratic society. Johannesen summarizes this perspective:

> Dialogical perspectives for evaluating communication ethics focus on the *attitudes toward each other* held by the participants in a communication transaction. Participant attitudes are viewed as an index of the ethical level of that communication. The assumption is that some attitudes (characteristic of dialogue) are more fully human, humane, and facilitative of self-fulfillment than are other attitudes (characteristic of

monologue). Dialogical attitudes are held to best nurture and actualize each individual's capacities and potentials, whatever they are.[57]

Characteristics of such dialogue include: authenticity, inclusion, confirmation, presentness, an ethos of mutual equality, and a supportive psychological climate.[58]

As articulated by communication scholar Charles Lawson, fundamental to this perspective is the duty of search and inquiry to attain and present accurate, complete, relevant evidence.[59] This involves the allegiance to accuracy, fairness, and justice in selection of ideals, arguments, language, and tactics employed, as well as the careful analysis of claims and probable consequences. A good example of a *violation* of this principle is the People For the Ethical Treatment of Animals' (PETA) controversial 2003 *Holocaust On Your Plate* campaign. The campaign, which traveled through more than 100 cities throughout the United States, featured photographs, some as large as 60-foot panels, of gristly scenes of holocaust victims paired with similar body shots of pigs, chickens, and cows. Headings on these pictures read "The Final Indignity," "Baby Butchers," and "To Animals, All People Are Nazis." One of their brochures explained that "We're asking people to recognize that what Jews and others went through in the Holocaust is what animals go through every day in factory farms."

On one level, the PETA campaign presents a potentially powerful analogy. If we were to accept this argument, many things would have to change in our society in the direction of PETA's goals. Thus, the ad is threatening as well as provocative. Elsewhere, PETA makes this clear when it states, "Like the Jews murdered in concentration camps, animals are terrorized when they are housed in huge filthy warehouses and rounded up for shipment to slaughter. The leather sofa and handbag are the moral equivalent of the lampshades made from the skins of people killed in the death camps."[60] The ad goes on to challenge us:

> Decades from now, what will you tell your grandchildren when they ask you whose side you were on during the "animals holocaust"? ....Will you be able to say that you could visualize a world without violence and realize that it began at breakfast?

Ads such as this can be expected to be controversial, but for many people, these ads went further—many viewers were sickened, not at the pictures, but at the comparison which can be read as demeaning and dehumanizing to humans, and trivializing of the tremendous calamity of the holocaust and its victims. Even people sympathetic to PETA were repulsed by this ad campaign; indeed, responses to this ad were so negative that PETA president Ingrid Newkirk was forced to apologize.[61]

Further aspects of a dialogical approach to persuasion ethics, as noted by Johannesen, involve the balance between the persuader's original/personal idea and how it is modified to achieve maximum impact with a particular audience and a willingness to submit private motivations to public scrutiny, toleration of dissent and divergence of viewpoints, and an acceptance of responsibility for the effects of our persuasive efforts.

As listed by Larson, the following are some typical ethical argument forms or perspectives that persuaders use in their appeals to audiences: internal authority perspective, ends justifies the means perspective, situational perspective, laisser-faire/caveat emptor perspective, prevailing conduct perspective, legal perspective, religious perspective, and human nature perspective.

Internal Authority Perspective: The stance of the persuader using this perspective is that something is "good/okay if *I* say so." The emphasis here is on the "I". The strength of the argument depends upon the credibility or authority of the individual making the statement. To assert that "I'll be the judge of that" is to imply that *I* have special resources or experiences which make *me* uniquely qualified to evaluate the situation. This argument form looks like: "Why did you do that?" Answer: "It was my personal feeling at the time." While this sounds self-serving and juvenile, and while it certainly can be perceived that way, it *is* the case that some people *are* in a position to make these sorts of judgment calls. For example, parents often argue like this to their children, and we expect them to do so; parental authority and responsibility mean precisely this. Along with certain types of status comes the power to make decisions. Parenthood, particularly of young children, is one such status. The responsibility of being a parent assumes this power—parental authority would be ineffective without it.

Faculty status is another example of this perspective. When an instructor gives a student a grade on an assignment, that instructor is judging—what makes that judgment authoritative is the status of the grader (i.e., her/his credentials and vetting by the university). As long as that faculty member is recognized as a member in good standing of a professional community, that person's judgment cannot be second guessed, even by other members of that community. Without some extenuating circumstance, such as overt hostility or bias toward a student by the instructor, it does not make sense for one instructor to evaluate the evaluation of another instructor. Similarly, it is not the job of the department chair or the dean of a college to interfere with an instructor's evaluation of a student without reasonable cause. The judgment of an instructor is authoritative by virtue of the fact that the instructor was hired by the department and university to teach the course and evaluate students.

Yet another important status under the internal authority perspective of persuasion is to be president of the United States. When a president comes on television to announce and justify a military action, or some other foreign policy decision, s/he is doing her/his job. The president's responsibility is to anticipate threats to the nation and to respond appropriately in leading the nation to meet the demands of such threats. The fact that George W. Bush defined Iraq as a threat is not in itself wrong (again, that is what he as president is expected to do), but the *manipulation* Bush used to convince us with false and fabricated information of the threat from Iraq was wrong. While Bush's responsibility is to assess threats to the United States, it is not to *manufacture* them. Once the president determines that a threat exists, her/his job is to convince the American people both that the threat exists and that the response proposed by the president is necessary to meet the challenges of that threat. All claims of "national security" to the contrary, in a democracy, this should be done directly, fairly, and openly.

To take another example, in early 2006 Bush defended his beleaguered secretary of defense, Donald Rumsfeld, against a public outcry against him, including eight retired generals. As an architect of the invasion of Iraq and as its chief civilian administrator, Rumsfeld, an arrogant and insensitive man, was an easy target for the public to express its dismay with Bush.[62] Hence, there were frequent calls for Rumsfeld's removal. Bush resisted such calls for a long time, as he did on April 18, 2006, when he declared:

> I say I listen to all voices but *mine's the final decision* and Don Rumsfeld is doing a fine job. He's not only transforming the military, he's fighting a war on terror—He's helping us fight a war on terror. *I have strong confidence* in Don Rumsfeld. I hear the voices and I read the

front page and I know the speculation but *I'm the decider* and *I decide what is best* and *what's best* is for Don Rumsfeld to remain as the secretary of defense.[63]

Such action is the president's prerogative and it is difficult for others to second guess his decision formally. By definition, the president alone is in the position to determine the best people for fulfilling his policy objectives. This does not mean we cannot criticize the president; on the contrary, we have an obligation to do that when appropriate, but such criticism must be made on *different* moral grounds. We cannot criticize the president for the authority that he wields. He has that power by virtue of his office which we, collectively, have given him. We do not have to like the president just as we do not have to like a particular instructor who has given us a bad grade, but we cannot deny that the job of such people is to evaluate and render an authoritative decision. If we do not like these decisions, our only recourse is to vote the president out of office (or impeach her or him) or, if enough students complain, not renew an untenured instructor's contract.

The Ends Justifies the Means Perspective: This is an argument from consequence. My goals/ends are so important that the means I use are justified or irrelevant. One may lie, cheat, steal, or kill for a greater good: save a life, unify the party, national security, compete, or preserve freedom. For example, "national security" is frequently held before the American people as a goal so worthy of protection that it often trumps all other factors in our moral calculus. In the "war on terror" in which we find ourselves, torture, assassination, indefinite detentions and the like are sometimes argued for under this rationale. On the one hand, it sounds like a good argument, as some things, such as our physical or national safety, are so valuable that they deserve to be protected in the most stringent fashion. However, it does not follow necessarily that any *one goal* can justify any *one specific mean*; the fact that the United States is at war does not mean that "anything goes" in pursuit of victory. Moreover, ethical theorists have long argued that evil means for a just end produce an evil end.[64] Things such as "national security" are valuable, but their value cannot be separated from the things that we do as a society to constitute that security.

Situational Perspective: Similar to the reasoning above, this argument maintains that certain situations require us to set rules/standards aside. Killing is usually wrong except during wartime, self-defense, to terminate an unwanted pregnancy, to release somebody of their suffering (i.e., euthanasia), and capital punishment. For example, in justifying its planned invasion of Iraq which resulted in tremendous loss of life, the Bush Administration argued repeatedly that attacking Iraq was justified because it had weapons of mass destruction, harbored Al-Qaeda terrorists, threatened its neighbors, and because the head of that nation was a tyrant who oppressed his own people. Furthermore, we had been attacked, and it was imperative that we fight the terrorists on the streets of Baghdad rather than in the streets of New York City. We were, said Bush, taking the fight to the terrorists. Thus framed, Bush's narrative made sense, although a different persuader could have framed the post-September 11 environment quite differently.

Laisser-Faire/Caveat Emptor Perspective: Persuaders who utilize this perspective assume, along with their audiences, that all human activity is basically game-like, so a person should not play if she or he does not know or understand the rules. The individual is at fault if she or he is deceived or taken in by a crafty persuader. If I believe that XYZ tonic will cure my baldness or help me lose weight, it is nobody's business to keep me from getting ripped off when the tonic is ineffective. This was largely the ethical approach to business prevalent in the United States prior to the Great Depression and the reinvention of government as an administrative, regulatory body by President Franklin Delano Roosevelt.

Prevailing Conduct Perspective: With this tactic, a persuader urges her/his audience to judge a particular conduct in terms of conduct that is being accepted currently by a specific community. For example, a member of Congress may or may not be ethically liable for taking a plane trip paid for by a lobbyist. Is this an industry standard? Are there other respectable people of the same status who engage in this behavior? In more colloquial terms, people who argue this way may say: "Everybody does it. Get with it! If I don't do it, someone else will. Times have changed. It's the only way to stay in business." Nations, in particular, argue this way when they fight diplomatically. That is, much of international law is premised on the assumption that certain conduct is or is not acceptable for a nation to take. Nations like Cuba, Iran, Syria, and North Korea are frequently condemned by the United States for acting in ways that "nations" as a class are not supposed to act. Economic sanctions or military force is often used to encourage such nations to behave in ways that are deemed acceptable in the international community.

Legal Perspective: According to this perspective, certain conduct is unacceptable by definition of statute or court decision. In other words, that which is not specifically prohibited by law is ethical. A good example of this would be laws regarding the permissibility or legality of drugs or alcohol. Alcohol is tolerated, even celebrated, in Western culture and is prohibited in many Muslim societies. On the other hand, drugs like marijuana and hashish are seen as morally inconsequential in some Muslim societies or in places like Amsterdam but are seen as grave moral offenses in other places, such as in the United States. When the government urges its citizens to blindly "obey the law," it is confusing the important distinction between positive and natural law (i.e., between law as a biased political instrument and law as a moral imperative). All laws are, by definition, laws, but that is not to say that all laws are moral or even beneficial to society; that determination is left to the individual and her/his conscious.[65]

Religious Perspective: When they think about ethics, most people turn immediately to this perspective. Here, a persuader grounds her/his ethical argument in a specific religious doctrine or tradition located in the Bible, Koran, Torah, Bhagavad Gita, Tao De Ching, Talmud, Book of Mormon, or other sacred text. These are certainly important grounds upon which to situate an ethical argument and people often take them very seriously (or too seriously), but we need to realize is that this is but *one* of *different* ways of grounding an ethical argument. Its value in argument, like any perspective, depends on what a particular audience is willing to accept.

Human Nature Perspective: Fundamental to the human nature perspective of persuasion ethics is the grounding of ethical claims in the argument that actions that harm humans in any way can be considered wrong or unethical, that treating human beings as objects to manipulate is both dehumanizing and immoral. Any technique that dehumanizes persons or groups according to racial, gender, age, ethnic group, or similar categories is condemnable. As Johannesen notes, "Communication that dehumanizes reinforces stereotypes, conveys inaccurate depictions of people, dismisses taking serious account of people, dismisses people as citizens worthy of participating in public discourse on public issues, and even makes people invisible for purposes of decision or policy."[66]

For example, in early 2001, while still a law student, I gave two lectures at two universities in two different parts of the country in which I criticized the practice of female genital mutilation, which had been a salient issue in the legal literature at the time.[67] To my great surprise, I was confronted, in both cases, by members of the audience (students and faculty alike) who complained bitterly that my critique was Eurocentric, that I was privileging Western values over non-Western ones. This surprised me, as I consider myself to have a wider, more progressive world view than their critique of me suggested. Later I published a book chapter discussing these incidences along with a defense—grounded in the human nature perspective.[68] Injunctions against cruelty, I argued, are not Western phenomena, and even if they were, such injunctions are based on a principle worth defending. My unqualified defense of gay and lesbian rights would also be grounded in this perspective, as well as for the autonomy and dignity of minority groups anywhere in the world. In my world view, the human nature perspective trumps other perspectives, such as the religious perspective on this and related social issues. This does not mean that I am right and others are wrong, but that I find arguments grounded in the alleviation of human suffering more persuasive (that is, morally compelling) than arguments based on religious prohibitions and condemnations. Others will have a different moral calculus and argue on different moral grounds.

∞ Mythical and Pseudo Events ∞

Many events presented for public consumption are not quite what they seem to be. Sometimes this is reasonable, as in the use of *mythical events*, in which the persuader tries to place us and things into a mythical/hypothetical but believable situation so that we become inclined to internalize the product into our emotions. In these cases, there is no covert manipulation involved. The intent here is not to deceive us, but to *seduce* us to believing that a product is grander or more spectacular than it is. For example, an ad for oral chemotherapy medicine for colon cancer depicts two senior citizens dancing joyfully on a pier, rejoicing in the love they feel for each other. The text reads, "Imagine being here rather than at the clinic."

Key to this tactic is the overt appeal to our imagination and to our innate desire for ever more increments of satisfaction. Imagine the power to . . . have romance, have the freedom, and have the security… We do not have to actually *do* these things the ads suggest—in fact, they are often times too fanciful to be taken literally, such as a man powering a lawnmower up a vertical hedge or a geeky nerd being smothered by the affection of a sexy cheerleading team. The fact is, we long for power, influence, and appeal, and products promise this, even if no one could possibly believe they can deliver on the magnitude promised. For example, an ad for the Nissan Pathfinder vehicle shows the SUV crushing through thick hedges alongside powerful equestrian riders leaping eloquently over the hedges. Clearly, we would never do this; but the text implies we could.

Other tactics are clearly manipulative and unethical, such as the *pseudo-event* in which the persuader creates an illusion that a "real" event is taking place or has taken place in order to mislead or fool an audience. The purpose of the pseudo-event is to *deceive*; as such, pseudo-events are per se unethical. As originally described by historian Daniel Boorstin, pseudo-events are "happenings" that take place solely for the purpose of being reported; they are designed to make a good photo opportunity for a client without providing any substantive material that can be used for the evaluation of that client. In other words, pseudo-events are vacuous forms that substitute for, or replace, substance.[69] Boorstin begins his discussion of pseudo-events with the following example:

> The owners of a hotel… consult a public relations counsel. They ask how to increase their hotel's prestige and so improve their business. In less sophisticated times, the answer might have been to hire a new chef, to improve the plumbing, to paint the rooms, or to install a crystal chandelier in the lobby. The public relations counsel's technique is more indirect. He proposes that the management stage a celebration of the hotel's thirtieth anniversary. A committee is formed, including a prominent banker, a leading society matron, a well-known lawyer, an influential preacher, and an "event" is planned (say a banquet) to call attention to the distinguished service the hotel has been rendering the community. The celebration is held, photographs are taken, the occasion is widely reported, and the object is accomplished.[70]

As in the above example, pseudo-events are "happenings" that have been caused to occur or staged to engender press coverage and public interest. They are events arranged or brought about merely for the sake of the publicity they generate. The pseudo-event is essentially an empty, meaningless occasion that has been given a false cultural significance by a persuader through the media. In so doing, the pseudo-event reshapes our very notion of the truth. In time, by thinking in terms of images and not ideals, we deceive ourselves. Politicians carefully script and act out events to craft believable images that are convincing of their sincerity but which are disconnected from the facts and/or circumstances situating a more honest response. In other words, pseudo-events create the illusion that we who watch them are "informed."

According to Boorstin, pseudo-events have four characteristics.[71] *First*, they are planned or planted. They are scripted and dramatic, intended to produce iconic images to serve a need, such as the Boston Tea Party in 1773 which was intended as political theatre in support of the American Revolution. Far from being spontaneous, the Boston Tea Party was carefully orchestrated to achieve maximum symbolic effect and easy accessibility to the media in order to inspire resistance to the British presence in North America.

Second, they are created or planted for a reason—that is, to attract media attention for a person or a cause. To do this, pseudo-events pander to the press and make it easy for reporters to cover them and editors to publish them. The spin surrounding the death of Captain Pat Tillman in Afghanistan and the capture/rescue of Private Jessica Lynch in Iraq are notable examples. Both soldiers were held out to the press by the military as "heroes" and their tragic experiences used to increase public support for the two wars. This is not to suggest that either Tillman or Lynch were not decent or even honorable people. Rather, the military exploited cynically their sacrifices for propagandistic effect in order to "sell" both wars. Specifically, the military reported that Tillman, a football star who gave up his lucrative NFL contract to fight in Afghanistan, earned a Silver Star when he died bravely fighting the enemy. It was later revealed that Tillman had been killed in a "friendly fire" accident. Lynch was falsely portrayed as bravely fighting off her Iraqi captors only to succumb to captivity where she was badly mistreated and perhaps sexually abused. She was rescued in an overly dramatic raid that misrepresented seriously her actual condition.[72] In both cases, the military cared more about the image of these two soldiers than for them as individuals. Both were reduced to objects to be manipulated, denigrating their actual service to our nation, belittling their sacrifices.

Third, the relationship between the pseudo-event and the underlying situation is ambiguous. Audience interest in the pseudo-event is grounded in this ambiguity, which becomes a resource for manipulation. When engaging a pseudo-event the question of "meaning" is unclear. So a hotel stages a banquet, as in Boorstin's example. What does this mean? We attend, we eat, we cele-brate, but what have we done? What have we come to know? While the news interest in a plane crash is, as Boorstin points out, in *what* happened and in the material consequences to the victims and their families and perhaps to its effect on the airline industry, the interest in a pseudo-event is always, in a sense, what might have been the motives behind its creation. Is the event what it appears to be? Whose interest does it serve? What really happened and what were we en-couraged to *think* happened? At the end of the day, we might have been dis-tracted from news or ideas that really mattered.

Fourth, pseudo-events are intended to be "self-fulfilling prophecies." An event becomes "real" when it is created by the media and given signifi-cance that it would not have, otherwise. In other words, a pseudo-event is the conscious, deliberate attempt of manufacturing news to make a policy, person, or event appear important to a neutral observer. When it is successful, the pseudo-event has established itself as culturally significant. A sense of impor-tance in an event has been created. Boorstin's hotel achieves a new level of prestige that it *did not earn.*

Probably the best example of a successful pseudo-event is the ill-famed "Torches of Freedom" march orchestrated by public relations pioneer Edward Bernays in 1930.[73] On Easter Sunday of that year, Bernays, who was working covertly for the American Tobacco Company, hired ten women, provided them with cigarettes, and instructed them to march down Fifth Avenue in New York City. He carefully instructed the marchers to display prominently their smoking and to hold themselves out as engaging in a spontaneous emancipatory activity. He coordinated this with apparently neutral spokespeople who explained that the women were marching for feminism and freedom.

Bernays invited the press, had the event photographed, and made sure it was reported widely throughout the country. This contrived event was pro-moted as "real" and was discussed in the papers nationally as a bold step for women in an era where women just recently received the right to vote. As a result of this publicity stunt, cigarette marketing opened up for women. Few events in the history of public relations have been so consequential to people's health. Generations of American women have seen their self images contami-nated, and their health sacrificed, thanks to Bernays. *But he sure sold a great many cigarettes!* It is because of examples like this that Boorstin remarked that "We are haunted, not by reality, but by those images we have put in place of reality."[74] He also warned that "We risk being the first people in history to have been able to make their illusions so vivid, so persuasive, so 'realistic' that they can live in them. We are the most illusioned [i.e., deceived] people on earth."[75] Battling such deception is an important part of approaching persuasion as a critical activity.

Other more recent examples of pseudo-events include the hype surrounding the 1995 film *The Blair Witch Project* as well as the "underground" marketing of the 1975 flop *The Rocky Horror Picture Show*.

Released in 1999, the film *The Blair Witch Project* was a Hollywood success. The grainy, home-made style film was made for only $35,000 but grossed $250 million worldwide.[76] What is most interesting about the film, which was, cinematographically speaking, unexceptional, was how it was marketed. To cultivate "grass roots" interest in the film, the studio falsely implied that the film was "real," that the students in the film had actually disappeared under mysterious circumstances, and that there had been a cover-up by the police. In effect, the studio intentionally blurred the distinction between fact and fiction in what the *New York Times* called "conjured folklore."[77] In this way, the film was promoted as if it were non-fiction, a mere crude documentary. To cultivate this false impression, fake official documents such as missing persons' fliers were released around college campuses.

Likewise, the *Rocky Horror Picture Show* (also a low budget production) released in 1975, owes its continuing success to a well-orchestrated pseudo-event. Long hailed as a classic cult film, the film has been shown continuously since its release over 35 years ago.[78] An entire subculture has grown up around it. Attending a showing with the attendant people's theater makes it appear that this was a "take back," a reclaiming of corporate art for the people, an authentic display of reverse cooption in which the people claim for themselves on their terms some prefabricated cultural kitsch. Unfortunately, this is not the case. After bombing upon its release, the studios made a decision to repackage the film for a midnight screening, and to encourage the audience behavior that has grown up around it.[79]

✂ The Art of Deception and How to Detect It ✂

In this chapter we have been discussing ethics, and our primary assumption has been that unethical behavior is rampant in our society and that a critique of deception is both necessary and beneficial. This, however, begs the question, what exactly is lying? Everyone agrees that lying is bad, but there is no agreement as to what it is or where to draw the line. To live in a world of perfect honesty, in the most technical sense, would be to live dysfunctionally. Like it or not, perfect honesty is often undesirable. At the very least, healthy relationships require some degree of deception.[80]

Moreover, definitions of lying are culture-bound. Interpretations of what a lie is and expectations concerning appropriateness of deceptive behavior differ from society to society and even from within different segments of society. Consider the word "lying." Everyone knows that lying is wrong but to assert this means nothing outside of the context in which we portray it. For example, the following words can be used to describe lying: *white lie, fib, joke, deception, falsehood, misunderstanding, bald-faced lie, misstatement, stretching the truth, slight/mere exaggeration, mistake, oversimplification* and *misunderstanding*.[81] Undoubtedly, readers can think of more.

To complicate matters further, we lie with more than just our words. A comprehensive discussion of this point can be found by rhetorical scholar George Yoos who notes that our "looks, our actions, and even our silence can lie."[82] We deceive by both implication and suggestion. As he notes, "to lie is not just to say only what is clear-cut and false. An analysis of lying involves, among other things, an analysis of motives, beliefs, and intentions… . Lying extends to all sorts of statements and behaviors that may be misleading, deceptive, and confusing."[83]

Why do people lie? While people may lie for many different reasons, development consultant Kathy Thomas-Massey has identified five predominant ones: *need, opportunity, feelings of dissatisfaction or mistreatment, feelings of inequity*, and the *perception that lying is widespread in society*.[84] Indeed, Thomas-Massey reports that, in a survey of 40,000 Americans, 93% admitted to lying "regularly and habitually in the workplace."[85] To personalize these statistics, think for a moment about what would you do in the following situations. Would you lie to make another person feel good? (e.g., tell someone they looked great or that they had a great sense of humor). Lie to enable another person to save face? Lie to get what you deserve but could not get any other way? (e.g., lie to get a well-earned promotion or raise). Lie to get yourself out of an unpleasant situation (e.g., an unwanted date, extra chore, boring conversation)?

Social scientists have taught us that there are certain behaviors associated with deception, such as increased blinking, more use of adaptors (e.g., scratching head, playing with an item of clothing, tracing objects), anxious pitch/vocal nervousness, pupil dilation, lack of immediacy with the audience, short messages, increased use of pauses.[86] People who lie tend to create a psychological distance between the message and her/himself; this includes leaning away, gazing less, pausing more frequently, taking more time to answer questions, nodding and smiling more.[87] However, it is important to realize that proficient con-artists may exhibit *none* of the above behaviors, that we can train our bodies to avoid telegraphing physiological clues, and that the more preparation time a liar has to practice and prepare for her/his performance, as well as the more motivation s/he has to lie, the more successful s/he is likely to be.

One interesting discussion of how lies work comes from the most unsavory source, German dictator and mega-mass murderer Adolph Hitler, who infamously identified the power of what he called the "Big Lie":

> [I]n the big lie there is always a certain force of credibility; because the broad masses of a nation are always more easily corrupted in the deeper state of their emotional nature than consciously or voluntarily, and thus in the primitive simplicity of their minds they more readily fall victims to the big lie than the small lie, since they themselves often tell small lies in little matters but would be ashamed to resort to large-scale falsehoods. It would never come into their heads to fabricate colossal untruths, and they would not believe that others could have the impudence to distort the truth so infamously. Even though the facts which prove this to be so may be brought clearly to their minds, they will still doubt and waver and will continue to think that there may be some other explanation.[88]

In other words, while most people suspect that politicians lie or are dishonest, we act as if the lies or dishonesty apply only to the *small* things. As we discussed earlier in this chapter, President Clinton lied about his sexual relationship with Monica Lewinsky, and President George W. Bush lied about the influence of Enron and other oil interests on the formation of his energy policies. So what? We excuse such lies because they are, in some sense, reasonable—they are part of the hazards of living the public life, and do not rise to the level of policy deception or criminal culpability. We understand; after all, we want our leaders to be human not saints. Few of the rest of us are completely honest, even with ourselves. We are all unique individuals with conflicting values, desires, and emotions, and we exist in various pressure cookers that often accentuate our less-than-flattering characteristics, and that is without the microscope of public scrutiny and the crushing pressures of high office. How many of us could retain our integrity, our perceived moral continuity, if we were thrust, suddenly, into the limelight with its attendant bootlickers, yes-men, and enemies that come out of the woodwork like cockroaches? Thus, we explain away minor falsehoods and illusions, believing that their existence is not a threat to our world view as a nation. However, when the stakes rise, when the illusions themselves become official policy, when the narrative vision of the nation is grounded in a lie, when our political and economic systems become vested in that lie, we become a society not unlike that described by Hitler, disconnected from the larger moral community and vulnerable to the greatest calamities.

The final concept discussed in this section is *visual deception*. Communication scholar Paul Messaris has identified five components of visual deception.[89]

The *first* is that the events that occur in front of the camera can be staged. If something looks like a natural image of a non-manipulated event, but has, in fact, been manipulated to embody such an appearance, then a form of deception has occurred. For example, deception exists when advertisers use props or alter a product so that it appears to perform in a particular way on television, but it could not perform that way in real life. Famous instances include Campbell's Soup Company placing marbles in the bottom of a soup bowl so that the soup's ingredients would rise to the surface, making it look chunkier, Volvo reinforcing the roof of its car with steel beams so that it could be filmed withstanding being run over by a huge truck, Palmolive Rapid Shave razors being shown shaving off sandpaper which was really sand on glass, or Dateline NBC rigging General Motors pickup trucks to make them appear like they explode on low speed contact. Each of these examples resulted in fines or other civil penalties for the producers of the deception.[90]

A *second* component of visual deception involves the tactic of altering the photograph. This used to be done crudely through cutting-and-pasting, but has grown increasingly sophisticated with new computer technology. Many examples of this from the former Soviet Union and from China can be discussed. Both China and the former Soviet Union were famous for their use of visual deception. The Soviets went through great pains to control popular perception of not only the Party, but of history as well. Photos were frequently doctored to remove disgraced and murdered officials. The Chinese government took this a step further when they not only *erased* disgraced officials from photos, but *left spaces* where the images had been; the idea being that an "undesirable" was not only erased from history, but everyone knows that the Party had the power to effectuate this goal. Such manipulation, rather than secretive, became an expression of omnipotent state power.

Third, Messaris notes that discrete images can be edited together to leave viewers with a false impression about the relationship between "real" events depicted in the images. Messaris provides the example of the Boston Harbor ad that was shown in 1988 when Vice President George H. W. Bush attacked Massachusetts Governor Michael Dukakis on his environmental record. The ad claimed that, because of Dukakis, Boston Harbor was horribly polluted. To emphasize this point, the ad, which had surveyed dirty and trash-ridden water in Boston Harbor, focused on a danger sign indicating the presence of radioactive contamination in the water. The voiceover states gloomily that "Dukakis promises to do for American what he has done for Massachusetts." This image and the voiceover are both powerful and convincing.

Yet, as Messaris reveals, "the radiation warning sign was not in Boston Harbor at all. It was in Boston Navy Yard, a facility that was under the jurisdiction of the federal government—that is, the same administrative entity in which Mr. Bush was at that very time serving as vice president."[91] According to Messaris, "The ad's words, together with the images surrounding the radiation sign, lead us to assume that the sign is in Boston Harbor and is Michael Dukakis's responsibility. Neither of these is true."[92]

A *fourth* component is that the photograph's value as evidence can be affected by the simple means of selection (i.e., what is left out of the image). For example, photographers typically take dozens or even hundreds of pictures of a subject (say at a press conference), later selecting the picture or two that they think is best for whatever purpose they have in mind. That particular picture or two then becomes the one we all see and, if it is iconic enough, comes to stand for the event being depicted. While people may gravitate toward that image and come to believe in it, that picture is no more a complete record of that event than any of the other discarded pictures. There is nothing wrong with this, we engage in selection with everything we do. This tactic becomes a problem only when we are encouraged to attribute to the picture more documentary evidence or power than is warranted by the integrity and claims of the photographer.

The *fifth* component of visual deception identified by Messaris is that the photograph can be mislabeled. An example of this can be seen in March of 2006, when Republican Howard Kaloogian, who was running for Congress in California, was forced to remove a picture from his campaign web site. Kaloogian had claimed that the photograph, showing a peaceful idyllic street scene in downtown Baghdad with happy shoppers strolling and mingling carelessly, was evidence that the news media was portraying an inaccurate portrayal of life in Iraq. The caption read: "We took this photo of downtown Baghdad while we were in Iraq. Iraq (including Baghdad) is much more calm and stable than what many people believe it to be. But each day the news media finds any violence occurring in the country and screams and shouts about it in part because many journalists are opposed to the U.S. effort to fight terrorism."[93] The photo, however, was later revealed to be from Istanbul, Turkey, a country currently at peace.

During the 2004 presidential elections a fake news clipping circulated on the internet, purporting to show democratic candidate John Kerry speaking on stage with anti-war activist Jane Fonda during the Vietnam War. While both Kerry and Fonda were well known for being outspoken critics of the war, Kerry was a decorated solider who had served in Vietnam and was a well respected member of the anti-war group Vietnam Veterans Against the War (VVAW). As part of VVAW, Kerry testified before Congress and appeared on television shows, such as Meet the Press, where he tried to explain how what we were doing in Vietnam was wrong. Fonda, on the other hand, was widely considered to be on the fringe (or "loony") left and had outraged many Americans by traveling to North Vietnam in July 1972 where she posed for pictures with the Vietcong on anti-aircraft guns aimed at American warplanes and engaged, via radio broadcast, in communist government propaganda against the U.S. Although she was never formally charged, cases have been made for prosecuting Fonda for treason.[94] By associating Kerry with Fonda, Kerry's critics succeeded, in part, in undercutting his authority to be president.

❧ Conclusion ☙

As mentioned in the Preface to this textbook, the Department of Communication here at the University of Colorado Denver views it as our mission "to guide students toward developing the skills, knowledge, and abilities necessary to use communication to create a more civil and humane world." Fundamental to this mission is the question of ethics or ethical communication. As a department, we recognize that ethics is an increasingly important subject to discuss across the communication curriculum, which I have attempted to do throughout this course in persuasion and in this textbook. This chapter is merely the most focused expression of our collective departmental concern.

As most readers of this chapter will acknowledge, few things are more important than the subject of ethics. Yet it is a subject that tends to get short-changed in many of our courses. There may be different reasons for this, but one important reason is that ethics is a notoriously difficult subject for students to wrap their minds around. On the one hand, we want to be cautious of any arbitrary and difficult-to-support absolutes, which I have tried to do in this chapter and throughout this course. On the other hand, we want to be careful not to disregard, totally, the social certainty that comes from such monolithic mandates. In other words, we still have to judge, but our judgment needs to be grounded in principles more nuanced and pragmatic than those commonly postulated by theists or moral metaphysicians. With this chapter, I hoped to strike a middle-ground between these two extremes and present my view of ethics as being an *argument*, expressed through persuasion and human action.

ഌ Notes രു

1. According to communication scholar Ronald C. Arnett, Aristotle's notion of *phronesis* has four components: "deliberation about the problem at hand and the 'good' toward which one should strive in a unique situation," "knowledge of universals (general theories) that provide a stance or position from which a situation can be viewed," "a willingness to modify a universal or theory to meet the demands of the particular situation," and "putting a decision" from the above process "into action." See, "The Practical Philosophy of Communication Ethics and Free Speech as the Foundation for Speech Communication," *Communication Quarterly, 38* (1990), 210.

2. Carol Kirby and Oliver Slevin, "Ethical Knowing: The Moral Ground of Nursing," in Lynn Baford, Oliver Slevin, eds., *Theory and Practice of Nursing: An Integrated Approach to Caring Practice* 2nd ed. (London, UK: Nelson Thornes, 2003), 212.

3. "Ethical Issues in Teaching," in Anita L. Vangelisti, John A. Daly, Gustav W. Friedrich, eds., *Teaching Communication: Theory, Research and Methods* (Mahwah, NJ: Lawrence Erlbaum, 1998), 460.

4. "Perspectives on Ethics in Persuasion," in Charles Larson, ed., *Persuasion: Reception and Responsibility* 7th ed. (Belmont, CA: Wadsworth, 1995), 28.

5. Ibid.

6. (New York: Harcourt, 2004).

7. David Cay Johnston, "The Gap Between Rich and Poor Grows in the United States," *International Herald Tribune* (March 29, 2007). Retrieved from http://www.iht.com/articles /2007/03/29/business/income.4.php.

8. John V. Pavlik, *Media in the Digital Age* (New York: Columbia University Press, 2008), 252–265.

9. Ibid.

10. Janel Alania, "The 'News' From the Feed Looks Like News Indeed: On Video News Releases, the FCC, and the Shortage of Truth in the Truth in Broadcasting Act of 2005,' *Cardozo Arts & Entertainment Law Journal, 24* (2006), 234.

11. David Barstow and Robin Stein, "The Message Machine: How the Government Makes News; Under Bush, a New Age of Prepackaged News," *New York Times* (March 13, 2005) 4. Retrieved from http://query.nytimes.com/gst/fullpage.html?res=9A03E5DD153CF930A257 0C0A9639C 8B63&scp=2&sq=&st=cse.

12. Ibid.

13. Martin Mayer, *The Greatest Ever Bank Robbery: The Collapse of the Savings and Loan Industry* (New York: C. Scribner's Sons, 1992).

14. Cited in Richard L. Johannesen, *Ethics in Human Communication* 4th ed. (Prospect Heights, IL: Waveland Press, 1996), 173.

15. A partial list of people responsible for the massive fraud of this era include: Samuel Waksal of ImClone, Dennis Kozlowski of Tyco, Alan Bond of Albriond Capital Management, and Kenneth Lay, Jeffrey Skilling, and Andrew Fastow of Enron.

16. *The Cheating Culture*, 13.

17. Kevin M. Hart, "Not Wanted: Thieves; It's Not Just Ne'er-Do-Wells Who Are Stealing," *HR Magazine, 53* (April 2008), 119–123.

18. U.S. Congress, Office of Technology Assessment, *The Use of Integrity Tests for Pre-Employ -ment Screening*, OTA-SET-442 (Washington, DC: U.S. Government Printing Office, Sep tember 1990), 1. I suspect that this number has grown substantially. I remember taking one of these tests in the summer of 1990 when I applied for a job as a security guard. After look- ing at my test results, the manager rushed out of his office and told me that he had never seen anyone score so well as I did and immediately hired me. I left wondering who it was that was applying for these jobs. Incidentally, the OTA was closed in 1995.

19. Ibid.

20. Ibid.

21. According to the U.S. Department of Justice on June 30, 2007, the United States housed 2.5 million prisoners. See http://www.ojp.usdoj.gov/bjs/prisons. This is the highest percent- tage of incarcerated people in the world. According to a report by The Pew Center on the States, released on February 28, 2008, one out of every 100 people residing in the United States is behind bars.

22. See Tara Herivel and Paul Wright, eds., *Prison Nation: The Warehousing of America's Poor* (New York: Routledge, 2002).

23. "'The Whole Operation of Deception': Reconstructing President Bush's Rhetoric of Weapons of Mass Destruction," *Cultural Studies <-> Critical Methodologies, 4* (2004), 152.

24. "The Contemporary Presidency: Presidential Lies," *Presidential Studies Quarterly, 29* (1999), 903.

25. *When Presidents Lie: A History of Official Deception and Its Consequences* (New York: Viking, 2004), 1.

26. James P. Pfiffner, "Did President Bush Mislead the Country in His Arguments for War With Iraq?" *Presidential Studies Quarterly, 34* (2004), 45.

27. Richard Shenkman, *Presidential Ambition: Gaining Power at Any Cost* (New York: Harper Collins, 2000), chapter 4.

28. Italics added. Cited in Donaldo Macedo, "Our Common Culture: A Poisonous Pedagogy," in Manuel Castells, Ramon Flecha, Paulo Freire, Henry A. Giroux, Donaldo Macedo, and Paul Willis, eds., *Critical Education in the New Information Age*, (Lanham, MD: Rowman & Littlefield Publishers, 1999), 125.

29. "The Atomic Bombings Reconsidered," *Foreign Affairs, 74* (1995), 147. Today, we would label this action, if undertaken by our enemies, "terrorism."

30. Why, if inducing Japan to surrender was the reason for dropping the bomb, was a second one dropped as well? Writes Bernstein, "Whatever one thinks about the necessity of the first A-Bomb, the second—dropped on Nagasaki [a few days later]—was almost certainly unnecessary." Ibid., 150.

31. Pfiffner, "The Contemporary Presidency," 913.

32. Stephen Kinzer, *Overthrow: America's Century of Regime Change From Hawaii to Iraq* (New York: Time Books, 2006).

33. "Iran-Contra Hearings; Boland Amendments: What They Provided," *New York Times,* (July 10, 1987). Retrieved from http://query.nytimes.com/gst/fullpage.html?res=9B0DE4DF103 9F933A25754C0A961948260&sec=&spon=&pagewanted=print.

34. Jonathan Marshall, Peter Dale Scott, and Jane Hunter, *The Iran Contra Connection: Secret Teams and Covert Operations in the Reagan Era* (Boston: South End Press, 1987).

35. Cited in William E. Pemberton, *Exit With Honor: The Life and Presidency of Ronald Reagan* (Armonk, NY: M.E. Sharpe, 1997), 191.

36. Harold Hongju Koh, "Begging Bush's Pardon," *Houston Law Review*, 29 (1992), 889–890.

37. The video can be retrieved from http://www.youtube.com/watch?v=KiIP_KDQmXs&feature =related.

38. *Presidential Studies Quarterly*, *29* (1999), 904.

39. "Sex, Lies, and Presidents," *Washington Monthly* 30, (October 1998), retrieved from http://w ww.washingtonmonthly.com/features/1998/9810.shenkman.sex.html. See also Richard Norton Smith, "The President is Fine' and Other Historical Lies," *Columbia Journalism Review*, (September/October, 2001), 30–32.

40. Kenneth Burke, *Permanence and Change* (Berkeley, CA: University of California Press, 1984), 192.

41. This is a central point made in Friedrich Nietzsche, *Thus Spoke Zarathustra* (New York: The Modern Library, 1995). Students interested in reading Nietzsche should start with the Walter Kaufmann translations of his work.

42. A classic example of this is *Yania v. Bigan*, 155 S.2d 343 (1959). Here the court held that the defendant was *not* liable in tort when he stood by and watched a man, with whom he was having a conversation, drown.

43. Hedrick Smith, "Reagan's Gaffe," *New York Times* (August 16, 1984), A4.

44. *The Arrogance of American Power: What U.S. Leaders Are Doing Wrong* (Lanham, MD: Rowman & Littlefield, 2006), 49.

45. "Bush: 'Bring on' Attackers of U.S. troops," *USA Today*, July 2, 2003, retrieved from http://www.usatoday.com/news/world/iraq/2003-07-02-bush-iraq-troops_x.htm.

46. Richard Saitz, "Unhealthy Alcohol Use," *New England Journal of Medicine*, *352* (2005), 596.

47. Brad J. Bushman, "Human Aggression While Under the Influence of Alcohol and Other Drugs: An Integrative Research Review," *Current Directions in Psychological Science*, *2* (1993), 148–152.

48. Leslie B. Snyder, Frances Fleming Milici, Michael Slater, Helen Sun, and Yuliya Strizhakova, "Effects of Alcohol Advertising Exposure on Drinking Among Youth," *Archives Pediatrics and Adolescent Medicine, 160* (January 2006), 18–24.

49. "WHO Wants Total Ban on Tobacco Advertising," http://www.who.int/mediacentre/news/releases/2008/pr17/en/index.html.

50. Kenneth E. Warner, Linda M. Goldenhar, and Catherine G. McLaughlin, "Cigarette Advertising and Magazine Coverage of the Hazards of Smoking: A Statistical Analysis," *New England Journal of Medicine, 326* (1992), 305–309. The study concluded that "cigarette advertising in magazines is associated with diminished coverage of the hazards of smoking. This is particular true for magazines directed to women." The authors added that "Avoidable suffering and premature death are the inevitable consequences."

51. The Enlightened Cigarette Company had two major problems that led to its failure. First, many advertisers would not sell the company ad space for fear of offending its much more lucrative mainstream cigarette advertisers. Second, and more importantly, the company had some legal problems involving tax laws in the European Union which, ultimately, doomed the company.

52. A reproduction of this ad can be found in Chris Jenks, ed., *Visual Culture* (New York: Routledge, 1995), 31.

53. *Ethics in Human Communication,* 4th ed., 146.

54. Ibid.

55. Ibid.

56. (New York: W.W. Norton Publishing, 1966).

57. *Ethics in Human Communication* 4th ed. (Prospect Heights, IL: Waveland Press, 1996), 64.

58. Ibid., 64–66.

59. *Persuasion: Reception and Responsibility* 11th ed. (Belmont, CA: Wadsworth, 2007).

60. Wesley J. Smith, "PETA to Cannibals: Don't Let Them Eat Steak," *San Francisco Chronicle* (21, Dec., 2001), D1.

61. The apology was issued on May 5, 2005, and it can be found at http://web.israelinsider.com/Views/5475.htm

62. For example, Rumsfeld's critics hold him responsible for the abuse of prisoners at the Abu Ghraib detention facility in Iraq. "Rumsfeld Okayed Abuses Says Former US Army General," *Reuters* (November 25, 2006), retrieved from http://www.alertnet.org/thenews/ newdesk

/L25726413.htm. Rumsfeld also drew criticism for not personally signing condolence letters to the families of dead U.S. soldiers (he used an impersonal signing machine). See Dana Milbank, "After Outcry, Rumsfeld Says He Will Sign Condolence Letters," *The Washington Post* (Sunday, December 19, 2004), A05.

63. Italics added. Reported in John O'Neil, "Bush Picks Trade Envoy as Budget Aide," *New York Times* (April 18, 2006). Retrieved from http://www.nytimes.com/2006/04/18/washin gton/18cndbush.html.

64. Georges Enderle, "Some Perspectives of Managerial Ethical Leadership," *Journal of Business Ethics, 6* (1987), 657–663.

65. For an elaboration of this point, see my "Natural Law, Positive Law, Slavery, and Nuremberg: Toward a Pragmatic Legal Criticism," *Bad Subjects: Political Education for Everyday Life, 69* (2004). Available from http://eserver.org/bs/69/swartz.html.

66. *Ethics in Human Communication*, 256.

67. This experience is discussed in more detail my "Hierarchy is Not Harmony: A View of the Traditional Chinese Family," in Xing Lu, Wenshan Jia, and D. Ray Heisey, eds., *Chinese Communication Studies: Contexts and Comparisons* (Westport, CT: Greenwood Press, 2002), 199–133.

68. Ibid.

69. *The Image: A Guide to Pseudo-Events in America* (New York: Vintage, 1992).

70. Ibid., 10.

71. Ibid., 11–12.

72. "Who Spread False Tales of Heroism?" *New York Times* (July 16, 2008). Retrieved from http://www.nytimes.com/2008/07/16/opinion/16wed2.html?_r=1&scp=1&sq=who%20sprea d%20flase%20tales&st=cse&oref=slogin.

73. This event is discussed in Scott M. Cutlip, *The Unseen Power: Public Relations, A History* (Hillsdale, NJ: Lawrence Erlbaum Associates, 1994), 210.

74. *The Image*, 6.

75. Ibid., 240.

76. David Carr, "Life After That Very Profitable Fake Witch," *New York Times* (April 24, 2008). Retrieved from http://www.iht.com/articles/2008/04/25/arts/24witc.php.

77. Ibid.

78. Bill Henkin, *The Rocky Horror Picture Show Book* (New York: Dutton Adult, 1979).

79. Ibid., *26.*

80. David B. Buller and Judee K. Burgoon, "Interpersonal Deception Theory," *Communication Theory*, *6* (1996), 203–242.

81. See Eve E. Sweetser, "The Definition of Lie: An Examination of the Folk Models Underlying A Semantic Prototype," in Dorothy Holland and Naomi Quinn, *Cultural Models in Language and Thought* (New York: Cambridge University Press, 1987), 52–54.

82. "Rational Appeal and the Ethics of Advocacy," in Robert Connors, Lisa S. Ede, and Andrea A. Lunsford, eds., *Essays on Classical Rhetoric and Modern Discourse* (Carbondale: Southern Illinois University Press, 1984), 90.

83. Ibid.

84. "The Whole Truth: Are people regularly and habitually lying in the workplace?" http://content.careers.msn.com/WorkingLife/Workplace/0101_wholetruth.asp).

85. Ibid.

86. Miron Zuckerman, Bella M. DePaulo, and Robert Rosenthal, "Verbal and Nonverbal Communication of Deception," in Leonard Berkowitz, ed., *Advances in Experimental Social Psychology* vol. 14 (New York; Academic Press, 1981), 1–59; Mark A. Turck and Gerald R. Miller, "Deception and Arousal: Isolating the Behavioral Correlates of Deception," *Human Communication Research*, *12* (1985), 181–201.

87. Ibid.

88. *Mein Kampf* (New York: Melbourne: Hurst and Blackett, 1942), 134.

89. *Visual Persuasion: The Role of Images in Advertising* (Thousand Oaks, CA: Sage, 1997), 142.

90. I discuss each of these cases in a Mass Media Law and Policy course, CMMU 4180.

91. *Visual Persuasion*, 150.

92. Ibid.

93. Cited by Daren Briscoe, "Baghdad. Istanbul. What's the Difference?" *Newsweek* (October 15, 2007). Retrieved from http://www.newsweek.com/id/47226.

94. See Henry Mark Holzer and Erika Holzer, *"Aid and Comfort"; Jane Fonda in North Vietnam* (Jefferson, NC: McFarland & Co), 1990. This book should be contrasted with Mary Hershberger, *Jane Fonda's War: A Political Biography of an Anti-War Icon* (New York: The New Press, 2005). It is interesting to note that pictures of Fonda in North Vietnam adorn the cover of both books. The one laying out the charge of treason has her looking naïve and childlike as she sits adoringly among Vietnamese soldiers. The other photo, which appears to be taken on the same day and in the same location, presents Fonda in a defiant, heroic pose.

CONCLUSION

Writing and teaching are, for me, acts of love. Teaching this course in persuasion and writing this textbook are ways that I connect with and give back to the communities and world in which I find myself. They are also ways for me to honor my own teachers and sources of inspiration. With one foot firmly in the past—their past—I write to meet the needs and demands of the future, the future exemplified in my students.

Specifically, in this textbook and throughout this course we have studied not only the nuts-and-bolts of persuasion—that is, the rules, perspectives, and suggestions for constructing our own persuasive messages—but also introduced ourselves as well to the philosophy of communication and to its practical implications for media literacy in our twenty-first century democracy. My goal has been to blur the distinction between the classroom and "real life" and between "textbook" and "popular literature," inviting students to see and apply what they learn in the classroom to the practical, everyday, and messy business of living their lives. To this end, my writing has been as jargon free as possible and direct, with many practical examples to illustrate the theories and principles discussed. My hope has been that the experience of this textbook and course has made students more conscientious as consumers and, perhaps, more engaged and critical as citizens in our vibrant twenty-first century society. Individually and collectively, the quality of our lives depends on our ability to make intelligent decisions at the polls, marketplaces, schools, and within our interpersonal relationships. To be most meaningful, democracy must start with *us*.

To conclude this textbook and course, I want to share with readers a presentation that I gave to an elementary school Parent Teacher Association (PTA) meeting in 1995 and have since updated and modified for inclusion here. The presentation sums up the view of communication and persuasion that I have been emphasizing in this course and throughout this textbook. Students with young children, or who are thinking about having children, should find the material to be particularly salient.

After I presented this speech, I was approached by a couple with young children. They told me that they were an inter-faith family (Jewish and Catholic) that had long struggled with the pressures of accommodating their different religious beliefs and values, particularly when it came to raising their children. They thanked me for the presentation which they said "saved their marriage." In other words, I helped them to see how our thoughts and actions are influenced by the language we use to describe the world, and that our lives become enriched the more that we expose ourselves to vocabularies different from our own.

❧ How Children See the World ☙

Being a parent is a wonderful thing; it helps me to appreciate what I have studied for years as a communication scholar, that human beings come into this world as blank slates whose identities are created through experience and education—that is, through communication, through talk (words and language and style), and through the stories they are told by their parents (in particular) about what it means to be human. By being sensitive to the environment in which our children receive messages about the world, we have a good chance of influencing intentionally the moral development of our children. This may sound obvious, but many parents, I believe, are remiss in their responsibility to consciously create moral, productive, and well-adjusted children. Too often we default to popular culture, mostly television, which uses and abuses our children. Or we do not reflect carefully enough about who we are as moral beings. We live daily with the consequences of this dereliction of duty; our children often hurt—often profoundly so—and that harm reverberates throughout society, reproducing itself in each generation. Rather than being forward-thinking people working toward a better future, we are often more interested in conserving the limitations of the past.

In this conclusion, I want to challenge such status quo. I believe we should be more strategic and thoughtful than we have been with our attitudes toward education, especially if we want our children to grow up different from the images of children presented to us by corporate interests. Our lives, and particularly the lives of our children, are becoming increasingly corporatized and homologized, and this condition cannot be considered beneficial. If we do not like what we see around us in terms of other people—their crassness and shallowness—this is our chance to do something about it. Parents *can* and *do* make a difference, both deleterious and beneficial. But to educate our children we ourselves have to be educated and, thus, it becomes crucial to determine, as critical theorists have long noted, who educates the educators.

As a parent, I have been extremely self-aware so as to be able to make conscious choices with regard to the development of my son, Avi. I regret no part of his education (or, should I say, creation). Part of my motivation for writing this textbook and teaching this course in persuasion is that I want to encourage others to appreciate the power and the responsibility they have in helping to construct their children's sense of self and her or his relationships with others. To do this, I must first explain that what we *think* we are giving our children, things such as their gender, race, religion, and nationality, are themselves *constructions*, and, as I argue below, a type of *limitation*. What I mean by this is that most of us hamper our children's emotional and cognitive growth by treating the world as prescribed, forcing our children to fit into neat little boxes that do not exist, except in our imaginations.

I begin with what many readers might consider to be a provocative claim: categories such as gender, race, religion, and national origin are not *givens*; they are not found in nature in ways that we commonly suspect. They are not structurally grounded in reality. They are not eternal or immutable. They are not gifts or designs from a deity; nor do they embody in-and-of-themselves any hierarchy of value—they are not to be confused as constituting the "essence" of people. Like playing cards, they have meaning only in terms of a particular game—other than that, cards are merely paper, plastic, and ink. The pleasure we get from playing cards comes not from the cards, but from the meanings we attach to them in the context of a set of rules. Otherwise stated, the cards are no different than the "coins" that philosopher Friedrich Nietzsche famously described in order to illustrate what he means by the contingency of truth.[1]

As we discussed earlier in this textbook, coins hold value only to the extent that their value is recognized by us; eventually, the pictures on the coins rub off through years of handling and matter to humans only as metal. This, in a nutshell, is a sense in which truth becomes understood from a pragmatic framework. Categories such as gender, race, and the like have importance only in small, localized ways. To attribute to them any greater significance is to argue for, and to accept, our own limitations and to impose those limitations on our children. As novelist Richard Bach warns, "Argue for your limitations and, sure enough, they are yours."[2] As individuals, we waste colossal amounts of our potential. Our children deserve better than this. The more they succeed, the better for all of us.

Restated, categories such as race, gender, religion, and national origin are superficial in the strongest sense of the term, created and maintained through language for the political economy they serve.[3] The fact that these terms exist means that they remain important in that economy. Terms that lose their cultural importance—terms such as "illegitimacy," "debtor's prison," "miscegenation," and "divine right of kings"—drop out of circulation, becoming the curios of the social historians. In other words, the categories we think we find in nature are *takens*, concepts humans have molded from the raw material of nature for their own use—they are conveniences for getting the human things we want done.[4] In a fundamental sense, we do not discover the world; rather, we create it.

To write that I am white, middle-aged, liberal, heterosexual, Jewish, American, working-class, and male is not to indicate anything of importance or special, nor is it to suggest that I can be "known" by the reader because of these traits; I am not interchangeable with other white, middle-aged, liberal, heterosexual, Jewish, American, working-class males. Nor should it be assumed that this list exhausts the potential labels that can be assigned to me, as I am actively trying to create new ones. To write that I have these traits is to share with readers how I have been positioned in the world by *others*; it is to acknowledge the rules of the game that I am forced to play to be able to communicate effectively with others. These are not necessarily the terms that I would choose for myself—history is rich with other possible identifications, many of which are quite appealing (for instance, I would love to be an ancient Chinese Taoist sage roaming an idyllic coastal countryside). I am also positive that there are new, yet unimagined identifications that may be preferable to the ones that exist today.

Nevertheless, I exist in time and space and so I am more or less comfortable with the self that I have. It has its advantages and disadvantages. I do not fear its contingency and I welcome the opportunity to change. Unlike people who accept their positioning as given, I view it as an accident, something to put up with when I am weak and tired and something *against* which to struggle when I feel healthy, rested, and zestful. Such struggle is a sign of health. We do not want our selves or our children to be *too* comfortable with their lives or with who they are. We want them to be inspired. Uninspired children make for degenerate citizens when they grow up. Society only progresses when people outgrow themselves and demand more out of their lives and of the world around them. The more that others grow, the greater the opportunity for the rest of us; thus, we all have an obligation to resist being pigeonholed. Social life should not be seen as a zero-sum game; we do not need "winners" and "losers." We are all resources for each other.

Of everything I will write in this textbook and state in this course, my claims regarding gender are probably the most difficult for people to accept; therefore, I offer the following analogy. When we engage with cats and dogs, we seldom make distinctions based on sex. To us, a dog is a dog and a cat is a cat. For the most part, we only care about the sex of our pets when we are concerned about biological reproduction—for example, their sterilization or breeding. Cats and dogs interact with each other in much the same way—their sex is important to them only in terms of reproduction—it has no symbolic value (e.g., only humans experience pornography and the sexual fetishisms of commodities). Humans are the ones who attach a significance to what we call gender, associating it with things that have little or nothing to do with biological reproduction (blue or pink colors, for example); in other words, we *invent* difference and use that difference to define much of the social experience of our children. In a biological sense, we do not need "women" and "men" except as producers of eggs and spermatozoa—we no longer even need women and men together for reproduction. We could, if we wanted, create a society that disconnects reproduction from social life entirely. If we did that, much of our reasoning for differentiating between women and men would vanish. We might wish to distinguish between tall and short people, strong or weak people, muscle mass, and the like, or between eye color or skin color. These are choices that we make. However we decide to slice things up, so little of who we are and how we think is dependent upon correspondence to how things are "really" in the world. Human prejudice belongs to us alone.

This disconnect between human culture and the survival of the human organism is further illustrated by a humorous passage in a well-loved novel, *Slaughterhouse-Five*. In this book, a work of science fiction, author Kurt Vonnegut, Jr. provides an interesting discussion of how humans reproduce, as perceived by Tralfamadorians, space creatures very much unlike ourselves. Ac-

cording to these creatures, at least *seven* sexes exist on Earth, all of which are
essential for human reproduction. We cannot discern this because much of the
sexual activity necessary for reproduction takes place in a fourth dimension,
well beyond our human-all-too-human perception. Understandably, Billy Pil-
grim, the novel's protagonist, has a difficult time processing this information:

> The Tralfamadorians tried to give Billy clues that would help him ima-
> gine sex in the invisible dimension. They told him that there would be
> no Earthling babies without male homosexuals. There *could* be babies
> without female homosexuals. There couldn't be babies without women
> over sixty-five years old. There *could* be babies without men over
> sixty-five. There couldn't be babies without other babies who had lived
> an hour or less after birth. And so on.[5]

Obviously, this is a work of *fiction*; neither Vonnegut nor I are suggesting otherwise. Rather, I take it as an excellent way of demonstrating my
point—what we make of our lives, our relationships, and our social practices
has little to do with "reality." We do not need to even know what "reality" is,
and we probably do not, as long as we do not neglect basic life-sustaining social practices, some of which we appreciate; others we probably do not appreciate. While we *think* we know and while we have been fairly good at getting
along this far, we must not mistake our past success with truth. The success of
our species thus far does not guarantee the "truth" of our actions or representations; nor does it guarantee future success. As Nietzsche frequently asserts, it
may be *error* and not truth that is most useful for us, and that if we knew the
truth, we would perhaps die from it.[6] Think of organized religion. If we are
asked to take the claims of any religion literally, all are based on error, but that
does not make them any less useful for inspiring large human populations or
civilizations. Alternatively, consider how Aristotle's system of physics, while
fundamentally "wrong" from modern notions of physics, was useful for navi-
gating ships in the ancient world.[7]

We learn from Nietzsche that there are "no facts, only interpretations,"
that all observations are theory-laden and anthropomorphic, and that what we
often call truth is error in relationship to error.[8] In other words, our understandings of the world are human through-and-through, forcing the others to conform to our prejudices. Education, therefore, in the sense that I am discussing it
here and throughout this textbook, should not be aimed at codifying these dis-

tinctions, since that would be a lie—such error in relationship to error—an attempt to box in and assign an essence to things, which, by our experience, change in relationship to us.

In less philosophical terms such error in relationship to error has traditionally been known as the "banking model" of education, in which the experts capture truth and transmit it through clear and unfettered channels of communication to intellectually prepared and screened students who are conditioned to accept it, as chicks, wide mouthed, accept nourishment from their parents. Instead, education should be seen for what it is, a radical act—it is the way by which we interpret the interpreter who, in turn, interprets us through the dialogic process. This is the dialogical approach to education.[9] In this way, we resist placing into our children our values so that the future may justify ourselves—for the most part, the banking model of education is wholly egotistical in that the educators teach to justify themselves rather than for their students to surpass themselves. Rejecting this view is disturbing to most people, who want the future to be no different from the past and who, thus, fear a dialogical and progressive education.

I argue that it is important that we learn to realize how our belief in "real" categories, such as race and sex, controls and often limits our experience of the world; we tend to see the world as women or men, or as black or white, Jew or gentile, etc. To many people these things matter, often profoundly so, and they are content with the identities they have inherited. But that does not mean that *we* should be content, that *we* should be beholden by the limitations of others. This is a serious matter because we "color" the experience of our children and transmit these limitations. This is our legacy to our children. In raising them, we color their world, affecting the way they think and feel. We would be foolish to say that we could or should stop coloring our children's expectations. We have no choice but to do this. We should embrace this, but become aware of what we are doing, mindful that this is the most wonderful thing that we do for our children as well as the most consequential. We create children in our own image, and this should make every parent proud. With this in mind, I encourage all of us to keep creating our children in terms of our visions of the world, but to do so in a more self-conscious way, a way that actually empowers our children to overcome the limitations of a particular way of coloring without losing the strengths of that perspective.

Each identification we have in the world—religious, political, social, racial, or gendered—brings with it a wealth of perspectives, as well as a wealth of limitations. The key is to realize, as the critic Kenneth Burke explains, that any one way of seeing blinds us from seeing something else; each coloring of the world, each identification, accentuates one aspect of reality, and blurs, or obscures, another.[10] Furthermore, there is no place where we can stand, or where we can teach our children to stand, that will give us the larger or more complete picture of the way things "really" are. The best we can do is to equip ourselves to see the world through different lenses, to experience the world from other points of view, and to encourage our children to do the same.

To help readers understand how this coloring of experience works, think for a moment about how a photograph or television works. When we contemplate a snapshot or watch television, we must be careful to not be led into thinking that the image before us represents or has captured a piece of the world-as-it-is. The pictures we receive on television or in the newspapers are nothing but perspectives; they are small ideologically mediated slices of the world that direct our thinking in conceptual and limiting terms. Since we cannot appreciate the total "essence" of the world, and because such an "essence" does not exist, it is useful and practical to have certain perspectives accentuated. Thus, we must never forget that the picture is not the "thing," just like we must never forget that any particular religious, political, or racial perspective is not the "correct" description of human nature. Rather, each perspective is simply one interpretation, one snapshot of a larger phenomenon called the human experience that cannot be represented accurately.

The point just made can be made in another way, as originally illustrated by Burke.[11] Take any object, such as a vase. Photograph that object with different colored filters. Do not move the camera, do not change the lighting. If we do these things, we will find that each picture will be different; the pictures will vary not only in color, but also in tone and texture. Each filter will accentuate a certain part of the vase and deflect our attention from another part. Also, the relationship between the vase and the background will change, depending upon the color of the filter. The vase does not only exist in time and space, it also exists in terms of our perceptions. It is "real" only to the extent, and in such a way, that we perceive it to be. In a similar fashion, our identifications of "gender," "race," and "national origin" affect the way we and our children see and interact with the world.

All this is natural, as I mentioned above. The key is not to stop our identifications from coloring our experience, since we cannot, but to realize what we are doing when we make decisions about how to think and feel. Correspondingly, the self-reflexive key is to learn ways of constantly broadening our identifications so that we can grow sensitive to the identifications of others. A clearer and final way to illustrate this notion of coloring and how it affects the way our children perceive the world, is to see each of our identifications as a "vocabulary." Our lives, in many ways, are scripted by the identifications we choose, and by the identifications that other people force upon us, which are sometimes quite negative. In an important sense, each of our identifications is composed of words, ways of talking. If our race and our gender are not "out there," then they have to be inside of ourselves or placed upon us by others, and the means of doing this is discourse (i.e., communication). Each identification, in short, exists because of a vocabulary. The set of the terms that define any particular identification is called, according to philosopher Richard Rorty, the *final vocabulary* of a culture or of an individual:

> All human beings carry about a set of words which they employ to justify their actions, their beliefs, and their lives. These are the words in which we formulate praise of our friends and contempt for our enemies, our long-term projects, our deepest self-doubts and our highest hopes. They are the words in which we tell, sometimes prospectively and sometimes retrospectively, the story of our lives.[12]

A person's or a culture's final vocabulary is not "final" in the sense that it is "Truth" or permanently fixed. Rather, it is "final" in the sense that it involves the terms that constitute our selves in a particular, but temporal way. It is, literally, the words that constitute who we are at any given point in time. The vocabulary provides the words that take us as far as we can go today without running around in circles. Once we get to the level of the final vocabulary, we have to say, "Well that is just what I believe, I cannot think any differently right now." This is fine; we all have that point at which our languages and self-concepts do not allow us to proceed any further with our thoughts. At a certain point, however, we reach the end of our tolerance and we can no longer continue forward without *hurting* ourselves in some fundamental way. Conversation usually breaks down at this juncture, and communication ends. Unfortunately, this is also the point at which much violence in the world begins.

Words position us, whether we like it or not, to be and to act in certain ways. Our final vocabularies are so central to who we are that we often treat them as if they were real and immutable, and we do not recognize that they affect us and influence how we conceive of the world. We see it as "common sense." For common sense is:

> ... the watchword of those who unselfconsciously describe everything important in terms of the final vocabulary to which they and those around them are habituated. To be commonsensical is to take for granted that statements formulated in that final vocabulary suffice to describe and judge the beliefs, actions, and lives of those who employ alternative final vocabularies.[13]

In other words, we often fail to realize that our final vocabularies serve as the "foundations" of our children's self-consciousness and sense of social being, preventing them from growing and maturing in different ways.

The point I wish to make about language and identification, and its relationship to people as parents, is that good parents are those who help their children to realize that they have been given a set of perspectives with which to interpret the world. Those perspectives, while good in themselves—at least to the extent that we, as parents, are good human beings—are nothing more than perspectives. They may be all that we have right now, and they are us in a very real sense, but they affect us in ways we may not be fully aware. Furthermore, good parents need constantly to challenge their children to question the final vocabularies that they have inherited so that they do not take them for granted or confuse them for being the only way to think. In other words, we want our children to become, in some respects, ironists, "never quite able to take themselves seriously because [they are] always aware that the terms in which they describe themselves are subject to change, always aware of the contingency and fragility of their final vocabularies, and thus of their selves."[14]

We do not want our children, I think, to stay up at night worrying if they are being "good Christians," "good Jews," or "good Americans." Likewise, our children should not be worrying themselves if they are being "Chinese enough" or "masculine enough." This is not to say that I think that any of these things are bad; rather, I argue that these identities do not *mean* anything in-and-of-themselves. So, what these children are really saying is that they want to be like the people around them who are Christian, Jewish, American, or Chinese. They are concerned about how they measure up to the gendered norms of their society. Their aspirations, however, says nothing about the *cha-racter* of the people whom the child is modeling. Instead of having these worries, my wish, following Rorty, is that any thoughtful child will spend her/his time "worrying about the possibility that she has been initiated into the wrong tribe, taught to play the wrong language game."[15] In other words, when we stop taking our identities for granted, when we historicize and criticize our inherited identifications, we find the resources to become better at being human. The best way to do this is to encourage reading. Literature, in particular, challenges us to question what we believe by exposing us to new and novel ways of being. Exposure to literature makes us better people.

In sum, words both constrain and liberate us. The stories we tell our children, stories about "God," "ethnicity," "culture," "politics," and "history," are just that—stories. They are the materials by which we constitute our lives. Because something is a story does not mean that it is not important. What it means is that the importance of things becomes constituted through language, through the stories we tell and the manner in which we discuss our lives. Thus, the more we read and encourage our children to read—to inquire about different people and different ideas—the more we realize that our final vocabularies are not the same as others', and that different vocabularies lead to different lives. Now some of those lives may not be what we would choose for ourselves, but it does not hurt to read about them. In fact there is no disadvantage to reading: reading opens the mind and gives us reason to think and believe like we do. The more exposure we have to competing visions of the world, the better we are able to understand how language positions us to act in certain ways.

If we love our children we will want them to have control of their own minds. In an important aspect, that is what love means. I am reminded of the idiom, "if you love somebody, set her/him free." Our children can only be set free to the extent that they understand their self-identifications and how those identifications position them in the world.

༄ Notes ༅

1. *The Portable Nietzsche* (New York: Penguin, 1976), 47.

2. *Illusions: The Adventures of a Reluctant Messiah* (New York: Dell, 1989). Other people I have seen use this quote, or some version thereof, attribute it to Abraham Lincoln and Henry Ford.

3. A good example is Ian F. Haney-Lopez, *White by Law: The Legal Construction of Race* (New York: New York University Press, 1998).

4. This idea is developed in John Dewey, *The Quest for Certainty* (New York: G.P. Putnam, 1929), 178.

5. (Delacorte Press, 1969), 99.

6. *The Will to Power* (New York: Vintage, 1968).

7. Discussed in Thomas S. Kuhn, *The Structure of Scientific Revolutions* 3rd ed. (Chicago: University of Chicago Press, 1996).

8. *The Will to Power.* 267.

9. Paulo Freire, *Pedagogy of the Oppressed* (New York: Continuum, 2000).

10. *Language as Symbolic Action: Essays on Life, Literature, and Method* (Berkeley: University of California Press, 1966), 44–62.

11. Ibid.

12. *Contingency, Irony, and Solidarity* (New York: Cambridge University Press, 1989), 73.

13. Ibid., 74.

14. Ibid.

15. Ibid., 75.